BOLLINGEN SERIES XXX

PAPERS FROM THE ERANOS YEARBOOKS

Edited by Joseph Campbell

Selected and translated from the *Eranos-Jahrbücher*
edited by Olga Froebe-Kapteyn

The Mystic Vision

PAPERS FROM THE ERANOS YEARBOOKS

Ernesto Buonaiuti · Friedrich Heiler · Wilhelm Koppers
Louis Massignon · Jean de Menasce · Erich Neumann
Henri-Charles Puech · Gilles Quispel · Erwin Rousselle
Boris Vysheslawzeff · Heinrich Zimmer

BOLLINGEN SERIES XXX · 6

PRINCETON UNIVERSITY PRESS

Translated by

RALPH MANHEIM

CONTENTS

CONTENTS

LIST OF PLATES

For Heinrich Zimmer, "The Indian World Mother"
following page 82

Note of Acknowledgment

Grateful acknowledgment is made to the following publishers for permission to quote as indicated: Allen & Unwin, London, for a passage from the *Tao Tê Ching*, translated by Arthur Waley, in *The Way and Its Power*; Harper & Row, New York, for quotations from *The Upanishads*, translated by Swāmi Nikhilānanda; Dial Press, New York, for a passage from Euripides' *Medea*, translated by Frederic Prokosch; Clarendon Press, Oxford, for passages from *The Apocryphal New Testament*, translated by M. R. James; Professor Jacques Maritain, for passages from his *Quatre Essais sur l'esprit dans sa condition charnelle* and his *Les Dons du Saint-Esprit*.

The photographs by Eliot Elisofon (Plates II and IV), taken for *Life* Magazine and reproduced in Heinrich Zimmer's *The Art of Indian Asia*, are copyright 1955 by Time, Inc.

The advice and assistance of Ilse Lichtenstadter and Hellmut Wilhelm are gratefully acknowledged. The late A. S. B. Glover made important bibliographical and editorial contributions to this volume, whose contents exemplify the broad range of his interests.

EDITOR'S FOREWORD

It is now forty years since Olga Froebe-Kapteyn built in the garden of her residence on the northern shore of Lago Maggiore the graceful lecture hall that has served, for the past thirty-five years, as the auditorium of the annual Eranos Conferences. There, year after year, successive companies of the greatest scholars of our time have assembled to compare and expound their views concerning those "elementary forms," informing themes and visions, creative urges and symbolic aims—the "archetypes," in short—that have inspired, and are inspiring still, the cultural evolution of mankind: and the Yearbooks in which their findings have been published by the Rhein-Verlag of Zurich (now numbering thirty-five, with more, year by year, to come) testify remarkably, in this period of universal discord, to such a prestigious "hidden harmony" through all the works of man as might be thought to promise a day of peace to come: or, if not that, then to point to a discoverable ground of peace in the context even of these conflicts—in the sense of thosè words of the Gnostic Gospel of Thomas, where the Saviour, answering his disciples' question "When will the Kingdom come?" replied: "It will not come by expectation. . . . But the Kingdom of the Father is spread upon the earth and men do not see it."[1]

The authors here presented are of the number of those whose genius, in the first years of Eranos, set the style and standard of the meetings. Heinrich Zimmer was at that time professor at Heidelberg of Sanskrit and Indology; Erwin Rousselle, director of the China Institute of the University of Frankfurt-am-Main; Father Friedrich Heiler, professor of the comparative history of religions at the University of Marburg; and Ernesto Buonaiuti had just

[1] A. Guillaumont et al., *The Gospel According to Thomas* (Leiden and New York, 1959), pp. 56–57; Log. 113 : 13–18.

xi

been deprived of his professorship in Rome for refusing the oath of loyalty to Mussolini. These four had been participants, in 1933, in the first "shared feast" (*eranos*) of the series, together with C. G. Jung, who continued to contribute until 1951, Mrs. C. A. F. Rhys Davids, president of the Pali Text Society, and Dr. Gustav-Richard Heyer, a distinguished neurologist and author. Henri-Charles Puech, director of studies at the Ecole des Hautes-Etudes of the Sorbonne, and Boris Petrovitch Vysheslawzeff, professor of moral theology at the Russian Orthodox Theological Institute in Paris, read their papers here translated at the session of 1936. Louis Massignon, of the Collège de France, president of the Institut des Etudes Iraniennes of the Sorbonne, arrived the following year for the first of his many appearances. Father Jean de Menasce, professor of ancient Iranian religion at the Sorbonne, and Wilhelm Koppers, professor of Indic and ethnological studies in Vienna, were together contributors to the distinguished meeting in 1944 on *The Mysteries*.[2] Professor Gilles Quispel of Leiden (now of Utrecht) made his first appearance at the Eranos meeting of 1947, and Erich Neumann—with the unforgettable paper here for the first time rendered into English—at the meeting of 1948.

The present is the sixth of our series of volumes of translated papers from the Eranos annuals. Volume 1, *Spirit and Nature*, was based largely on the meetings of 1945 and 1946; Volume 2, *The Mysteries*, on 1944; Volume 3, *Man and Time*, carried papers chiefly from the meeting of 1951, the last of Professor Jung's participation, which marked, as many of those present realized, the closing of one stage of the project and opening of a new. Volume 4, *Spiritual Disciplines*, returned to authors of the years 1933 to 1945; after which Volume 5, *Man and Transformation*, based largely on the session of 1954, presented together a number of those—Ernst Benz, Henry Corbin, Mircea Eliade, and Adolf Portmann—who have continued as guiding contributors to the present. Frau Froebe died in 1962 at the age of 81, but the Eranos festival that she inspired and for thirty years directed is continuing in her spirit—

2 Most of the other papers of that year have been presented in English in Volume 2 of the present series.

and, if a word were sought to characterize it, it were best found, perhaps, in Lao-tse, in whose concept of the Tao she had her being:

To know the always-so is to be Illumined;
Not to know it, means to go blindly to disaster.

He who knows the always-so has room in him for everything;
He who has room in him for everything is without prejudice.

To be without prejudice is to be kingly;
To be kingly is to be of heaven;
To be of heaven is to be in Tao.

Tao is forever and he that possesses it,
Though his body ceases, is not destroyed.[3]

It remains for me, in closing, only to thank sincerely the distinguished directors of Bollingen Foundation, through whose kindness I was accorded the great privilege of participating in this venture; to recall with grateful affection the trust and sympathetic guidance of Frau Froebe in the first years; and to acknowledge with admiration my debt as editor both to Mr. Ralph Manheim and to Mr. R. F. C. Hull for their masterful translations, and to the members of the Bollingen Series editorial and production staff, who through their unstinting care and labors brought these six volumes through to publication.

"Matters be ended as they are befriended."

JOSEPH CAMPBELL

New York City
Easter, 1968

3 *Tao Tê Ching*, XVI (in part), tr. Arthur Waley, *The Way and Its Power* (London, 1934), p. 162.

THE MYSTIC VISION

Boris Vysheslawzeff

Two Ways of Redemption: Redemption as Resolution of the Tragic Contradiction

I

A philosopher must first of all admit his membership in that group of men who are still searching for the philosopher's stone. A scientist is tempted to look for this stone in his own science: in chemistry, mathematics, mechanics, biology, and, most recently, in psychology. But here he can never find it, for wisdom, *sophia,* transcends all specialized disciplines with its all-embracing unity, with its ultimate interpretation and decision. The philosopher's stone can indeed be found only in philosophy, which subordinates all the findings and techniques of the specialized sciences to its own purposes. The philosophical aim, the ultimate aim, transcends all the sciences. A positive science, based on the principle of causality, can never come to grips with the problem of ultimate aims; it cannot embody an ultimate interpretation. A technical method always implies an axiology, presupposes values which are tacitly recognized. The techniques of medicine and psychoanalysis possess no axiology but merely select from the hierarchy of values such isolated values as health or physical and mental "normalcy." But no one knows what is "normal," for what is the "norm" of man? The answer depends on what man *wants to be,* on what he *ought to be.* In any event, it is not "normal" for man to think of nothing but his health. For the ultimate decision and interpretation we must sum up the whole meaning; we must presuppose (clearly or obscurely, consciously or unconsciously) the whole system, for the interpretation consists precisely in our attitude toward the "whole," toward the all-embracing "symbol" of the absolute, toward the ultimate unity of opposites.

3

But the ultimate question, the question of the meaning of life, arises from the depths of self-reflection when the self finds itself in a *tragic contradiction,* when it clashes with an absurdity, a catastrophe, an injustice.

The solution of the tragic contradiction cannot be logical, theoretical, technical; it cannot be arrived at by any immanent science or rational consciousness; it requires a *redemption* that comes from the realm of transcendence, from the kingdom that is "not of this world." All great religions have been religions of redemption. The misery and suffering of life, the tragic contradiction, create the need for redemption:

> Who never ate his bread in sorrow,
> Who never spent the darksome hours
> Weeping and watching for the morrow,
> He knows ye not, ye gloomy powers.[1]

Such redemption and salvation from a tragic contradiction, from the *aporia* (perplexity) in which no way is discernible, cannot but be experienced as a miracle, a "revelation." The solution comes to us from the ultimate hidden unity of the absolute, from the *Deus absconditus,* who dwells "behind the wall of the coincidence of opposites" (*intra murum coincidentiae oppositorum*) and miraculously combines the opposites, so that, clash as they will, they cannot destroy each other, so that conflict is suddenly transformed into a harmony—for "from contradictions arises the most beautiful harmony."

This solution is never rational; it is "religious," for it is arrived at through our tie (*re-ligio*) with the transcendent, through our sense of dependence on the absolute. But this sense of dependence with all its wealth of meaning, this sense of being rooted in the ultimate source of the absolute, can be expressed only in a rich and mysterious *symbol.* Only in a symbol can the supraconscious speak to the conscious and subconscious, as a transcendent father to his this-worldly son.

The *symbolic wisdom* of the redeeming word cannot be explained by any rational science; it can only be surmised by a *divinatio* or interpreted by a philosophical prophecy. The love of

---

1 Goethe, *Wilhelm Meister,* tr. Thomas Carlyle.

divine wisdom, philosophy itself, is the "mirror" in which redeeming wisdom appears—though in a cryptic and "fragmentary" way. *Intuition* and *dialectic* constitute the method of philosophy; the mysterious symbol of the solution is perceived intuitively in the infinite richness of its potentialities, and then dialectically developed in its antinomic ambivalence and polyvalence. Philosophy deals always with the ultimate unity and with the antinomies, with the absolute and the coincidence of opposites. Hegel is right in saying that the object of philosophy is the same as the object of religion.

Wisdom is to be found where philosophy and religion meet. It is in the field of the infinite, the unconditional, the absolute that antinomies arise and dialectic begins. But dialectic is the art of dealing in contradictions, of discovering and resolving antinomies. Everyone who speaks of the coincidence of opposites enters into the sphere of philosophy, even if it is in his own science that he encounters the problem.

II

As we have said, all great religions are religions of redemption, that is, solutions of the tragic contradiction, of the fundamental antinomy of life. When we intuitively perceive and emotionally experience their symbols in all their depth and richness, we become immediately aware of the profound cleavage between the European and Asiatic worlds, between the Indian and the Christian-Hellenic idea of redemption. Two types of solution are possible a priori, and there are in fact two possible attitudes toward the tragic contradiction:

1. To withdraw, to evade the contradiction; to flee from the contradictory world, allowing this world to dissolve into an "illusion."

2. Or to thrust oneself into the objective contradiction, into the battle of opposites, to oppose the hostile forces as a tragic hero, to fall without fear, to "rise" from every defeat with firm faith, with a hope that hypostasizes all our profoundest desires (ἐλπι-ζομένων ὑπόστασις) .

This second approach implies that every practical contradiction is soluble, if not here and now, then in the "hereafter." This is the Christian–Hellenic attitude. We find the opposite in Hinduism: the contradictions of life and the world are insoluble in principle; to develop the contradictions and combat them is to involve oneself in conflict and suffering; on the contrary, we must withdraw from the contradictions.

The fundamental experience of the tragic is different for the Indian and for the Christian–Hebrew–Hellenic mind; there are different degrees, different levels of the tragic. Every tear, every sorrow, every pain is tragic in itself. (Does the Apocalypse not promise that "God will wipe away all tears"?) But there are different kinds of tears and varying degrees of sadness. Buddha saw the tragic in the visions of sickness, old age, and death. That man must suffer and die—therein lies the essence of the tragic in the Hindu conception—but this is not the supreme experience of the tragic. It is more tragic to suffer and die unjustly, like Prometheus, Socrates, Job, and Christ. Here the contradiction is perceived more profoundly. Man wants to live and must die; he wants to be healthy and happy and must suffer. This, to be sure, is a tragic contradiction, but there is another and far deeper one—that formulated by Socrates in his *Apology:* a man deserving of the highest honor is sentenced to death. The tragic increases with the injustice: the suffering and condemnation of the innocent, the meritorious, the saint—and finally of the demigod. This is the extreme of the tragic: the precious, the sacred, the divine, is trampled, humiliated, destroyed. The height of the tragic is attained in Golgotha. Here the Christian mind finds the archetype of the suffering God, the archetype of the tragic situation. Here all tragic situations are epitomized: the unjust sentence, the treachery of the mob, the inquisition of the priests, the failure to recognize the sublime and godly in the "son of man," the disloyalty and betrayal of the disciple, and finally God-forsakenness, the silence of the heavens. In this extreme situation, the tragic contradiction becomes intolerable to man; accordingly it is here that the solution—redemption—must be found.

Before we can ask how this is possible we must reflect on the profound paradox of the tragic: it does not utterly crush the soul but calls forth a feeling of redemption, a "catharsis" that is difficult to define. Consolation is always present in the depths, although one

6

cannot apprehend it. The spirit of the Paraclete is present in the tragic, but it is something imponderable and unknown. In the presence of the tragic, courage is not lost but becomes tension, upsurge; it is elevated (ἀναγογή) to the sphere of the unknown, as in a *divinatio*—hence our sense of the sublime. This strange phenomenon presupposes and hints at the possibility of a solution to the contradiction; the new symbol, the symbol of a new interpretation, is born from the transcendent.

Thus a remarkable dialectic can be found in the tragic: an *unbearable* tragic fate is borne by the tragic hero, the holy martyr, the suffering God: he does not bow and he does not take flight—to lesser values and deficient values he opposes his higher value. The just will cannot be annulled by injustice. The greater the injustice the more sublime becomes the unjustly suffering holy will. In the condemnation and death of Socrates man's greatest disgrace coincides with his greatest glory. On the heights of Golgotha his profoundest fall from grace coincides with his supreme "justification" and glorification in the God-man.

At one and the same moment God might say that he repents of having made man—and that he does not repent after all. This is *redemptio*, justification: the divine *fiat iustitia* need not mean *pereat mundus, pereat homo*. There are values which "redeem" all failings.

This is the first "cathartic" sense of the tragic: in tragedy, authentic and false, meaning and absurdity, value and deficiency—the greatness and the wretchedness of man—coincide.[2] There is a certain consolation in the mere fact that everything cannot be reduced to absurdity and meaninglessness, that utter despair and resignation prove unfounded, that existence need not be totally condemned (*pereat mundus, pereat homo*), since the sublime, the sacred, the transcendent is inherent in every tragic situation. Yet it is a sad consolation, for the "ideal realm" is always present, but only "in so far as we do not possess it" (Fichte). The true, the sacred, the transcendent is "mere idea." And when one who is able to perceive the idea, who may be regarded as an embodiment of this idea itself, descends into the dark cave of this world to liberate

2 Also essentially in the comic, as Socrates and Aristophanes surmised in the *Symposium*.

the prisoners who lie here in chains and lead them up to the sunlight, he is, like Socrates, killed by the prisoners; for he *contradicts* everything by which the prisoners live; he stands in tragic conflict with everything he finds here below. When a god wishes to descend into this world that is "immersed in evil," he must *suffer and die.* But that is no solution, for the "suffering god," the dying god, is a contradiction. God is blessed and immortal. Hence he must rise again; he must transcend the tragic contradiction of suffering, death, and sin; he must transcend this evil world itself, in order to manifest the realm "that is not of this world."

III

This "transcending" in its fine dialectical ambiguity, perceived by Hegel, shows us the two roads of redemption. The Hindu redemption "transcends" the world with its tragic contradiction by annihilating it, by dismissing it as illusion. The contradictory dissolves in illusion. Christian redemption transcends [*aufhebt*] the world by preserving it at a higher level, by a transfiguration, a *theosis.* It is a "leading upwards," an *anagōgē,* a sublimation.

Anagōgē, sublimatio, represents a fundamental philosophical category. It found its first, inspired elucidation in the Platonic Eros, and a more sober expression in Aristotle's hierarchy of form and matter; in these two traditions the notion was preserved and utilized throughout the Middle Ages. Aquinas' famous maxim, *"gratia naturam non tollit sed perficit,"*[3] embodies the principle of sublimation. Alexander of Hales employed the same term: *"sublimatio creaturae super naturam."* The Aristotelian hierarchy of forms and the *anagōgē* are developed and given dialectical foundation in Hegel, who retains their substance in his notion of the higher category which transcends the lower. Nietzsche prized this philosophical category, particularly in its ethical application, and even made use of the term "sublimation."[4] And today we find the same tradition in Nikolai Hartmann's "Überbauungs- und Überformungsverhältnis" (hyperedification and hyperformation) of the categories. *Überformung* is neither more nor less than sublimation.

3 "Grace does not take the place of nature but perfects it" (*Summa Theologica,* I, q. 1, art. 8, obj. 2, resp.).
4 See, for example, *Thus Spake Zarathustra,* Part I, ch. 5, Joys and Passions.

Freud was perfectly right in applying the term "sublimation" to psychoanalytical theory and practice, particularly in connection with the Platonic Eros. But in so doing, he incurred an obligation to take this term in its best and profoundest sense, as fixed by the vast dialectical labors of philosophy; this he did not do. Consequently, "sublimation" has become a practical, popular term among the psychoanalytic public. Philosophically, it lends itself in this usage to the vulgar positivism which attempts to reduce all higher values to the sexual urge by the "nothing but" method (a *spéculation à la baisse* after the manner of Marxism).

This leads to the very opposite of philosophical sublimation, of "hyperedification and hyperformation" of the categories. For if the higher level can be reduced to the lower and explained in terms of it, the successive stages of development lose their qualitative independence. What does sublime mean? What is "higher" and "lower" form? What is sought and found in the uplifting of the psyche?

Here all these questions find no answer. Important philosophical and psychological problems are concealed and ignored in the popular term "sublimate." Jung had good reason not to content himself with this usage but to search farther for the true meaning of sublimation. With Aristotelian sobriety he said: What we are seeking is the middle road; that is, the issue from an *aporia,* a dilemma, a contradictory situation. It is extremely difficult to find that issue, for it is the solution of a contradiction in which a *tertium non datur.* This third which is not given, and which is seemingly impossible, must, however, be found, and it can only result from an entirely *new* synthesis of opposing forces or directions. This is an operation, a discovery, which transcends the level of warring opposites, of contradiction, and finds in another dimension a synthesis that was impossible at the earlier stage. This new synthesis and stage are called higher only because here all the positive forces and elements that were previously in conflict are retained, but they have entered into a new combination which solves the contradiction.[5] This precisely is sublimation; this is hyperformation, the discovery of a higher form. Without the solution of the "middle

---

5 The spatial relation of "height" means only that the "higher" stage embraces and contains the "lower"; it presupposes the lower—but not conversely.

road," without the unity of opposites, without the "dialectic method," sublimation cannot be understood and cannot be put to practical use.

Modern analytical psychology strives to bring about "mental health"—that is, to overcome the conflicts of the psyche. This in itself relates it to the "problem of salvation," since it, too, seeks a solution of the tragic contradiction. What desires to be saved and "redeemed" is above all the soul; but tragic contradictions can make themselves felt in other provinces of being as well. There are cosmic catastrophes as well as biological, sociological, juridical, ethical, and national conflicts. But the soul has its own ways of rationalizing dissonance, of assimilating and transforming it into tragic experiences. Injustice is as much a tragedy of the soul as of the state and of the law.[6] The same principle of tragic contradiction is determinant for both macrocosm and microcosm.

Opposition and contradiction are not psychological categories but universal ontological principles, having their application on all levels of being and in all fields of knowledge (including psychology). Anyone who speaks of opposition and contradiction embarks on a dialectical process and enters the sphere of philosophy. And here, too, the problem of the tragic is present.

IV

We cannot understand the tragic contradiction and the nature of its solution without developing the whole problem of contradiction. This is and remains the fundamental problem of philosophy, both Hindu and Hellenic–European. The problem is raised in the philosophical myth of the *Ṛg Veda* (10.129); it runs through all the Upaniṣads, and it finds its definitive formulation in the great philosophical systems of India. The primeval archetype of the birth of contradictions signifies also the birth of philosophy. European dialectic begins with the *elimination* of things from the *apeiron* of Anaximander, and with the Pythagorean table of opposites. The principle of *"Schiedlichkeit"* (Jakob Boehme), of "disjunction," of the *"Durch"* (Fichte), or simply of the *"dia"* is at the base of all being and thinking. A is made possible only by not-A. This

6 For it is the same idea of justice which, as Plato said, is inscribed in large letters on the state and in small letters on the soul.

simple principle contains within it all the complexities of the dialectic as it developed from Heraclitus, through Plato and Aristotle, to Jakob Boehme, Kant, Fichte, Schelling, and Hegel. The ultimate mysteries of being are antinomic. Antithesis and synthesis constitute the eternal theme of philosophy; and in this sphere nothing is static—not since Aristotle and not since Hegel. The coincidence of opposites embraces many wonders and revelations. The philosophical dialectic makes possible new discoveries in the realm of opposition, polarity, contradiction.

It suffices for the present to discuss three aspects of the relationship of opposites.

1. *The indifferent coincidence of opposites.* All opposites are, as Plato said, connected with their ends. But the nature of the connection varies: on the one hand we have a fixed, eternal, ontological connection; on the other hand a soluble, mobile, imposed connection. The first applies approximately to the relation of opposites which Aristotle calls "$\tau\grave{\alpha}\ \pi\rho\grave{o}s\ \tau\acute{\iota}$." Here we have such antitheses as the part and the whole, north and south, cause and effect, substance and accident, positive and negative. The spatial and temporal antitheses of here and there, now and then also belong to this group. We have called this coincidence "indifferent" because it is unchanging: the part is always part of a whole, just as the cause is always the cause of an effect. The connection between these antitheses is rigid and immutable; it reveals no qualitative or quantitative differences. The connection is given, and the antitheses have no need to adapt themselves to one another or to concern themselves with one another in any way. In this sense, the connection between them is "indifferent."

But there are two other modes of connection which represent not a stable tie but a dynamic activity of binding; here the antitheses do not coincide indifferently but adapt themselves continuously to one another and concern themselves with one another in an attitude either of battle or reconciliation.

These are:

2. *The repugnance (or battle) of opposites.* Individual examples are unnecessary, because the whole world that is "immersed in evil" provides an example. All the conflicts in the outward or inward world and all the conflicts between these worlds are examples. And

11

because this aspect of the dialectical development of opposites is *everywhere* to be found, Heraclitus could say that war is the father of all things. In this relation the opposites are also bound, one may even say chained, to one another, but the bond is not stable and at rest; they are not *indifferently* connected but connected by "hate." "Φθαρτικὰ γὰρ ἀλλήλων τὰ ἐναντία," says Aristotle, "opposites destroy one another."[7] In his strange dialectic of society, Hobbes calls this state of affairs "a time of Warre, where every man is Enemy to every man" (*Leviathan*, Part I, Ch. 13).

To this category of antagonism belongs also the tragic contradiction, which demands solution and promises redemption. In dialectical terms, the nature and meaning of this opposition can be expressed as follows: *a reciprocal exclusion*, an *either–or*, an inability to coexist. The mutual exclusion may be actual or ideal; it may be judgments—or things, forces, or living creatures—that cannot coexist. Both belong to the same comprehensive mode of opposition. There is actual repugnance and logical repugnance; Kant uses the same term for both. Essential and determinant for this whole category of opposition is the *repugnance,* despite all possible differences in its actual or ideal application. Thus it is by no means correct to say that there is only a "logical" and no "actual" contradiction: living men can oppose one another, and conflicting ideas can wage an actual war and manifest a very actual repugnance.[8]

---

7 *Physics*, 192 a.

8 The most widespread fallacy consists in making a total distinction between ideal and actual repugnance, in disregard of the category of repugnance which lies at the base of both. The total separation of the actual and ideal is in itself false. Contradiction [*Wider-Spruch*] and conflict [*Wider-Stand*, literally "resistance."—Tr.] share this category of contrariness [*Widereinander*], which is by no means common to all modes of opposition. For opposition does not necessarily mean conflict. The first group gave us a different category of opposition, for north does not "conflict with" south, any more than an effect can "conflict with" a cause, although the two are opposed. But the close connection between "contradiction" and "conflict" is revealed by any lawsuit, for the two sides contradict one another, each one saying: "This is mine and not yours," and this contradiction is actual conflict, or even battle and warfare. The mutual exclusion is here both ideal and actual. Total distinction between "logical" and "actual" opposition is always directed against Hegel and his contrary fallacy, namely failure to consider these two modes of repugnance—contradiction and conflict. Here we cannot go more deeply into this distinction, for it raises a highly complicated problem to which we are devoting a special work. But we must stress this one point: Hegel's fallacy

Intrinsically, contradiction is a negative value; we seek to avoid it. Since the opposites cannot tolerate one another, it becomes *intolerable*. In this sense, it is the source of suffering and tragedy. One cannot calmly accept this contradiction; it cannot be recognized as "definitive." A different connection between the opposites is called for. And if contradiction means repugnance, hence struggle, the solution can only mean peace. This brings us to another relation between opposites.

3. *The harmony of opposites.* Harmony is not identity; it is opposition and articulation. For "opposites concord and divergences give rise to the finest harmony, and all through struggle." So said Heraclitus (τὸ ἀντίξουν συμφέρον καὶ ἐκ τῶν διαφερόντων καλλίστην ἁρμονίαν καὶ πάντα κατ' ἔριν γίνεσθαι) .[9] This is a new relation of opposites, in which the opposites do not exclude or destroy one another; they do not devour but mutually nurture one another— ἐναντίος δὲ τροφεῖ τ'ἀναντίον (Aristotle) . "Whence rises friendship, the harmony of love," asks Plato. "From sameness or from opposition?" And he answers: "The most contrary is most attracted to the most contrary" (τὸ γὰρ ἐναντιώτατον τῷ ἐναντιωτάτῳ εἶναι μάλιστα φίλον, *Lysis,* 215 E) . From struggle arises harmony, and the greater the conflict the profounder and firmer the union which transcends it.[10]

The very same elements of being which have been at war, here enter into another, *complementary* relation. A new and fortunate combination is found, which in alchemy was called *hieros gamos,* a sacred marriage of the elements. This fortunate relation is really a miracle, a *tertium datur;* it is the birth of a new stage of being, which was not previously present. We do not fully understand how this is possible, for the transition, the mutation, is at certain

is much less serious than that of his opponents, since he recognized the comprehensive unity of repugnance, while his adversaries had no inkling of it. His achievement lies in his recognition of "actual contradiction"; his fallacy, in his belief that this justified him in neglecting or rejecting the logical law of identity (and of contradiction) . But both must be retained in accordance with Plato's dialectics (particularly in *The Sophists*) .

9 Heraclitus in H. Diels, *Die Fragmente der Vorsokratiker* (Berlin, 1938) , Frag. 8.

10 We must not forget Spinoza's psychological explanation (see *Ethics,* III, props. 43, 44) of why enmity can turn into the strongest friendship and love (the theme of *Romeo and Juliet, Tristan and Isolde*) . That the enemy is a potential friend and that enmity is transcended by love is the essence of the Christian injunction to "love thine enemy."

moments quite unconscious and even irrational. We can be sure of only one thing: this is the source of creative resurgence, of sublimation, of the transcending of the lower by the higher. The whole "hyperedification and hyperformation" of being—in its ascent from the atom to the living cell, and from animate life to the living spirit with its forever new conflicts and solutions—is possible only because the third mode of opposition, the harmony of polarities, lies at the base of the whole process. It is here that we must seek the philosopher's stone, for if it were contained in the first mode of opposition, in indifferent coincidence, we should not have to look for it, we should find it in every pebble on the road. But to seek it in the second mode, in that of conflict and contradiction, would be an absurdity, for its function is precisely to supersede this state and deliver us from it. The absurdity of contradiction achieves meaning when we transcend the contradiction and arrive at a solution. The meaning of struggle lies in the new harmony of peace. To seek meaning in war for its own sake would be perversion and demonism, for this would be calm acceptance of an actual contradiction.[11]

All living creatures, all intellectual conceptions are such *systems of harmonious polarity;* the development of thesis, antithesis, and reconciling synthesis merely constitutes the principle and rhythm of the highly complex differentiation and integration. Jung's greatest philosophical and psychological achievement is to have discovered in the mind a system of harmonious polarity, and in particular the polarity of conscious and unconscious. But this discovery leads the psychologist to the "dialectical method"; he must engage in dialogue with the philosopher; and at the same time dialogue with the great psychologist becomes incumbent on the philosopher.

The system of the mind is no stable equilibrium, no given harmony, but one that is merely projected—it is always present and never present; it is in constant development and disintegration, a continuous transcending of conflict. The soul is harmony and dissonance; it is a system of opposites which "nourish" and "devour" one another, an antinomy in constant process of solution.

11 The contradiction of war is expressed in the words "All they that take the sword shall perish with the sword" (Matt. 26:52).

Hence the need for redemption and the inner tragedy of the soul. The opposites bound together in repugnance and harmony stand in no fixed relation but in a relation which continuously dissolves, binds, and changes. The harmonious systems arise from struggle and disintegrate through struggle—clashing, battling, or integrating themselves with one another. This is the Heraclitean flux of becoming and passing away, of struggle and harmony, of death and birth, of war and peace. And we find this rhythm of conflict, this rhythm of development, solution, and dissolution, in every sphere: in biology, psychology, sociology. Has this play of opposites a meaning? Or does eternity "play with the world as a child with sand" (Heraclitus)? The alternating rhythm leads one to doubt whether the process has any meaning or direction. It may signify eternal repetition as well as development or decay. Here the ultimate interpretations and decisions of the great religions diverge.

If there is a direction, it can only lie in the transition from the second to the third mode of opposition, that is, from repugnance to harmony. This direction is a question of value. Here lies the immanent axiology of being.[12]

But this axiology points to the infinite, because every differentiated harmonious system stands in conflict with another system and demands an integration, that is, a superordinate system of systems. The direction is ultimately determined by the idea of actual-infinite integration, by the idea of universal harmony. Leibniz was right and will always be right in defining perfection as the greatest unity of the greatest diversity, or as extreme integration of extreme differentiation.[13]

But universal harmony is the philosophical term for the Christian kingdom of God, for which the last two chapters of the Apocalypse give a symbolic picture. Similarly in Plato the reign of justice is conceivable only as the harmony of opposites, as "symphony and symmetry." But to this must be added an idea which is lacking in classical Greek thought: the idea of the actual-infinite. It is however contained in the "Messianic kingdom" and in the symbol of the "Pantocrator": God will become *all in all*. This

12 An axiology which not only feels or discovers values but also thinks or understands them.
13 Also as *magna potestas in exiguo volumine.*

idea of concrete totality is also known to Neoplatonism: the ἕν καὶ πᾶν, the "one and all." Nicholas of Cusa explored and elucidated the actual-infinite by means of the Greek and Byzantine dialectic of opposites and equated it with the Christian kingdom of God. Thus he arrived at a magnificent *coincidentia oppositorum:* God governs his kingdom in that he holds together the infinite multiplicity of opposites by their coincidence. Leibniz epitomizes these ideas by linking his notions of mathematical infinity and of perfection, and so arriving at the idea of a *harmonia universalis.* But the Kantian dialectic formulates a fundamental opposition which was disregarded by Nicholas of Cusa and Leibniz: the opposition of that which is and that which ought to be. For him, too, allness (the all-embracing synthesis, "universal law") is a value; however, it is not given but only aimed at; "it exists only in so far as one does not possess it" (Fichte) ; it *is* not but only *ought* to be. We must hold to this idea with a tragic courage and an ethical faith, "even if it is never realized."

Since it never is realized, one can lose faith and come to regard the "infinite task" as an impossible task, as a "bad infinity" of genesis and passing away. Every harmony must experience the tragic fate of dissolution, and there is no sense in trying to reverse the wheel of life. This is another conception of life, the Hindu conception.

V

In India universal harmony, the "kingdom of God," is regarded as an illusion, a fundamental fallacy. And not only in Buddhism, which formulates elaborate proofs of the non-existence of God, but also in the Upaniṣads and in the philosophical systems of Vedānta and of Yoga, where the absolute (Brahman) or even God (Īśvara) is recognized as true being. Īśvara, the Lord God, dwells aloft in his eternal transcendence; far below him flows the stream of world and mankind in Saṁsāra, in eternally recurrent cycles of genesis and passing away. And here the errant soul is lost in worldliness. This world wanders on from *kalpa* to *kalpa.* Never does it become a "kingdom of God," a place of the sublime or of glory to God. It remains forever concatenation without goal or end, forever worthless, never imbued with value, never transfigured. For India the world and history have no value and no *telos.* This is in total contrast to Christianity with its positive evaluation of the world.[14] The *theosis,* the "restoration of the all," the kingdom of God, are here without meaning.

This Hindu attitude is based on a particular conception of opposition and polarity. The first mode of coincidence is almost disregarded;[15] there is no belief in the third mode, the mode of harmony; the second, that of repugnance and contradiction, is looked upon as the only true mode of opposition. The Hindus do not believe in harmony, because it represents a passing state, because every system must suffer and collapse under an inner or outer shock. This is proved by the experience of sickness, old age, death, suffering. All these phenomena are variants of the basic contradiction.

In the Indian conception, every opposition leads in principle to a repugnance, a conflict, to hate and suffering. Only the absolute, the Brahman in its identity, is free from contradiction, unsuffering and immortal.

> No, my dear, it was Being alone that existed in the beginning, one only without a second (*Chāndogya Upaniṣad* 6.2.2).[16]
>
> Everything else but this is perishable (*Bṛhad-āraṇyaka Upaniṣad* 3.4.2).
>
> He goes from death to death who sees in It, as it were, diversity (*Bṛhad. Upan.* 4.4.19).

Most typical is the following maxim of the Yogi Patañjali:

> *Duḥkha—anuśayī—dveṣaḥ* (*Yoga Sūtra* 2.8).

Hauer translates as follows: " 'Duality caused by hate appears in the consciousness as pain.' Or, more briefly, we might say: 'Opposition is conflict, disunity, and pain.' "[17]

> This world suffers forever from the dichotomies (*Rāmāyaṇa* 2.84.20).[18]

14 See the excellent comparison by Rudolf Otto in *India's Religion of Grace,* tr. F. H. Foster (London, 1930) , pp. 68–70, 72–74.

15 Hence the lack of science and technology in India, for these are built on such categories of opposition as cause and effect and the polarity of forces.

16 Tr. Swāmī Nikhilānanda, *The Upanishads* (4 vols., New York, 1949) . [All translations from the Upaniṣads in this paper are from this work, unless otherwise noted.]

17 J. W. Hauer, *Der Joga als Heilweg* (Stuttgart, 1932) , p. 112.

18 [Tr. from the author's German.]

The solution of the basic contradiction is impossible in so far as we hold fast to oppositions. The only solution and redemption is the dissolution of oppositions in identity or indifference, or a radical annulment of opposition itself. This is the famous *Kevalādvaita* of Vedānta—the doctrine of absolute nonduality. Multiplicity is a great cosmic illusion, a delusive mania (*avidyā*). We find this idea throughout the Upaniṣads:

> Therefore the non-dual position does not conflict with the dualist's position. This unborn (changeless, non-dual Brahman) appears to undergo modification only on account of Maya (illusion) and not otherwise. For, if this modification were real, the Immortal (Brahman) would become mortal (*Māṇḍūkya-Kārikā* 3.18, 19).[19]

> That which you see as other than righteousness and unrighteousness, other than all this cause and effect, other than what has been and what is to be—tell me that (*Kaṭha Upan.* 1.2.14).

Freedom from opposition is the essence of true being, of Brahman:

> Through the mind alone is Brahman to be realized. There is in It no diversity. . . . It should be realized in one form only. The Self is free from taint . . . (*Bṛhad. Upan.* 4.4.19, 20).

In the ultimate unity of the absolute, all opposition and contradiction vanish; hence there is no suffering:

> (This Ātman is) all peace, eternal effulgence free from activity and fear and attainable by concentrated understanding (of the Jīva). In that Brahman which is free from all acts of mind there is neither any idea of acceptance nor any idea of giving up (of anything). Established in the Ātman (Self), knowledge attains to the state of birthlessness and sameness, that is to say, changelessness. This Yoga, which is not in touch with anything, is hard to be attained by all Yogis (in general). The Yogis are afraid of it, for they see fear in it where there is really fearlessness. . . . When the mind does not merge in the inactivity of oblivion, or become distracted by desires, that is to say, when the mind becomes quiescent and does not give rise to ap-

19 Tr. Nikhilānanda, *The Māṇḍūkyopaniṣad, with Gauḍapada's Kārikā and Śaṅkara's Commentary* (Mysore, 1936). [This translation is used for all quotations from the *Māṇḍūkya Upaniṣad* in this paper.]

pearances, it verily becomes Brahman (*Māṇḍūkya-Kārikā* 3.37–39, 46).

In approaching the absolute, with which he ultimately becomes identical (for Ātman is fundamentally identical with Brahman), the sage achieves freedom from opposition, nonduality, the only possible "redemption":

> By the wise, who are free from attachment, fear, and anger and who are well versed in the meaning of the Vedas, this (Ātman) has been verily realised as totally devoid of all imaginations (such as those of Prāna, etc.), free from the illusion of the manifold, and non-dual. Therefore, knowing the Ātman to be such, fix your attention on non-duality. Having realised non-duality, behave in the world like an insensible object (*Māṇḍūkya-Kārikā* 2.35, 36).

This flowing-together and dissolution of all things in the ultimate identity of nonduality can be attained in different ways: through the affective identity of universal suffering, through sympathy (*tat tvam asi*—thou art that), and by the theoretical identity of the non-differentiation of subject and object. My "self," the Ātman Self, is such a point of identity, out of which all oppositions develop and into which they can retreat. "I" *transcends* all oppositions, even the fundamental opposition of knowing subject and known object. If the self, Ātman, remains in this transcendence and develops no oppositions, then "there is no second, other, different thing that it can see, smell, taste, speak to, hear, think, feel, and know," as we read in a famous passage of the *Bṛhad-āraṇyaka Upaniṣad*.

Objectness is here abandoned, but with it also subjectness, the conscious ego, with its functions of cognition, sensation, feeling, with its fear, desire, and suffering.

> For when there is duality, as it were, then one smells another, one sees another, one hears another, one speaks to another, one thinks of another, one knows another. But when everything has become the Self, then what should one smell and through what, what should one see and through what, what should one hear . . . speak . . . think . . . know and through what? Through what should one know That owing to which all this is known—through what, my dear, should one know the Knower? (*Bṛhad. Upan.* 2.4.14).

19

But if opposition is annulled, all oppositions and all objects vanish with it; the world of objects vanishes, but so likewise does the world of subjects:

> No Jīva is ever born. There does not exist any cause which can produce it. This is the highest Truth that nothing is ever born (*Māṇḍūkya-Kārikā* 3.48).

If there are no opposites, the concept of change vanishes, the rhythm of genesis and passing away, of death and birth. The illusion of diversity, the illusion of the outward and inward worlds, is dispelled like a dream.

What then remains? Mere *nothingness?* Does "redemption" signify a dissolution into nothingness? Southern Buddhism does not hesitate to draw this inference. But the Upaniṣads and the systems of Vedānta and Yoga that are based on them take a different view: the state of redemption is not nothingness but something very positive—the highest salvation; it is not a void but a fullness:

> Where one sees nothing else, hears nothing else, understands nothing else—that is the Infinite. Where one sees something else, hears something else, understands something else—that is the finite. The Infinite is immortal, the finite mortal (*Chāndogya Upan.* 7.24.1).

What remains—after the dissolution of all oppositions and all worlds—is the "self," Ātman, *puruṣa* ("man as such"), but in an unusual state which seems rather strange and forbidding, even to "the Yogi himself." Even the wise Maitreyī is thrown into confusion when her husband tells her that in this state there is *no consciousness:* "after attaining [this oneness] it has no more consciousness" (*Bṛhad. Upan.* 4.5.13). This state is often likened to a deep dreamless sleep (ibid. 4.3.19ff.), but it is distinguished from such sleep as a higher, rarer state, difficult to attain, is distinguished from a lower, common, and general state.

The *Sarva Upaniṣad* (5.8) distinguishes four states of Ātman: waking, dreaming, deep sleep, and the fourth: *turīyam*. This last is defined as "the spiritual which stands to being as an onlooker, but which in itself signifies an indifference liberated from all being."

But there can be no definition and description of the "self" in the state of its ultimate transcendence and redemption. Even that which we have just quoted is very inadequate. The *Bṛhad-āraṇyaka Upaniṣad* ends with a negative definition, a "not this, not that" (*neti, neti*), as in an apophatic theology, and this is perhaps the profoundest statement of all that can be said of it. It is a state which must be attained and experienced by the methods of Vedānta or Yoga, or of some other school of mysticism. The comparison with deep sleep, however, contains an important indication: the "self" in its highest state is no ego consciousness; it is the unconscious. But deep sleep is something base and common; it might be called the subconscious, compared to which the "self" (Ātman, *puruṣa*) would be the superconscious.

The similarity with deep sleep, with death, lies in the loss of consciousness ("it has no more consciousness"). But there can be another, hyperconscious state of the "self." When the "self" transcends all oppositions and rises above them, it transcends also the opposition of conscious and unconscious. True, this is a very modern inference which was not drawn by Indian philosophy. But it did explicitly formulate another conclusion: the *transcendence of the self,* the transcending of oppositions, means not death but immortality; for death is an opposite of birth. Death and birth, genesis and passing away, form a chain of opposites which can be suspended by the nondifferentiation of *advaita.* The "self" transcends the rhythm of death and birth, hence it is in this state undying, but one might equally well say "unliving," for in freeing itself from the rhythm of death it also liberates itself from the rhythm of life. All this is very different from the Christian idea of immortality and salvation.

This idea of the dissolution of opposition, of nonduality (*advaita*), which we find in the Upaniṣads and in Vedānta, is the basis of the whole Indian *Weltanschauung.* "Freedom" from oppositions, "imperviousness to oppositions" (*nirdvandva*) —everywhere we encounter this path of redemption: in the *Book of Manu,* in the *Bhagavadgītā,* in the whole *Mahābhārata.* And the system of Yoga defines the supreme state of bliss, *samādhi,* as "imperviousness to oppositions." (Hauer translates *samādhi* as "Einfaltung" [folding inwards]—the opposite of the "Entfaltung" [unfolding] of oppositions, objects, diversity.)

21

> When in the "world of the soul" the conscious relation
> to each object ceases and a concentration-on-the-one begins,
> this is the movement of consciousness that is called *samādhi*.
> (Patañjali, *Yoga Sūtra* 3.11) [20]

This "folding inwards" is freedom, as it were, "from the opposition
of consciousness and object of consciousness" (Patañjali, 3.3 and
1.43).

The "unfolding" of diversity, and most particularly the opposition of subject and object is annulled.

> When mind's activity is controlled, illumination results,
> mind reflects the nature of either the seer, the seen, or the
> seeing, as pure crystal reflects the color of whatever is
> placed on it (ibid. 1.41). [21]

This "folding inwards" is attained by "inversion," by an attitude of
self-communion, by "concentration upon inner unity." This is the
Yogi path of salvation. Here, too, nonduality is recognized as a
principle and a method: "Perception of the Two, in which they
appear fully identical" (Patañjali, 3.53).

Here in classical Yoga we recognize the recurrent Hindu theme:
the world is dissolved by the dissolution of oppositions, and with
it vanishes "world involvement," the "cause of servitude" (2.24);
man's "thirst is slaked" (3.50), the "eating of the world" ceases
(3.35) and with it "the anxious, convulsive will to live" (2.9).
Suffering is defeated, but by *indifference*. Such redemption by the
identity and indifference of oppositions is diametrically opposed to
the Christian notion of salvation, the "new heaven and new earth,"
as also to the Hellenic harmony of opposites. Deussen is absolutely
mistaken when he identifies the profound pessimism of the Upaniṣads with Christianity and, following Schopenhauer, defines the
ultimate aim of both as "redemption from this existence." [22] Christianity is not resignation but tragic optimism—tragic hope, tragic
faith, and tragic love.

20 Tr. Hauer, *Der Joga als Heilweg*, p. 105. [This passage may be translated
somewhat more simply: "When mind rejects all objects but one, illumination
results" (Purohit Swami, *Aphorisms of Yoga*, p. 62).]
21 Tr. Purohit Swami, *Aphorisms*, p. 42.
22 Paul Deussen, *The Philosophy of the Upanishads*, tr. A. S. Geden (Edin-
burgh, 1906).

VI

The Hellenic-Hebraic idea of redemption is diametrically opposed to that of the Hindus. The Hebrew-Christian element is the idea of creation. The world is not illusion; it is a work of art, fashioned by God, a "cosmos." All the diverse forces and elements of being are intrinsically good and valuable: "And God saw that it was good." Only an attitude of mutual annihilation, of strife, is bad. The idea of creation *affirms the world*. An ultimate "yes" unfolds the whole of being, with all its oppositions and degrees, in a single undivided love.[23] Love belongs to the very substance of being. And, accordingly, the creative power of man—that is, his art and culture—is recognized to be "godlike" and intrinsically valuable.

The Hellenic-Christian element is the dialectic of oppositions and their fusion in harmony. We have said that the perception of harmony always represents the miraculous solution of a riddle, a *divinatio*, a stroke of magic. Therein precisely consists the miracle of creation, the miracle of art.

To common sense, it would seem at first sight that we can solve an antinomy, an actual contradiction, only by effacing the thesis or the antithesis—wholly or at least in part. The one or the other is only "partly" posited and recognized. But this is a poor solution; it is unacceptable to dialectical reason. Kant saw that in a true antinomy thesis and antithesis must both stand in full force, both properly demonstrated. If both remain true, we have discovered the unity of opposing statements with regard to one and the same thing.[24]

Analogously, the conflicting forces and elements must not be "mixed" or quantitatively diminished, for this provides no solution but only a diminished or concealed conflict. Likewise, the total separation of the elements (in contrast to "mixture"), after the manner of the Manichaean separation of spirit and matter, is no solution but merely an admission that a solution is impossible. Only where opposing forces develop wholly, where the tension of conflict is

23 On the philosophical idea of creation, see Heinz Heimsoeth, *Die sechs grossen Themen der abendländischen Metaphysik* (Leipzig, 1934), pp. 26ff.
24 Man is free and not free; he is an immanent (empirical) and transcendent being.

realized to the full, can harmony arise. It is something entirely new, something that has never before existed, something that suddenly comes into being where before there was only conflict and destruction and "inhibition."

Harmony is hard to learn and harder to understand. A remarkable symbol of Heraclitus permits us to apprehend and visualize the third mode of opposition in its mysterious polyvalence. It is the symbol of the bow and the lyre.

Οὐ ξυνιᾶσιν ὅκως διαφερόμενον ἑωυτῶι ὁμολογέει: παλίντροπος ἁρμονίη ὅκωσπερ τόξου καὶ λύρης.

(They do not understand how that which differs with itself is in agreement: harmony consists of opposing tension, like that of the bow and the lyre [Diels, Frag. B 51].) [25]

The bow is a system of conflicting forces; the greater the tension of the polarity, the better the bow. To diminish or destroy the conflict between the two extremities would be to destroy the bow itself. But the cord of a bow can become the string of a lyre. The lyre is built on the same principle as the bow. It is a many-stringed bow, a transformed, one might say a "sublimated," bow. Here we can see and hear how "from conflict the finest harmony arises." The beautiful and the good, the whole καλοκαγαθία, the system of values, rests on this principle. This symbol is as rich in meaning, as all-embracing as the Platonic Eros, with which it is fundamentally related. The classical and Hellenistic ages sensed its meaning and developed it dialectically. We find it in Plato and Aristotle, in Plutarch, in Simplicius, and even in Synesius.

To the Greek mind, harmony had a cosmic significance. The philosopher could hear the harmony of the spheres.[26] The cosmos was "beauty," hence a "symphony and symmetry" like the lyre:

According to Heraclitus, the harmony of the cosmos had its changing tones and modes (παλίντονος, παλίτροπος) like the lyre and the bow (Plutarch, Frag. Mullach. 38).

For the cosmos is not a simple unity, but a unity formed of many, and its parts are friendly and hostile to its parts (Synesius, *De insomniis* 133 A).

25 Tr. K. Freeman, *Ancilla to the Presocratic Philosophers* (Oxford, 1948).
26 A Pythagorean symbol.

And not only the cosmos but art and architecture as well apply the principle of the bow (the arch) and of conflicting forces (the buttress).

It was not so simple to discern the same principle in the inner world, the microcosm. It was first discovered by Plato, who represented the soul as a chariot drawn by a white and a black horse, and in it perceived the conflict or possible harmony of opposing psychic forces. And as the strings are attuned in the lyre, so in lyric poetry are the forces of the soul attuned. This "tuning" is always a tension of opposites, and the concrete richness of the soul is never fixed and simple but always ambivalent, often contradictory, and at best contrapuntal.[27]

The bow and the lyre are in principle "identical" and yet opposed, like life and death (for life is a harmony). Heraclitus expressed this rhythmic play of opposites as follows: "The name of the bow is life, its work is death" (βίος, life; βιός, bow; Diels, Frag. 48). Heraclitus, like Hegel, perceived the deepest mysteries of dialectics, but both indulged in dialectical play and dialectical mischief. "Identity of opposites" is an ambiguous, false term, for *coincidence* is not identity, and the opposites are not identical but opposed.

Plato remains the great dialectician, for he declined to play with oppositions and sternly refused to transgress against the law of contradiction, though he was profoundly aware of the hidden meaning of the Heraclitean symbolism. He has preserved the Heraclitean dictum in the following form: "The one, the divergent (διαφερόμενον) unites with itself (αὐτὸ αὑτῷ ξυμφέρεσθαι) like the harmony of the bow and the lyre" (*Symposium,* 187 A).

And his interpretation runs: Here Heraclitus has expressed himself erroneously, although he has in mind something true. The incompatible and conflicting cannot be united in a harmony when, and in so far as, they do not accord (ibid., 187 B). A particular art, such as music or medicine, is required to join the hostile and incompatible in a loving accord and so establish a harmony (187 C).

27

> Zwei Seelen wohnen, ach, in meiner Brust,
> Die eine will sich von der andern trennen. . . .

(Two souls strive, alas, in my breast; the one strives apart from the other. . . . Goethe, *Faust, Part I.*)

Thus Plato preserves the law of contradiction; for if the contradiction is not perceived as contradiction, the solution and harmony lose all meaning and value. The bow and the lyre are *not identical,* for the lyre is a new invention, a transformation and sublimation of the bow. The harmony is a new and different relation between opposites, a third kind of opposition. On it, in Plato's view, rest health and beauty, medicine and music; on it rests also the complementary relation of man and woman, and here it takes the form of love and Eros.

Thus it is not permissible to confuse and identify opposites that mutually nourish one another with those which devour one another, and so proclaim an "identity of opposites" which suspends the law of contradiction. When this is done, serious dialectical method is turned into a sophistical game, as in the pitiful imitation of Hegel's style and Hegel's errors by his epigoni.[28]

Aristotle also provides a dialectical investigation of "the most beautiful harmony that arises from opposition and conflict." We find the famous maxim of Heraclitus in his ethics. He raises the Platonic question: Between whom do friendship and love exist, between equals or between opposites? In answer he first quotes Euripides: "The dry earth loves the rain (ἐρᾶν) —and the sky likes to fall to the earth in rain," and continues with the passage from Heraclitus (*Eth. Nic.,* Bk. VIII, Ch. 1, end).[29] Aristotle gives his own solution much later (VIII, Ch. 8); it runs as follows:

> But perhaps there is no real attraction between opposites as such, but only accidentally, and what they actually desire

28 We find this particularly in F. Lassalle's long monograph on Heraclitus, *Die Philosophie Herakleitos des Dunklen von Ephesos* (Berlin, 1858). Despite his erudition and copious quotations, he failed to understand the symbolism of the bow and the lyre, for he supposed that the fundamental principle of Heraclitus is the "identity of opposites." He simply uses the terms "identity of opposites" and "unity of opposites" promiscuously. When this is done, everything is lost: The bow and the lyre express an "identity of opposites"; conflict and harmony are one and the same thing (I, 90). This vitiates everything that is true and profound in Hegel. Plato has an acute passage attacking the Heracliteans and Sophists, but it is equally applicable to the Hegelians and to all those who play with antinomies and seek to demolish the law of contradiction: "To prove that identity is an opposition and opposition an identity—that the large is small and the like unlike and to take pleasure because oppositions keep cropping up in discourse—this is no true dialectical method but the pastime of an apprentice who has scarcely learned to understand logical analysis" (Soph.).
29 The famous passage is quoted above, p. 13.

is the mean between them (since this is for Good) ; the dry for instance striving not to become wet, but to reach an intermediate state, and so with the hot, and everything else.[29a]

Thus he construes the harmony of opposites as a *mean*, and it is clear from the context that this "mean" signifies a desirable synthesis of opposing elements and forces. His "golden mean" has often been misunderstood and disparaged as "mediocrity." But Aristotle's "middle" is a center, a target, and to strike this target is no mediocre, simple task but an extremely difficult one—the marksman must take good aim. Aristotle himself states that his "mean" does not signify mediocrity, but a summit, an *extreme* (ἄκρον). It is by no means a middle ground between virtue and vice, between value and deficiency—that would indeed be "mediocrity"; it is the middle ground between two opposing vices.

With this last definition, Aristotle thought he had found the right path. But this is not the case. Between two opposing vices or deficiencies there can only lie a dead point, an indifference, and by no means a golden mean. His μεσότης, his mean, becomes sound and useful only when it dominates and combines two opposing forces or impulses.[30]

This relationship is amply illustrated by an example from Aristotle's doctrine of virtue. Generosity in regard to money (the virtue of ἐλευθεριότης) is not a dead point between avarice and extravagance but a synthesis of two functions, both of which have a positive value though they work in opposite directions, namely, the functions of acquisition and expenditure, of *production* and *distribution*. Without either of these functions a patron of the arts, a Lorenzo de' Medici, is unthinkable. But avarice as well as extravagance constitutes a *real contradiction* between the same functions: the expenditure is not in keeping with the acquisition. This example has a profound psychological significance, for a very similar situation prevails with regard to the accumulation and expenditure of libido, of psychic energy. These functions, too, can stand to one another in a relation of contradiction or in a relation of harmony.

29a Tr. H. Rockham (LCL, rev. edn., 1934) , p. 485.
30 It is in this way that he actually meant it, and it is in this sense that his dialectic must be developed. This was discovered by Nicolai Hartmann, who proves the point with brilliant precision in his *Ethics*, tr. Stanton Coit (London and New York, 1932) , II, 407–17.

The true and profound sense of the "golden mean," the middle path, is already contained in the Heraclitean symbol. The middle path means the transition from the repugnance to the harmony of opposites, and to find this path is a great art.

The symbol of the bow and the lyre has still many other implications. The arrow is placed at the middle of the bowstring and is intended to strike the middle of the target. Apollo is represented with bow and lyre, he is the "God who leads the Muses," Apollo Mousagetes, but at the same time he is an archer who knows the art of always striking home (Plato, *Cratylus*). Eros also carries bow and arrows. Pausanius describes a famous image in which Eros after shooting the arrow lays down the bow and takes up the lyre. The lyre is another of his attributes; he is, above all, "lyric."

VII

Now in conclusion we must raise a last question: Is this Greek dialectic of opposites, this coincidence of opposites, really Christian? Can it be applied to a Christian idea of redemption? The greatest of the Greek church fathers answered this question in the affirmative; they were Greek dialecticians who believed in Christ and conceived of him as a coincidence of opposites—of the divine and the human. According to the Chalcedonian formula, these opposites are "inseparable and yet not merging" in the son of man. (The relation of the divine and the human is solved quite differently in Vedānta: here the opposites merge as a drop of water with the ocean.)

Christianity is dialectical through and through; it moves in the realm of ultimate concepts, which are antinomic; it discovers and experiences the ultimate antinomies of world and soul, of immanence and transcendence, and it promises, hopes, and trusts to find their solution. St. Paul was the first Christian philosopher and the greatest of Christian dialecticians. Luther had good reason to say: *fides est quaedam dialectica*. The ultimate unity of the ultimate oppositions—the unity of the absolute and the relative, of heaven and earth, of God and man—constitutes the ultimate problem of dialectic and the first experience of Christian revelation.

The transition from the first to the third mode of opposition, from repugnance to harmony, from the tragic to solution and redemption constitutes the essence of the gospel. How is it possible to make from duality and strife, from conflict, war, and hate, a harmony of opposites—to make peace and love? That is the most elementary and most fundamental problem of man in every province of his outward and inward world. Christ himself is a living answer, for he is a living harmony of opposites, he is *peace*. This was St. Paul's understanding of him:

> For he is our peace, who hath made both one, and hath broken down the middle wall of partition between us; having abolished . . . the enmity . . . for to make in himself of twain one new man, so making peace; and that he might reconcile both [opposites, τοῦς ἀμφοτέρας] unto God in one body by the cross, having slain the enmity thereby.

St. Paul saw the essence of Christian doctrine in the abolition of enmity, in peace, in universal harmony. "And came and preached peace. . . . (Ephesians 2:14–17; cf. John 14:27).

The New Testament applies the principle of the harmony of opposites to the inner world as well as the outer and social world. "From whence come wars and fightings among you? come they not hence, even of your lusts that war in your members?" The passions contradict one another in the heart of man as in his social relations; the inner conflicts of the soul are transformed into outward conflicts and draw the whole man into *tragic contradiction:* "Ye lust, and have not: ye kill, and desire to have, and cannot obtain: ye fight and war, yet ye have not, because ye ask not. Ye ask, and receive not, because ye ask amiss, that ye may consume it upon your lusts" (James 4:1–3). Here we find the dialectic of mutually devouring opposites. And to all this "confusion" is opposed the harmony which is contained in wisdom (σοφία) and justice, and which signifies peace (James 3:16–18).

But nowhere is the inner conflict of the soul expressed with such force as in Romans 7, for here we have the fundamental conflict of the conscious ego with the unconscious; antiquity had already formulated this tragic contradiction of the soul: *"video meliora, proboque, deteriora sequor"* (Ovid). There is a consciousness of the law but also an unconscious resistance. That is the fundamental thesis of the apostle. The law is recognized "by my reason" (νόμος τcῦ νοὸς μοι), and I am aware that it is good and precious, I have the conscious will to do what is good and lawful—and yet I do the opposite. Everything happens contrary to my consciousness:

29

"For that which I do, I allow not: For what I would, that do I not. . . ." That is, I act unconsciously and against my will. But for Paul the "I" is nothing other than the center of consciousness and reason. And so he concludes quite consistently that it is not the "I" which acts here, but something else: "Now then it is no more I that do it, but sin that dwelleth in me." But where does it dwell if the conscious ego is filled with good intentions and respect of the law? It can dwell only in the unconscious. Paul did not have this term at his disposal, and so he spoke of "captivity to the law of sin which is in my members." It is easy to show that he is here referring to a province of the mind, for he speaks of desires and "lusts."

With his remarkable dialectic of psychological conflict, Paul had discovered the law of unconscious resistance: ". . . another law in my members, warring against the law of my mind. . . ." (Rom. 7: 23). This is the law of the forbidden fruit, or the *"loi de l'effort converti."* Essentially it is neither more nor less than an expression of the conflict between conscious and unconscious. And, according to St. Paul, this conflict is solved by the harmony of opposites, by sublimation, by the spiritualization of body and soul.

Now it is evident that the ancient dialecticians, with all their ingenuity and astuteness, could not but turn their attention to the tragic conflicts and mystical antinomies of Christianity and strive to render the Christian solutions "thinkable." Pseudo-Dionysius and Maximus the Confessor were classical dialecticians in the Platonic and Neoplatonic style. Here we need only mention certain aspects of this tradition. For Maximus sin and evil are an ontological cleavage, a duality in cosmos and microcosm, and the mission of man is to transcend this conflict. Christ has shown by his example how this is possible. He is a true *coincidentia oppositorum.*

> He is the wisdom (σοφία) and the thinking (φρόνησις) of the Father, who holds together the whole of existence. . . . He himself bridges the contradictions (εἰς ἓν ἄγων τὰ διεστῶτα δι᾽ ἑαυτοῦ), dispels the war of existence, and binds all things together in peace and love and unassailable harmony (πρὸς ἀδιαίρετον συνδέων ὁμόνοιαν).[31]

31 Maximus the Confessor, *Ambiguorum Liber;* Migne, *PG,* XCI, 1313.

VIII

Thus there is a necessary ascent from the Heraclitean lyre to the idea of universal harmony; and this ascent (ἀναγωγή) is by a dialectical path. It leads from the despair of classical tragedy, from Hindu resignation, to the *tragic optimism* of Christianity. The postulate of a "new heaven and a new earth" remains in force, stronger than ever. And the idea of universalism is no abstraction, but a true actuality. There are no isolated, self-sufficient harmonious systems, no autarchies—not in any sphere, whether in psychological, national, or political life. All things are bound up with all things, all things "breathe together" (σύμπνοια πάντα), "all men are responsible for everything and are guilty of everything" (Dostoyevsky). Salvation can come only through a *medicina catholica* (to use an alchemistic term), through *universal* deliverance and redemption. For a European alchemist of today, whether he be a psychologist, a sociologist, or simply a philosopher, the *lapis philosophalis* can mean nothing other than the principle of universal harmony. And it is easy to understand why Jakob Boehme found the philosopher's stone in Christ himself.

Wilhelm Koppers

On the Origin of the Mysteries
in the Light of Ethnology and Indology

1. Introduction

By way of introduction, I wish above all to make it clear that nothing more than a contribution to the study of this theme is intended. We cannot aspire to more because we are entering on what is largely new territory; of the little that has been published on the subject, a good part is none too helpful. The works I have found most useful—and I should like here to express my gratitude to their authors—are those of F. Gräbner,[1] W. Schmidt,[2] D. Kreichgauer,[3] A. Gahs,[4] F. Kern,[5] L. Walk,[6] and Karl Prümm.[7] These names should provide a sufficient indication that my remarks will

---

1 "Ethnologie," in P. Hinneberg, ed., *Die Kultur des Gegenwart,* part III, section 5, "Anthropologie" (Leipzig and Berlin, 1923), pp. 435–587. *Das Weltbild des Primitiven* (Munich, 1924).

2 "Initiations tribales et sociétés secrètes," *Compte-rendu analytique, Semaine Internationale d'Ethnologie Religieuse, III⁶ Session, Tilbourg, 1922* (Enghien and Vienna, 1923), pp. 329–40. Schmidt and Koppers, *Völker und Kulturen* (Regensburg, 1924). W. Schmidt, *Der Ursprung der Gottesidee* (12 vols., Münster, 1926–55).

3 "Die Religion der Griechen in ihrer Abhängigkeit von den mutterrechtlichen Kulturkreisen," *Jahrbuch von St. Gabriel* (Mödling), II (1925), 107–51.

4 "Blutige und unblutige Opfer bei den altaischen Hirtenvölkern," *Compte-rendu analytique, Semaine Internationale d'Ethnologie Religieuse, IV⁶ Session, Milan, 1925* (Paris, 1926), pp. 217–32.

5 "Die Welt, worein die Griechen traten," *Anthropos,* XXIV (1929), 167–219; XXV (1930), 195–207, 793–99.

6 "Initiationszeremonien und Pubertätsriten der südafrikanischen Stämme," *Anthropos,* XXIII (1928), 861–966.

7 "An Quellen griechischen Glaubens: Die 'Mutterreligion' des ägäischen Kreises," *Biblica,* XI (1930), 266–90. "Muttergottheiten," *Zeitschrift für katholische Theologie,* LIV (1930), 572–80. "Neue Wege einer Ursprungsdeutung antiker Mysterien," ibid., LVII (1933), 89–102, 254–71. "Materialnachweise zur völkerkundlichen Beleuchtung des antiken Mysterienwesens," *Anthropos,* XXVIII (1933), 759–76. *Der christliche Glaube und die altheidnische Welt* (Leipzig, 1935), vol. I. *Christentum als Neuheitserlebnis* (Freiburg i. B., 1939). *Religionsgeschichtliches Handbuch für den Raum der altchristlichen Umwelt* (Freiburg i. B., 1943).

32

be made from the standpoint of a historically oriented ethnology.

Yet if I look upon the mysteries as a historical phenomenon and attempt to treat them and interpret them in the light of universal history, which embraces also the so-called prehistoric times, this does not mean that in my eyes a psychological study or a philosophical-religious evaluation of the same phenomenon would have no value. It goes without saying that I am profoundly convinced of the contrary. But I am certain that a psychological-philosophical-religious study of the mystery complexes will have a much greater prospect of success if the relevant data can previously be established and fixed in their historical contexts.[8]

When an ethnologist turns to the problems surrounding the ancient mysteries, he soon becomes aware of two things, or at least this has been my own experience. He admires the sum of intellectual endeavor that has already been devoted to this question by a great many authors. And, at the same time, it occurs to him that perhaps these phenomena are not alien to the field of ethnology and that a good deal might be said about them from an ethnological standpoint. Our task then, will be to search methodically for a bridge, a reliable contact, between the two fields, the ancient mysteries and ethnology. And we proponents of historical ethnology believe that we have such a bridge in that cultural-historical method which in its core and essence is nothing other than a genuine adaptation of modern historical method to prehistoric cultures and to primitive peoples without writing.[9] This is not the place for a detailed discussion of the conceptions and methods of his-

---

8 Cf. W. Schmidt, *Handbuch der kulturhistorischen Methode der Ethnologie*, mit Beiträgen von W. Koppers (Münster, 1936), p. 256. A. E. Jensen, "Das Weltbild einer frühen Kultur," *Paideuma*, III (1944), 1–83, has illustrated (pp. 56–58) the need for this method in the field of ethnology by a concrete example. He discusses the remarks of C. G. Jung in "The Psychological Aspects of the Kore" (CWJ, 9i; 1959). Jensen concludes his critical judgment with these words: "Here we can learn by a single example that psychology is unable to solve the problem of 'ethnological parallels.' At best it can point to contents of our own consciousness which make it easier for us to understand a foreign cultural manifestation" (p. 58). In other words, ethnological (cultural-historical) problems as such must primarily and essentially be solved by ethnological and historical methods.

9 F. Gräbner, *Die Methode der Ethnologie* (Heidelberg, 1911). W. Schmidt, *Handbuch* (above, n. 8). W. Koppers, "Was ist und was will die völkerkundliche Universalgeschichte?" *Histor. Jahrbuch der Görres-Gesellschaft* (Cologne), LII (1932), 40–55. Koppers, "Le Principe historique et la science comparée des religions," *Mélanges Franz Cumont* (Brussels, 1936), II, 765–84.

torical ethnology. But the very nature of our undertaking will require us to touch upon the basic questions of method where the material under treatment demands.

I believe that I may presuppose a knowledge of the constantly recurring elements in the mysteries of antiquity.[10] However, it seems worth while, for the purposes of our paper, to take up this question briefly. It has repeatedly been recognized that there are still grave gaps in our knowledge of this field. First, let us devote a few words to the terms "secret" and "mystery."

We shall do well to bear in mind that there are different ways in which a thing can be "secret" or a "mystery." Perhaps only certain persons who are in some way elected may be admitted to the ceremonies in question and initiated in them. This is often the case in the male secret societies typical of certain primitive peoples. Or perhaps only a certain section of the population, such as minors, are barred from certain ceremonies and for pedagogic reasons kept in uncertainty as to what takes place in them. This is the case, for example, with regard to the initiation of the youth among primitive peoples. Here we can speak only of a temporary secrecy. A third meaning of "secret" or "mystery" may reside in the content of a belief. This may be true of any conception or doctrine—for example, of the theory that all human and animal life as well as all foodstuffs arose in some mysterious way from the fragmentation of the lunarized original being (or creature), and so on. It is clear that these and similar conceptions usually involve the idea of magic. And behind all magic lurks some "secret"; in any event, the magician and his followers—sometimes, to be sure, the followers more than the magician—believe this to be the case.

Finally, certain Christian doctrines are designated as mysteries. Here again the reason is to be sought in their content. These doctrines are looked upon as secret, or, rather, mysterious, in so far as their content transcends natural understanding; they are therefore ascribed to the intervention of a higher power, specifically the power and will of God. And Christianity has its "mysteries" of revelation, which by their very nature cannot be conceived as

---

10 A short but serviceable survey is presented by B. Heigl, *Antike, Mysterienreligionen und Urchristentum* (Münster, 1932). Cf. also the works on the subject by K. Prümm (above, n. 7).

secret but can only accidentally (for historical reasons) be submitted to a discipline of the arcanum.

There is general agreement among modern scholars regarding
certain characteristics of the ancient mysteries. I should like to
mention briefly a few of these characteristics, and in the course of
our discussion I shall come back to them as necessary.

Today, as far as I know, it is generally agreed that:

1. The ancient mysteries are pre-Indo-European and pre-Semitic
in character.

2. The cultures of these prehistoric peoples were essentially
agrarian and matriarchal.

3. In the center (or background) of the various mystery complexes there usually stands (or once demonstrably stood) a female
deity, in whom, at least if she is considered from the standpoint
of comparative mythology, lunar elements are more or less clearly
discernible.

4. Though the mystery cults have as their aim some sort of
better lot in the afterworld for their initiates, the ethical motive
plays a very minor role in these religions.

5. Fertility rites and conceptions connected with fertility play a
dominant role in most of the mystery cults; other common elements most often connected with it are magical conceptions and
practices, as well as excesses of a sexual and orgiastic nature.

2. Tribal Initiations and Secret Leagues among Primitive Peoples

Certain of the secret tribal initiations and rites of the secret societies among primitive peoples suggest a parallel to the ancient mysteries. In the course of the last decades ethnological science has
come to distinguish the following principal forms or stages:

1. First of all, an initiation of the youth, or rather a course of
training, to which boys and girls approaching maturity are subjected. Essentially we find here no secrets and certainly no secret
societies. Secrecy is maintained at most toward children who have
not yet been initiated and toward persons outside of the tribe.
In the light of our present ethnological knowledge this simple
form of initiation or training of the youth must be regarded as the
oldest known institution of this kind. We find it among distinctly

primitive peoples. Its purest form seems to occur among the Indians of Tierra del Fuego, of whom I shall speak later on in greater detail. But a similar institution is found among the Kurnai (an aboriginal tribe of southeastern Australia), among the Andamanese (a pygmy group living in the Andaman Islands, in the Bay of Bengal), and among certain primitive tribes in the northwestern part of central California. In every case the primary aim of the educational measures is to make good men, good fathers and mothers, of the candidates. Tribal interests as such are less stressed because at this stage the tribal feeling and above all the tribal organization are not yet highly developed. In general there is no question of bodily deformation (circumcision, etc.). The earliest ethnological stage, with its economic basis in "primitive" hunting, fishing, and fruit-gathering techniques, reveals neither marked patriarchal nor marked matriarchal tendencies. By and large the sexes enjoy equal rights: and accordingly both girls and boys participate in the youth initiations.

2. Secret initiations of boys, often culminating in circumcision, appear commonly among those primitive peoples characterized by the phenomenon of totemism.[11] Here, as a rule, a so-called higher hunting technique forms the basis of economic life. In general the tribal idea is more pronounced. This finds its expression, on the one hand, in the highly developed clan system; on the other hand (at least in part), in a highly developed system of age classes. The growth of the tribal (state) idea benefits chiefly the male sex. At this stage accordingly we usually find only an initiation for boys. Circumcision, originally performed at the age of puberty, is in some way related to sexual life. Through the influence of sheep- and cattle-raising peoples, the significance of circumcision often changes: it is performed in infancy and assumes the character of a sacrifice of first fruits. As a rule the female members of the community are rigorously excluded from the rites in which the boys are initiated. Here, then, we can actually speak of secret initiations or rites. At the end of the initiation the candidates are not infrequently accorded a period of sexual freedom. Among some of these peoples the girls undergo

11 W. Koppers, "Der Totemismus als menschheitsgeschichtliches Problem," *Anthropos*, XXXI (1936), 159–76.

an initiation analogous to that of the boys. For the most part the two initiations are held separately. Often the girls are subjected to an operation corresponding to the circumcision of the boys.

It is evident that this initiation of boys stands in a genetic connection with the youth initiation of the aboriginal stage. But it presents important new factors not to be overlooked: one-sidedness, limitation to the one sex, circumcision, and emphasis on sexuality. And the element of secrecy is here clearly manifested for the first time.

3. In primitive agricultural societies, where the labor is performed largely by women, the development is of an entirely different nature. Here we find the institution of the secret male societies, whose original connection with this form of culture was first clearly recognized and elucidated by W. Schmidt on the basis of the essential spade work of H. Schurtz and others.[12] The ethnological findings argue for the belief that it was woman who developed the plant gathering of the aboriginal period into agriculture. She made the soil valuable and consequently became its owner.[13] First economically and then socially she achieved a dominant position: the complex of matriarchy developed.

The none too pleasant situation, into which men had thus been thrust, provoked a reaction. This is manifested in the male secret societies, whose secrecy and terror were directed primarily against the female part of the population. The males attempted by intellectual and religious-magical means to retrieve what they had lost in economic and social life. The matriarchate brought female deities to the fore; often the supreme deity is conceived as female, as primal mother. Of this we shall encounter the most extreme manifestations, but only in connection with certain later cultural-religious developments. Mythology is at this stage dominated by lunar conceptions. The primal moon mother has two brothers (or

---

12 Particularly W. Schmidt in Schmidt and Koppers, *Völker und Kulturen*. Cf. H. Schurtz, *Altersklassen und Männerbunde* (Berlin, 1902). G. Höltker, "Männerbunde," *Handwörterbuch der Soziologie*, ed. A. Vierkandt (Stuttgart, 1931), pp. 348–53. That the "lunar conception of the world" first arose "in the cultural complex associated with the beginnings of agriculture" is also the opinion of Jensen (op. cit., p. 71).

13 W. Schmidt, "The Position of Women with Regard to Property in Primitive Society," *American Anthropologist*, XXXVII (1935), 244–56.

sons), who personify the (clever) bright moon and the (stupid) dark moon.

A typical ancestor and spirit cult develops (animism and fertility rites are characteristic of this stage), and we encounter also the skull cult (head-hunting), cannibalism, and the cultic use of masks.[14] Admission to the secret male societies is usually limited by selection. They often exhibit propagandistic tendencies, passing beyond the confines of the tribe or state and seeking friends among outsiders. In western Africa and Melanesia, for example, we find the same societies encompassing diverse tribes and peoples. And presumably the sexual (pederastic, etc.) excesses which frequently occur in the male societies are connected with a striving for emancipation from women.

In my opinion there can be no doubt that among primitive rites it is those of the male societies which most remind us of the mysteries of antiquity. However, we should not be justified in speaking of any direct contact between the mysteries and the secret societies. The secret societies constitute a very ancient phenomenon in the history of mankind. They seem to have been founded by self-assertive men not very long after women had introduced the earliest agriculture. This may well have occurred in the Mesolithic Age.[15] It is indeed generally recognized that the mysteries which became widespread in the classical world must have had their roots in an earlier pre-Indo-European or pre-Semitic population.[16] But this does not take us back to that more tangible prehistoric age when the first secret societies arose.

Thus for the present we cannot establish a direct relationship between the two. And yet in principle the possibility is not precluded, and I believe that it can be realized through a study of the

---

14 H. Baumann, in *Schöpfung und Urzeit des Menschen in Mythus der afrikanischen Völker* (Berlin, 1936), shows that in Africa, too, primitive agriculture (pre-eminently carried on by women), matriarchy, the use of masks, manism, animism, a female (earth) deity, and gods of the underworld occur together.

15 O. Menghin, *Weltgeschichte der Steinzeit* (Vienna, 1931). R. Pittioni, *Urgeschichte* (Leipzig and Vienna, 1937), pp. 30f. F. Kern, *Die Anfänge der Weltgeschichte* (Leipzig and Berlin, 1933).

16 Here, by way of example: H. Krahe, "Die Indogermanisierung Griechenlands," in *Antike: Alte Sprachen und deutsche Bildung* (1943), pp. 2–13. W. F. Otto, "The Meaning of the Eleusinian Mysteries," in *The Mysteries*, PEY 2, p. 16. How, on the other hand, solar mythologems are still prevalent, even among the Hamites of Africa, is shown by the investigations of H. Baumann (op. cit., p. 391).

historical links and mixed forms. The pre-Indo-European or pre-Semitic peoples from whom the Greeks took their mysteries represent relatively young cultures. The mysteries peculiar to them are not original in every respect but involve all manner of mixtures, developments, and modifications brought about by the new ruling class (in this case Indo-European).[17] And this interpretation is often fully confirmed by ethnological findings. Among primitive peoples the mixed and transitional forms of the secret rites are likewise far more frequent than the original pure components, and this circumstance corresponds to general cultural conditions. We frequently find the initiation of boys combined with the rites of the male societies, and we encounter religious-magical confraternities, clubs, associations of shamans which are characteristic of a more advanced stage than the above-mentioned mixed forms but which at the same time clearly reveal their connections with older secret societies.

In the foregoing remarks I have aspired only to characterize the general situation and suggest profitable lines of research. As for particulars, almost everything remains to be done. The task here facing historical ethnology is so vast that in my opinion a great many scholars might well devote their lives to it.[18] This may seem a little discouraging. But, on the other hand, it is comforting to think that something remains to be done by future generations of scholars.

3. The Tierra del Fuegians Throw New Light on the Subject

I should now like to give two concrete examples showing what work must, in my opinion, be done to advance our understanding

---

17 It is in this light that we must understand the peculiar position that Baumann (p. 394) assigns to the Mediterranean Magna Mater as opposed to the female earth goddess of the primitive African peoples.

18 This is recognized by K. Prümm. He believes, however, that for the present the work cannot be undertaken on such a vast scale. This may be true, but then we must not forget that we are making a virtue of necessity (*Zeitschrift für katholische Theologie*, LVII [1933], 269). Up to a certain point, O. E. Briem (*Les Sociétés secrètes de mystères*, Paris, 1941) recognizes the historical problem involved in the study of the mysteries, but then simply puts the whole problem aside (p. 25). Briem has done conscientious work but cannot be said to have advanced us in any crucial point. Cf. the same author's study *Zur Frage nach dem Ursprung der hellenistischen Mysterien* (Lund and Leipzig, 1928).

of the ancient mysteries. My examples have to do with the institutions of Tierra del Fuego and India, two regions where I myself have been engaged in research. I shall first take up Tierra del Fuego.

I spent the years 1921 and 1922 in Tierra del Fuego, studying the inhabitants of the extreme southeastern region in collaboration with M. Gusinde.[19] In Tierra del Fuego live, or rather lived, three primitive tribes: the Yamana [Yaghan] in the extreme south, to the northwest of them the Halakwulup [Alacaluf], and in the northeast the Selk'nam [Ona]. The Yamana and the Halakwulup are clearly related in their origins, while the Selk'nam reveal ties with the Patagonians to the north. It is generally recognized that the Tierra del Fuegians are extremly primitive tribes. Their cultural level seems to be about that of the prehistoric Mousterian period at the end of the Upper Paleolithic Age.

The Indians of Tierra del Fuego have long been held to be the oldest inhabitants of America—a hypothesis favored by their geographical position. If the early population can only have come to America by the land route, the ancestors of those tribes which were driven farthest south were presumably the first to have migrated from northeastern Asia to northwestern North America. In the light of recent studies, this hypothesis has become a relative certainty. W. Schmidt's penetrating studies of religions[20] provide new arguments for it, and it is also supported by recent analyses of blood groups.[21] For, whereas the prevalence of the O blood group among most American Indians reveals a tie with the Mongoloids of eastern Asia, the southernmost inhabitants of America, the Yamana and Halakwulup, deviate from this group. Among them the B group is predominant, and in this they accord with the peoples of central Asia. This would seem to suggest an old racial tie interrupted by the impact of a later, predominantly

19 W. Koppers, *Unter Feuerland-Indianer, Eine Forschungsreise zu den südlichsten Bewohnern der Erde* (Stuttgart, 1924). Idem, "Sur l'Origine de l'idée de Dieu: A propos de la croyance en Dieu chez les Indiens de la Terre de Feu," *Nova et Vetera* (Fribourg, 1943), pp. 260–91. M. Gusinde, *Die Selk'nam (Ona)* (Mödling b.W., 1931). Idem, *Die Yamana* (Mödling b.W., 1937). Idem, *Anthropologie der Feuerland-Indianer* (Mödling b.W., 1939).
20 *Der Ursprung der Gottesidee*, VI (1935).
21 M. F. Ashley Montagu, "Genetics and the Antiquity of Man in the Americas," *Man*, XLIII (1943), 131–35, n. 105.

Mongoloid migration. It seems probable that ten to twenty thousand years ago the ancestors of the Yamana and the Halakwulup were the first to step onto American soil. Scholarship is fairly well agreed that the first human settlement in America dates from the end of the last ice age, though, in recent years, to be sure—on the basis of new prehistoric findings, particularly in New Mexico (Folsom and Yuma cultures)—the belief has gained ground that the first settlement of America may have taken place during the last ice age.[22] This, as I have said, is believed to have taken place between ten and twenty thousand years ago. These figures are in general supported by the archaeological and volcanic investigations carried on in Tierra del Fuego in the last ten years.[23] According to these findings, Tierra del Fuego was settled between three thousand and five thousand years ago. All indications are that the first settlers of the extreme south were the ancestors of the Yamana.[24] It must have taken five to six thousand years (if not more) for them to be driven from the northwestern corner of North America to the southernmost tip of South America.

Now let us have a look at those of our studies in Tierra del Fuego which concern the topic of our present paper. We shall

22 There are increasingly strong indications that man was living on the American continent before the end of the ice age (dated at 10,000 years ago) roughly 20,000 years ago. The inhabitants in question were the representatives of the above-mentioned Yuma and Folsom cultures. These men hunted, among other animals, mammoths and camels—beasts that soon died out on the American continent. See C. B. Schultz, "The First Americans," *Natural History* (New York), XLI (1938), 346–56. Hence it has lately come to be considered probable that the first immigration took place during the last ice age: W. Krickeberg, *Die grosse Völkerkunde* (Leipzig, 1939), pp. 19ff.; M. Gusinde, *Anthropologie der Feuerland-Indianer*, pp. 403ff.; W. Koppers, "Die Erstbesiedlung Amerikas im Lichte der Feuerland-Forschungen (Ethnologie, Prähistorie, Anthropologie, Blutgruppenuntersuchung)," *Bulletin der Schweizer Gesellschaft für Anthropologie und Ethnologie*, XXI (1945), 49–63.

23 Junius Bird, "Before Magellan," *Natural History*, XLI (1938), 16–28, 77, 79. Idem, "Antiquity and Migrations of the Early Inhabitants of Patagonia," *Geographical Review*, XXVIII (1938), 250–75. Väinö Auer, "Der Kampf zwischen Wald und Steppe auf Feuerland. Die finnischen Expeditionen in Feuerland und Patagonien," *Petermanns Mitteilungen*, LXXXV (1939), 193–97.

24 The prehistorical investigations of J. Bird have made it as good as certain that the Yamana were the first settlers in their principal territory (central and eastern shores of Beagle Channel, the islands to the south of it, Navarin, Wollaston, etc.). According to Bird's reckoning, the Yamana reached this last territory, from which further retreat was impossible, only approximately 1800 years ago.

start with the Yamana, who, as we have seen, may be regarded as
the oldest inhabitants of America. The Yamana perform two
secret rites in which my colleague and I were permitted to take an
active part. For details, those who are interested may consult the
publications mentioned above (note 19). All in all, Gusinde and I
published more than 4,000 pages. Here I shall mention only the
salient points essential for our discussion. The two secret festivals
of the Yamana are a youth initiation and a festival of men.

The youth initiation represents essentially a course of education
administered to the young people, girls as well as boys, under the
guidance of adults. Their distinct purpose is, as the Yamana say,
to make *good* people of the candidates, to train them for a harmonious social life and a happy family life. Thus the youth initiation is also a tribal initiation. Those who have successfully completed it are regarded as full-fledged members of the tribe. This of
course applied also to us, a circumstance most helpful to us in our
researches. As members of the tribe, we had rights as well as duties.
The other members recognized our rights and took all conceivable
pains to acquaint us with the secrets of their social and religious
life.

To what degree can this youth initiation be called a secret youth
initiation? Since all members of the tribe, boys and girls, participate in it, not only once but repeatedly, we may speak of secrecy
not with regard to the rite, but only with regard to certain parts
which are kept secret from children and outsiders. The children
are constantly being frightened by references to an evil spirit
named Yetáita. They are told that Yetáita, who is represented as a
kind of earth spirit, metes out tortures and punishment in the
initiation hut, especially to bad children. In the ceremony itself,
Yetáita appears in the form of a man in fantastic dress. Finally
the secret is revealed to the frightened candidate: in the supposed
Yetáita he sees a man from among the circle of his intimates. He
is then admonished: "You are frightened, but remember, the real
Yetáita is much worse. And you must not speak, especially to children and the uninitiate, of what you have just learned about
Yetáita."

Up to a certain point, the knowledge of a myth dealing with a
culture bringer may be regarded as a secret of the youth initiation.

The myth concerns two brothers named Yoálox (pronounced Yo-ah-lokh), who taught the ancestors of the Yamana how to organize their lives. The elder Yoálox was the stupid brother; the younger one was clever. But cleverer still was their older sister, Yoálox-Tarnukipa. In the light of comparative mythology there can be no doubt that here we are dealing with a lunar conception. The clever brother is the bright moon, the stupid one the dark moon, while the woman (the older sister of the two brothers) embodies the moon as a whole. A superficial knowledge of the Yoálox story is general among the Yamana, even among the children. On the occasion of the youth initiation, the myth is divulged in some detail. I myself heard only fragments of it in the first months of 1922, but more was revealed to me in March, when I took part in the youth initiation. But the myth is fully divulged only in the men's festival of Kina, of which we shall soon have more to say. This suggests that the Yoálox "mystery" is originally bound up with the male festival and appears only in a secondary, hence incomplete and weakened, form in the youth initiation.

All things considered, there is nothing especially secret about the youth initiation of the Yamana. Both sexes participate in the whole initiation, essentially as equals. Here there is little to remind us of the ancient mysteries. This becomes particularly evident when we consider what things are not kept secret from the candidates for the youth initiation, what elements are peculiar to this rite, and what elements are lacking in it.

The Yamana make no secret of their faith in a supreme deity, who is called Watauinéwa (the Eternal) or Hitapúan (my Father). Every child learns of this god as soon as he reaches the age of discernment. And Gusinde and I heard all about this god before we participated in the youth initiation in March 1922. Watauinéwa is held to be the supreme and final authority behind the youth initiation. He wishes it to be held; he wishes the teachings and regulations imparted in it to be observed; and he punishes disregard of them with sickness and early death. I do not believe that in any of the ancient mysteries a similar supreme deity (Zeus, for example) plays such a part. In the mysteries the emphasis is always on various forms of the mother goddess, often with her son, lover, or satellite at her side. There is no suggestion of any such female deity in the youth initiation of the Yamana, or, for that matter, in their faith as a whole.

But apart from the absence of a female deity, the youth initiation of the Yamana is lacking in other elements characteristic of the mysteries. There is no spirit cult or cult of the dead. There is no use of masks, no physical mutilations, bloody rites, no ceremonies stressing the sexual and the obscene. The idea of death and resurrection, associated with many of the mysteries, is absent, and so likewise are vegetation and fertility rites.

Thus the youth initiation of the Yamana is distinguished from the mystery complexes of antiquity by both its positive and its negative characteristics. What seems to be the only exception consists in the instruction which in both cases (for this is true of certain mysteries) is imparted to the candidates. Yet this characteristic can be regarded as implicit in the nature of both rites, so that surely no one will construe it as a basis for historic-genetic dependence.

This youth initiation of the Yamana, whose salient characteristics I have set forth, finds its exact companion piece in a corresponding rite of the neighboring tribe, the Halakwulup. This fact supports the view that we are here dealing with an aboriginal element of the Tierra del Fuegian tribes. And other important factors argue its extreme antiquity. Youth initiations of the same or similar character, as I have pointed out in the first part of my paper, are found in various other parts of the world, among certain primitive tribes in the northwestern part of central California,[25] in southeastern Australia,[26] and among the pygmies of the Andaman Islands.[27]

In every case, we have to do with tribes who, because of their isolation, tend to retain archaic institutions. And all the tribes in question represent pretotemistic and prematriarchal cultures. Consequently, we must accept the thesis, first propounded by W. Schmidt, that this youth initiation constitutes the oldest form of communal education known to us. Once again I wish to remind

---

25 W. Schmidt, *Der Ursprung der Gottesidee*, vols. II, V, and VI.
26 Ibid., III, 594ff., 991ff.
27 E. H. Man, *On the Aboriginal Inhabitants of the Andaman Islands* (London, 1885). Schmidt and Koppers, *Völker und Kulturen*, pp. 180ff.

you that it contains nothing to remind us of the ancient mysteries. But this is not the case when one turns to the second secret festival of the Yamana, in which we were also privileged to participate.

The Yamana call this second festival Kina. Here the term "secret" is quite applicable; for the Kina is observed only by men. Women may not take part in it, and, indeed, the whole institution is directed *against* the women. The men are painted and masked to represent spirits, and the women are supposed to take them for real spirits. Thus the men consciously deceive the women, and, in principle at least, the death penalty attaches to betrayal of the secret of the Kina to women or the noninitiate.

This secret consists primarily in the myth which in a sense justifies the rite. It is a clear and distinct astral myth, according to which the women, led by the moon woman, Kina, formerly enacted the very same rite now enacted by the men. This servitude of the men was forcibly broken by the sun man. Led by the sun man, the men (of that time) killed all the women but spared the little girls in order to provide for the survival of the tribe. When the little girls grew to be women, they knew nothing of all these events; particularly, they knew nothing of the Kina mystery. And, in their own interest, the men still keep the women in ignorance. The rule is that only those young men who have twice taken part in the youth initiation may be admitted to the Kina festival. This is to make certain that they will know how to keep silent.

This male festival of the Kina, as the Yamana themselves know, is not indigenous to the Yamana but came to them through their northern neighbors, the Selk'nam. It has recently been possible to confirm this through archaelogical studies which show that some thousand years ago a new form of house, the conical hut, was introduced into the territory of the Yamana from the north. The male festival is connected with this conical hut. It can only be celebrated in such a hut, while the festival of the youth initiation must be enacted in the older, beehive-shaped hut.

Thus the Kina of the Yamana finds its prototype in the Klóketen, the male festival of the Selk'nam. The Kina appears to be an attenuated offshoot of the Klóketen. Even feebler is the form found among the third Tierra del Fuegian tribe, the Halakwulup. Here we need only mention in passing that the Klóketen of the Selk'nam reveals ties with a ceremony performed farther north, among the Indian tribes of Patagonia. Unfortunately no detailed investigations in this matter have been carried on in Patagonia.

It is interesting to note that the element of secrecy is much stricter among the Selk'nam than among the Yamana. The Yamana admit individual women known to be close-mouthed to the festival, and thus to the secret of Kina. The mere thought of such an exposure, endangering the whole secret, infuriates the Selk'nam men. The Klóketen of the Selk'nam—or so the women are led to believe—is presided over by the female earth spirit, the evil Xálpen (pronounced Khal-pen). This Xálpen corresponds to the spirit Tánuwa of the Yamana. Among the Yamana, the sex of this spirit fluctuates —emotionally, at least—although Tánuwa literally means "earth man." Despite the meaning of the name it cannot be doubted that Tánuwa goes back to an older female form. Thus—fictitiously, to be sure—the male rite of the Selk'nam and Yamana rests on the power and domination of a female spirit.

I say "fictitiously" because this is what the men tell the women and the noninitiate. They themselves are perfectly well aware that they suffer nothing at the hands of the evil earth woman. But this circumstance clearly indicates that among the Tierra del Fuegian tribes as a whole, not only the Yamana but the Selk'nam as well, Klóketen-Kina constitutes a foreign element.

This view is supported by the following considerations:

1. The female spirit which, fictitiously, at least, presides over the Klóketen-Kina is without significance in the ordinary life of the Selk'nam and Yamana. Moreover, both tribes have the conception of a supreme male deity, Watauinéwa (the Eternal) among the Yamana and Temáukl among the Selk'nam. General observations leave no doubt that in both tribes this conception of a supreme deity must have existed before the introduction, or borrowing, of the secret male festival.

2. Like their other institutions, the male festival of the Tierra del Fuegians is entirely lacking in a cult of the dead, not to mention a skull cult or the usages of head-hunting and cannibalism. The brightly painted and masked spirits are the men and boys themselves. But to the noninitiate they are represented as spirits. The whole then has a strong quality of masquerade and comedy.

3. Fertility rites and rites with a sexual and obscene emphasis are not entirely lacking—but the Klóketen of the Selk'nam has more of this than the Kina of the Yamana. But, relative to the other scenes and ceremonies, these rites play a subordinate role, particularly among the Yamana—and this is significant in view of the fact that their form of the male festival is only a feeble copy.

4. There are no rites of death and resurrection and no idea of redemption in any form, although both tribes believe in a survival of the soul after death. Participation in the Klóketen-Kina has no effect whatever on one's lot in the hereafter, either in a favorable or in an unfavorable sense. The supreme being punishes crimes (including offenses against the teaching and laws of the secret institutions) in this life with sickness and early death.

5. An interesting particular, which reminds us especially of the Eleusinian mysteries, is the following: The Selk'nam in particular lead the wives and mothers to believe that Xálpen, the evil spirit woman, carries off the candidates beneath the earth, where she torments and assaults them sexually. The men are perfectly well aware that this is not the case. The child Ketérnen is shown to the women as the product of this union. To make him look as young as possible, the youngest and weakest of the candidates is chosen for the role. He is painted from top to toe with red earth paint; he is covered with downy feathers and a pointed mask. At sight of him the women burst into rejoicing, just as the divine boy, product of the sacred marriage, is greeted with exultation in the Eleusinian mysteries. As for the mother of the miraculous child, the agreement could not be greater: Xálpen (as goddess of the Klóketen) corresponds to Demeter (as goddess of Eleusis). But it would be quite incompatible with Indian conceptions to make the supreme being Temáukl or Watauinéwa (corresponding to Zeus) the child's father. Both Temáukl and Watauinéwa are considered as celibates and are not drawn into this myth. And since there are no priests as there are in Eleusis, one of the candidates is represented to the women and other noninitiates as the father of the boy.

6. There is no doubt that in connection with the male festivals a specific wave of magic and shamanism found its way to the Yamana and Selk'nam. We have here a peculiar type of singing and sucking medicine men, who reveal few or none of the proper-

ties which characterize a younger, ecstatic shamanism. The Selk'nam are much more strongly infected with this magic than the Yamana. And, again, the authors who have written about the ancient mysteries make it clear that here, too, magic played a considerable part. As for the phenomenon of shamanism, it may well be said in passing, certain of its characteristics place it close to the male societies and the mystery cults, so that a satisfactory study of the whole complex of shamanism would in principle require a similar approach. In any case, every specialist realizes today that there are different forms of shamanism from a historical and ethnological point of view. But so far there has been little detailed and systematic work in this field.

As we have seen, the Selk'nam are more serious than the Yamana about keeping the secret of the men's festival and terrorizing the women. But in neither tribe have permanent male societies been formed. The evident reason for this is that the social and economic life of these peoples is not and never has been dominated by women. The hostility to women expressed by the men's festival is without social and economic foundation; it exists in a vacuum. The male festival, rooted in an agrarian, matriarchal culture, was at some time taken over by the Tierra del Fuegian tribes, but they never went so far as to adopt and assimilate the institution of male societies, because there could be no basis, need, or understanding for it among primitive hunters and fishermen. Here, then, we have a classical example of an institution originally belonging to a higher cultural stage being taken over by a primitive or aboriginal culture. The institution is not simply copied, but *quidquid recipitur secundum modum recipientis recipitur*. Moreover, this example seems to attest the propagandistic force inherent in the male secret societies. An institution probably originating in the broader or more restricted confines of the ancient classical world or of southern Asia has sent forth its emanations not only to America, but to its southernmost and most remote corner.

In this connection it should particularly be noted that the Yamana and Halakwulup have not permitted any infringements on the independence of their venerable custom of youth initiation. This is, no doubt, one reason why the men's festival never assumed any great significance and influence among them. Among the

Selk'nam to the north, however, the men's festival has struck deeper roots. And it is possible that a more ancient youth initiation was absorbed in it. This is suggested by the numerous pedagogic exercises to which the candidates are subjected in the Klóketen. These measures, of course, affect only the boys, since the girls and women are excluded from the rite.

A similar discussion of the institutions of southeastern Australia might not be unprofitable, but unfortunately we have not sufficient time at our disposal. I shall limit myself to a few words. The Kurnai tribe of southeastern Australia constitutes a kind of parallel to the Indians of Tierra del Fuego, particularly the Yamana and Halakwulup.[28] The Kurnai are also an aboriginal people of pretotemistic and prematriarchal character. They also have a youth initiation, which in many essential points resembles that of the Yamana and Halakwulup, and which has also been influenced by neighboring tribes. But the neighbors are of a very different sort—revealing fewer matriarchal and more totemistic, patriarchal elements than those of the Tierra del Fuegian Indians—and this is reflected in the culture of the Kurnai, particularly in their youth initiation. It is for these reasons, we may assume, that the female sex is excluded from at least a part of the ceremonies. Only the boy candidates, and not the girls and women, are permitted to see the two bull-roarers, or to know of their existence. These bull-roarers are believed by the Kurnai men to represent the ancestors of the tribe. Here again we find an indication that the aboriginal peoples know a youth initiation or a course of education in which both sexes participate on an essentially equal footing, while male festivals and men's societies constitute essentially alien phenomena. Unfortunately this is all we have time to say of the Australian institutions, which are as complicated as they are interesting.

4. Our Question in the Light of Indological Research

The student of Indian culture and religion faces special difficulties but enjoys special advantages. He should, where possible, be

---

28 W. Koppers, "Die Frage eventueller alter Kulturbeziehungen zwischen dem südlichsten Südamerika und Südostaustralien," *Proceedings of the 23d International Congress of Americanists, New York, 1928* (New York, 1930), pp. 678–86.

trained in Indology as well as ethnology. And today he must be familiar with the Indus cultures of Mohenjo-Daro, Harappa, etc. that have been brought to light by the excavations of the last twenty years. He is highly favored by the circumstance that the foreign invaders and conquerors, who poured into India over a period of thousands of years (Aryans, Mohammedans, etc.), did not fully succeed in suppressing and assimilating the indigenous element.[29] Especially in the remoter sections of the Asiatic subcontinent which India represents, the old has frequently survived side by side with the new, so that the student who is sufficiently at home in both Indology and ethnology has before him, in a manner of speaking, a rich and vast museum of cultural and religious history. On the basis of my expedition of 1938–39 among the primitive tribes of northwestern central India, I have endeavored to promote this ethnological-Indological research to the best of my ability.[30] Here I shall only attempt to state briefly what India has to tell us with regard to the mysteries and related questions.

Today it seems very likely that in the Indus culture, which flourished about 2500 B.C. in the northwestern sections of India, there prevailed religious conceptions and cults similar to those of the pre-Semitic and pre-Indo-European population of the Near East and the Aegean region. This would still be true even if Hrozný's thesis that the language of Mohenjo-Daro is related to that of the Hittite hieroglyphics should be confirmed.[31] For this linguistic discovery (even if confirmed) will not alter the fact that the Indus

---

29 Cf. H. Zimmer, "The Indian World Mother" (the following paper in this book) : "Stone Age civilization, elsewhere the rubble of archaeology, is in India living reality." To this we might add that it is not only a "living" but in good part an ethnological reality, which as such still requires careful study.

30 A few of W. Kopper's works in this field are: "Meine völkerkundliche Forschungsreise zu den Primitivstämmen Zentralindiens, 1938–1939," *Internat. Archiv für Ethnographie*, XLI (1942), 141–52. "Bhagwān, the Supreme Deity of the Bhils," *Anthropos*, XXXV/VI (1940/41), 264–325. "Monuments to the Dead of the Bhils and Other Primitive Tribes in Central India," *Annali Lateranensi* (Rome), VI (1942), 117–206. "Probleme der indischen Religionsgeschichte," *Anthropos*, XXXV/VI (1940/41), 761–814. "India and Dual Organization," *Acta Tropica* (Basel), I (1944), 72–93, 97–119.

31 Bedřich Hrozný, *Die älteste Völkerwanderung und die protoindische Zivilisation* (Prague, 1939) ; "Inschriften und Kultur der Protoinder von Mohenjo-Daro und Harappa," *Archiv Orientalni*, XII (1941), 192–259, XIII (1942), 1–102; "Kretas und Vorgriechenlands Inschriften, Geschichte und Kultur," ibid., XIV (1943), 1–117.

culture is fundamentally non-Indo-European in character. And finally, it is not without significance that, even in the light of Hrozný's thesis, the Mohenjo-Daro culture nevertheless points in some way to the "Taurian corner," which in recent years has quite justifiably attracted the attention of those concerned with a better understanding of the mysteries.

Valuable in this connection are the recent art historical studies of Heinz Mode.[32] According to his findings, two distinct lines of influence emanate from an important center of multi-colored ceramic (pre-Sumerian, pre-Indo-European, and pre-Semitic) culture in northern Syria: one to the Indus culture, and the other to Crete. There are strong indications that the religion of this culture is generally dominated by the mother goddess complex.[33] The worship of Śiva, or let us rather say proto-Śiva, in Mohenjo-Daro has also been shown to be probable. Thus not only does the Indus culture give forth an "atmosphere of mystery," but it also seems more than likely that we here encounter genetic relations which in some way connect Mohenjo-Daro with the main focuses of the mother goddess cult and the related ancient mysteries.

In 1922 I published a study on "Buddhism and the Theory of Cultural Spheres."[34] At that time no one knew of the Indus culture, and so I ascribed the obvious influence of matriarchal conceptions on the development of Aryan-Indian philosophy and religion exclusively to the mother-right of native primitive tribes, particularly those of northeastern Hindustan. I hope soon to show, with the help of Ehrenfels's *Mother-Right in India,* that in all probability a matriarchal social order prevailed in the Indus culture. In any event, it is clear that there was no lack of religious manifestations rooted in a matriarchal religious and cultural order. And if the religion of the Indian Aryans was influenced by indigenous peoples oriented toward matriarchy, Mohenjo-Daro must also be taken into account.

32 *Indische Frühkulturen und ihre Beziehungen zum Westen* (Basel, 1944). See also V. Pisani, "L'unità culturale indo-mediterranea anteriore all'avvento di Semiti e Indoeuropei," *Trombetti-Festschrift* (Milan, 1936), pp. 199–213.

33 This was already the belief of Sir John Marshall (*Mohenjo-Daro and the Indus Civilization,* London, 1931, I, 57ff.).

34 W. Koppers, "Kulturkreislehre und Buddhismus," *Anthropos,* XVI/XVII (1921/22), 442–58.

As for the Aryan Indians who invaded India from the northwest in approximately 1200 to 1000 B.C., it seems quite certain that they, like all Indo-Europeans, had no mysteries in a strict sense. The same is true of the Semito-Hamitic and Turko-Mongolian peoples, but this is only incidental; we shall concentrate our attention on India. It is a matter of general and, in my opinion, well-founded belief that female deities were virtually unknown to the Aryan Indians before the invasion. They certainly lacked the idea of a female supreme deity. And, as usual among the Indo-European peoples, this absence of female deities was bound up with the dominance of father-right or patriarchy. The Indo-European peoples may well have derived both their male supreme deity (*Dyaus pitar*, Ζεὺς Πατήρ, etc.) and their patriarchal social order from their own pastoral culture indigenous to central Asia.[35] This explains, among other things, why the ἱερὸς γάμος was originally unknown to the Aryan Indians, as well as to other Indo-European peoples.

On the other hand, I believe that I have at least shown the likelihood that the old Indo-Europeans had a mystery of the world's creation[36] centered around the horse, which, however, almost certainly had as its prototype the bull or cow of the "south." The "southern" component, whose presence in the religion of the original Indo-Europeans I believe I have demonstrated, shows clear ties with the ethnological complex of the secret societies and mysteries. In Old-Aryan (Vedic) India, these phenomena are grouped around the horse sacrifice (*aśvamedha*), the king's initiation (*rājasūya*), and the Soma cult.[37] If no rituals and institutions recalling mysteries in the stricter sense developed in this period, it is, in my opinion, because the Indo-European spirit (above all, the supreme deity was not yet feminized; see below) was still dominant. The "southern" influence became stronger at a later

---

35 W. Koppers, "Urtürkentum und Urindogermanentum im Lichte der völkerkundlichen Universalgeschichte," *Belleten*, No. 20 den ayrı basim (Istanbul, 1941), pp. 481–525.

36 W. Koppers, "Das magische Weltschöpfungsmysterium bei den Indogermanen," *Mélanges . . . offerts à Jacques van Ginneken* (Paris, 1937), pp. 149–55. Idem, "Pferdeopfer und Pferdekult der Indogermanen," *Wiener Beiträge zur Kulturgeschichte und Linguistik*, ed. Koppers, IV (1936), 279–411.

37 See, in addition to the literature mentioned in the preceding note, A. E. Jensen, "Das Weltbild einer frühen Kultur" (above, n. 8), with quotation from H. Lommel on pp. 36–39.

date, and this explains why it is Śaktism, a younger religious complex, which shows the most striking similarities to the mysteries of the classical world.

At the center of Śaktism,[38] or the religion of the Śaktas, stands the Śakti, meaning feminine force or energy. The supreme deity is conceived as a primal feminine power. A male principle is indeed juxtaposed to her. This male principle always takes the form of Śiva, "lord of the demons," so that evidently there is a primal relation between Śaktism and Śivaism—a circumstance both characteristic and important. But in the sphere of Śaktism, Śiva plays only a secondary role, he is merely a counterpart to Śakti. The female principle is predominant; it is the active principle, while the male principle is passive. How, when, and where did this Śakti cult arise in India, and wherein consist its coincidences and similarities with the mysteries of classical antiquity?

Śaktism, as we have intimated, includes both indigenous and Aryan-Indian elements. We shall gain a better understanding of it if we give some attention to the relation between the two. The Aryan invaders of India often found it necessary to make concessions to the native population, not least in respect to matters of culture and religion. In this process the adopted elements were often exaggerated as a means of impressing the natives and holding them in subjection. This can be demonstrated in connection with the system of endogamy and exogamy which today still prevails in Hinduism. The characteristic group- or gotra-exogamy[39] represents an exaggerated version of the clan organization and strictures against exogamy that are characteristic of totemic peoples. There were and still are numerous totemic peoples in India.[40] But it was not only in a sociological but also in a religious respect that the Aryans were influenced by the native population. The strong inclination toward magic (*Atharva Veda* and later the system of Tantrism), as well as the tendency to solarize and pantheize the concept of God (Upaniṣads, Vedānta), so conspicuous in Brahmanism-Hinduism, all emanate, at least in part and up to a cer-

38 For literature see Koppers, "Probleme der indischen Religionsgeschichte" (above, n. 30).
39 S. V. Karandikar, *Hindu Exogamy* (Bombay, 1929), esp. p. 172.
40 H. Niggemeyer, "Totemismus in Vorderindien," *Anthropos*, XXVIII (1933), 407–61, 579–619.

tain degree, from the same source.[41] But these conceptions owed their systematic development, their form if not their existence, to the workings of the Aryan-Indian mind.

There can be no doubt that among the indigenous population of India patriarchal totemism and mother-right existed side by side, that of the two matriarchy was by far the stronger and more widespread.[42] In the sociological sphere, the Aryans may be presumed to have borrowed many institutions from this indigenous matriarchy—for example, the important position which the maternal uncle occupies in the marriage ceremonial. But what is more important, especially in this context, is that the Aryans probably gained their closer acquaintance with female deities from this same source. We have seen that the Indus culture must be considered in this connection. But even E. Mackay admits that the cult of the primal mother was probably known in India before the Indus culture[43] and an ethnologist cannot doubt this for one moment. By the end of the Vedic period the concessions to indigenous conceptions become evident. This development continued and found its culmination in the religion of Śaktism.[44] Śaktism originated in cen-

41 H. Zimmer ("Death and Rebirth in the Light of India" [orig. 1938], PEY 5, pp. 326–52) shows by interesting and instructive examples how in the period of the Upaniṣads, particularly in connection with the doctrine of reincarnation, lunar conceptions gradually gave way to solar attitudes. Zimmer, however, ascribes this solely to a Sumerian-Babylonian influence, and here we must wonder if he has not taken a too one-sided view of things. A progressive solarization did, to be sure, take place in the ancient world (see Koppers, "Pferdeopfer," pp. 374, 384ff.), and this may have exerted an influence on India. But it must also be borne in mind that the Hindu system of exogamy was borrowed from totemism. This suggests that the solarization of the concept of God (Viṣṇu) and related conceptions (liberation from the eternal, moonlike alternation of birth and death and acquisition of never-ending sunlike immortality) may, in part at least, have arisen from the same totemic source. For in the light of universal ethnology totemic religion reveals a preference for solar conceptions.

42 O. R. Ehrenfels, *Mother-Right in India* (Oxford and Hyderabad [Deccan], 1941). H. Zimmer, "Die vorarischaltindische Himmelsfrau," *Corolla Ludwig Curtius* (Stuttgart, 1937), pp. 183–86.

43 E. Mackay, *The Indus Civilisation* (London, 1935), p. 97.

44 "The underlying conception [of Śaktism] that forces conceived as female deities directly or indirectly govern the world process and the process of salvation has strongly influenced Indian thinking of the last 1500 years and set its stamp more or less deeply upon the most diverse religious and philosophical systems, so that to a certain extent it can be designated as one of the great ideas to which all sects and schools equally pay tribute" (H. von Glasenapp, "Tantrismus und Śaktismus," *Ostasiatische Zeitschrift*, n.s., XII [1936], 127). In Śaktism this conception is not a mere component; it is the "actual principle of salvation."

54

tral India, but it was in Bengal and Assam to the northeast that it developed the special form to which the term Śaktism without modifier refers.

It developed in this particular place—the ethnologist will see this more clearly and directly than the Indologist—because of an especially characteristic form of (pre-Aryan) matriarchy which predominated in northeastern Hindustan and is in part still evident today (Khasi, Garo). Also, the number of Aryans penetrating these regions was relatively small. Thus, existing conditions virtually forced the invaders to make strong concessions to the native element. The tendency to see the supreme deity as a female was indeed present among the pre-Aryan population; the exaggeration of this tendency, however, such as that expressed in its systematization, Śaktism, was principally the work of the Aryan newcomers. Experts in the field agree almost unanimously that this developmental process reached its climax between A.D. 700 and 800 in the regions of Bengal and Assam.

As for the elements in Śaktism which recall the mysteries of classical antiquity, we have already spoken of its central principle, the conception of the supreme deity as female. I believe that this idea has nowhere else been so systematically fostered and over-emphasized. Only in Indian Śaktism has the supreme female principle been so one-sidedly and exclusively conceived as the active principle in contradistinction to the passive principle represented by the male.[45] It should be taken into account that even in Tibetan Buddhism (Lamaism), which has otherwise absorbed the Śaktist system, what strikes us as a more normal relation between the two principles prevails: here the male principle is active while the female is passive. And it might be mentioned in passing that this is the relation between the two principles Yang and Yin in ancient China. It should not surprise us that the strict adherents of Śaktism not only conceived of the supreme deity as female but went so far as to teach that the aim of every man should be to become woman.[46]

---

45 Here I cannot discuss, but can only call attention to, the likelihood of a relationship between Śaktism and the classical *Sāṁkhya* (active *prakṛti*—inactive *puruṣa!*).

46 R. G. Bhandarkar, *Vaiṣṇavism, Śaivism and Minor Religious Systems* (Strasbourg, 1913), p. 146.

This brings us to redemption, another element common to
Śaktism and the mysteries. Here we must recall that some of the
oldest hymns of the *Ṛg Veda* are prayers to Varuṇa, the supreme
deity, for redemption from sin and its fetters.[47] But this idea of
redemption by a god is soon replaced by the characteristically
Indian idea of self-redemption through true insight. In this, as in
the related doctrine of rebirth, Śaktism reveals a universal Indian
(Hindu) orientation. The object of the crucial insight changes in
accordance with the philosophical-religious trend of the individual.
In addition to the knowledge of the secret of the *aśvamedha* and
the (lunar) nature of the Soma,[48] the following main trends are
found: idealism, materialism (*sāṃkhya*), Buddhism, and Śaktism.
The idealist believes that he can achieve redemption by recognizing his own identity with the universal being (Ātman-Brahman); the materialist sees the decisive factor in the knowledge of
an absolute distinction between the spiritual and material principle (*puruṣa* and *prakṛti*); the Buddhist finds it in the knowledge
that all life and all action are suffering, that the consciousness of
self is an error, and he hopes by totally transcending all this to
achieve his nirvaṇa.[49] Śaktism stands philosophically with idealism,
the doctrine of the one in all. But the universal being is seen as
female. For the strict Śaktist, the knowledge of the profoundest
unity with this female universal or primal power signifies redemption. But, as we shall soon see, this conception has peculiar implications.

There is, in my opinion, good reason to believe that about
600 B.C. the idea of redemption, which had already taken distinct

47 Poul Tuxen, in "Die Grundlegung der Moral nach indischer Auffassung"
(*Acta Orientalia*, XIV [1936], 1–25; see p. 2), has shown that here we are
dealing with conceptions which are related to our own and seem strange in
relation to the general religious and ethical content of the Veda (Forgive us
the sins of our fathers and those which we ourselves have committed).

48 Cf. Koppers, "Pferdeopfer," pp. 329ff. (Ein Stück Geheimbundcharakter im
Brahmanentum) and p. 359. H. Oldenburg, *Die Religion des Veda* (2nd edn.,
Stuttgart and Berlin, 1917), p. 177: "Here as we see [Oldenburg is referring
to the great nuptial song, *Ṛg Veda* 10. 85] the Soma-nature of the Moon is
represented as a secret known only to the Brahmans."

49 See H. von Glasenapp, *Unsterblichkeit und Erlösung in den indischen Religionen*, Schriften der Königsberger Gelehrten Gesellschaft, 14. Jahrgang
(Halle a.d. Saale, 1938), pp. 1–72. I have thought it permissible to leave out
of account the teachings of the theistic systems of India, according to which
redemption derives from the grace (*prasāda*) of God.

form in India, found its way to the West, thus entering into the sphere of the ancient mysteries (or their forerunners).[50]

Here again we have communication between the two worlds, but in the reverse direction. If the idea of redemption generally prevalent in the world of classical antiquity differs more or less from the Indian conception, I believe it is primarily because in the West the personal gods retained their identities and no such deep-seated pantheization of the idea of God occurred as in India.[51] It is the gods, always conceived in some sense as personal, who give the *mystes* redemption, which is seen as a blissful life in the hereafter. Here again our old axiom applies: *Quidquid recipitur secundum modum recipientis recipitur.* We cannot enter here into a detailed discussion on the origin and itinerary of the idea of redemption. But to me it seems probable that the religious history of India will have much to tell us regarding the genesis and growth of the notion of self-redemption. Here I can merely note that there would seem to be a relation between the specific development of this idea in India and the struggle which the Aryan Indians thought it necessary to wage against indigenous religious conceptions. It would appear that in this way they strove to rid themselves of spiritual-religious forces which they felt unable to master in any other way.

Beyond question the element of magic so prevalent in the ancient mysteries is vastly exceeded in Śaktism. One good reason for this is that Tantrism, the grandiose system of magic which had previously developed in central India, must be regarded as one of the foundations and essential elements of Śaktism. I believe that I have shown in one of my papers how the shamanism and magic which in Śaktism revolve around the great and terrible goddess Kālī-Durgā gained power over large sections of the aboriginal Indians.[52] This extreme, highly systematized magic constitutes a development that must definitely be characterized as "from above" and not, as was generally thought, "from below."

Once again the propagandist force inherent in such phenomena

---

50 F. Kern, "Die Welt, worein die Griechen traten," *Anthropos*, XXIV (1929), 212ff. K. Prümm, *Religionsgeschichtliches Handbuch* (above, n. 7), pp. 128, 670.

51 Prümm speaks of a tendency toward pantheistic conceptions in the ancient world, about 300 B.C. (op. cit., p. 301).

52 W. Koppers, "Probleme der indischen Religionsgeschichte" (above, n. 30).

is noteworthy. H. Goetz even goes so far as to postulate a link between the European witchcraft of the Middle Ages and Tantrism. This idea had frequently occurred to me, but I had never ventured to express it. Recently I discovered that Goetz stated it some years ago, in the following words:

> These few brief though characteristic excerpts represent only an infinitesimal fragment of that gruesome chapter in Indian religious history which we should prefer to pass over in silence if, with its strange, forbidding mixture of crass superstition and hair-splitting logic, of unrestrained license and true, self-sacrificing piety, of purest ethics and every erotic error, it were not among the most interesting cases in all the pathology of religious thought. But there is still another reason why Tantrism is important to us. It has left its traces everywhere. Neither present "northern" Buddhism nor Hinduism can be understood without it. But, more than that, it is the main source of our witchcraft. Our ancestors, to be sure, knew of witches and magicians; but compared to the fantasies of the high Middle Ages these creatures are pale shadows. Only when in the migration from central Asia the Huns, Avars, Magyars, Bulgars, Khazars, and Mongols carried the ideas of Tantrism, along with other things such as dress and weapons, across the steppes of southern Russia to the West, did all those specters appear which were to give rise to the burning of witches and the persecution of heretics. All those goblins which are only too well known from the *Malleus Maleficarum* and similar works had their source in Tantrism. These are no longer the witches of the Germanic peoples and Slavs, but Indian-Tibetan *ḍākinīs*. From stupefying salves and brews made of children's corpses, excrement, etc. the witches obtain the power to fly naked through the air to the witches' sabbath; they are the paramours of devils and kiss the posterior of Satan himself—and the Tantrists by association with the *ḍākinīs,* by intoxicating liquors and the most repulsive human slaughter, obtain the gift of Siddhi, the magic of flying through the air, etc. The *ḍākinīs* fly through space at night and when they pass water it rains (weather witches!) ; they cohabit with the devil, as in the witches' sabbath or as a witch with an incubus; they murder and eat humans, killing with knife or fire, or like the succubi by exhaustion from erotic excesses. They can make themselves invisible and are invulnerable—here

consider all the notions about the illusory body of witches, the *sigillum diaboli* and the witches' sleep. And this is far from all. The orgies of the black mass, which Huysmans describes in *Là-bas*, are mere echoes of a Tantric ritual which has been preserved in a Śivaite-Śaktist form in the cult of the Vāmachāris and which is said to be still practiced in secret.[53]

As in the mysteries, there is a strong esoteric element in Indian Śaktism—and not only in Śaktism, though here in a special sense. The "one in all" doctrine of the Upaniṣads was treated as a secret doctrine. The Ātman-Brahman could, of course, only be understood and appreciated by a limited number. The same is true of the central doctrine of Sāṁkhya-Yoga and Tantrism. The teacher (guru, yogi) is forever initiating into the ultimate secrets of the system those adepts who are hungry for knowledge and salvation and who are found fit. In Śaktism there is a twofold secret. On the one hand, the great Śakti is the all-encompassing, primal being; on the other hand, the initiates may, indeed must, know that extramarital relations, otherwise regarded as illegitimate, can be a means of union with Śakti, the primal mother.[54] And this brings us to the erotic-sexual element, which, in one form or another, is by no means alien to the ancient mysteries.

By way of explaining these extravagances of Śaktism, earlier writers have correctly pointed to the pantheistic basis of the system. The idea of inner union, self-identification with the female supreme deity, the notion already developed in Tantrism that for those who have fully achieved this union good and evil no longer exist, and the belief that at this stage evil may be overcome by evil (passion by its exercise) —these adequately account for the monstrosities which are a source of constant horror to scholars. They explain, for example, the Tantric assertion that the initiate need not shun sexual relations with mother or daughter.

It was Aryan Indians, as research has amply shown, who developed the theory and practice of Tantrism in such extreme forms. But there is a somewhat extenuating factor which should not be

53 H. Goetz, *Epochen der indischen Kultur* (Leipzig, 1929), pp. 308ff.
54 J. Woodroffe, *Shakti and Shākta* (2d edn., Madras and London, 1920), p. 376. Some of the doctrines here described were never meant for the general body of men.

overlooked. As we have seen, the Aryan Indians found themselves in the midst of indigenous peoples characterized by a matriarchal orientation. The sexual mores of these peoples were in general free to the point of license, while the Aryans brought with them a relatively high moral standard, which they defended to the best of their ability against the freer conceptions and practices of the matriarchal natives. There is good reason to believe that, in order to do away with free choice on the part of the girl and with premarital sex relations, they ultimately introduced the custom of child marriage, which still prevails in a good part of Hindu India.[55] This, too, was of course a grave excess, but to the Aryans it no doubt seemed the best way out of what they held to be an intolerable situation.

In the case of Śaktism, the excess was quite in the opposite direction; native conceptions and customs rooted in matriarchy were carried to the utmost extreme.

But in the interest of justice it must be said that by no means all the Aryan Indians succumbed to Śaktism. Quite the contrary. In India itself, Śaktism encountered much opposition. Its sworn opponents were the Viṣṇuites and the supporters of the doctrine of Bhakti (Bhagavatas). The schism that took place in Śaktism may be regarded as a consequence of this opposition. The leftward trend (vāma-mārga, "road to the left") was countered by a milder rightward trend (dakṣiṇa-mārga, "road to the right"). The "rightists" strove to assimilate themselves to the local Hinduism; in their cult they eschewed sexual excesses, bloody sacrifices, and the enjoyment of meat and alcohol.

In connection with bloody sacrifices we are again reminded of the ancient mysteries—some of them at least. In the mystery of Dionysus a bull was torn to pieces and devoured, and Cumont believes that the bull replaced a child who had originally been sacrificed. We are reminded also of the taurobolium in the Phrygian cult, etc. In India, bloody sacrifices were not, and are not today, limited to Śaktism, but in Śaktism they were carried to unequaled extremes. I need only point to the present center of the Śaktist sacrificial cult in Kālīghāt-Calcutta, where day after day the blood

55 See Koppers, "Probleme," p. 782.

literally flows in streams. These bloody sacrifices (which included, and still occasionally include, human victims) are made chiefly to the great goddess Kālī-Durgā, who thirsts for blood and delights in blood. It is characteristic of India with its feminine orientation that only male animals (particularly he-goats, buffalo bulls, and cocks) are sacrificed, while female animals are under all circumstances excluded, just as they may not be used as beasts of burden. There is no more impressive indication of how profoundly the idea of the mother-goddess has influenced and still influences the life and thinking of India.

Let us for a moment go back to the time in which typical Śaktism developed. We have seen that this occurred about A.D. 700. In view of this date, it goes without saying that the typical Śaktism of India cannot be regarded as a forerunner of the ancient mysteries. The matter is not so simple. We must make distinctions. The background of Śaktism, particularly the mother-goddess complex, seems, as we have shown, to disclose ancient contacts between the Indus culture and the (pre-Semitic and pre-Indo-European) Near East. In India, the Aryan Indians—first through the influence of this Indus culture, then on the basis of association with characteristic matriarchal peoples, particularly in the northeast—developed the typical form of Śaktism, which, as we have seen, has many elements in common with the mysteries. On the one hand, we find common, ancient, origins, while on the other hand, the recent phenomenon of typical Śaktism is itself, in a sense, an analogue to the mysteries. By analogue we do not, of course, mean an attenuated version; on the contrary, the common elements, particularly the female conception of the godhead, are carried to the extreme in Śaktism. And this seems only natural when we consider that the typical Śaktism of India has a twofold matriarchal base: the Indus culture and the prehistoric matriarchal peoples.

In any event the typical Śaktism of India attained its highest development in connection with classical mother-right, and this throws new light on the older thesis to the effect that the mysteries of classical antiquity were ultimately rooted in an agrarian-matriarchal society.[56] But whereas, with the full development of Christi-

56 A. E. Jensen (op. cit., above, n. 8, pp. 6of.) has very much underestimated the significance of matriarchy for the spiritual and religious development of

anity, approximately 1500 years ago, the mysteries of antiquity came to an end, in India, for reasons which I have already stated, the process has more or less continued down to our own day.

5. Summation and Conclusion

What I have said in this paper concerning the origin of the mysteries in the light of ethnology and Indology may perhaps be summed up as follows:

1. Our ethnological-historical question is not yet susceptible of an exhaustive answer. With regard to many of its aspects, the necessary spade work has not yet been done. We can, however, gain significant insights into the question.

2. From an ethnological point of view there are typological and, in the broader sense, genetic relations between the ancient mysteries and the secret societies of agrarian-matriarchal primitive cultures.

3. The mysteries, however, cannot be directly connected with the primitive secret societies, for the mysteries include more advanced developments and mixtures.

4. The advanced character and mixtures are above all due to the influence of a new stratum of conquering peoples (Indo-European in Greece and India). Mysteries and institutions similar to mysteries were originally unknown both to Indo-Europeans and to Semites.

5. Such secret societies are not (and never were) characteristic of those present aboriginal cultures which are accessible to ethnological inquiry (Tierra del Fuegians, southeastern Australians, Andamanese, etc.). The "secret" festivals we do find among them are essentially limited to educational measures in which both sexes are included. They are not, strictly speaking, esoteric.

6. The male secret societies found in agrarian-matriarchal primitive cultures were first interpreted by W. Schmidt as a reaction to the social and economic domination of the woman. In the light

---

a great part of mankind. Above all, Jensen fails to see that the "lunar world conception," which he himself has described quite well as it applies to a number of peoples, is essentially rooted in the feminization bound up with the social phenomenon of mother-right. Cf. also what we shall have to say on this point below.

of the most recent research, this interpretation still seems highly plausible.

7. The propagandistic force inherent in the institution of secret societies is well demonstrated by the fact that even the primitive aborigines of Tierra del Fuego felt their influence.

8. In Śaktism we have, beyond any doubt, that religious phenomenon which, more than any other in India, recalls the Greek mysteries. Both Śaktism and the mysteries have as their basic component an agrarian-matriarchal culture, Śaktism most probably in a twofold form (Indus culture and prehistoric matriarchal tribes); in both cases a new (Indo-European!) ruling class brings about developments and modifications. As the circumstances might lead us to expect, this development takes on an exaggerated form in India. Extremes of a nature elsewhere unknown are the consequence. Specifically, we have seen that the extreme pantheistic conception of God, which was taken over by Śaktism and applied to the female supreme deity, was an important contributory factor.

9. Just as the social institution of matriarchy is prerequisite to the secret male societies, it is also the essential factor in the change of sex of the supreme deity. The aboriginal peoples, it is quite well established today, do not know of a female supreme deity. This shift occurred in the sphere of agrarian-matriarchal cultures. Here we recall the role played by the female deities, particularly the female supreme deity, in the secret societies and mysteries. We have then arrived at a crucial conclusion: Like the earliest agriculture, carried on by women, and the mother-right which went hand in hand with it, the feminization of the deity and the formation of secret male societies are not primary phenomena in the history of man and his religion. They are secondary and not universal. This applies particularly to the mysteries, which were relatively late developments. Hence it is not permissible to make deductions with regard to primal man and primal religion, etc. on the basis of the mysteries.

10. Thus, viewing things as a whole, we stand here in the presence of a paternal and a maternal mind, such as Bachofen recognized in the world of classical antiquity. The fundamental difference between our view and that of Bachofen is merely that in the light of modern ethnological and archaeological research, it

63

is evident that the paternal form did not arise from the maternal, but that the paternal, though in simpler form, has existed since the beginnings of human society and has developed without break, while the maternal with its mother-right culture must be regarded as merely an episode, though an important one, in the development of human thinking and religion.

11. In concluding, let us inquire into the contribution of the secret societies and mysteries to human thought and religion. Here of course we must bear in mind the limits imposed by the present state of research. We can, however, arrive at certain conclusions— of a predominantly negative character, to be sure—which I believe will stand up under future inquiry. Beyond doubt, the root of all evil lies in the lunarization and feminization of the concept of the godhead and in the related growth of spirit cults, cults of the dead, fertility rites, etc. The first part of this thesis has been formulated by that eminent student of ancient religious history, M. J. Lagrange: "As soon as . . . the Goddess appears, the assimilation of the divine to the human is an accomplished fact."[57] W. Schmidt has expressed the second part, with special reference to his penetrating studies of the early American Indians: "Nowhere and never has a spirit cult contributed anything toward deepening and purifying man's faith in the supreme being; on the contrary, it debases it and dilutes it."[58] Greece, to be sure, succumbed in large measure to matriarchal conceptions, but this is not what made it great; on the contrary, the greatness of Greece was assured when, beginning about 600 B.C., its ruling classes moved away from this "Taurian heritage" and succeeded in largely overcoming it.[59] It is an irony of fate that later, and, strange to say, at the dawn of the Christian era, large sections of the civilized world came very close to drowning in a wave of new mystery cults. Then, as we all

---

57 Lagrange, *Études sur les religions sémitiques* (2nd edn., Paris, 1905), p. 119. Quoted from K. Prümm, "Muttergottheiten," *Zeitschrift für katholische Theologie*, LIV (1930), 575.

58 W. Schmidt, *Der Ursprung der Gottesidee*, II (1929), 171.

59 F. Kern (above, n. 50), pp. 217ff. Cf. H. Zimmer, "The Indian World Mother" (following paper in this book). Also, H. Krahe, "Die Indogermanisierung Griechenlands" (above, n. 16), p. 9: "For there is one Indo-European god's name which the Hellenes never relinquished—and we may regard it as a symbol that this one name is that of the supreme deity, who dominates and outshines all others: Ζεὺς Πατήρ, the heavenly father, the Indo-European god of light, who governs the day."

know, Christianity played the leading part in halting this development. Within a relatively brief period it put an end to the Hellenistic mysteries.

In view of the vast importance of this question for the history of mankind, I shall perhaps be forgiven for quoting from a review which I published some years ago of O. Höfler's well-known book, *Kultische Geheimbünde der Germanen* (Frankfurt a. M., 1934). What I then said about the Germanic peoples (and Greeks) is applicable to our present subject:

> The greatness of the Greeks was based not on their mystery cults, often so dark and dismal, but on their crystal clear science and art; and, similarly, I very much doubt whether Höfler is right in attributing so much cultural importance to the "male societies" of the Germanic peoples. Generally speaking, ethnology does not support his theory. Though it is true that the secret societies and the related mysteries and shamanist cults possessed a great propagandistic and internationalizing force, it is quite evident that such magical irrationality did not provide a soil from which world civilizations and world religions could spring forth. And basically the true Indo-European peoples showed themselves to be relatively free from such irrationality. This was one of the principal foundations for their particular world calling. The Greeks succeeded in transcending the pre-Greek mysteries, in part on the basis of their higher and purer Indo-European thought, and in part, later and more completely, with the help of Christian ideas and energies. The Germanic peoples drew, whether directly or indirectly, from essentially the same sources, but they too transcended the spiritual and religious irrationality inherent in them, as well as the catastrophic political fragmentation which, in part, at least, was bound up with that irrationalism. Touched by Christianity and to a certain degree renewed and exalted in their original faith in the god of heaven, they were enabled in great measure to assume the leadership of the world. Thus, upon closer examination, we must look upon the suppression of the old Germanic secret societies, along with their ideological foundations and the various phenomena which accompanied them and resulted from them, as a prerequisite for any true progress.[60]

60 *Anthropos,* XXX (1935), 273.

And what of India? Charles Eliot, one of the foremost students of the subject, has spoken of the characteristic sterility of Śaktism as follows: "It acquired great influence both in the courts and among the people of northeastern India but without producing personalities of much eminence as teachers or writers."[61] I am assuredly the last to underestimate the cultural achievements of India in the most varied fields. But these achievements cannot generally be reckoned to the account of Śaktism. It provides food for thought that precisely where the supreme deity is conceived and worshiped as a primal feminine force and as the source of all fertility the worshipers themselves have in large measure succumbed to spiritual sterility. It would seem that the reversal of the original and proper order (a paternal, not maternal, and a causal, not generative, relation of the supreme god to the world) was in this way bitterly avenged. Nothing less than the "intactness" of the supreme being was here at stake; in fact it was lost, and with it much else was endangered. We have seen that in India the situation was made much worse by the previous pantheization of the idea of God. There is no doubt that for large sections of the Hindus (and not only for the adherents of Śaktism) this whole development led to a kind of spiritual softening, which, in my opinion, explains in part how it has been possible for the English, with their truly paternal organization, to rule a people of several hundred million souls for nearly two hundred years.[62]

But, in spite of all this, there is ground for reflection that millions and millions of people, not only in India but in many other parts of the world as well, have time and time again succumbed so completely and willingly to the female conception of the deity. Here we encounter something which evidently touches on the depths of human nature. The female element in religion obviously has its positive aspects, provided it remains in its natural subordinate place. Christianity, under higher, divine guidance, as it believes, has found such a solution. We shall shortly return to this point.

12. My last points are not intended to deprecate the importance

61 Charles Eliot, *Hinduism and Buddhism* (London, 1921), II, 274.
62 In his paper "The Indian World Mother" H. Zimmer has eloquently and impressively expressed the belief that the pronounced orientation toward the female-motherly brought with it an "impoverization of the life melody."

of studying the mysteries. The very theme to which this volume is devoted, the Ancient and Christian Mysteries, forbids any such attitude. It reminds us that in spite of everything the mysteries have a very special significance for us Western men and for this reason have in many different periods aroused a lively interest. It is not my task, however, to speak on this topic in the more restricted sense; I leave that to other, better-equipped speakers. In this connection I only ask leave to make two brief concluding remarks, which in a sense follow naturally from the vast, world-encompassing, historical vision implicit in the topic of my paper.

First, in view of the male concept of God, so markedly manifested in the Old and New Testaments, we can hardly expect to find any particular relation between Christianity and the mysteries. If the Indo-European concept of the god of heaven, the father god (*Dyaus pitar*, Ζεὺς Πατήρ, etc.) excludes any such relation,[63] this is all the more true of the idea of God prevailing in the Old and New Testaments. But independence in essential matters does not, of course, preclude the possibility of a relation in peripheral matters (rites, usages, the obligation of silence, etc.).

Second, a connection has sometimes been found between the female supreme deity (Terra Mater, etc.), who plays so prominent a part in many of the mysteries, and the cult of Mary, which developed in Christianity. But here there are two factors that have often been overlooked. First, there was no particular emphasis on the cult of the Virgin in the first period of Christianity. The true central figure of Christianity was and remains Christ, from whom it took its name. Secondly, it must be said that in the christological discussions of the first centuries, the emphasis was upon the *human* character of Mary and her son (in so far as his true and perfect human nature was to be emphasized).[64] She was the mother of God, but she was not the goddess-mother or mother-goddess. As an ethnologist I can only say that in pagan religions and mythologies the figure of Mary would have developed into the latter rather than the former.

63 No less a scholar than Max Müller (*Anthropological Religion*, London, 1892, p. 82) called the etymological equation of *Dyaus pitar*, Ζεὺς Πατήρ, etc. the "most important discovery of the 19th century."

64 K. Prümm calls our attention to this and related points ("Muttergottheiten," pp. 578ff.).

As an indication of this we may point to the development in the Lower Congo. In the sixteenth and seventeenth centuries Portuguese missionaries were active in this territory; after that their activity could not be continued. With the relapse into paganism Mary was soon either identified with the earth mother or transformed into the mother (i.e., goddess-mother) of the old supreme deity Nsambi.[65] Here I should like to repeat: The female element in religion has its positive value, provided it remains in its natural subordinate place. Such phenomena as these from western Africa are looked upon by Catholic Christians as proof that the fundamentals of religion cannot in the long run be sustained without a central locale of instruction and guidance from above.

Permit me to conclude my remarks with the apposite and beautiful words which were spoken in this very place some years ago by none other than the late Heinrich Zimmer:

> The subjection of the earthly-maternal life principle by Heracles (and Theseus), by the victory of Apollo and the Olympians as described by Bachofen, finds its Christian correspondence in the Savior, who tramples the head of the serpent underfoot. This Christian victory of the male-celestial principle over the maternal is expressed in tenderly transfigured form in certain Sienese representations of Mary's death. Mary, the maternal, lies lifeless on her bed, surrounded by the Apostles; the divine son has descended amid a glory of angels to gather up her soul. He stands by her bed and holds her soul like a little child in his arms: the son presses his diminutive mother to his breast, just as in the manger his mother held the diminutive newborn babe. The earthly-maternal principle, of which the divine had to partake in order to descend from its heavens, in order to live as a mortal in the flesh, has become the *mater purissima,* the *vas spirituale,* the "spiritual vessel," removed from all the earthly demonism of avidly luxuriating and self-devouring vital forces. Thus the divine son takes his earthly mother with him into his heaven as an innocent child, to crown her: the earthly-

---

65 H. Baumann, *Schöpfung und Urzeit* (above, n. 14), pp. 246, 397. In the church history of the fourth century we read of cases in which uneducated or inadequately instructed believers worshiped Mary as a goddess side by side with Christ. "But the bishops of the Catholic church were on their guard, and these heretical usages never became church practice" (W. Krebs, *Gottesgebärerin,* Cologne, 1931, p. 15).

maternal is annulled by the male-celestial counterforce—annulled and fused with the higher, contrary sphere. The triumphant Kālī, trampling the corpselike Śiva, is the corresponding gesture of the Indian world; and it is directly antithetical to the Christian Sienese Madonna, carried aloft to heavenly life in the arms of her son.[66]

66 Zimmer, "The Indian World Mother"; see pp. 82–83 following.

Heinrich Zimmer

The Indian World Mother

I

The *Hitopadeśa* ("Instruction in what is profitable")[1] includes the story of a Rajput who offered to serve a certain king with his person and his sword for the exorbitant price of four hundred gold pieces a day. He was employed for a trial period. Each day he donated half his wages to the gods and the Brahmans and one quarter to the poor; the remainder served to keep him and his wife and son. With sword in hand he stood before the king's gate and left his post only when the king sent him home.

Then, in the night of the new moon, the king heard the sound of a woman lamenting and sent the warrior to investigate. The soldier departed fearlessly into the black night, and the king decided to follow him; unobserved, he became the witness of strange events. The Rajput followed the plaintive sound until he came to the city gate, and there he found a splendidly appareled woman weeping. She was the king's good fortune: for long years this deity had lain like his wife in the shadow of his arm, but now she must leave him—through a thoughtless transgression he had aroused the anger of the Great Goddess, and therefore he was to die within three days. She was weeping for his end, which would deprive her of her master. Can he not be saved? Yes, there was one way: If with his own hand the Rajput were to cut off the head of his only son as a sacrifice to the goddess, the king would live a hundred years and his good fortune might remain with him.

---

[1] A collection of popular fables and tales, a variant of the famous *Pancha Tantra*. These two works, in numerous translations, are the sources from which world literature has derived many Indian themes. See Charles Wilkins, tr., *Fables and Proverbs from the Sanskrit, being the Hitopadeśa* (London, 1885).

The Rajput went home at once, awakened his wife and son, and told them of his encounter. The son was fully prepared to give his life, for this was in keeping with the spirit of the warrior caste; the mother understood the sacrifice as the price of her husband's kingly wages. All three hastened to the temple of the goddess "adorned with all the signs of fortune"; here the warrior struck off his son's head in accordance with the ceremonial and offered it to the goddess as the price for restoring her favor to the king. But then, just as deftly and solemnly, he cut off his own head—he had requited his master for his princely wages, but to go on living without his son seemed to him vain and empty. His faithful wife did not lag behind; she took up his sword and cut off her own head as well. A sea of steaming blood lay before the image of the goddess.

Thereupon the king, who had observed all this unseen, seized the sword and cried: "Paltry beings like me are born and die each day, but never before has there been one like him, and never will there be again; what avails me the glory of my kingdom without him?"—and he prepared to sever his own head. But the goddess, contented with the bloody drama and with so much spirit of sacrifice on every side, appeared before him in the flesh and stayed his hand. The king, however, consented to remain alive only if the goddess would restore to life those who had died for him. This she promised to do, and he departed to avoid being seen by the others when they returned to life.

The goddess brought the beheaded family back to life; mother and son returned home, and the warrior took up his place at the king's gate as though nothing had happened. And the king, also as if nothing had happened, cried out from above: "What of the weeping woman?" But the hero replied only: "Nothing at all; just as I reached her, she vanished in the darkness." The following day the king publicly celebrated his deed and gave him the overlordship of the land.

This bloody tale, which is enacted each night in the temple of the goddess Kālī—with a happy ending, because all the participants [*pl.* 1] satisfy the blood lust of the goddess with their boundless spirit of sacrifice—is one among many. It is also found in the well-known story collection, the *Kathā-sarit-sāgara,* the "Ocean of streams of story," in which Somadeva gave definitive form to many old Indian legends. Here it stands among the twenty-five stories told by a specter in a corpse that a king has been ordered to cut down from the gallows.[2] Among these stories related by the specter in the corpse there is another, a kindred tale, which however must also be considered in the version of the poet Shivadāsa for a full understanding of its import.[3]

Two friends undertook a pilgrimage to a bathing place sacred to Kālī and there saw a beautiful girl. One of them fell sick with love and was certain that he would die unless he obtained the girl for his wife. His friend spoke to his father, who negotiated with the young girl's parents, and the marriage was arranged. Soon after the wedding, the young couple and the friend set off for the home of the young wife's parents. On their way, they came to a temple of Kālī. The young husband bade his wife and friend wait outside, while he went in to honor the goddess.

When he saw her bloody, triumphant image, crushing furious demons with eighteen mighty arms, her lotus foot planted upon the bull demon, an illumination—so fate decreed—befell him: "The people honor the goddess with many sacrifices of living creatures; shall I not obtain her grace and be saved if I immolate myself before her?" In the silent cella he then found a sword and cut off his head.

When he did not appear for some time, his friend went into the temple to look for him. Overcome with despair at the sight—the severed head, the pool of blood—the friend seized the sword and cut off his own head. Finally the young woman went into the temple to look for the friends, and when she saw the two headless bodies lying in a sea of blood she rushed out in horror to hang herself by a vine from the nearest tree. But the voice of the goddess bade her desist and enjoined her to restore the two to life by setting their heads back on their bodies.

This she hastened to do, but in her distraction she placed her husband's head on his friend's body. To whom then did she be-

---

2 Vetāla Tales, No. 4.
3 Vetāla Tales, No. 6. Shivadāsa's version: "Die vertauschten Köpfe" (The Transposed Heads), in *Vetālapantschavimshati,* tr. into German by H. Uhle (Meisterwerke orientalischer Literaturen, vol. 9, Munich, 1924), p. 47.

long? The shrewd king, confronted with this question by the specter in the corpse, replied that the one bearing her husband's head was her husband, for just as woman is the highest of delights, so is the head the highest part of the body.

Thus she was wedded to the friend's body, beneath the visible sign of the husband. Was the young woman guided by a secret desire in transposing the heads? Was the marriage unhappy; was it this that made the husband so ready for death, so eager for salvation? The story says not a word to indicate the answer but merely tells what happened. The strange mistake with its underlying motives stands unexplained.[4]

The Western reader of these tales is astounded and repelled by the bloody sacrifice, the terrifying alacrity with which the protagonists immolate themselves to the goddess. To the Hindus all this seems perfectly natural. The cults and myths of the Great Goddess are distinguished by the streams of blood that are shed in her honor. In Devī-Pattan, the "city of the goddess"—today a village in the Gonda district of Oudh—the mother-goddess has one of the oldest shrines in northern India; architectural ruins from the Gupta period at the end of the fourth century A.D. show that her primordial cult had been Brahmanized even at that time. Here Mother Earth is worshiped as Durgā, the "Unapproachable" [pl. 11] and "Perilous," or as Pārvatī, "daughter of the mountain," i.e. of the Himālayas. Her great temple festival in the spring—for the refertilization of nature—is attended by pilgrims from the surrounding plain and from the mountains which enclose it. An Englishman who attended the festival in 1871 reported that each day twenty buffalo, two hundred and fifty goats, and the same number of pigs were slaughtered in the temple. Under the sacrificial altar there was a deep pit, filled with fresh sand, which absorbed the blood of the beheaded beasts; the sand was renewed twice a day, and when drenched with blood it was buried in the earth to create fertility. Everything was very neat and orderly; there were no bloody remains or evil smell. In preparation for the new agricultural year, the life sap, the blood, was intended to give renewed strength and fertility to the nature goddess, the bestower of

---

4 [Thomas Mann's novel, *The Transposed Heads* (New York, 1941), was inspired by this passage of Zimmer, with its interesting query.—ED.]

all nourishment, the daughter of the mountain, whose gigantic generative strength is made tangible in the towering mountains.

Today the temple of Kālī at the Kālīghāt in Calcutta is famous for its daily blood sacrifices; it is no doubt the bloodiest temple on earth. At the time of the great autumn pilgrimages to the annual festival of Durgā or Kālī (Durgāpūja), some eight hundred goats are slaughtered in three days. The temple serves simply as a slaughterhouse, for those performing the sacrifice retain their animals, leaving only the head in the temple as a symbolic gift, while the blood flows to the goddess. For to the goddess is due the life blood of all creatures—since it is she who has bestowed it—and that is why the beast must be slaughtered in her temple; that is why temple and slaughterhouse are one.

This rite is performed amid gruesome filth; in the mud compounded of blood and earth, the heads of the animals are heaped up like trophies before the statue of the goddess, while those sacrificing return home for a family banquet with the bodies of their animals. The goddess desires only the blood of the offerings, hence beheading is the form of sacrifice, since the blood drains quickly from the beheaded beasts. That is why the characters in the tales of the *Hitopadeśa* and the *Kathā-sarit-sāgara* cut off their heads, though it is also true that the head signifies the whole, the total sacrifice.

In her "hideous aspect" (*ghora-rūpa*) the goddess, as Kālī, "the dark one," raises the skull full of seething blood to her lips; her devotional image shows her dressed in blood red, standing in a boat floating on a sea of blood—in the midst of the life flood, the sacrificial sap which she requires that she may, in her gracious manifestation (*sundara-mūrti*) as the world mother (*jagad-ambā*), bestow existence upon new living forms in a process of unceasing procreation, that as world nurse (*jagad-dhātrī*) she may suckle them at her breasts and give them the food that is "full of nourishment" (*anna-pūrṇā*).

An ancient conception, extending back as far as the Stone Age: Nature must at every step be given a helping hand; even she can accomplish nothing by herself. She is no more self-sufficient than man. Nothing takes place of itself, either in the cosmos or in human beings. Man must perform clamorous rites in order to

74

liberate the moon from the clutches of the eclipse, to dispel its demons; and if the sun is to be released from its winter feebleness and rise ever higher with the rising year, a young girl, symbolizing the sun, must swing higher and higher into the sky. In order to bear fruit and nurture life, the earth mother demands to be fertilized and strengthened by potations of blood, the vital fluid. Just as primitive man requires his *rite d'entrée,* his little magic spell, before he can undertake anything whatsoever, just as he must be stimulated and strengthened before he can become a hunter, a warrior, a lover, so the primal forces must be awakened, attuned, stimulated, and fortified forever anew if they are to fulfill the function wherein resides their eternal essence.

Thus the Khonds renewed the fertility of the earth with human blood until the British authorities put a stop to it; the Meriahs made human sacrifice to the earth-goddess Tārī Pennu for good harvest and protection against plagues and sundry calamities. The victim had to be purchased; he was well fed, and banquets preceded the sacrifice. He was anointed with butter, oil, and curcuma, ceremonially paraded, and finally strangled. His flesh was distributed among the participants in the festival, who buried it in the fields or burned it and scattered the ashes over the countryside—and thus it fertilized the soil. Every part of the victim—hair, spittle, etc.— had some miraculous efficacy; consecrated by magic he ceased to be a man like any other and became the incarnate spirit of fertility.

The chief deity of the central provinces is Dhārni Deotā, "earth, the deity"; her husband and companion, Bhātarsi Deotā, is a god of the hunt, related to Śiva, the archer, lord of the wild beasts and the jungle. A three-sided wooden pole represents the goddess; this is the symbol of the womb (*yoni*) and of the divine world energy (*śakti*) in the Tantras, hence of the Great Goddess. A stone figure at its feet, related to the *liṅga* characteristic of Śiva, designates the male god. The stone is sprinkled with the blood of a buffalo that has replaced former human victims. In Kalahandi it is a lamb that is sacrificed, and strips of its flesh are dug into the fields to make them fertile. Bāna's *Kādambarī,* a Sanskrit romance of the seventh century A.D., suggests human sacrifice in its description of the temple of the "Angry Goddess" (Chandikā); and the fifth act of Bhavabhūti's pathetic drama of love, the *Mālatī-mādhava,* shows a priestess of Chamundā—a cruel aspect of the goddess—attempting to sacrifice a young girl whom she has carried off to her temple. The goddess, representing universal vital energy, is as inexorable as life itself; she feeds on the blood of her own creatures.

Thus the origins of the goddess lie in prehistory, which, as far as the popular customs and peasant fertility cults are concerned, is still the present. Her earliest idols have come to light in Mohenjo-Daro, where excavations have disclosed a protracted pre-Aryan civilization in the valley of the Indus, during the third millennium B.C. Here we find a number of motifs which later assumed great significance in Hinduism. These include the image of a divine Yogi, antlered lord of the beasts, comparable to Śiva, and the divine cult symbols of the sexes: *liṅga* and *yoni*.

The goddess made her entry into the Brahman world of the Aryan invaders in one of the younger Upaniṣads of the Veda, which effects an important compromise between the exclusive priestly tradition of the newcomers and the ancient heritage of the Indian earth: here the nature of *brahman*, the mysterious, all-moving, highest force, is elucidated through the basic motif of Indian mythology in a parable concerning the eternally renewed struggle of the gods and demons for domination of the world.[5] *Brahman* gained victory for the gods, but, unaware of this, they boasted: "Ours is this victory, ours is this glory." Then the mysterious force became visible to them, but they did not recognize it, and said among themselves: "What strange, miraculous being is that?" They sent the fire god to investigate; he named himself and boasted that he had power to burn all things, but he was unable to harm a blade of grass that *brahman* pointed out to him. Then came the wind god, who carries all things off in his whirling blast, but he could not move the blade of grass. Then the gods bade Indra, their king, to discover the nature of the strange, miraculous being; he set off, but while still in the heavens he encountered a magnificent goddess, Umā, daughter of Himālaya. He questioned her: "What is that strange, mysterious being?" And Umā, or Pārvatī, "daughter of the mountain," alien to the world of the Vedic gods, but through her father primally indigenous to the Indian earth,

5 *Kena Upaniṣad* 3.

knew the secret of the miraculous being: "It is *brahman*," she said, "you are claiming the glory of *brahman's* victory for yourselves."

The goddess alone knew of the all-moving, secret world energy which had helped the gods to victory; it was the power within them, of which they were unaware. They believed that they were strong in themselves, but without this force, or against it, they could not so much as harm a blade of grass. The goddess knew of the universal force, which the Vedic priests called *brahman* and which the Hindus call *śakti*, for *śakti*, i.e. energy, is the essence and name of the Great Goddess herself, hence she could explain the mysterious being to the gods, she could teach them its secret—for it was her own secret.

Later, in Hinduism, the gods are all aware of this highest, female world force. They know that their male intelligence and pride can accomplish nothing without her—and this is disclosed in a myth concerning the genesis of the goddess.[6] On this occasion, the gods are defeated in their battle with the demons; a bull demon has seized dominion over the world; driven from their seats in the universe, the helpless immortals betake themselves to Viṣṇu and Śiva, the two great gods who, exalted above the world drama and its vicissitudes, descend into the struggle between its divine and demonic forces only when it is necessary to restore the balance of the divine order. Furious flames of wrath burst from their faces when they hear that the antigod has triumphed; and impotent rage bursts forth in flames from the bodies of the other gods; the searing flame becomes a radiant figure and the Great Goddess stands before all eyes in the flesh, as the union of their profoundest forces. She takes the weapons and implements of all the gods with her many arms, and adorns herself with all their charms and emblems: as the epitome of all cosmic forces which, divided among many god manifestations, had succumbed to the immeasurable force of the bull demon, she goes forth to battle and subdues him, although like Proteus, like the vital abundance of nature itself, he keeps changing his body as he faces her.

Here all the gods, by renouncing their weapons and emblems—

6 In the *Devī Māhātmya* of the *Mārkaṇḍeya Purāṇa*. [English tr. in H. Zimmer, *Myths and Symbols in Indian Art and Civilization* (New York, Bollingen Series VI, 1946), p. 190.]

borrowed substance that flows back to its rightful owner—admit that all the divine energy of the universe, in its multiple manifestations, is gesture, emanation, form of the one primal force: the *śakti* and World Mother.

The myth cannot actually reveal the genesis of the great mother-goddess, but only the manner in which she makes her appearance, for the myth knows of her beginninglessness, which is implicit in the term "mother": it knows that as mother she existed prior to any of the things to which she has given life. In the conception of the myth, any inquiry into her origins seems as childish and presumptuous as the act of that reckless adept who undertook to lift the veil of the goddess at Saïs and was stricken everlastingly dumb with horror and fear. For the statue at Saïs is the image of the mother-goddess who says: "τὸν ἐμὸν πέπλον οὐδείς πω θνητὸς ἀπεκάλαψεν" ("No one has raised my veil") —meaning the dress that cloaks her feminine nakedness; the term "veil" is a product of the prudery of later tradition. No one has lifted my dress and seen, that is, mastered, my nakedness. I am the mother without a husband, the primal mother, all are my children. He who presumes to lift my dress desecrates the mother. (And he must atone for it, like Ham, who was cursed because he had looked upon the nakedness of the patriarch Noah.)

One cannot speak of her origin, her birth, but only of her multiple manifestations, sum of the rage and fire of all the gods who pour back their borrowed force that she may concentrate herself into one all-conquering form; or as she appears in the firmament to initiate Indra and the gods into the strange, miraculous power which has suddenly become visible to them and made them feel their own impotence, the power which is essentially the secret of the goddess herself.

Intangible and all-embracing, she holds the universal god Viṣṇu in her power; she is his Great Māyā (Mahā-Māyā) or *yoganidrā,* the dream force of his universal sleep, by which, as a yogi manipulates his inner visions, he moves all the fullness of the world within himself. On the lotus throne that springs from the sleeper's navel sits Brahmā, the projection of his purest clarity. He prepares to unfold the world; but from the ears of Viṣṇu arise two mighty demons, devouring passion and bestial stupor, whose interplay will drive the world forward through all its splendor and wildness, through battles, horror, and annihilation. They attempt to tear Brahmā, their pure counterpart, into pieces, but, lest the drama of the universe end before it has begun, Viṣṇu must rouse himself from his slumber and rescue Brahmā. Brahmā invokes the dark goddess, bidding her release the sleep-intoxicated Viṣṇu: "Great wisdom," he invokes her, "great blindness, primal stuff of the universe and night of the world death, might of all beings, sublime motherly goddess!" And she rises like smoke from the sleeper's mouth and nose, so that he awakens to subdue the two demonic emanations of his universal being.[7]

To all the gods the Great Goddess is wedded as the power peculiar to them, the power which moves them and without which they can do nothing, but by virtue of which they can do what it is their nature to do. As the feminine power (śakti) of Brahmā, she is the goddess of flowing, abundant discourse (Vāc, Sarasvatī), and of revelation and wisdom; she is pre-eminently called Viṣṇu's māyā, because Viṣṇu, the preserver, and his avatars dominate the myth of Hinduism in its golden age, while in the last age of the world Śiva, the bringer of the end, overshadows him, and finally the Great Goddess, Śiva's consort, surpasses them both.

As Gaurī, the "radiant white one," she rests on Śaṅkara, Śiva the peace-bringer, the redeeming death which lies spread out beneath her, as rigid and dead as a mountain. As his vital energy (śakti), she holds him in her insatiable embrace and takes her pleasure of him, just as in the Egyptian myth Isis, in the form of a female sparrow-hawk, perches grieving and passionate upon the dead Osiris and rouses his dead force to new life until at last she conceives the child Horus of him. The eternal embrace of the divine pair, Gaurī and Śaṅkara, is manifested in the Gaurishankar, the highest of the glacier caps, as it embraces the jutting peak with its glittering whiteness.

As Kālī, the black one, wreathed with the severed heads and hands of her victims instead of flowers, she stands upon the dead Śiva, holding in one hand an opened lotus blossom, the womb of life, and in the other the sword of death (or the shears of the

7 Ibid. German tr. in H. Zimmer, *Māyā, der indische Mythos* (Stuttgart, 1936), p. 476.

Parca). Without her, Śiva is nothing but a corpse (śava): his force
has exceeded him, he lies lifeless beneath her; but her foot touches
him, and thus in the Tantric miniatures of the allegory he often
appears twofold[8]: on the ground he is a bearded ascetic, rigid in
death, the resting-in-itself of the divine principle that is not acti-
vated; but, somewhat raised, turned toward the goddess, gently
animated by her foot, he is a youthful figure, the eternal youth of
the god. She stretches out her arm as in a dream and gently touches
his head; for the goddess unites the deathlike eternity of the world-
removed god and the eternal vitality of divine energy as the drama
of the world.

Elsewhere, in the myth of Andhaka,[9] the "blind demon," the
goddess becomes the entire primordial chorus of the mother-
goddesses, characteristic of the pre-Aryan popular religion of
India. Andhaka, "the blind one," was an *asura,* an antigod or
demon, embodiment of blind, unrestrained vital energy (*asu*),
in opposition to the gods, who possess more intelligence and clarity
than brute force. He was black as mascara and by ardent asceticism
had achieved immortality. Once he overheard the Great Goddess
in her love play with Śiva and attempted to ravish her. A battle
began between god and demon, but Śiva, with his magic weapon,
the "arrow of the lord of the beasts," could only wound but not
subdue his adversary. Every drop of blood from Andhaka's wounds
was immediately transformed into another blind demon. They
swarmed around Śiva by the hundreds and thousands, and whenever he struck them with his arrows, new hordes, generated from
their blood, flung themselves upon him.

In his distress, the god brought forth hosts of mothers to drink
the blood of the demons. These Terrible Mothers, who were the
[*pl.* III] forces of all the gods and named after them—the boar-headed after
Viṣṇu as boar, the windlike, the sunlike, and the moonlike (the
tale mentions over 190 different names) —hurled themselves on the
blood and drank it up; but the life sap that they drank made them
fertile, more blind demons surged up from within them, and

8 Published and interpreted by Sir John Woodroffe: "The Indian Magna Mater" in *Indian Art and Letters* (India Society, London), II, No. 2 (1926),
66–89. Plate VII, "Kālī on Shiva Shava."
9 After *Matsya Purāṇa,* Adhyāya 179.

these too attacked Śiva. Then Śiva appealed to Viṣṇu, the preserver; and Viṣṇu brought forth the "barren Revatī"—in one moment she drank up the blood of all the demons, but the more she drank, the more barren she became. She was the death of searing drought in which no life germinates. Thus all the blind demons were killed except the first, who was immune to death. Śiva lifted him on his trident, but Andhaka begged for mercy, and the god gathered him into his wild horde of spirits.

But the host of the mothers screamed in unstilled blood lust; they were intent on devouring all the worlds, including gods and demons alike. In vain Śiva cried out: "It is your mission to shelter all creatures; desist from your gruesome sport!" They gave no heed. Again Śiva was compelled to invoke Viṣṇu, the preserver, to oppose the forces of destruction which he himself had unleashed. Viṣṇu's destructive manifestation (*ghora mūrti*), "half-man, half-lion" (*narasiṁha*), tearing the flesh of his fallen enemy with his paws,[10] countered their terror with a salutary fear. From his tongue he brought forth the "mistress of discourse" (Vāc, Sarasvatī, Brahmā's *śakti*); and from his heart he brought forth the *māyā*, his own world-maintaining *śakti*; and from his sexual part he brought forth "her who is wreathed in the flowery garland of the forms-of-becoming" (Bhavamālinī); but from his bones he brought forth Kālī, the dark one, all-consuming time, the bone-wreathed mistress of the place of skulls. It is she who is said to have drunk the blood of the blind demons, and who on earth is called the barren Revatī. These goddesses flung themselves upon the raving mothers who had sprung from Śiva and compelled them to implore the aid and protection of Viṣṇu. Viṣṇu commanded them: "Just as men and beasts long shelter the young that they bear, so shall you shelter the worlds, protect the pious, and fulfill their desires." Thus the Terrible Mothers were conciliated; and they renounced their blind, enraged wildness. The myth tames their primal horror by establishing a relation between it and the preserving god: they enter into the sphere of the beneficent deities, approachable by pious humans, through rituals. It is a conciliation similar to that effected in the Greek myth by the transformation

10 On the mystery of the "lion-man," see Zimmer, *Māyā*, pp. 142–94.

of the bloodthirsty earth-mothers, the Erinyes, into the "friendly" Eumenides.

Andhaka, the demon of inexhaustible life, who multiplies with every drop of blood that pours from him, recalls the hydra, the chthonian serpent of vital energy, which grows seven heads for each one that is cut off. Only Heracles, wielding a brand from the fire which Prometheus has stolen from heaven, can wither the fury of this earthly exuberance. In the Indian myth, there is no Heracles to discipline the blindly luxuriating vital force in the course of his wonderworking journey from earthbound existence to Olympian apotheosis—the defeat of the hydra is only one link in the chain of his labors which, taken together, all signify the arduous conquest of his arch-enemy Hera, the mother-goddess and earth-mother, who, unwilling to release him, attacks him even in his cradle with the serpents of earth, against which the infant Heracles first demonstrates his superhuman powers.

The subjugation of the hydra and of the "blind demon" disclose opposing destinies. In Hellas the maternal principle is overcome, while in India it is appeased, conciliated, and included among the sacred forces. And the mothers lose none of their stature and power in the process.

The subjection of the earthly-maternal life principle by Heracles (and Theseus), by the victory of Apollo and the Olympians as described by Bachofen, finds its Christian correspondence in the Savior, who tramples the head of the serpent underfoot. This Christian victory of the male-celestial principle over the maternal is expressed in tenderly transfigured form in certain Sienese representations of Mary's death.[11] Mary, the maternal, lies lifeless on her bed, surrounded by the Apostles; the divine son has descended amid a glory of angels to gather up her soul. He stands by her bed and holds her soul like a little child in his arms: the son presses his diminutive mother to his breast, just as in the manger his mother held the diminutive newborn babe. The earthly-maternal principle, of which the divine had to partake in order to descend from its heavens, in order to live as a mortal in the flesh, has be-

11 For example, "The Death of Mary" by Duccio Buoninsegna (Museo dell' Opera del Duomo); same title by Taddeo di Bartoli in the Palazzo della Signoria, and by Spinello Aretino in the Accademia delle Belle Arti.

Kālī. Southern India, XIX *cent.*

I

Durgā on the buffalo-demon (*Mahiṣāsura-mardinī*) . *Java,* XIII *cent.*

II

The boar-headed mother goddess Vārāhī, as śakti of the boar-headed Viṣṇu (Vārāha).
Relief, northern India, VII cent.

III

The White Tārā as Prajña Pāramitā. Java, late XIII *cent.*

IV

come the *mater purissima,* the *vas spirituale,* the "spiritual vessel,"[12] removed from all the earthly demonism of avidly luxuriating
and self-devouring vital forces. Thus the divine son takes his earthly
mother with him into his heaven as an innocent child, to crown
her: the earthly-maternal is annulled by the male-celestial counterforce—annulled and fused with the higher, contrary sphere. The
triumphant Kālī, trampling the corpselike Śiva, is the corresponding gesture of the Indian world, and it is directly antithetical to
the Christian Sienese Madonna, carried aloft to heavenly life in
the arms of her son.

II

The idea of redemption is everywhere associated with the cults
and mysteries of the Great Mother—is it not to be expected that the
soul, in its highest aspiration, should turn to the great ancient
goddess and, childlike, look to her motherliness for what it feels
incapable of obtaining by its own strength? To be sure, the omnipotence of the mother, as Great Māyā and inexhaustible womb
of created things, raises the question: "Who will redeem the world
from the mother?" Or: "Who will redeem the mother from herself
—from the mute demonism of her vital urge toward herself?—
from her enraged motherhood, as all-devouring as it is all-nourishing?"

Heracles and Christ are two male Western answers to this question: yoga, which experiences all gods as *māyā*-imprisoned rulers
of cosmic realms and raises itself to detachment from the world
through total integration of its involvements and contents (*kai-
valya*), is the male road of India—in the figure of Buddha a source
of inspiration for the whole world.

The myth of Buddha also hints at the transcending of the
mother: she dies on the eighth day after the birth of the redeemer,
and in one tradition her name is Māyā. The Buddha does not, like
common mortals, issue from his mother's womb; like other bringers of a new world age—such as Indra in the Vedas—he springs from
her flanks, and from his very first breath he has knowledge of himself. He takes the ceremonial steps in all four directions, and says:

12 In the Litany of Loreto: "Mater castissima, inviolata, intemerata. . . . Virgo
veneranda. . . . Vas insigne devotionis," etc.

"I am the oldest, I am the highest in the world!"—transcended is the primal husbandless mother as beginning of all being, and transcended is the venerable womb which no eye has seen.

In Pālī Buddhism, the female relative who raises the orphaned Buddha bears the name of Mahā-Prajāpati—the name becomes intelligible when read in Sanskrit as *Mahā-prajāvatī*, the "great woman rich in creatures," and becomes meaningful only when it is taken as "Māyā," thus making the mother of Buddha a likeness of the great primal mother herself—the transcended mythical, original force: "The great woman rich in creatures" is a most natural designation for the great World Mother. And the spell which for eons has driven her to keep bringing forth the same life in more and more creatures, and taking it back again, is broken by the illumination of Buddha.

Indeed, the Great Mother would not be the all-moving universal energy (*śakti*) that is represented in all the figures of the Indian pantheon with their spectrum of gestures, the energy that is generated in every creature and in every impulse of every creature, if she were only the skeleton with murderous weapons in upraised arms, only the blood-quaffing destroyer. In the introductory prayer of the *Kālikā Purāṇa*, she is celebrated as "she who in the mind of all yogis leads out (*tarati*), beyond the darkness of bondage, the causal force of self-mastery and redemption"—and in the same breath the goddess becomes "she who deludes and enchants (*vimohinī*) the host of creatures and is therefore the *māyā* of the unfolding god, which destroys clear consciousness in the creature." As *māyā* and delusion (*avidyā*) the all-accomplishing force enchants and ensnares, while as illuminating knowledge (*vidyā*) she leads outward (*tarati, Tārā*).

The function expressed in the word *tar*, i.e. to "lead out" of dangerous defiles and menacing terrors, across roaring rivers without bridges, to guide the soul across the river of Saṁsāra, has been associated with tutelary deities since the Vedas. It is used in connection with such redeemers as the *tīrthaṅkaras* of Jainism, the "preparers of the ford," who point out a ford leading to eternal salvation through the rolling waters of the Saṁsāra, and it is applied also to the related Buddhas and Bodhisattvas.

Tārā is the Great Goddess as protectress and redemptress. *"Tarati iti Tārā,"*—she leads happily across, hence she is called *Tārā.*"[13] A relief of Tārā (executed in A.D. 1096) represents her as a helper in all distress: she protects against water, fire and wind, elephants and snakes, demons, and danger on the high seas, against imprisonment, thieves, and—kings. The *Brahmāṇḍa Purāṇa* calls Tārā (in her manifestation as Kurukulla) the "mistress of boats" (Naukeśvarī) , "capable of suppressing floods."[14] She has in her service innumerable boat women, similar to her, who go about in barks rescuing the shipwrecked. In this she resembles the Madonna as *Stella Maris,* to whom Christian mariners pray for protection and aid. She who saves all, says of herself: "The eminent sages in the world call me Tārā, because, O Lord! I take [my worshipers] across the ocean of various dangers."[15]

In her sacred gesture, as the initiating wisdom that redeems from the Saṁsāra, she is archetypally related to the Christian-Gnostic Sophia. Just as Lakṣmī, the lotus-throned goddess of earthly happiness and prosperity, sprang from the ocean of the cosmic life milk, when the gods churned it to obtain the potion of immortality, Tārā came into being when the sea of knowledge, of which she is the quintessence, was churned.[16]

In her eternal, loving embrace the great Māyā, in her aspect as the "redeeming one" (Tāriṇī) , holds Śiva, the "imperturbable," who in the glassy unapproachability of his yogi immersion is the divine representation of the attitude of the redeemed one (he has his double in the cosmic Buddha Akṣobya, who bears the same name) .

As "perfection of knowledge"—Prajñā Pāramitā—which confers [*pl.* IV] illumination and *nirvāṇa,* Tārā is sublime womanhood in the circle of the Buddhas and Bodhisattvas, especially revered in matriarchal

13 Cf. "Tārā-Upanishad" in Sītārām Shāstri, ed., *Kaula and Other Upanishads,* Tantrik Texts, ed. Arthur Avalon, vol. XI (London, 1922) .

14 Cf. (as also concerning inscription of 1096) Hīrānanda Shāstri's monograph, "The Origin and the Cult of Tārā," *Memoirs of the Archaeological Society of India,* No. 20 (Calcutta, 1925) .

15 Quoted from "Arya-Tārā-bhattārikā-nāmāshtottarasataka-stōtra," ibid., p. 24.

16 According to the *Todalatantra:* "At the time when the ocean was churned there arose a deadly poison, O Goddess! and all the gods and goddesses felt very much disturbed. But as Shiva drank the deadly poison without any tremor, therefore, O Goddess! he is called Akshobya (The Imperturbable) and with him Mahāmāyā 'the great Illusion' Tāriṇī always enjoys herself."

Tibet. Tārā is regarded as the *śakti* of the redeemer Avalokiteśvara (Chinese Kuan Yin, Japanese Kwannon), in so far as this Bodhisattva is manifested as a male. In Tāntric Buddhism, she rises to the very zenith of the pantheon: as Prajñā Pāramitā, she is the mother of all Buddhas; she signifies nothing other than the illumination which makes one into a Buddha; *pāram itā*, i.e. "gone (*itā*) to the other shore (*pāram*)"—she leads the soul across the river of Saṁsāra to the far shore, which is Nirvāṇa. Her emblem as the wisdom of illumination is the book resting on a lotus blossom beside her shoulder, and her hands form a circle signifying the inner contemplation of the true doctrine (*dharmacakramudrā*). Thus, finally, just as she is the Great Māyā of Viṣṇu and the *śakti* of Śiva in his role as universal God, she becomes the *śakti* of Ādi Buddha, the cosmic primal Buddha, the temporal and timeless one, of whose transcendent reality the Buddhas and Bodhisattvas of all the worlds are as mirrored reflections, casting their light into the phantasmagoria of transient existence.

The Buddhist initiated in the Tantras obtains a vision of the Buddhas in Nirvāṇa, in eternal embrace with their *śaktis*, just as the Hindu beholds the divine pair, Gaurī and Śaṅkara. This timeless, loving embrace is the highest, "fourth" body of the Buddhas, above the three others, which are: the sensory world in which the Buddhas appear to the outward eye; the inner vision with which the supramundane Buddhas reward the immersion of yoga; and the "diamond sphere" of crystal-clear detachment, which signifies illumination and freedom.[17] These Buddhas, coupled with their *śaktis*, spiritualize and transfigure the tradition of the Stone Age pairs representing the mother-goddess or earth-mother with her male companion (demon of fertility, celestial god, lord of the beasts, etc.), transfigured in spiritual transcendence. But the erotic symbol implicit in the pair signifies the triumph of the feminine

17 *Nirmāna-kāya*, the body of the Buddhas in the world of sensory appearance; *sambhoga-kāya*, the manifested body of the visions of super-sensory world spheres; *vajra-kāya*, the diamond body of transcendent authentic reality; and *mahāsukha-kāya*, the body of the highest pleasure in the Nirvāṇa of the loving embrace of Buddha and Śakti (in Tibetan the pair is called Yab-Yum). On *mahāsukha* in lamaistic art, see H. Zimmer, *Kunstform und Yoga* (Berlin, 1926), plate 29/30 and pp. 74–86.

principle over the masculine, ascetic spirituality of Buddhism, just as in late Buddhism the ascendancy of the Great Goddess as *śakti* over Brahmā, Viṣṇu, Śiva, and all male gods of the Brahman pantheon, signifies the victory of her archetype over all others in India.

The "Perfection of Knowledge"—Prajñā Pāramitā—is regarded as the white form of Tārā; another beneficent aspect is the green one, but the "redeeming" mother has also three hideous, terrifying forms: the blue, the yellow, and the red. Blue-black is the color of death; the blue Tārā rides on a corpse, carries sword and shears in her hands, and wears a necklace of skulls. With gnashing jaws and dangling tongue, with squat trunk and hanging belly, she represents the dark, destructive aspect of the Universal Goddess, which counterbalances her beneficent forms. The bright, redeeming colors are only a part of the spectrum of her being and stand in an intimate relation to their counterpart—to the darkness which merits equal reverence as a reality of life and is fully as close to man.

The enchantress, the Great Māyā, who delights in imprisoning all creatures in the terrors of Saṁsāra, cannot be pronounced guilty in her role of temptress who lures souls into multiform, all-embracing existence, into the ocean of life (from the horrors of which she unceasingly saves individuals in her aspect as "boat woman"), for the whole sea of life is the glittering, surging play of her *śakti*. From this flood of life caught in its own toils, individuals ripe for redemption rise up at all times—in Buddha's metaphor, like lotus blossoms that rise from the water's surface and open their petals to the unbroken light of heaven. The others are contented in the lower region, which is full of all manner of monsters and sodden darkness, but glittering also with gems, pearls, and corals. The goddess, who "consists of all the beings and worlds" (*jaganmayī*) is herself the pregnant salt womb of the life sea, holding all forms of life in her embrace and nourishing them; she herself casts them adrift in the sea and gives them over to decay, and in all innocence rebuilds them into forms forever new, which devour one another. He who thus comprehends the mother does not ask to be delivered from her, but rather to be released from himself, to be freed from the presumption of his ego in inner devotion to her eternal power.

Once Viṣṇu was riding through the air on the sun bird Garuḍa,

his steed, and both of them, filled with their sense of self, saw in
Viṣṇu the highest, most irresistible and universal being.[18] They
flew past the Blue Mountain, the throne of the Great Goddess as
"Mistress of All Desires and Joys,"[19] but they gave her no heed—
"Fly on, fly on," said Viṣṇu to Garuḍa. Then the Great Māyā
paralyzed them, and they could not stir from the spot. Viṣṇu was
filled with rage against the Blue Mountain, shook it with both
hands, but could not move it. Enchanted and frozen by the *māyā*
of the Great Māyā, they fell into the world ocean; Viṣṇu sank to
the bottom-most depth and strove in vain to work his way upward.
Unable to stir a muscle, he lost consciousness. Because he failed
to honor the *śakti,* the world force that confers all motion, whether
of limb or of spirit, it magically withdrew itself from him: and he
became rigid, defenseless, lifeless.

Brahmā, the creator, went in search of him and found him at
last on the bottom of the sea, as though dissolved and returned to
the primal substance. Brahmā seized him and tried to lift him from
the sea, but was unable. Enchanted by the *māyā* of the goddess, he,
too, to his infinite amazement, grew rigid under the same magic.
And the same fate befell all the gods who went with Indra in search
of the first two and tried to raise them from the bottom of the sea.

Then Bṛhaspati, the priest and spiritual guide of the gods, finding their spheres deserted, betook himself to Śiva's solitude upon the
Himālaya, and respectfully inquired where the gods had gone. Only
Mahā-deva, the Great God, knew the secret of the Great Goddess,
whose consort he was, and to the priest of the gods (who are themselves unknowing in the face of the highest force in the universe)
he said: "They have slighted the Great Goddess, the Mahā-Māyā,
from whom the world is made; therefore Viṣṇu and all the gods have
been enchained by her *māyā* and dwell at the bottom of the sea. I
will go with you and set them free; without me, you would suffer
the same fate as they."

The two of them went to the gods at the bottom of the sea, and
Śiva asked them: "Why are you dwelling here? How did you become rigid and lifeless and shorn of consciousness like substance

18 *Kālikā Purāṇa,* Adhyāya 76.
19 Kāmeśvari, or, in the abbreviated form, Kāmākhyā: "she who takes her name
from *kāma,* the desires and joys."

without animation?" Under his questioning, Viṣṇu, who had sunk
to the deepest bottom of unconsciousness, slowly regained his speech;
indeed, he now understood what had happened to him and why.
He bade Śiva lead them all to the Great Māyā, the "trance of yoga,"
who held them enchanted at the bottom of the sea, in order that
they might do homage to the gracious one (śiva) and obtain her
grace.

This Śiva promised to do; but to make it possible he taught all
the gods how to fashion in their own flesh the magic "defense" or
"armor" (kavaca) of the "Mistress of All Desires and Joys," and
thus release themselves from her māyā and saturate themselves once
more with her strength. It was this "armor" that protected him
against enchantment by the māyā, so that he did not suffer the fate
of the other gods; and he who fashioned it in undivided devotion
could behold the goddess. It helps toward the realization of all
desires. By a laying of hands on all the limbs and organs, from the
head to the heels, by an invocation of the many forms of the
omniform śakti that is effective in them, the whole body enters piece
by piece into her safekeeping—or, rather, the all-governing force,
hidden within it, is aroused limb by limb to beneficent efficacy. By
this ritual of daily worship the believer enchants and exalts himself
into an aggregate of the multiform divine forces of the Great Māyā;
he transubstantiates his created nature into her hallowed vessel.

When Viṣṇu and the gods had distributed this "armor" through
their bodies by the laying on of hands amid mumbled invocations,
they rose from the watery depths, thanks to the force of the Great
Māyā, and betook themselves to the Blue Peak. When Viṣṇu approached the "Mistress of All Desires and Joys," he was overcome
by the knowledge of her greatness and worshiped her as the mother
of all worlds and beings, as primal substance and creatrix of the
universe, and as the knowledge that confers redemption. Then the
goddess revealed herself in the flesh and bade all the gods drink
of the waters of her womb and bathe therein: "Thus will you be
free of imprisonment in your ego and filled with supreme heroic
might, and thus will you move to your place in the zenith of heaven."

This ceremonial of drinking and bathing in the womb of the
goddess does not mean subjection to the higher feminine principle,
nor does it mean an imposed humble acceptance of the over-

whelming sovereignty of the womb, for this act of subjection and pious devotion had already been performed through the ritual of the "armor"—he who dons it has already been transformed by enchantment into a vessel of the goddess—and full recognition of the Great Goddess in her overwhelming greatness had already been expressed in the words of worship from the mouth of the great god-maintainer. The ceremonial signifies nothing other than the solemn self-revelation of the veiled image at Saïs: in the Indian gesture, the primal womb, whose cloak no one has lifted, reveals itself in a sublime act of grace, and invites to solemn communion. The gods—and as always in India, men following their example— are held worthy to bathe and drink in the divine source of the world's life, to find rebirth and a higher life in its waters. Thus pilgrims throughout India gather the water of life from sacred wells, or communicate in sacred pools and bathing places with the miraculous power of the god who is present in them—with the seed of Śiva, for example, in the Pool of the Golden Lotuses belonging to the great temple of Madura.[20] Each one of them is a *tīrtha,* a ford, by which to cross the waters of Saṁsāra to the opposite shore, the shore of beatitude in God and release from the ego.

And so Viṣṇu and the gods bathed in the womb of the Great Goddess and drank of it; thus beatified and dismissed by the Great Goddess, they returned to the highest heaven. There they saw the "Mistress of All Desires and Joys" hovering high in space and round her thousands of blue mountains, their slopes touched by her and dotted all up and down with wombs. The sacred bath and place of pilgrimage—the *tīrtha* of the *yoni*—had reproduced itself a thousand times.

The vision recalls Rabelais. Panurge, the tutor of Pantagruel, once spun the fantasy of a wonderfully fortified, absolutely impregnable city: the stones of its walls consisted entirely of yonis; and thus the city was able to withstand the masculine assault of whole armies. This grotesquely obscene fantasy originated in age-old mythical conceptions of central and southern France; suppressed by the Church during the Middle Ages, they raised their head for the last time under a comic cloak in Rabelais' unique work, in the freest

20 On the origin of the Pool of the Golden Lotuses in the seed of Śiva, see Zimmer, *Māyā,* p. 456.

hour of the Cinquecento, before the Medicean Renaissance of the Valois with its classicism and humanism preparing the way for the ideal of the courtier in the age of Louis XIV completely excluded such motifs, as did also the Calvinistic asceticism of the Huguenots and the spirit of the Counter Reformation. This animal exuberance and joy of life is generally associated with the *esprit gaulois,* but fundamentally it is the matriarchal structure of pre-Celtic France, comparable to that of pre-Aryan India, that speaks in Rabelais. In the Middle Ages this same matriarchal element made its appearance in the tale of *Aucassin and Nicolette,* which indicates for example that the custom of *couvade* still existed in southern France (as in southern India today).

In an instant the gods climbed the thousands of Blue Mountains and, drinking and bathing in their sacred pools, happily repeated their communion with the womb of the goddess. Thereby they were seized with incomparable delight. Relieved of all sorrows, filled with beatific amazement, they praised the womb of the "Mistress of All Desires and Joys," gave thanks to Śiva, and went their way.

The communion with the vital essence of the goddess washes away all sorrows. In the end, Śiva, who had taught the gods the "armor" of the goddess and its ritual, reveals that once a man has bathed in the womb of the goddess and drunk of it, he will never be reborn on earth but will attain to the highest Nirvāṇa. Through this communion an alchemical transformation takes place in him; he is transubstantiated into the divine. The womb of the goddess contains the alchemical essence of the philosopher's stone; moreover, according to the words of Śiva, the maternal blood that nourishes the fruit within it contains red arsenic (*manaḥ-śilā*), the mineral that trickles from the rocks of Himālaya and is said to possess the alchemical power of transforming copper and other base metals into gold. Quicksilver, as the seed of Śiva, possesses the same virtue and confers divine immortality.

On all levels there are rituals capable of transforming man. But it is everywhere the tradition and trend to rank the spiritual, sublime practices above the sensual and magical ones, since the general course of cultural development has favored the spiritual element over the material and feminine. This development has taken place under the predominance of the male principle. But with the cult of the Great Goddess in late Hinduism, the archaic heritage of sensual earth-bound rites rises once again overwhelmingly to the zenith. The old World Mother is "Redeeming Knowledge," "She Who Saves," the force of illumination in the yogi; but at the same time she relinquishes none of her power over the tangible world, every form and gesture of which is the self-revelation of her enchanting, world-creating, world-deluding force. Just as the gods are beatified and fulfilled by honoring her world-bearing womb, the cult of the pure vital forces in Tāntric Hinduism represents the sanctification of created nature as the everywhere-tangible revelation of the undying maternal force amid the transient bloom of creation.

Thus the emblems of the sexes, the *liṅga* and the *yoni,* become supreme cultic symbols—or, rather, they have maintained their symbolic rank from antiquity down to the most recent times. This lends the love life of the Hindus, at least where the cult of Śiva prevails, a sacramental quality, sharply contrasting with the total secularization of the erotic in the Moslem and Western worlds. In the teaching of the Tantras man and woman should approach one another with the feeling that they are meeting the godhead. The husband represents for the wife—as the teacher and initiator for his pupil—a human form of Śiva. To belong to him utterly is to her mind the epitome of her religious duties. The long myth of the goddess' love and marriage with Śiva, the dramatic vicissitudes of separation and re-encounter extending over eons, the jealousy and sacrificial death of the goddess, her ascetic striving for the ascetic god,[21] present the Hindu woman with her whole canon of exemplary behavior—including voluntary sacrificial death.

It is the foundation of this mythical ritual of the sexes that spouses do not look on one another as persons and individuals but as the human form of the divine world force, whose male and female aspects meet in Śiva and the goddess and are paired in all creatures. Here we have an archaic situation comparable to the ritual in which king and queen, as the embodied deities of sun and moon, solemnly enter into a fruit-bearing union which is a source of blessing to land and people—a ceremonial in which the personal element of affection and enjoyment can play no part.

21 See Zimmer, *Māyā,* pp. 426–89.

Later man, who has achieved greater self-awareness with the definite emergence of the ego, can no longer, as dancer or mime, thus transform or enchant himself into the divine, and this is characteristic of his situation. He knows the dividing line between godhead and man and has experienced it as immutable. Hence the resignation of modern man, growing out of the development of his persona. He has found consciousness and reflection, critique and restless inventiveness, material and technical domination over a world that is losing its gods, the sentimental ideal of eighteenth-century humanitarianism, and the cold practice of twentieth-century technological inhumanity. And he has lost his early paradise full of fear and trembling, limitless flights and transpositions, blood-lust and innocence.

In the sphere of Hinduism, the male looks upon all womanhood, beginning with the little girl, as the self-revelation of the goddess in the world of appearances. In the esoteric ceremonial, girl and woman take the place of the cult image of the goddess, and in the secret orgiastic ritual of the Tantras, reserved to the initiate, the erotic sacrament of the sexes stands above the enjoyment of meat and drink as the supreme intoxicant by which men can attain redemption in their lifetime. Though distrusted, excoriated, and subjected to wise limitations, it remains the natural and primal fulfillment of the cult of the Great Goddess.

In one of the Tantras Śiva says to the goddess:[22] "Just as the Goddess Discourse and Brahmā (the epitome of creative wisdom) are inseparably fused, so also the elect (*vīra*) with his *śakti* (the female companion of his initiation). A thousand vessels of intoxicating liquor or a hundred heaps of meat will not content me if the essence of immortality (*amritam*) from womb and *liṅga* is lacking." Not Viṣṇu's discus is the sign over this world, not Brahmā's lotus, or Indra's thunderbolt; *liṅga* and womb are its signs, and its essence is Śakti and Śiva. Whenever the union between Śiva and Śakti takes place (i.e., the erotic communion of the initiate with his feminine companion in sacramental form, which makes them the earthly image of the divine pair), which is the

---

22 Tārānātha Vidyāratna, ed., *Kulārnava-tantra*, Tantrik Texts, vol. V (London, 1917), 8th Ullasa, verses 106–08.

true act of worship of the initiate (*sā sandhyā kulanishthānām*),
then the true union with the godhead is effected in immersion
(*samādhi*).

The Stone Age gesture of the old earth-mother and her male
companion has descended from the cosmic sphere and become the
valid, esoteric sacrament of initiated human pairs, a sacrament
which high Brahman tradition was compelled to acknowledge in
the Tantras. In the later age the weapons of the victorious male
gods are no longer the dominant signs: not Indra's thunderbolt,
opening the way for the Aryan invaders, shattering the fortified
cities of the indigenous population, preparing the victorious march
of the conquerors into the plain of Hindustan; no longer is it
Viṣṇu's discus that played so great a part in the mythical battles of
gods and demons, or Brahmā's lotus blossoming to renewed creation, or any of the dominant symbols of the classical Hindu myth.
Liṅga and *yoni,* the age-old symbols of the sexes, have reascended
after episodic eras and stand again at the zenith of valid revelation,
as in the Stone Age beginnings and in their timeless survival in the
realm of popular customs.

The ring has closed and may be turned over for contemplation.

The all-sustaining, all-nourishing goddess is first embodied in the
earth (*dharaṇī*); hence, she is the daughter of the great mountains, the Himavant (*Haima-vatī*), and is their mistress; she has her
throne upon the Vindh-ya Mountains (*Vindhyavāsinī*).

But she is also the darkness of temporal death (*kāla-rātrī*) and
she is the womb of all life, which is to say, the fury of growth
fighting for every hand's breadth of air and earth, the mute rage
of the creature, the rage of passion and the urge to conceive, the
inexorable urge to bear fruit without end, which drives the creature
through life and death, in forever-changing form; the striving of
the unborn for the light and the tyrannical cry of newborn life for
food and warmth, the discord among brothers and generations—
she is the entire struggle for the pasture of life, whether silent or
cloaked in pathos. The war-god is her son, and so is the plentiful,
jovial god of the rice fields, the elephant-headed Gaṇeśa, whose
function is to remove all obstacles to life. The struggle for life,
with its inexorable, strangling embrace, is represented by the Angry
One (Chandikā), the horror of existence, striding through the

gigantic, overpopulated country, through withering heat, dusty wind, and steaming sultriness; and in her many arms she bears all the weapons of destruction: plague, famine, and tumultuous war. Under her feet stately residences, populous cities, flowering country-sides are trampled in the dust: "A thousand years a city, a thousand years a wilderness," says an Indian proverb.

Every being has a twofold aspect, reveals a friendly and a menacing face. All gods have a charming and a hideous form, according to how one approaches them; but the Great Goddess is the energy of the world, taking form in all things. All friendly and menacing faces are facets of her essence. What seems a duality in the individual god, is an infinite multiplicity in her total being.

Her terrible traits are exemplified in the Mothers of southern India, the plague goddesses: as thou hast given life, thou bringest death. For the infant the mother is all-powerful, her face radiates all-embracing love, but also fury, cold, and death. She is the inexorable womb. Hence the melancholy of all those bound to the cult of the mother; life is as it is, with its alternating play of light and shade, its resurgences and declines, now exposed, now sheltered.

She is the inexorable actuality of life, the flowing circle of its forces and forms, racing headlong, changing and merging with one another. Who will escape from her? And she is its perfect counterpart: the forces that raise us above it, Tārā, the savioress, who guides us out of Samsāra, out of the raging circle into the resting center, out of the transience of all forms, into the permanence of the eternal force which hurls itself into those forms as water hurls itself into waves, bubbles, and foam. She is the mute security of life in itself; from the ashes of burned forests she raises eager fresh flowers whose decay is pregnant with new life, a new life which all around it sees only life in its transitions and transformations with no shadow of death, just as we ourselves, when we sink our teeth into a ripe fruit, or draw a living plant from the garden, are without awareness of death.

Whatever you do, in waking or sleeping, consciously or involuntarily in the cycle of your flesh to the accompanying music of your soul; whatever you do as your body builds and destroys, absorbs and excretes, breathes and procreates, or bestows joy infringing on the limits of rage and pain—all this is a mere gesture of the Great

Mother, *jaganmayī* (consisting of all worlds and beings), who unremittingly does likewise with her world body in endless thousands of forms. And the spirit, which comprehends all this and appropriates it as redeeming knowledge, is not her counterpart but merely one of her gestures: captivating or liberating, double-faced like everything that is and moves.

To see the twofold, embracing and devouring, nature of the goddess, to see repose in catastrophe, security in decay, is to know her and to be saved. The utter transience of things, the bitter taste of forgetting the ruins and rubble as they lie forsaken and overgrown in the pitiless heat of noon, is an illuminating gesture of the Mother, with which the knowing believer saturates himself. A joyful sense of the bitter and pitiless finds reverent appeasement in her spirit and scorns conciliation through the clever transitions of embellishing thought. She is the perfect figuration of life's joyous lures and pitiless destruction: the two poles charged with extremest tension, yet forever merging. How narrowed and attenuated all this has become in the modern, nationalistic "Mother Earth" of India, raising her arms in warlike patriotism, resisting foreign domination and shielding the "children" of her own land!

The potential superiority of the womanly over all other gestures of life—conferred by simple motherhood; by the mother beast in man and its ability to meet all situations in its fulfillment of the trivial central function of renewing life; raised above all other spheres in its tension, intoxication, pain, and fervor; seen as an elemental destiny giving and demanding fulfillment—for late Hinduism this function, which carries magic power, which fulfills and hallows, is embodied in everything feminine. Thus girl child, maiden, and matron all have a shimmer of superhuman dignity, as vessel and symbol of the supreme natural force (*śakti*) of the mother-goddess, to whom all things owe their existence.

This overwhelming trend toward the feminine principle greatly impoverishes the melody of life—what then becomes of the male prototypes and heroes in this exaltation of the mother above all else, in this late revival of an early matriarchal age? If motherhood is the answer to the riddle, then we have returned to childhood and cast off the male principle, for it is precisely by relinquishing childhood and stressing the male principle that a man becomes a man, a hero and warrior, a creator and a philosopher, a transcender, finding and transcending the woman, who is not yet a mother, but will become a mother through none of her own volition, overpowered by the new man.

The cult of the World Mother and Mother Earth extends into the present from the ethnic childhood of the Stone Age, which has survived for thousands of years among the pre-Aryan masses of the Indian peninsula. Stone Age civilization, elsewhere the rubble of archaeology, is in India living reality; and the inarticulate popular cults have even acquired a literary language in the Purāṇas and Tantras. The world becomes a vast kindergarten, hence exceedingly democratic: in the presence of the sheltering maternal principle, the little men are very little and helpless—an emasculated culture of peasant masses, bound and bent to the earth, unwarlike, without the adventure of the spirit.

Here we are still in an age anterior to the great battle of the sexes which constitutes the leitmotiv of Bachofen's mythological history of the ancient world; the male has not yet rebelled against the hegemony and natural tyranny of the woman and mother. He has not yet done violence to the feminine—carried off the Sabine women (as prelude to the foundation of the Roman empire) or made woman his domestic chattel.

The cult of the pure vital principle in its womanly-maternal form is democratic, while the spiritual male cults lead to aristocratic hierarchies. The helpless cry for the mother is a democratic renunciation of the male principle, a casting off of the individual values which grow out of man's profound inner development on his road to maturity, and which he elaborates through achievement and experience, self-discipline and mastery. The cry for the mother is regression to the elementary form of subordination and dependence; it is the suckling reflex of the baby, the return to infancy.

Here all masculine glory is renounced: that of the conquerors in Vedic battles and songs, of the bloody warrior aristocracy in the *Mahābhārata*, of the demi-god hero and savior in the *Rāmāyaṇa*, who is able to save himself and the world from menacing monsters because the helping powers of the universe extend a hand to him, because the beasts of the wilderness, which are alien and menacing to others, become his best friends. Even the illuminated, spiritual transcender, the yogi, and his most sublime form, the Buddha, are renounced—or else we might say that all these figures and symbols have passed by this world without transforming it, as though on another stage, as though they had failed in their role of models for human mastery over life, as though they had all been unequal to the full horror of life, of the life that is the Mother herself; or as though since the dawn of the last and darkest age of the world there had been no adepts capable of filling in the outlines sketched by such figures, of traveling their roads to an end; and as though all other gods had faded and been reabsorbed by the Primal Mother, and their seers and sages with them. A circle of the ages of the world has closed, as in the prelude to *Götterdämmerung*, when the cord breaks in the hands of the Norns, when in answer to the question: "Knowest thou how it will be?" the wise women fall silent and, embracing one another, depart into the depths:

> Zu End ewiges Wissen!
>   Der Welt melden weise nichts mehr.
> Hinab zur Mutter! Hinab!
>
> (Here ends all of our wisdom!
>   The world marks our wise words no more.
> Away! To mother! Away!) [23]

The self-reliant male with his uniqueness as hero, transcender, master, with his grand gestures, is here renounced as impotent. The sole object of reverence becomes the hungry maw of life, which gobbles and crunches all things, all the life that has burst from its own womb, which murders its own creatures with a somnolent indifference: the vital process of the world body.

The regression to the maternal, the homecoming from the adventures of the male principle, whose great heroes and models are swept away and shattered, remains a profound enigma. The melancholy songs of the eighteenth-century Bengali mystics, of Rāmprasād and other singing yogis, describe in ascetic devotion the consolation and hopelessness of this trusting childhood. The Mother is as merciless as she is merciful, since she is life itself, and life remains as it is, whether man raises the plaintive cry of "Mother!" or clenches his teeth to withstand the aspect of its

---

23 English tr. from Richard Wagner, *The Dusk of the Gods,* tr. H. and F. Corder (Mainz and London, n.d.), p. 10.

Gorgon's head. It allows itself to be called "mother," and for one moment the sound of the word may relieve our heart of its boundless fear of the silent horror of life, unceasingly grinding its blossom in its jaws; but our cry does not change the Mother. She remains the dark figure adorned with the severed hands and heads of countless victims, raising the blood-filled goblet to her lips, quaffing the steaming sap of life with her broad, tigerlike tongue.

Even in the most fervent appeals to her motherly embrace, the melancholy knowledge emerges that she remains what she is: the totality, maintaining its balance by contradictions: sheltering maternal womb, silently nurturing, generous breast and hand, and devouring jaws of death, grinding everything to bits.

The wisdom of Rāmprasād in his *Songs to the Mother* bids us find repose on the thorny bed of this bitter, bright-dark insight:

> Mother, how often will you drive me round and round the Wheel of Being, like a blindfold ox that grinds the oil? Binding me to the log of the world, you urge me round incessantly. For what guilt have you subjected me to six oilmen [The Six Passions]? After wandering though eighty lākhs [i.e., eighty times 100,000] of rebirths in form of beast and bird, still the door of the womb is not closed to me, but sorely hurt I come again. When the child weeps, uttering the dear name of Mother, then the mother takes it in her lap. Throughout the whole world I see this comes to pass, I alone am excepted. Crying Durgā, many sinners have attained to pardon.
>
> Take this binding from my eyes, that I may see the Feet which banish fear. Countless are the evil children, but who ever heard of an evil mother?
>
> Mother, this is the hope of Rāmprasād, that at the end I may find station at your Feet.[24]

Resumption of the childlike relation to the mother necessarily implies an ironical element: the notion that the continuously child-bearing World Mother may exempt her child from the timeless circuit of birth and death, which is nothing other than the substance of her motherhood. But who, if not the goddess, "consisting of all worlds and beings," will respond to the cry of her child?

24 Rāmprasād, 1718–75. See Edward J. Thompson and A. M. Spencer, eds., *Bengali Religious Lyrics*, The Heritage of India Series (Calcutta and London, 1923), p. 49.

The maternal world force can only strive silently, unquestion-ingly, for the unremitting rebirth of every creature; the monotony of life, with its cyclical, unepical recurrences, its round of seasons, ages of life, generations, is the substance and meaning of the whole; the unique, masculine individual rises above it; there is no his-torically incisive, epoch-making event, nothing to divide one season from another in the vegetative cycle, no hero setting out for ad-venture, no savior descending to earth.

Since male gods and heroes have paled during the latest histori-cal period of Hinduism, the Indian sphere has been overwhelmingly influenced by this age-old spirit of melancholy flowing from the monotonously murmuring river of life which engulfs the people of a matriarchal culture. It is this, in the final analysis, that has given rise to what Westerners have called Indian pessimism.

Over and over again this absurd springtime, this deadly serious-ness about the same old divine foolishness with its personal excite-ments and crises—merely in order that Jack and Jill may meet and the necessary miracle occur, the silent ritual pleasing to the World Mother. Over and over again the struggles and spasms, empires trembling and frontiers bursting asunder, thrones rising and falling —and the consequence is the inevitable: biography and history con-tinue. And each time it is as never before: paeans of praise, bells of peace, flags of victory over city and countryside; always magically new as in Tristan and Isolde—never have man and woman loved one another as we do—flights over the Milky Way and back again to the childbed—for once again, without our willing, the good World Mother, the old cosmic matchmaker, the Great Māyā, has been driving at just this.

Thus life renews itself with joy and depletes itself with victories, drunk with the magic of its unchained demons—that is, the drunken, self-intoxicated dance of the World Goddess with her free-flowing hair, virgin seductress in the full radiance of her slender charms, whiplash driving the team of life through the night of the universe.

Forlorn is the lot of the World Mother's child. Rāmprasād sings:

> Is motherhood then a mere word of the lips? Bringing forth does not make a mother, unless she can understand the griefs of her child.

Ten months and ten days a mother endures sorrow. But now, though I am hungry, my Mother does not ask where her child is. Earthly parents correct their sons, when they have offended.

Though you see Death, that dreadful ogre, coming to slay me, you are untroubled.

Twice-born Rāmprasād says: Where did you learn this conduct? If you behave like your father [*himālaya:* stony], do not take upon yourself the name of World Mother.[25]

This passionate impetus toward the mother may arouse all that is childlike in the worshiper of Kālī and raise it to formative dominance; in this regression to (or persistence in) the mother–child relationship, he may perhaps find the same form of shelter as the believer finds in the bosom of Mother Church, and the aspect of the Mother's rending horror, counterbalancing her all-nourishing motherhood, may serve as an unconscious model for the unclarified demonism of his nature, helping it to live from day to day in childlike innocence, unconsciously at home in the multiplicity of the goddess, mutely secure in her ghastly archetype, as a fish in water.

But the true adept of the mother-goddess, less naïve, since he seeks consciously and with all his strength to penetrate her secret, must renounce every gesture of maternal love and care on the part of the mother to whose worship he has dedicated his life, if he is to effect the dark balance of renunciation and yearning in the melancholy, inexorable knowledge which, through contemplating the hour of his death, he feels ready to accept. It is thus that Mahārāja Rāmkrishna of Nātōr, a contemporary of Rāmprasād, sings to Kālī and Śiva, in his preoccupation with his last hour:

> When my mind is failing, then the name of Kālī whisper in my ears, as I lie on my bed of sand. This body is not mine, the passions sweep it along. O Forgetful One [Śiva], bring my rosary when I float in Ganges.
>
> Rāmkrishna, fearful, says to the Forgetful One: Thou art careless for my welfare, careless as to my fate.[26]

Śiva, the "gracious," is the "great forgetful one," who has no thought of his faithful in life and death—that is the truth of which the believer is convinced and which consoles him by its very bitter-

25 Ibid., pp. 31f.
26 Ibid., p. 75.

ness. Thus Śiva is the true consort of Kālī: she too is "forgetful," self-intoxicated as the Great Māyā with her never-ending play; eternal genetrix, she devours her children unceasingly; in child-bearing and tender nurture she is indifference and forgetfulness, for to her one child is as another.

The godhead is the great forgetful one. To remember all things, let alone to write them down—*liber scriptus proferetur, in quo totum continetur*[27]—is utterly alien to the divine. In masculine epochs and cultures there arises the phantasmagoria of the epic and dramatic as the highest interpretation of existence; as the hypothesis and illusion of the unique, the heroic, and tragic; as the continually renewed experience of extraordinary figures, grace-inspired heroes, gods descended on earth. But the maternal consciousness of India sees them all as the recurrence of the eternally same: a blurred, monotonous series of Buddhas, a spinning cycle of avatars.

Every young hero, borne by the Mother, experiences and dominates the world anew, as an individual, but the Mother looks on with indifference; the same games have been played by so many other sons whom she has forgotten: the maelstrom of life is forever fresh and forever the same in its cyclic, grinding eventlessness.

The transfigured image of this oppressive idyl of the world of the Mothers is Nirvāṇa: in Nirvāṇa the mute urge to life has been cleansed of its oppressive fury and become crystalline silence; the world of the Mothers, where, despite constant creation and negation, nothing happens, is transfigured and rests from its own labors.

But he who is caught and spellbound by the circling of this world can, in sustained contemplation of the irreconcilable contradictions of maternal love and maternal ruthlessness as the unity of life and death, become permeated with the essential secret of the Great Māyā, and thus obtain release from the love and fear of his own transience. In the unity of the momentary and the timeless, he may experience the whirling wheel in which he moves as standing radiantly still.

27 *Dies irae* sequence from the Mass for the Dead, Roman Missal.

Erwin Rousselle

Dragon and Mare
Figures of Primordial Chinese Mythology

The great basic ideas of Chinese culture and religion were present in remote antiquity and even then had a long history behind them. As in ancient Egypt and in all early history, we here come into contact with that vast stratum of the human mind for which the gods were still animals and the animals were still men and gods. Divine beings and spirits, even ancestors and heroes, were almost without exception conceived of as animals or in animal form. An animal cult, sometimes revealing totemic features, gives this lapidary culture a primal force of expression which in many ways reminds us of Egypt—a force which is so often lacking in the classical Greeks, whose "spiritualization" had transformed, transfigured, and muffled the primordial.

The "God of Heaven" (T'ien) or the "Lord on High" (Shang-ti) is far removed from man, but the gods in their animal forms presided as godparents over the cradle of a kindred mankind. And in each one of us, in dreams, in visions, in metaphors, the animal gods still live today, an age-old metaphysical heritage. For they are the representatives of the primordial source and its manifestations, good and bad. Only when the animal world was divested of divine associations by the human mind did it cease to seem mighty, awe-inspiring, and full of secret wisdom; only then did it come to appear base, evil, and stupid. Ever since then the animal has suffered in silence through man, and the *creature* has yearned for redemption.

But in olden times, when the gods were still animals and the animals were still men and gods, a wonderful sense of the prodigious permeated human civilization. In embodiments of profound meaning, the world of the animal gods embraced the heights and depths of the universe and of the human spirit; the animal gods glittered in the constellations above us; walking alone or in packs, they populated woods and mountains; they conferred blessing and at the same time inspired spectral awe; they rose up from the darkest depths with the heady smell of earth; they dwelt in the fog and mist in springs and streams, lakes and oceans.

In the very midst of this animal cosmos stood man—for the animal was very close to him, and yet in some way entirely different. On all his fateful days the voices of divine animals spoke to him with the simple power of gigantic primordial forces. A religion of this kind gave rise to a monumental culture—in China, among the American Indians, in Egypt, and elsewhere.

Later, when the animal was dethroned, when the world was spiritualized and humanized, and the animals were reduced to companions, messengers, attributes of the gods, the prodigious— that noble sense of something boundless and yet plastically complete, that sense of an animal beauty and primal wisdom—was repressed and thrust back into the darkness of oblivion. But, in the secret dreams and visions of our nights, the holy animals still appear to us.

The record of this primordial world in China has come down to us only in fragments.[1] But the force and clarity of the Chinese mind rest precisely on a living historical rapport between the days of the animal gods and the most recent wisdom, and this applies both to the culture as a whole and to the individual. The Chinese have never lost their original knowledge of those forces which are the vehicles and movers of the world process.

Among the abundance of forms—among the bears, tigers, deer, foxes, horses, steers, sheep, swine, owls, cicadas, fishes, tortoises, snakes, and the giant army of the fabulous beasts—we shall turn our attention to two sacred and noble animals which stand in a special relation to the first two signs of the *Book of Changes,* to Ch'ien, the Celestial, and to K'un, the Earthly: these two beasts are the dragon and the mare.

1 As a result of the incomprehension of later "spiritualized" ages, and most particularly of the orthodox school. But a certain light is shed by comparison with the other descendants of the paleo-Asiatic culture (in Siberia and America), and with Australasian and Austronesian parallels.

1. The Dragon

The *Book of Changes* begins with the hexagram Ch'ien, the sign of celestial activity (God). It consists of six unbroken lines, to be read from the bottom upward. The basic text begins literally as follows:[2]

Ch'ien is creative and persevering,
Furthering and supplying security.

Nine at the beginning means:
Submerged dragon. Do not use.

Nine in the second place means:
One sees a dragon on the field (of the kettle drum?).
It furthers one to see the great man.

Nine in the third place means:
The superior man[3] maintains all day long an attitude of
    attentiveness,[4]
At nightfall as if beset with cares.
Danger (but) no mistake.

Nine in the fourth place means:
And then the jumping up (of a dragon) in the abyss
    (of the watery world).
(Especially this) no mistake.

Nine in the fifth place means:
Flying dragon in the heavens.
It furthers one to see the great man.

Nine at the top means:
A dragon flying too high. There will be repentance.

2 [*Note on the translation:* Rousselle originally made his own German translation from the *I Ching* for publication in the 1934 *Eranos-Jahrbuch*. The present English version has been provided through the kindness of Professor Hellmut Wilhelm. It is based on the German translation by Professor Wilhelm's father Richard Wilhelm, modified to retain particular renderings essential to Rousselle's interpretation. The complete text may be found in *The I Ching or Book of Changes*, the Richard Wilhelm translation rendered into English by Cary F. Baynes (3rd edn., Princeton and London, 1967) ; hereafter referred to as Wilhelm/Baynes.—ED.]

3 Here, in the pre-Confucian sense of "prince," "ruler," "lord," and not yet the figurative sense of "noble, spiritual man." Cf. A. Conrady and E. Erkes, "Yi-king-Studien," *Asia Major* (Leipzig), VII (1931), 409ff. The words for "field," "depths," and "heavens" rhyme in the ancient Chinese.

4 In this meaning *ch'ien-ch'ien* should perhaps be pronounced *hsin-hsin* (see Conrady and Erkes, p. 426), though it may have been pronounced *ch'ien-ch'ien* because of the rhyme. The verse in question falls out of rhythm because of the addition of "superior man."

Uses of nines (only) :
One sees only dragons without heads.
(Just for this reason) good fortune.[5]

We further read in the "Commentary on the Decision":

> Being abundantly clear as to the end and the beginning,
> as to the way in which each of the six stages completes
> itself in its own time, one mounts at times to heaven on
> a six-in-hand of dragons.[6]

Without attempting a detailed inquiry into this sage exegesis of
the venerable and impressive text, let us merely point out that in
every line—with the exception of the third—the sign of "celestial
power" is manifested by the form and activity of the dragon. Thus
the dragon embodied the qualities of the Ch'ien, the Celestial.
The ideogram for Ch'ien means the warmth of the sun, under
whose influence the vapors of the earth rise shimmering upward.
This influence of the mighty light of heaven is beneficent—without
it there can be no life—but it also parches and destroys.[7] This same
prodigious ambivalence of power and strength is also that of the
dragon. It is the "noblest among the 360 scale-bearing animals,"
indeed among all fabulous creatures, and at the same time the most
terrible of monsters. The dragons call forth great summer thunderstorms with their beneficent rainfall, and they also produce the
destructive turmoil of the elements. In winter the dragon rests
"submerged"[8] in the watery depths beneath the earth (first, i.e.
bottom-most, line) , and the thunderstorms also rest.[9] In the spring
it ascends in noble flight (fourth line) and flies through the
heavens (fifth line) to send down rain clouds and thunderstorms
during the warm season. In the autumn it returns—no longer
proudly stretching forth its head, but in a sense "headless"—to the
depths. The rule of Yin has begun; the dragon wisely assumes a

---

5 [Cf. Wilhelm/Baynes, pp. 4ff.]
6 [Ibid., p. 371.]
7 Accordingly, this sign, in the pronunciation *kan*, has the meaning "dry."
8 The Chinese word for "submerged" is written with the classifier "water."
  The same is true of the sign for "abyss" in the fourth line.
9 The sign for "field" in the second line, which also occurs under "rain" in the
  sign for "thunder," also has the meaning of "big drum." Cf. *Shih Ching*
  IV.2.5. Since time immemorial the skin of large drums has been decorated
  with the picture of a dragon. The thunder of the drum is the thunder of
  the dragon.

conciliatory attitude (sixth line). Thus the cycle of the sacred year with its successive contrasts finds its expression in the dragon.

A particularly magnificent conception of the dragon as the lord of thunderstorms has come down to us in a record whose sources clearly go back to primeval times. The "pool of thunder" (*Lei Tsê*) is represented in the *Shan-hai-ching* (Chapter 13) as the home of a dragon who is the thunder god. This is a swampy lake south of the present course of the Huang-ho in the prefecture of Ts'ao-chou (Shantung). Ts'ai Chen quotes from the *Shan-hai-ching*, "the canon of the mountains and seas," as follows: "In this pool there is a thunder god; he has the body of a dragon and the face of a man; when he beats his belly, there is thunder."[10] But in *Huai-nan Tzŭ* (Chapter 4), the account does not end with the word "thunder" but with the word *"hsi"*—"to gleam, or lightning; to be happy, to burst out laughing."[11] Accordingly, the account reads: "He beats his belly and laughs a beaming laughter." To beat one's belly is a Chinese gesture expressive of the primitive joy of life. The ninth book of the *Chuang Tzŭ* has this to say of the golden age:

> In the days of the (old emperor) Ho-hsü, the people stayed home and did not know what to do; they went out and they did not know whither; when their mouths were full, they beamed with joy (*hsi*), beat their bellies and went walking—this was all the people knew how to do. But then came the "saints" and fabricated rites and music with a view to regulating the shape of the world, and they afflicted the people with the aims of "humaneness" and "duty," in order to give consolation to the hearts of the world. And then the people began to run and stumble in their search for knowledge and to fight in their chase after gain, until there was no rest. And all this was the fault of the "saints."

Just as the people of the blessed old times beat their bellies, the thunder dragon beats his belly and laughs. Let us pause for a moment and contemplate this truly grandiose picture of the old Chinese imagination. In the primal joy of existence the monster, the dragon, lifts its enormous greenish-blue body from the pool,

10 See Edouard Chavannes, *Les Mémoires historiques de Se-ma Ts'ien* (5 vols., Paris, 1895–1905), I, 110.
11 See Marcel Granet, *Danses et légendes de la Chine ancienne* (Paris, 1926), II, 510ff., in the section under K'ouei. I have drawn on Chapter 6 of the *Huai-nan Tzŭ* for the interpretation of the word *hsi*.

so that the white underside of its belly glistens. In its primordial sense of well-being, the beast thumps resoundingly on its belly and far and wide the thunder re-echoes from the mountain slopes. At the same time, it laughs its terrible dragon laugh, and lightning spurts from its mouth. The storm wind lashes the rushes on the lake, and the crest of the rain drives long furrows through the water. The rain pours down and brings fertility and blessing— but also flood; the lightning destroys and brings death. In this sovereign beast good and evil are still unparted. The animal god is still beyond good and evil; he is great, and that is all.

This laughing joy, which the divine dragon shows in the expression of its fecundating and annihilating power, epitomizes the whole spirit and being of the old Chinese animal gods. True, at a more spiritualized stage people took umbrage at the animal god: in the crypts of the noble families of the Han period, the dragons assume a more subordinate position. The thunder god appears in human form, dressed as a lord, sitting in his war chariot and drawn over the clouds by spirits. He beats the drums of his chariot and brings forth the thunder. The wind god, the rain goddess, the spirits of lightning—all in human form—are his vassals; only the rainbow is represented by two dragons whose tails are tied together by a spirit of lightning, This is the union of Yin and Yang.[12] The thunder god is no longer associated with the dragons; but the cloud dragons are still prominent among the beasts—cloud birds, griffins, etc.—that adorn the walls of these crypts.

Moreover, the connection of the dragon with the cult of the Lord on High (Shang-ti) or the God of Heaven (T'ien), a cult originating in an entirely different sphere, was never so close as to efface the distinction between this god of the higher regions and the divine animal. The lofty ethical qualities which we find ascribed to the Lord on High, in the "Book of Songs" (Shih Ching) for example, bear witness to a higher religious attitude, contrasting with the popular faith for which the animal gods and spirits remained primordial powers beyond good and evil.

Dragons were the ancestors of the oldest Chinese dynasty, the house of Hsia; one of its emperors, the tradition has it, acquired a

---

12 Cf. E. Chavannes, Mission Archéologique. Textes (Paris, 1913), I, 84, 210, 212 and Figs. 48, 152, 153.

magic power by eating dragon's flesh, and one branch of the family had the privilege of breeding dragons. Later—under the Han dynasty—the dragon became the symbol of all imperial sovereignty, and this it has remained down to our own times.

The Chinese—and in this he has remained true to his heritage of age-old wisdom—has never forgotten the fearful aspect of everything that is truly great, and in tales and legends the magnificent primordial monster rises again and again to his consciousness. There is, for example, the story of the dragon-like spirit of Stallion Mountain:[13]

A peasant has dallied at the market and is a little tipsy as he starts on his ride homeward. As he approaches the ridge of Stallion Mountain, he suddenly sees a monster sitting by the brook, lapping up water. Its enormous face is blue; its eyes bulge out of its head like those of a crab. Its mouth gapes from ear to ear and has the aspect of a vat full of blood. Its fangs, growing in irregular clumps, are two or three inches long. The peasant is terrified, but the monster does not look up. Profiting by this, the peasant starts on a wide detour around the terrible ridge.

As he rounds a bend, he meets the son of a neighbor, who calls to him. The peasant tells him briefly that he has just seen the monster nearby, and the neighbor's son asks leave to ride with him. The peasant, eager to carry him as fast as possible from this awful place, lets him mount behind him. As they are riding along, the neighbor's son asks him in a crafty voice: "What exactly did the monster look like?" The peasant feels ill at ease and replies beseechingly: "I'll tell you everything when we get home." But the other persists and says: "Turn around; perhaps I look like the monster." A cold shiver runs through the peasant and he cries out: "Don't make evil jokes. A man is not a spirit." But the other jeers and repeats: "Turn around." The peasant refuses and the other pulls him around by the arm. And the peasant looks into the face of the monster and falls unconscious from his saddle.

Thus suddenly, beneath the mask of everyday, the mask of the neighbor's son, the horror which lies at the primal source of being —the monster by the stream—suddenly confronts man. He tries to

13 Brief summary after R. Wilhelm, *Chinesische Volksmärchen* (Jena, 1914), pp. 134ff.

escape but cannot. He carries the monster with him; it attacks him from behind, and in the dread of recognition man loses his senses, falls headlong into the depths.

Once upon a time, in the sea near the island of P'u-t'o-shan, there lived a dragon which had the power of turning itself into a beautiful lotus blossom. Many women, desirous of attaining quickly to the beatific depths of Buddha's paradise, hurled themselves into the perilous waters of the sacred sea. But they did not gain the desired goal; the dragon devoured them. At last an aged wise man flung a dead pig, in which he had hidden many sharp knives, into the sea: the dragon hungrily devoured the pig—which is itself a voracious, sensual beast—and died a wretched death. Though this profoundly meaningful legend is an extremely late one, it shows how a sense of the dragon's evil power survived, even amid Buddhist trappings.[14]

But the dragons, expression of the divine and virile creative power of the luminous Yang, are also playful. In the Chinese popular belief, the dragon king has nine sons. Each year he sends a certain number of his sons up to heaven to regulate the weather for that year. If he sends only two, it will be a very wet year, for the dome of heaven and the square of earth are so immense that the two seldom meet; consequently, they do their duty and send down ample rain. But if, for example, he sends up eight of his dragon sons, the year will be very dry, for these eight are constantly running into one another; they play games and forget their duty. And it is true that because of the extraordinary regularity of the Chinese climate, its rhythms and cycles, the "wisdom of the calendar" does often provide a correct weather forecast for a given year.[15]

From the waters of the abyss, from the springs and wells, the rivers and swamps, the lakes and oceans, the dragons rise up. The element of life is theirs; from heaven, to which a divine impulse draws them in the spring of the year, they send down their fecundating waters in the form of rain. They combine the heights with the depths; they guard the treasures of the sea and support the

14 Cf. S. Förster-Streffleur, *Was Li-Pao-Ting erzählt* (Vienna, 1924), pp. 28ff.
15 For the year 1935 the calendar announces: "Six dragons govern the water." In other words, a rather dry year.

celestial dwellings of the gods. They are truly divine beasts which encompass and largely regulate the cycle of the year.

The different activities of the dragons permit us to distinguish four classes: (1) the celestial dragons, which support the dwelling place of the gods; (2) the spirit dragons, which send wind and rain; (3) the earth dragons, which control the springs and rivers; and (4) the treasure-guarding dragons, which for the most part dwell in the depths of the sea.[16]

In conclusion let us turn to those dragons which guard treasures. If we look up at the central panel in the ceiling of a Chinese throne room or a temple, we see, usually in an angular, lantern-shaped little cupola, a dragon playing with a silvery pearl. This is the animal symbol of the celestial activity of the Lord on High and of the Son of Heaven, which causes the pearl of divine wisdom and power to operate. In the esoteric doctrines of Buddhism and Taoism, the dragon signifies the secret activity of that luminous force within us which unites the upper and lower cycles and which possesses the treasure, by which all desires are fulfilled, of our true, eternal nature and the seed of the deathless "diamond body."

The dragon is not only the guardian of the divine pearl but is also its bestower. Thus the dragon king of Buddhist legend holds the secret wisdom of Buddha stored in his underwater palace and later hands it down to the great founder of the doctrine and magic of the Mahāyāna, to Nāgārjuna, the "dragon tree" (*Lung-shen*) or "dragon hero" (*Lung-meng*).

According to a more recent Chinese legend,[17] the Lady of the East (Kuan-yin), appeared in earthly form as the princess Miao-shan, "miraculous goodness," who lived at the end of the third millennium B.C. Miao-shan preferred a contemplative life to worldly splendor. Her father attempted by forcible means to make her abandon this mode of life, and at length, when all manner of torture proved of no avail, he had her beheaded. Her lifeless body was then carried off into the mountains by the tutelary deity of the place, who had assumed the form of a tiger. She descended

16 Cf. Fred. Lessing, "Über die Symbolsprache in der chinesischen Kunst," *Sinica* (Frankfort), IX (1934), 148.
17 Cf. Arthur Waley, "Avalokiteśvara and the Legend of Miao-shan," *Artibus Asiae* (Dresden), II (1925), 130–32. Here the first literary record of this legend is placed in the 17th century.

to hell, visited the lord of the underworld, and by the magic force of her essence liberated the souls of the damned. On her return to the upper world, Buddha appeared to her on a cloud and advised her to retire to the island of P'u-t'o-shan and live a life of meditation, and he gave her a peach from the celestial gardens, to assure her immortal life.

The god of the island assumed the form of a tiger and carried her to the sacred isle with the swiftness of the wind. After nine years of meditation and worthy deeds, she achieved the rank of a Buddha and adopted her first acolyte, the boy Shan-ts'ai, "the nobly talented." Then one day the third son of the dragon king, having assumed the form of a fish, was caught in a net, and was to be sold in the market. Miao-shan, who was clairvoyant and saw what had happened, sent her boy to buy the fish and set it free. The dragon king, moved by her kindness, sent her his grand-daughter, the "dragon maid" (*Lung-nü*), with the pearl which shines in the darkness and enables one who studies the holy tradition at night to read and understand.[18] But the dragon maid was so charmed by Miao-shan that she wished to achieve the state of perfection and asked leave to stay with her forever as her second acolyte. This Miao-shan willingly granted.

Miao-shan later converted her own parents and became a "redeemer of men" with power to remove all the obstacles which stand between man and Amitābha's light-flooded paradise. She herself, however, refused to enter into it as long as any human being was excluded.[19] This extraordinarily beautiful and meaningful legend shows the path of the soul through introversion, death, and rebirth in Miao-shan's turn to an inward life, in her painful death and journey to hell, in her meeting with Buddha and her return, in her removal to the sacred isle and achievement of Buddhahood. A fine psychological and transcendental understanding of the male and the female, of consciousness and the unconscious, of the truly divine, and of their interrelation is revealed by

18 The dragon maid with the pearl appears also in the *Lotus Sūtra* (Chinese version, ch. XII). Buddha eliminates all the obstacles which her feminine nature places in the path of her Buddhahood by his ability to turn her into a boy.

19 See Alice Getty, *The Gods of Northern Buddhism* (2nd edn., Oxford, 1928), pp. 83ff.

this legend in its interplay of Madonna and dragon, in the entanglement of the dragon king's son as a fish and his liberation, in the boy acolyte, and in the dragon maid, who brings Miao-shan the pearl and is enchanted by the divine nature of the Lady of the Sea. All this has inspired the profoundest interpretations, full of true practical wisdom and metaphysical insight, interpretations which reveal themselves spontaneously to those endowed with understanding.

In Chinese art the Stella Maris of the Orient, Nan-hai Kuan-yin, "the Kuan-yin on the southern sea," is often represented sitting in a grotto, in an attitude of "regal lassitude," deeply immersed in meditation; before her the waves of the sea surge up, and the dragon emerges to do obeisance to her. Sometimes we also see the boy and the girl, "the gold boy" (*Chin-t'ung*) and "the jade girl" (*Yü-nü*) as the Taoist-alchemist symbolists call these aspects of the luminous Yang and the dark Yin.

There are female as well as male dragons. But the dragons have only one pearl, for ultimately there is but one. It is everywhere essentially the same, eternal pearl. Back and forth the dragons toss one another the living germ of eternal life—for the pearl is looked upon as a living thing! Through the depths, and in the celestial regions over the depths, they circle together and their play with the pearl that fulfills all desires is the blissful play of both genii with the sacred treasure—an authentic expression for the Chinese sovereignty of the spirit.

2. *The Mare*

The second sign in the *Book of Changes* is the counterpart of the first, celestial sign—it is the sign of K'un, the Earthly.

The "judgment" regarding the sign, which consists of six broken lines, read from the bottom upward, begins with virtually the same words as the text on the sign of the Celestial: "K'un (the Chthonian) is creative and persevering, furthering and supplying the security of the mare."[20]

20 [Cf. Wilhelm/Baynes, p. 386.] The word "to supply security" has also to be understood in the meaning of "to bring to a good end." The word is written with the sign for "tortoise oracle." The security, of course, is proper not only to the mare but also to the solid, boundless earth.

Only the fourth statement differs from the corresponding one concerning the celestial activity: the chthonian does not confer security in general but specifically "the security of the mare." Just as the celestial was expressed by the dragon in nearly all six lines, here the chthonian is represented in the judgment text by the mare. It may be presumed that we here have to do with an old form of the great mother-goddess of the earth, who was represented in the form of the noblest beast of the steppes, just as the activity of the heavens was represented by the noblest of all the fabulous beasts and scale-bearers. An oracular response inserted here interprets the chthonian as follows: "The superior man has nowhere to go. If he leads, he goes astray; if he follows, he finds guidance."

In this oracular counsel the character of the mare is employed as a *tertium comparationis*. Stallions are always playful, full of incalculable whims, while mares—though sometimes moody—generally show a tranquil, intelligent power and adaptability, so that the rider is easily and safely carried to his goal. The "superior man" is bidden to act like a mare. The text continues: "It is favorable to find friends in the west and south, to forego friends in the east and north: quiet supply of security! (This is) good fortune."

West and south are the quarters of the heavens, in which the chthonian acts obediently for the celestial in the summer and autumn. And here we have another reference to the security given by the mare—the guarantee of success: "Quiet supply of security! (This is) good fortune."

The "Commentary on the Decision," which briefly explains the four statements about the chthonian, has the following to say concerning the phrase "furthering and supplying the security of the mare": "A mare belongs to the creatures of the earth; she roams the earth without bound: flexible, pliable, furthering and supplying security."[21] If it should be true, as the Chinese tradition maintains, that the core of the *Book of Changes* goes back to the days before the Chou dynasty and originally—under matriarchal influence?—began, not with the sign of celestial activity (No. 1) but with the chthonian sign (No. 2), this would provide additional

---

21 [Cf. Wilhelm/Baynes, p. 387.] The Chinese word for "flexible" is written with the classifier "wood." The word for "pliable" has the classifier of the "pliable river" or "water-course" next to the sign for "head."

proof that an age-old tradition underlay this veneration of the earth-goddess[22] under the symbol of the mare.

An echo of the great age of sacred animals, attested in the *Book of Changes,* is found also in the celebrated sixth ode of the *Tao Tê Ching.* In the *Book of Changes* the mare is named P'in (Pi) Ma, "female horse"; in the *Tao Tê Ching,* which is attributed to Lao-tse or, at least in part, including the part to which we are here referring, to the mythical prehistoric emperor Huang-ti, the animal goddess is called Hsüan P'in (or Hsüan Pi), "the dark female animal"[23]—or, as we might translate more freely but also more aptly, "the dark animal goddess." Thus, she too may be conceived of as a mare, a "dark"[24] mare, which is identified with the "Valley Spirit." But the Chinese, as the sign indicates, conceive of a "valley" not as a dry depression but as a valley with a spring or river. And in the ode this establishes a connection with the womb of the mother-goddess. But in the *Tao Tê Ching* the womb of all being is not the mother-goddess Earth but the Tao, mother of heaven and earth. And throughout the book this Tao reveals distinctly feminine features:

> The Valley Spirit never dies.
> It is named the dark animal goddess.
> And the doorway of the dark animal goddess
> Is called the root of Heaven and Earth.
> Like an endless thread she (the goddess) is as if persevering
> And accomplishes[25] effortlessly.

A wonderful verse, charged with plastic and mythical power! But nowhere else in the *Tao Tê Ching* is the Tao referred to as "the dark animal goddess." And the passage quoted is intended

22 The fusion of the deities of the "land" and the "harvest" with the goddess "earth" (*Li*) is demonstrable since the 17th century B.C. See Chavannes, "Le Dieu du sol dans la Chine antique," appendix to *Le T'ai chan. Essai de monographie d'un culte chinois* (Paris, 1910).

23 Conrady, rightly in my opinion, related the two passages in the *I Ching* and the *Tao Tê Ching* and rejected as secondary the very late exegesis: Hsüan (dark) = "celestial Yang" and P'in = Yin. See Conrady, "Zu Lao-Tze Kap. 6," *Asia Major,* VII (1931), 150ff.

24 The word *hsüan,* dark, is, to begin with, to be taken literally and only in a later and more profound understanding as mysterious.

25 If it is permissible to take the word for "use, apply" (*yung*) in the weighted sense of "to practice, to be active, to be efficacious." Cf. in *Chung Yung:* Tzu yung "agir par soi-même sans conseil" (F. S. Couvreur, *Dictionnaire Classique de la langue chinoise,* Hokien Fou, 1904, sub "Ioung"). Otherwise the meaning is "One uses her [the goddess] without difficulty."

only to root the Tao in the ancient heritage of proverbs.[26] The dark animal goddess is designated also as the "mother (of the deities) of Heaven and Earth," a term which in this book is otherwise applied only to the Tao (cf. Ode 1).

> Unnamable it (i.e. the Tao) is the one giving birth
> to Heaven and Earth.[27]
> Namable it is the mother of the ten thousand creatures.

Elsewhere Lao-tse also designates the Tao as mother of all the creatures (of this visible reality) or as "mother of the world"[28] (*t'ien-hsia mu;* Odes 25 and 52). In Ode 25:

> There is a creature accomplishing incomprehensively
> That came into existence before Heaven and Earth.
> So quiet, so empty,
> Alone it stands and does not change,
> In a circle it goes without peril.
> One may also consider it the mother of the world.
> Not knowing her name, I assign the name Tao to her.

The Tao, the origin of the world, is for Lao-tse the maternal and eternal feminine principle as perennial genetrix and giver of nourishment, acting through "images" and the "seed" of all being, but it is also the ultimate home and refuge of all creatures. Here the animal cult ceases and its inner meaning appears transfigured on a higher spiritual plane.[29] Lao-tse finds truly moving words in which to speak of the feminine nature of the world origin. And indeed, what he says of the Tao is intelligible only if its feminine characteristics are taken into consideration.

For man must undertake the "journey to the mothers" when

26 The Valley Spirit is otherwise (Ode 39) classified on a cosmologically important but considerably lower level, among those "things that from of old have
   achieved the One": sky, earth, deities, the abyss (i.e. the Valley Spirit), the
   ten thousand creatures, kings, and princes. One should live after the manner
   of a "valley" (Ode 28).
27 Literally, "beginning." But the classifier of the word is that for "woman."
28 "World" in this connection is always to be taken essentially as "the earth,"
   literally "that which is under the heavens."
29 Other sacred animals (some of them of later origin) are stallions: the "ten-
   thousand-mile horse" racing through all the heavens (a shamanistic survival?)
   or the Buddhist "white horse" (one of the seven Indian treasures of the world
   ruler) which bears the wishing treasure (this steed has also taken on shamanistic features). The "white horse" that brought the holy scriptures from India
   to China was also a stallion.

rational clarity fails him and when in consternation at the irruption of objective destiny he encounters the depths of his own unconscious and from there the glittering depths of the universal night. Then in dreams and visions the silvery figures of primordial ages rise up again, as they are innate in us, handed down from generation to generation, for through them alone can man apprehend the *mysterium tremendum et fascinosum* of the godhead. And then the image of the World Mother shines before him, for to the soul of man, as vehicle of her being and repository of the holy, transcendent wisdom, the female-maternal symbols appear as elements opposite to his own active, rational nature. Often they take on a shadowy existence in the mysterious darkness of the semi-conscious. And in his bottom-most depths man encounters the dark animal goddess and the "black Madonna" (who is black not only because of the age of the ivory).

Here, too, lie the sources of power, the possibilities of rebirth through a wisdom transcending time. The *divinum quoddam atque providum,* "the divine, clairvoyant something in the woman" becomes the symbol and vehicle of the true *sophia,* the divine wisdom.

In his twentieth ode, Lao-tse represents this encounter with the great maternal goddess at a time of profound emotional upheaval, and through this experience finds transcendent consolation, self-awareness, and support in his melancholy:

All men, indeed, are wreathed in smiles,[30]
As though feasting after the Great Sacrifice,
As though going up to the Spring Carnival.
I alone am inert,[31] like a child that has not yet given sign,
Like an infant that has not yet smiled.
I droop and drift,[32] as though I belonged nowhere.
All men have enough and to spare;
I alone seem to have lost everything.
Mine indeed is the mind of a very idiot,
So dull am I.
The world is full of people that shine;

30 "Wreathed in smiles" (*hsi-hsi*) is the same word that has been used of the thunder dragon and the men of the golden age; see above, p. 107 and n. 11.
31 The word for "inert" uses the water classifier and means the lying still (at anchor) of ships. Hence, "unable to proceed."
32 The Chinese sign means "travel, vehicle."

I alone am dark.[33]
They look lively and self-assured;
I alone, depressed.
I seem unsettled as the ocean,
Blown adrift, never brought to a stop.
All men can be put to some use;
I alone am intractable and boorish.
But wherein I most am different from men
Is that I prize no sustenance that comes not from the Mother's
  breast.[34]

Yet he who has found the World Mother sinks into her arms, and his death is as a homecoming. The circle of life is closed. It begins with the feminine principle and leads back to it. With the mother of life, birth and death are one. Hence Lao-tse says (Ode 52):

> The world[35] has something that gives birth[36] to it.
> This is the mother of the world.
> He who has found his mother
> Thereby apprehends that he is but a child.
> When he has apprehended that he is but a child
> And again clings to his mother,
> He will be without danger when the body perishes.
>
> .   .   .   .
>
> Seeing the very small means clarity;
> Maintaining flexibility means strength.
> He who uses his light
> In order to revert to his clarity
> Will lose nothing when the body perishes.
> This is called: to be garbed in eternity.

Here, the Tao, the primal source of life, is no longer the dark animal goddess but the great mother-goddess. In the depths of his own soul, the most profound philosopher of Chinese antiquity experiences the feminine principle as a transcendent being which sustains him, nurtures him, gives him strength, refuge, and roots, and grants him the solace of homecoming.

Animal cult, totemism, matriarchy have vanished. The bright

33 "Dark" is written with the sign for dusk.
34 By a different reading: "But I hold it worthy to seek nourishment with the Mother."
35 Literally, "that which is under the heavens" (cf. n. 28 above).
36 Again, the same sign for "beginning" as in Ode 1 (above, n. 27).

day of the masculine spirit and its domination has begun. Its radiance still endures. The animals recede into the darkness and mystery of nature. The masculine mind sees the world in the bright—but at the same time dangerous and blinding—light, and believes that it can understand and regulate it.

Ernesto Buonaiuti

Christ and St. Paul

The central problem of Christian history is the relation between the personality and teachings of Christ and the personality and teachings of St. Paul presented in the New Testament.

In the first half of the second century this problem appeared in all its urgency, for Marcion, in his effort to restore the gospel to its original purity, took as his guide what we may call St. Paul's "hatred of the Law"; he strove to isolate Christ's message from any Judaizing admixture and also to defend the teachings of Paul against imitation and pseudo-Pauline falsification.

When in the fourth century Paul was rediscovered by Ambrosiaster and St. Augustine, Manichaeism had been at work for a whole century in the deepest strata of the Christian consciousness: the predominantly historical dualism of the first Christian generation (the New Testament dualism of "our time" and the "time to come") had given way to an anthropological dualism, from which followed the sinful lust and restorative grace of the anti-Pelagians and the social dualism of St. Augustine's *De Civitate Dei*. The outcome of this twofold dualism was the Middle Ages.

The Reformation revived the problem of the relations between Christ and St. Paul in all its scope and stressed the soteriological doctrine of St. Paul as the only means of preserving and interpreting the word of Christ.

Today the problem of the historical and doctrinal relations between Christ and St. Paul arises solely among students of textual criticism and comparative religion. That is to say, we are eager to establish the relations between Galilee and Judaea, between the teachings of Christ and the interpretation of the Galilean master's overpowering message of indubitable and imminent palingenesis, which Paul gave to the non-Palestinian world.

The problem can be projected against the background of a comparative study of the religious development of the Mediterranean world, if by this term we mean the region extending from the Iranian high plateau (whence Zoroaster—the first great religious reformer—descended to the lowlands in the first centuries of the first millennium B.C.) to the western shores of the Mediterranean.

First of all: did Paul know Jesus personally? This possibility seems precluded. In one of the most vivid and moving passages of his epistles to the Corinthian converts, Paul writes that he had not known Christ in flesh and blood (a privilege of which so many others boasted) and continues almost contemptuously to say that now, in full possession of his spiritual experience, he would not hesitate to renounce such a physical encounter, for from the spiritual and charismatic point of view it would be totally meaningless.

However—he seems to imply—he could not boast of any such renunciation, for the possibility of a physical meeting was purely hypothetical. Actually—although he may have been in Jerusalem at the time of Christ's conviction—he had never met Christ and had never had occasion to meet him. In accordance with God's will, the face of Christ had appeared to him incorporeally, as he tells us briefly but incisively in the epistle to the Galatians. And, indeed, when in this epistle Paul touches briefly on the drama of his conversion, he registers none of the details that are repeatedly adduced by the compiler of the Acts of the Apostles, but merely says summarily, "And when it pleased God . . . to reveal his son in me"—from which we can infer that Paul knew the teachings but not the person of Christ, and that a first hearing of Christ's words had dazzled and shaken him like a supernatural light; that in them he had seen the face and heard the voice of an eternal being, which through the law and death had conquered the law and death, of a *spirit* resurrected in the concrete solidarity of the faithful who lived in expectation of the day when the resurrected one would carry them all upon the clouds to the dawn of God's eternal triumph in his kingdom.

121

Since a personal meeting between Christ and Paul seems precluded, the problem of their relations can refer only to the likeness or divergence of their teachings. The Christian tradition has created an inseparable bond between Christ and St. Paul. But where, how, and when did this bond arise, which united the two names more firmly than any common experience? Where do we find such a bond in the New Testament, and what is its nature?

Modern liberal criticism has not failed to expose the obvious divergencies between the doctrine of Jesus (as arrived at through a strict critical sifting of the evangelical tradition) and the doctrine of St. Paul, as reconstructed from the authentic epistles. And, building (not without a certain bias) on these divergencies, various scholars have, in different ways, come to the conclusion that St. Paul was the true and authentic founder of Christianity—if by historical Christianity is meant that definite dogmatic and disciplinary content which is the common characteristic of the various Christian denominations.

In passing from the analysis of the gospels to the study of the Pauline epistles, we are inevitably impressed by their clarity and immediacy. It is true that in a certain sense the apostle dimmed the dazzling light which seems to surround the preaching of Christ: his gospel of the kingdom of heaven which could be brought about by absolute devotion to the commandment of love. We can no longer doubt that the authentic words of Jesus were saturated with apocalyptic spirit. According to his teachings, the kingdom of God would suddenly be at hand; it would upset the whole order of things even before the original apostles could reach the borders of Palestine. In this kingdom, the house of Israel may be said to have enjoyed an unassailable privilege. And the whole original character of Christianity is contained in this proclamation of the kingdom of God with all its consequences for the hopes and dreams of men.

Paul sharply rejected the strict geographical and national limitation of Jesus' perspective. With dauntless courage he crossed the borders of Palestine. In a solemn gesture that was to have immense historical consequences, he flung open the gates of the kingdom of heaven to Adam's whole posterity throughout the world. And it can be said that by a strange spiritual paradox every day of delay in the coming of the kingdom of God was a day gained for the conquests of the Pauline apostolate.

But did not the vision of the kingdom, this mirror of man's self which had filled the first generation of believers with so much joy and enthusiasm, in time lose much of its richness and strength of feeling? Did this vision, which had burst forth like a tongue of flame, unforeseen and in no way calculated for the increasing mass of converts, not lose in intensity? In order to rule, to endure, to sustain itself among wider and wider circles, did it not require intellectual and doctrinaire supports and expedients which would only have been made superfluous by the assurance of a swift and providential realization in time and by a foreordained limitation in space?

Paul found it necessary to forge and perfect the implements of conquest in accordance with the needs of his apostolate. Such implements were his personal christological, soteriological, sacramental, and ecclesiastical doctrines, on the basis of which traditional Christian dogma was to develop.

But did such creations not open a gulf between the historical Jesus and his interpreter and apostle, Paul? This has been assumed in various quarters and in various ways. But, we repeat, an abrupt distinction between the teachings of Paul and the teachings of Christ may perhaps be no less arbitrary than the orthodox tradition, which, with a frivolous unconcern for distinctions, identifies the teachings of the apostle with the teachings of the master and—in disregard of the very core of the historical tradition—combines them into a single essence.

Today we ought perhaps to consider the relation between the two doctrines in a much broader context, projecting it against the background of the religious evolution of our whole Mediterranean world. I believe that in the light of our studies in comparative religion, the historical religions can be divided into two basic types: religions of initiation and religions of conversion.

The devotees of the religions of initiation feel and believe that phenomena are governed by an unalterable law of proportion and causality; accordingly they seek to captivate the influences of the invisible world with the help of liturgical gestures and formulas which they believe to be endowed with infallible power. At certain crucial moments the life of the individual is eminently fused with that of the collectivity: on these occasions, the religions of initiation envelop men and events in a sacral atmosphere wrought of faith and magic practices. Birth, puberty, marriage, childbearing, death—these are the occasions which the religions of initiation consecrate with their rites of passage. The theory and practice of the religions of initiation are based on the notion that social relations can be infallibly governed and regulated by an external discipline.

One day men discovered that the regulation of collective life cannot be entrusted solely to the empirical norms of outward collective action or magical liturgy, and that there is another, more reliable magic power: the voluntary sacrifice of the individual, the spiritual service of the collectivity, the long militant chain of divine action oriented toward the good—that action which is performed in patient silence in a sphere removed from the visible network of social phenomena. On this day was born the idea of inner conversion—in contrast to the purely sensory experience of the biological process.

For the Mediterranean countries, the doctrine of Zoroaster marks the birth of the religions of conversion. They found their classical form in the experiences and teachings of the Hebrew prophets.

The doctrine of Jesus is a religion of conversion in the most authentic sense, for this conversion is not linked with an improvised act that consecrates a new life unconnected with the life that preceded it and requiring no further changes. This conversion is rather a continuous renewal, from moment to moment, of man's relation to earthly, sensory experience, which must be continuously negated and transcended with a view to the miraculous manifestation of the divine kingdom. This is the original nucleus of the evangelical message.

The prophetic and apocalyptic traditions had spoken of a palingenesis on the day of the Lord; life would be completely made over and placed under God's immediate guidance. It is unceasingly impressed upon the minds of men that conversion is the indispensable prerequisite for the coming of the angel who will bring the Lord's full message.

Malachi had prophesied:

I have no pleasure in you, saith the Lord of hosts, neither will I accept an offering at your hand. For from the rising of the sun even unto the going down of the same, my name shall be great among the Gentiles; and in every place incense shall be offered unto my name, and a pure offering: for my name shall be great among the heathen, saith the Lord of hosts. . . . Behold, I will send my messenger, and he shall prepare the way before me: and the Lord, whom ye seek, shall suddenly come to his temple, even the messenger of the covenant, whom ye delight in. . . . But who may abide the day of his coming? and who shall stand when he appeareth? for he is like a refiner's fire. . . . And he shall sit as a refiner and purifier of silver. . . . And I will come near to you to judgment; and I will be a swift witness against the sorcerers, and against the adulterers, and against false swearers, and against those that oppress the hireling in his wages, the widow and the fatherless, and that turn aside the stranger from his right. . . . For, behold, the day cometh, that shall burn as an oven; and all the proud, yea, and all that do wickedly, shall be stubble: and the day that cometh shall burn them up . . . that it shall leave them neither root nor branch. But unto you that fear my name shall the Sun of righteousness arise with healing in his wings; and ye shall go forth, and grow up as calves of the stall. And ye shall tread down the wicked; for they shall be ashes under the soles of your feet in the day that I shall do this, saith the Lord of hosts (Mal. 1:10–11, 3:1–5, 4:1–3).

The cruel and cynical rule of the Herodians had rekindled the flame of prophecy from the depths of the old ashes. And in the days of Herod Antipas, partial heir of Herod the Great, the voice of a new preacher suddenly rose from the lower Jordan valley. He called himself John, and the people gave him the epithet of "the Baptist," because he immersed in the river those who came and listened to his admonitions and desired a visible sign of their inner renewal.

The Baptist's words sounded hard and merciless:

O generation of vipers, who hath warned you to flee from the wrath to come? Bring forth therefore fruits meet for repentance: And think not to say within yourselves, We have Abraham to our father: for I say unto you, that God is able of these stones to raise up children unto Abraham.

> And now also the axe is laid unto the root of the trees:
> therefore every tree which bringeth not forth good fruit is
> hewn down, and cast into the fire (Matt. 3:7–10).

Jesus' preaching is never so angry and menacing as when he
flays the unctuous hypocrisy and false piety of the Pharisees, the
guardians and interpreters of external, casuistic legalism. But it
was these very utterances which brought about a decisive change
in our spiritual attitude toward the world of tangible values and
earthly criteria. Jesus shared the Baptist's belief in the kingdom of
God, so dear to all prophetic tradition, and his doctrine of rebirth.

The idea that the kingdom of God was at hand was in the background of all his sermons and admonitions. But his kingdom—and
this is what was new in the doctrine of Jesus—had been shorn of all
its national and social characteristics; it had been transformed and
sublimated into a pure, transcendent vision of an order permeated
solely by the radiance of God's will and of his supreme law—which
is love.

Like the Baptist, Jesus called upon all the abused and disinherited to rise up, and spoke of a liberation from the hardship
and misery of life. But the force which he invoked as the instrument of liberation was transfigured and active goodness; and the
joy which he promised was the transcendent joy of the Father.

Sometimes Jesus seems to recognize a divine paternity which
embraces solely the chosen people of Israel. He replied to the Ca-
naanitish woman who asked him to heal her daughter: "I am not
sent but unto the lost sheep of the house of Israel. . . . It is not
meet to take the children's bread, and to cast it to dogs" (Matt.
15:24–26). That is to say: to take the miracle of grace from the
house of Israel and give it to the heathen. And at first sight the
manner in which Jesus speaks of God seems to differ in no way
from the Jewish tradition. The phrase "Our Father which art in
heaven" or "the heavenly Father" occurs no less than twenty times
in the Gospel of St. Matthew. But the similarity is entirely external
and superficial. In the conception of God which underlies the
works and the prayers of Jesus and which he taught to his disciples,
there is something so intimate, so personal, so rare and new, that
it is easy to understand how it could give rise to a religious impulse
of such breadth and power.

His invocation of God is not the cold external formula of the professional clerics, who content themselves with stereotyped formulas or unctuous, circumspect expressions of humility, which only conceal their coldness and superficiality. Jesus apprehends God and speaks with him as though he were present, as though he were inseparably mingled with the good deeds and the active love which partakes of our sufferings and our struggles; it is God who subjects himself to the battle with Satan in this base world of injustice and evil—in the expectation that, thanks to our humble but resolute help, he, the Father, who watches and awaits the illumination and conversion of the universe, will celebrate his ultimate triumph.

As Matthew tells us in his record of the sermon on the mount, Jesus in unfolding his program of rebirth to the disciples, thrice invokes the Father's participation in the good and selfless deeds of men. Good deeds should be kept secret because it is the Father who rewards them (6:4). Prayer should not consist of monotonous, repetitious babbling, because our Father knows what things we have need of (6:8). Men must forgive one another before they can be forgiven by the Father (6:14–15).

Here we have the evangelical theodicy, sustained and safeguarded by its epic form. And the idea of the Father is transfigured and fortified through men's love for one another. This intimate fusion between religion and the living conscience of moral law, and the idea of active self-abnegation, are the new and unique elements of the New Testament message.

This fusion is so profoundly anchored in the subconscious that a blinding intuition gives rise to a kind of ideal union between the word of Christ and the most sublime inspirations of universal prophecy: in these realms the whole of life becomes a profound striving for extinction, for the sake of a return; a sacrifice, for the sake of resurrection; an affirmation of death, for the reconquest of life. "Blessed are ye who beg for joy, for peace, for love"—who see the central functions of life as a varied mendicancy; for in what measure you espouse poverty, in that measure will you be enriched.

In the light of this profound and all-embracing feeling for a life which is a constant rejection and transcending of the self, the idea of conversion ceases to be merely a special manner of apprehending and measuring the values of life; it ceases to be a mere injunction to inner renewal. It has now become second nature to see the snares of the evil one in every living impulse; the striving for conversion is also a striving to escape these snares by raising oneself in each passing moment to a higher sphere of life; and this sphere is the unfolding of God's paternal act, the preparation for his ultimate victory.

Seen in this way, conversion consists not in an external, purely spatial removal from the world. Christian conversion is an inward removal from the busy turmoil of empirical life—an approach to the profound, unwritten laws of a collective life that has its own primal discipline and intangible dialectic; it is brotherhood in communion with that divine force of the good, which suffers and struggles with all its strength for the conquest of the highest justice.

But those who live by the message of Christ will not make a display of contrition and gloom. The affectation of contrition is the affair of the Pharisees and their accomplices. Those who are reborn into the kingdom will march merry and festive, gracious and smiling, like the virgins in the parable, who go to meet the bridegroom on the day of the great adventure.

The joy of their countenance is not and cannot be synonymous with frivolity and superficiality. He who expects God to restore the good, and yet is at every moment beset by the snares, the guiles, the mimicry of the evil one, does not bear in his face the signs of his fear and trembling. His features reveal only the light of confidence and the pure clarity of joy. But in his heart he will feel the bitter pain of the unceasing battle to the death that is life in this world, where the cause of the good is so unremittingly exposed to the most grievous dangers.

However, the faithful whom Jesus has summoned to prepare his kingdom—the preparation lies in the act of faith itself—do not by any means consider that their task is done merely because they anticipate the coming kingdom of God with yearning hearts. Evangelical expectation means blind surrender to the conditions of total self-abnegation and uncalculating devotion. The light that pours down from the torch that is faith in the kingdom, without which the kingdom could not find its own way, is the light of the olive, the typical tree of the Mediterranean world—the true world of Christianity. The olive tree draws its life from the destruction caused by its roots deep down in the rock, and its power to give light and food is increased a hundredfold by merciless pruning. The light of God's kingdom is nourished and increased by sacrifice and renunciation.

If from the teachings of Jesus (and particularly his parable of the prodigal son) we try to glean a conception of the world, we may say that for Jesus the world is divided into two realms: the realm of the father, who, shading his eyes, peers down from the heights for the return of his sons who have heedlessly hurled themselves into distant perils; and the realm of the swineherd (for the Israelite the pig is an object of digust, the embodiment of impurity), who maintains in his service wretched creatures unable to sate their voracious appetites with the food offered by the unclean herd.

The two realms are at war. It is absurd and blasphemous to suppose that the father is insensitive to the sufferings and disillusionment of the prodigal. And it would be equally absurd and blasphemous to suppose that he means to call the repentant sinner to account for his disastrous adventure. For the soul of the father —essence of all fatherhood—is the realm of the absurd and inconsequential. The son sets out foolishly to seek his fortune, the father cannot forbid him to squander his own wealth; but now, forgetful of all his sorrow and care, he is filled with rejoicing when he sees in the distance the livid face of his returning son, ravaged by the hardships of his adventure.

Amid all the uncertainty that surrounds him, man, whether dying or doomed, needs always the rule of the father, who watches over him as over a child and with his inexhaustible creative power holds man's wretched fragility safely poised above the abyss of nothingness. But in his immaturity and inexperience man may presumptuously demand of the father the right to enjoy his inheritance in his own way. He knows nothing of the perils involved in his overweening heedlessness and does not suspect that in his adventures upon the roads of life he will be cut off from his bond with the father or that, in squandering those forces which are by no means his slaves but sisters of mortal fear and death, he will end in the service of the swineherd. For the swineherd has prepared a pen for his foul creatures in the world; here he lodges the presumptuous renegades from the house of the father and abuses them like swine.

But curse upon curse—the renegade can become doubly renegade. After demanding from his father his share of his inheritance and shamelessly wasting his substance, he may sink so far as to suppose that his sufferings are solely his own and not also those of the father; he may presume that on his return home he will find only a judge and avenger—and not a father. A son can fling no viler insult in his father's face than this: to ignore his fatherly tenderness and debase him to the level of a taxcollector and policeman.

True, man can demand of God the independent use of that which is his; but this independence reduces him to impotence and shipwreck. And man's suffering is the grievous suffering of God. The shipwrecked mariner, who on the wreckage of his own bitter disillusionment seeks to reach the heaven of salvation, should—as a Christian—feel only one thing: that now, in returning to the bosom of the father, he must not anticipate the false, humiliating existence of a hireling, for by his homecoming he will be giving back joy and peace to the father, who until now has been scanning the horizon in a torment of expectancy.

Life, according to the gospel, is the solitary return of the despairing and hungry, who bear in their ravaged bodies and flayed souls the sacred battle to the death, the wakeful hope in God.

The teachings of Jesus throw a clear light on the problems which, stated abstractly, form the object of theological speculation: the problems of human freedom, of religious merit, of the possibility of reconciling grace and free will. There is in man nothing autonomous with respect to God: but there is nothing in God which can exist without the response and help of man.

To the keen eye of Jesus nature presents an ambivalent polarity in the mystery of perpetual life. There is a perfect correspondence between the dialectic underlying animal and vegetable life and the dialectic of the miracle underlying the rhythm of spiritual life. With what subtlety and certainty Jesus chooses his metaphors from the cycle of seed and harvest!

The transcendent revelation, the embodiment and the synthesis which have given it the prophetic name of "kingdom of heaven," come to the soul by the common paths which are sometimes opened to the wanderer. History, too, knows its seasonal cycles; and when the plough has torn the earth open and freshets of autumn rain have softened the sun-parched earth, the sower, as we have heard, goes forth to sow. Once the seed is sown, the growth of the seedlings is no longer the business of man: it is the business of God and his grace. And God governs in silence beneath the ice of winter, in those depths to which the whirlwinds of the earth's surface do not penetrate. He who has sown the seed of the kingdom in good soil can turn to the concerns of his day. The seed of the kingdom, profoundly embedded in the ferment of the unconscious, prepares the fruit deep in the dark ground; nothing that comes from outside must enter this hidden zone, which is wisely separated from everything that is transient and questionable: the grain that in the fall was buried in the earth is slowly resurrected by God and his grace. The harvest time comes automatically and without fail. Hence the tiller of the soil has two indispensable implements, the plough and the scythe, and two unfailing seasons, sowing time and harvest time. And how striking is the contrast between the richness of the harvest and the frugal humility of the sowing!

Here the Christian message seems to bear within it the greatest conceivable inner contradiction. In order to attain God's grace the Christian must undertake the severest exertions in his service. And, at the same time, he must be aware of the futility and inadequacy of his own accomplishment; he must be aware of God's grace, which is the seed of the kingdom.

In the constant temptation to overemphasize his own accomplishment and to forget the transcendent rule of God, the Christian, according to Jesus, must unceasingly renew his "conversion"; he must withdraw from the spell of the external things which lead men to forget God; he must perseveringly raise his eyes to the mystery of the divine kingdom which approaches, without outward fanfare, solely through our belief in it.

Once we have thus reduced the teachings of Christ to their essentials and fitted them into their place in the general evolution of religion—from a body of magical and initiatory rites down to a continuous effort at conversion from empirical life to the life of transcendent values—the problem of the relations between the experience and doctrine of Jesus and the experience and doctrine of Paul appears in a clearer light.

We must examine the problem in its many prismatic aspects. First we might formulate it in this way: how would it be possible to sustain the gospel of "conversion," in all its stormy, creative vitality when the faithful were compelled to defer their hope in the coming of God's kingdom? For had this hope not fed and sustained the enthusiasm of the Lord's first, immediate disciples?

Eschatological zeal remains a crucial characteristic of the teachings of Paul, as of Christ. The dawn of the kingdom is the central motif of the apostle's first two epistles, the two letters to the Thessalonians. It might almost be said that from this moment on the development of Paul's ideas can be traced (we are in the year A.D. 50 and have the oldest of the New Testament documents before us) to the setbacks incurred by this still exuberant apocalyptic faith.

When Paul appeared in Macedonia and founded the first congregations of converts, he seems to have preached almost exclusively of cosmic rebirth and the imminent dawn of God's kingdom on earth. He succeeded in arousing so blind and staunch a faith that the sudden death of this or that convert filled the brethren and relatives of the departed with alarm; for what was to be the destiny of those who perished before the dawn of God's kingdom on earth, which, Paul had assured them, was at hand?

Paul heard in Corinth of the state of mind into which the Thessalonians had fallen and felt impelled to bolster their morale. He wrote:

> For if we believe that Jesus died and rose again, even so them also which sleep in Jesus will God bring with him. For this we say unto you by the word of the Lord, that we which are alive and remain unto the coming of the Lord shall not prevent them which are asleep. For the Lord himself shall descend from heaven with a shout, with the voice of the archangel, and with the trump of God: And the dead in Christ shall rise first: Then we which are alive and remain shall be caught up together with them in the clouds, to meet the Lord in the air: and so shall we ever be with the Lord (I Thess. 4:14–17).

The moment of this overwhelming return is unknown. But let no man therefore give himself over to fear and vacillation. For henceforward there can be no doubt, mankind is sharply divided into two groups: on the one hand, the sons of darkness—those who stubbornly close their eyes to the truth; on the other hand, the sons of light, who have opened their souls wide to faith and whose ultimate triumph, dead or alive, has been sealed by God's unalterable decision, against which there is no appeal.

Such express assurances were bound to call forth certain evils. The converts of Thessalonica began to reason as follows: "If God infallibly calls all the faithful to his bosom, if there is no longer a 'day of wrath,' but a perfect assurance of redemption, so that the faithful, waking or sleeping, dead or alive, are by the mystery made forever alive in Christ, who has been resurrected for all and who, even now, is busy separating his own from the vast mass of the sons of darkness—then there is no need to concern ourselves with a material existence which will shortly crumble away. Nothing remains to be done; we need only fold our hands and await the cosmic drama whose brief acts have been made known to us in advance and whose epilogue will find most of the converts alive."

St. Paul heard of this paradoxical and comfortable interpretation of his own message of hope (could Greeks after all be expected to think like Semites?) and wrote once again to the converts of Thessalonica. This second of the canonical epistles addressed to them is a strong admonition to active patience. Here Paul informs the congregation that the crisis which will usher in the kingdom of heaven is not as simple or imminent as the Thessalonians liked to think. It presupposed events and circumstances which could follow only from the acts and exertions of those who believed in the impending kingdom of God. With his circumspect phrasing and subtle, carefully worded, arguments (which come very close to diplomacy and were dictated by the need to protect the conveyor of the epistle as well as its recipients from stern measure on the part of the Roman authorities), Paul gave only a vague intimation of the events which would precede and pave the way for the great day of the Lord.

According to the words of Christ, the kingdom of God should have come suddenly and shatteringly upon the world, even before the first apostles reached the borders of Palestine with their preaching. And the house of Israel should have enjoyed unassailable, exclusive rights in the kingdom. Both geographically and with regard to the exclusion of the heathen Paul shattered this limitation of the Messianic message; he passed beyond the borders of Palestine and solemnly opened the gates to all Adam's posterity throughout the world.

But now that the gospel of the kingdom was addressed to vast multitudes, who moreover were subject each day to greater disappointment at their fruitless waiting, supports and safeguards were needed. It was necessary to find guarantees which would be as trustworthy as the physical presence of the "prophet" Jesus, who was personally in evidence with his original doctrine, both as herald and founder of the kingdom.

That the expectation of the kingdom of heaven remained one of the most conspicuous supports of Paul's teaching is understandable, although this expectation brought the greatest reverses of his apostolate; it was the source of all the unrest in the groups of converts which he had founded on his missionary travels, of all the spiritual and ideological difficulties in the congregations which he had established in Syria, Anatolia, Macedonia, and Achaea.

From Thessalonians to Philippians, the epistle that may be regarded as a kind of testament with which St. Paul set the seal to his apostolic career in Rome, all the Pauline writings, without notable variation, overflow with the certainty of God's coming. The apostle's last words are an invitation to rejoice in the imminent liberation: "Rejoice in the Lord alway: and again I say, Rejoice. . . . The Lord is at hand." (Phil. 4:4–5) . And the original Christian congregations, all filled with the impending kingdom of heaven, took as their motto the happy tidings: "The Lord is at hand."

This naïve certainty of the impending metamorphosis made each of the Christian-Pauline congregations a center of ferment within the Roman world. (Christ in his wisdom had called Christianity the leaven of the world, the light shining into the cosmic darkness.) And it is inconceivable that the congregations could long have remained in this state of ebullient unrest if they had not supplied themselves with trustworthy supports of a hope which—if we consider the enduring, instinctive dialectic of the human spirit—could not but automatically become a faith.

The conversion of the new recruits to Christianity was something fundamentally different from the conversion of the apostles whom Jesus, in his dramatic inauguration of the kingdom at Jerusalem, had chosen as his direct successors. Paul himself, the one trustworthy witness to his own conversion, had a very peculiar conception of this conversion. It was the vision of the resurrected Christ who miraculously appeared to fortify Paul's certainty of Christ's impending triumphal return from heaven; and he taught this conception to his converts, who expected justice and peace only from God. In the face of all the empirical forces of so-called human civilization, the former zealot, the irreconcilable Pharisee with his dream of the restoration of the kingdom of Israel, had transcended his hopeless disappointment and risen to faith in a spiritual kingdom. And it was not from human arts and instrumentalities that he expected salvation and the return of goodness.

In justifying his own antilegal message by way of admonition to the backsliding congregations of the Galatians, Paul touched on the extraordinary event which at one stroke had dispelled all his former ideals and aims:

> I certify you, brethren, that the gospel which was preached of me was not after man. For I neither received it of man, neither was I taught it, but by the revelation of Jesus Christ. For ye have heard of my conversation in time past in the Jews' religion, how that beyond measure I persecuted the church of God, and wasted it; and profited in the Jews' religion above many my equals in mine own nation, being more exceedingly zealous of the traditions of my fathers. But when it pleased God, who separated me from my mother's womb, and called me by his grace, to reveal his Son in me, that I might preach him among the heathen; immediately I conferred not with flesh and blood (Gal. 1:11–16).

From this we can measure the greatness and difficulty of the Pauline program. Those who had been "called" to conversion by Jesus had in him not only the herald of a divine kingdom which they expected to inherit, but also the visible and tangible pledge of the kingdom, which he, the messenger of God and the son of man, was to inaugurate according to the vision of the prophet Daniel.

But those called to conversion by Paul had no visible and tangible figure to sustain their hope in the kingdom: they had only the ideal image of the resurrected one, whom Paul claimed to have seen in a vision; but they themselves could not boast of any such miraculous vision.

Now how was it possible in such an unstable and difficult spiritual situation to prevent the religion of "conversion" par excellence, a religion built on the expectation of a God-willed cosmic palingenesis which would establish in the universe a hierarchy of true values constituting a direct antithesis to the hierarchy of false values—how was it possible to prevent this religion from degenerating into a magical religion of initiation? This was the immense task undertaken by St. Paul.

If we look upon the relation between the doctrine of Christ and the doctrine of Paul in this light, we shall avoid biased simplifications of the problem. The doctrines of Christ and St. Paul do not coincide as the orthodox tradition would have us believe, but neither are they as far apart as the liberal critics suppose. There is an indissoluble bond between Christ and Paul: their common program of transforming religion into an eternal and continuous dynamic of "conversions" and "rebirths," by which man is enabled to escape from the prison of material values into the sphere of spiritual values.

A pessimistic view of the world is the very basis of joyful faith in the kingdom of God. (Religious optimism is always the surprising consequence and unhoped-for fruit of an original and fundamental pessimism.) And the teachings of Jesus are entirely permeated with this pessimism. He came to put an end to the realm of Satan, for this world in all its manifestations has utterly succumbed to the corrosive rule of the evil one. And in the Semite Paul, raised in Hellenistic Tarsus, this same pessimism became a hideous vision of the realm of sin and death, from which man can escape only by raising up his own self to the realm of truth, light, and love.

In St. Paul are fused the two traditional Biblical and Hellenistic views of guilt as an inevitable taint upon successive generations and the whole universe.

Of the four basic emotions which combine to form the roots of religious life—love, pain, repentance, and fear of death—repentance, the bite of conscience, is assuredly the profoundest and most enduring. We are never without a vague, instinctive sense of guilt and a feeling of being punishable. At the root of our moral being we feel a laceration, a wound; our very first step into social life seems to have been tainted with brother's blood.

The Yahwist of Genesis has embodied this sense of guilt for all eternity in a magnificent myth which crystallizes our instinctive knowledge that human civilization had its origin in blood guilt and in an inexpiable curse that lies over all nature:

> And the Lord said unto Cain, Where is Abel thy brother? And he said, I know not: Am I my brother's keeper? And he said, What hast thou done? the voice of thy brother's blood crieth unto me from the ground. And now art thou cursed from the earth, which hath opened her mouth to receive thy brother's blood from thy hand. When thou tillest the ground, it shall not henceforth yield unto thee her strength; a fugitive and a vagabond shalt thou be in the earth (Gen. 4:9–12).

And Cain took stones and built a wall against the inexorable pangs of his conscience—and thus arose the first city. Man's technical civilization is an inventive effort, an increasingly frenzied endeavor to raise up a stone bulwark against that terrible, primeval cry, which went up from the earth to God, calling for vengeance and reparation for that first, forever renewed fratricide. But the steel walls do not muffle the cry; the voice of man's conscience is only increased a thousandfold.

The Greeks also knew the mystery of the physical world's participation in man's guilt, of the taint which passes from man's crime to material things. Pausanias relates, for example, that Alcmaeon, after murdering his mother Eriphyle, sought haven at Psophis in Arcadia. But his conscience found no rest. And so he went to Delphi, and there the Pythia revealed to him that the only place where Eriphyle's cry of vengeance could not rend and devour his reason was the little bit of earth which had been under water at the time of his matricide and hence had not been touched by the blood-guilt which had sullied the whole earth.

Apollodorus relates that Bellerophon, described by Homer in the epilogue to the *Iliad,* was stricken with a mysterious gloom after he had unwittingly killed his brother. He went to Proetus in search of purification and peace. But he found no peace. Proetus sent him to the king of Lycia; and Iobates sent him to the one spot on earth that could receive him, because it had no contact with the contagion of his fratricide: the new land in the Cilician plain, which had risen from the sea after his crime. And Aeschylus in his Orestes cycle gave magnificent artistic form to the conception of a hereditary guilt, passing from generation to generation. His trilogy is perhaps the most powerful artistic endeavor to inspire the fratricidal heart of man with horror of violence and hate, and to kindle the flame of mercy and forgiveness.

The Biblical myth of Adam may be said to schematize man's consciousness of the original sin which coincided in time with the formation of the first human societies. But even though the whole Biblical tradition is permeated with an awareness of man's innate sinfulness, the myth of Adam is not mentioned in the passages which recall that inherent guilt—such as the Book of Job or the most pessimistic passages in the Psalms.

Jesus himself, whom the author of the fourth gospel calls "the lamb," who was sacrificed to atone for the guilt of mankind—Jesus himself, who was so filled with a pessimistic consciousness of evil —never mentioned Adam. He was so entirely committed to the fulfillment of the kingdom which would end evil in the world, that he did not feel, as it were, the need of descending to the original source of evil.

It was Paul who created the doctrine of original sin in the belief that each individual bears his share of responsibility in the first human guilt. He formulated it in his polemic against the Platonist Apollos, who denied that human flesh could participate in the eternal beatitude of the kingdom. In Galatians, where Paul tells how man is liberated from the law by death and resurrection in baptism, he had spoken of Abraham, our father, the ancestor of all those who put their hope in God's unfailing justice, who live by confidence and expectation. In his polemic against Apollos, about the Corinthian "converts" who had been guilty of insubordination and incitement to vice, he went back still farther in man's history.

The coming of Christ, the proclamation of the new law establishing spiritual bonds between men who are mysteriously freed from the old bonds of flesh and blood—all this had created an unbridgeable gulf between the old, Adamite man and the new, Christian man. St. Paul wrote:

> The first man Adam was made a living soul; the last Adam was made a quickening spirit. Howbeit that was not first which is spiritual, but that which is natural; and afterward that which is spiritual. The first man is of the earth, earthy: the second man is the Lord from heaven. As is the earthy, such are they also that are earthy; and as is the heavenly, such are they also that are heavenly. And as we have borne the image of the earthy, we shall also bear the image of the heavenly. Now this I say, brethren, that flesh [including all the ephemeral institutions of our time] and blood [with all its false compromises and empirical ties] cannot inherit the kingdom of God; neither doth corruption [including human knowledge] inherit incorruption. Behold, I shew you a mystery: We shall not all sleep, but we shall all be changed, in a moment, in the twinkling of an eye, at the last trump: for the trumpet shall sound, and the dead shall be raised incorruptible, and we shall be changed. For this corruptible must put on incorruption, and this mortal must put on immortality. So when this corruptible shall have put on incorruption, and this mortal shall have put on immortality, then shall be brought to pass the saying that is written, Death is swallowed up in victory. O death, where is thy sting? O grave, where is thy victory? (I Cor. 15:45-55).

Has death a sting? And sin a power? Yes, the sting of death is sin; the power of sin is the law.

This comparison of Adam and Christ, touched upon in Corinthians and the polemic against Apollos, seems to have lingered on in Paul's subconscious and later brought forth surprising fruit. It is in the epistle to the Romans, this authentic work of anthropology and soteriology, that these fruits spring forth in all their abundance. Here we see that it was not the doctrine of original sin

139

which brought Paul to faith in Christ the redeemer—it was, on the contrary, his boundless confidence in the saving power of Christ which (in defiance of all formal logic) led Paul to abandon his doctrine of universal responsibility for the fall of Adam. It is only with a view to magnifying the light and the joy brought by Christ that Paul represents mankind past and present as groaning in the dark hell of damnation.

Let us recall the picture he draws of mankind in Romans:

> As it is written, There is none righteous, no, not one: There is none that understandeth, there is none that seeketh after God. They are all gone out of the way, they are together become unprofitable; there is none that doeth good, no, not one. Their throat is an open sepulchre; with their tongues they have used deceit; the poison of asps is under their lips: whose mouth is full of cursing and bitterness. Their feet are swift to shed blood: Destruction and misery are in their ways: And the way of peace have they not known: There is no fear of God before their eyes (Rom. 3:10–18).

With an almost pathological pleasure Paul searches the whole Biblical literature for passages which, taken together, yield the most repugnant and realistic picture of the world's evil. With the passion of an anatomist who thrusts his hands into diseased entrails and finds the cankers he is looking for, Paul probes into the moral decay which corrupts human society. Let them have their just reward, those presumptuous observers of the law, who look arrogantly down upon those whom in their self-righteousness they call "sinners," namely the heathen. They possess no other claim to distinction than their greater guilt. Even in the slightest transgression, they are doubly responsible: for their guilt and for their knowledge of the law. They are all steeped in utter baseness. And the signal for the recapitulation of the world's sins follows the unnatural degeneration of human instinct. God has surrendered mankind to the disgrace of a shameless sexual perversion. And here lies the most damaging proof of the total shipwreck of human society on the shoals of bestiality.

This was destiny. The periods in the development of human civilization are marked by the redeeming power of faith and not by enlightenment or superimposed, external knowledge. Salvation does not come from the law: God is not a debtor, from whom, the law in hand, one collects what is due. Against such presumptuous demands for payment, God has endowed the law with its terrible power of revival, its power to magnify guilt and sharpen the sting of death.

Still uncircumcised, Abraham found grace in the eyes of Yahweh for his childlike, trusting simplicity. He is the symbol of an incalculable, consoling mystery. He needed no cutting of the flesh to find grace in God's eyes. What then was the need for institutionalized Judaism with its mechanically repeated prayers and its babblings about caste, nation, and the purity of the law? Justified by faith, every man, regardless of any legal ordinance—every man justified by faith who is able to say that he has lived according to the example of Abraham—can experience anew the great drama of death in the flesh and rebirth in grace.

But each one of life's smallest manifestations is a brief epitome of life. When we come into the world we bring with us, deep in our innermost selves, the same trust and expectancy for which justice was done to Abraham. And when our destiny is fulfilled, when the moment comes for us to pass from living creature to life-engendering creature, that moment which all religions alike cloak in terrible rites of passage—then suddenly we become aware of the atavistic sinfulness and the questionable nature of our own life. For birth implies death. Paul spoke in the name of every human being when he said:

> For I was alive without the law once: but when the commandment came, sin revived, and I died. And the commandment, which was ordained to life, I found to be unto death. For sin, taking occasion by the commandment, deceived me, and by it slew me. Wherefore the law is holy, and the commandment holy, and just, and good. Was then that which is good made death unto me? God forbid. But sin, that it might appear sin, working death in me by that which is good; that sin by the commandment might become exceeding sinful. For we know that the law is spiritual: but I am carnal, sold under sin (Rom. 7:9–14).

No eye has ever looked deeper into the abyss of the subconscious, where man's innocence, in its hope, faith, immediacy, and hence justice, is ensnared, sullied, wounded by the fatal limits of the law and the impossibility of transgressing it without guilt and death.

> For that which I do I allow not: for what I would, that do I not; but what I hate, that do I. . . . For I know that in me (that is, in my flesh) dwelleth no good thing: for to will is present with me, but how to perform that which is good I find not. For . . . the evil which I would not, that I do. Now if I do that I would not, it is no more I that do it, but sin that dwelleth in me. . . . But I see another law in my members, warring against the law of my mind, and bringing me into captivity to the law of sin which is in my members. O wretched man that I am! Who shall deliver me from the body of this death? (Rom. 7:15–24).

But Paul would not have asked this anguished question if he had not long carried the joyous answer in his heart. Only great optimists have the need to descend into the abysmal darkness of pessimism. And he who has no feeling for the tragedy of life cannot behold the glad vision of the kingdom of heaven. It was his certainty of Christ's saving grace that impelled Paul to conceive of the life about him and indeed of all creation as shrouded in a dark cloak of suffering and injustice. For creation itself groans in the chains of mortality, which cannot be broken until the day when God's grace shines upon his children in all its radiance.

The irrefutable proof of this? Here it is. St. Paul's absolute certainty that Christ the Lord stood high above the wretched millennial heritage of laws and sinners: his belief in freedom and salvation by faith were so overwhelming that he finally arrived at the most sublime formulation of the antithesis between Adam and Christ. He begins with Adam, for Christ, being ever present, is unseen, while only Adam, the adversary, meets the eye. "Therefore, as by the offence of one judgment came upon all men to condemnation; even so by the righteousness of one the free gift came upon all men unto justification of life" (Rom. 5:18). Logic would have required Paul to continue as follows: "And so justice came into the world through one man, and through justice life." But for Paul there was no further need to praise the justice and lifegiving power of Christ. These were embodied in the Christian rebirth.

142

St. Paul, and with him his converts, was perfectly certain of rebirth. Now it was far more important to hammer into their minds the idea of sin and death, concentrated and embodied in Adam as in a single lump of damnation. And Paul, carried away as it were by the tumult of his pessimistic experience, repeats illogically: ". . . and so death passed upon all men, for that all have sinned." This incisive passage in Romans is the source of the whole church tradition of original sin and redemption.

But how prevent this anthropological, almost excessively pessimistic but strictly individualistic attitude from degenerating into another of those religions of initiation which Christianity, the religion of conversion par excellence, had defeated and done away with forever? This is the most difficult problem raised by the experience and doctrine of St. Paul: here lay the greatest threat to the future development of Christian expansion (*propaganda christiana*).

St. Paul withstood the danger unharmed, thanks to his experience of the mystical working of Christ in the Church; and Christianity might also preserve itself from the danger by a process of continuous transformation and regeneration. But how? And when?

Ernesto Buonaiuti

Christology and Ecclesiology in St. Paul

The most authentic and original achievement of the Apostle Paul is no doubt his conception of the mystical Christ, which is entirely consonant with his ecclesiology (Doctrine of the Church). Through this mystical christology and ecclesiology, St. Paul saved himself from relapsing into the type of religion of initiation which it has been the millennial function of all prophetic religious reforms to overcome, and created a basis on which historical Christianity might avert the same danger.

St. Paul's christology and ecclesiology represent a unique and highly original fusion of moral imperatives—not in the juridical or legislative meaning of the term, but in the sense of those unwritten laws which govern the growth of social life—with mystical vision, eschatological intimations, and a rare insight into those laws, subject to no mechanical definition, which control and cement the relations of men with one another.

As an example of this Pauline mystical christology, we shall cite a characteristic passage from the epistle to the Philippians. When he wrote it, Paul was a prisoner in Rome. Rome! Paul had yearned to go there to make his personal contribution to the establishment of that evangelical congregation which was destined to play so stormy a part in the history of Europe's spiritual life. Instead, he arrived there as a political prisoner, accused by his own kinsmen before the tribunal of that "son of godlessness," of whom he had never ceased to speak in terms of irreconcilable condemnation.

A stranger, more paradoxical situation is scarcely conceivable. The preaching of St. Paul was only the logical and natural culmination of the hopes which had sustained the spiritual life (*idealità*) of his people down through the centuries. His political imprison-

144

ment actually bore witness to the traditional hopes of Israel. But it was Israel that had dragged him before the tribunal of a ruler who was detested in Judaea as a tyrant, as the ravisher of Zion. He was accused of rebellion against the emperor. But in reality Paul was a new prophet who, stirred by the life and message of Christ, had become an interpreter of the Messianic tradition on a purely spiritual plane.

When Paul arrived in Rome under military guard, he could harbor no illusions. No understanding or leniency was to be expected from the government of Nero—a government which sought to conceal its profound corruption and brutal injustice under a surface of barbaric splendor. Yet even in chains Paul preserved his confidence in his calling. Though under constant military supervision, he enjoyed relative freedom in Rome. He made use of this freedom to approach the leading members of the Jewish community, whose intervention might help him in his impending trial, and strove to show them the continuity between Old Testament tradition and his own doctrine. And perhaps he had some opportunity to approach the Christian congregation which already existed in Rome. However, the prisoner's thoughts seem to have been chiefly with the little congregations which he had sown so plentifully along the highroads of the empire. In this solemn twilight of his life, he wondered what his first friends in Antioch were thinking; in what state of mind were the recalcitrant congregations of Galatia, his beloved brethren of Macedonia, the regenerate Christians of Achaea, and his loyal followers in Ephesus on the Ionian coast.

At this point Paul received an unexpected visit. Brother Epaphroditus had come to Rome from distant Macedonia in the name of all the congregations of Philippi, to seek information about the trial and to bring money. Paul was moved to the bottom of his heart, filled with tender memories which softened the bitterness and anguish of his imprisonment. He remembered how, spurred on by the Spirit, he had landed on the Macedonian coast, more than a decade earlier. He recalled the faces of the first European converts. He thought with emotion of the gentle, zealous soul of Lydia, the wealthy purple dealer who had offered her most generous hospitality to him and his companion, the bringers of an astounding

145

message. He wrote to thank his beloved congregation, and it may be presumed that Epaphroditus himself carried back the apostle's letter, this legacy of his heart, which even in the face of death was full of love and tenderness for his companions in faith and hope.

In this epistle, so full of memories and hopes, Paul formulates his christological faith with unequalled clarity:

> If there be therefore any consolation in Christ, if any comfort of love, if any fellowship of the Spirit, if any bowels and mercies, fulfill ye my joy, that ye be like-minded, having the same love, being of one accord, of one mind. Let nothing be done through strife or vainglory; but in lowliness of mind let each esteem other better than themselves. Look not every man on his own things, but every man also on the things of others. Let this mind be in you, which was also in Christ Jesus: who, being in the form of God, thought it not robbery to be equal with God: but made himself of no reputation, and took upon him the form of a servant, and was made in the likeness of men (Phil. 2:1–7).

Now this christological faith differs sharply from that which we find, for example, in the fourth gospel. St. Paul speaks of Christ's divinity, his "being in the form of God," solely in order to emphasize his humility, his making himself "of no reputation" when he "took upon him the form of a servant and was made in the likeness of men." Paul wished above all to instruct his converts in humility and brotherhood. His vision and his ministry are imbued with a kind of cosmogonic speculation, Jesus is not the word of God, serving as an intermediary between Him and the multiple realities of the world; he is a divine form of the Father, who has condescended to take on our carnal form solely in order to show us by his living example and message that we have no other duty than humble and devoted service to our brothers who, as the prophets said, are flesh of our flesh and blood of our blood.

Thus the cardinal doctrine of St. Paul formulates one goal, one striving, one criterion. It is a plan to convert man's innate impulses into a fervid bond of love through a unique collective mysticism, which is realized by the total annulment of the individual personality and its sacramental sublimation in Christ.

The early patristic tradition imputes to Christ a saying which, though it is not included in the canonical gospels, fully reflects the Christian attitude toward collective life: "Dost thou love thy brother? Thou seest thy God. Kneel down and worship."

The author of the first epistle of John says just this when he calls it a hypocritical lie to claim to love the invisible God if you are unable to love the visible God, your own brother. And Christ —in Matthew's report of the sermon on the mount—pointed, not without a certain irony, to this same virtue when, seeking to engrave the supreme law of charity in the hearts of his disciples, he paradoxically reversed the conventional order of punishments and transgressions:

> Ye have heard that it was said by them of old time, Thou shalt not kill; and whosoever shall kill shall be in danger of the judgment. But I say unto you, That whosoever is angry with his brother without a cause shall be in danger of the judgment: and whosover shall say to his brother, Raca, shall be in danger of the council: but whosoever shall say, Thou fool, shall be in danger of hell fire (Matt. 5:21-22) .

In the eyes of God, offense to one's brother is a transgression meriting the penalty of death. The highest piety consists in recognizing brotherly love as the divine life blood which circulates through the social organism. To disturb this supernatural flow is to taint one's hand with blood as though one committed murder.

With all his soul and all his ethical feeling, Paul, who had not seen Christ in the flesh, who must have discerned the divine face of Christ in the first collection of his sayings, espoused this tempestuous revelation of the absolute sanctity of the bond between human beings. Thence his instinct must have led him to his conception of evangelical conversion and of his mission to purge the faithful of every claim to privilege—whether of race, caste, or religious creed—and to his particular view of brotherly love between individuals artificially divided by rancour, rivalry, prejudice, and all those obsolete misunderstandings which permeate empirical politics and the technique of social organization. For St. Paul christology and ecclesiology were inseparably intertwined. The more he came to value the bond of grace created by the Church as a mystical organization of men redeemed from the law of sin which is the law of hatred and death, the higher he exalted the figure of the mystical Christ, who went through death in order to free men from death and who constitutes the invisible bond between the present age and the age to come. It would be foolish to create water-tight compartments within the apostle's rich and varied experiences, which occurred at a time when rebirth and redemption were thought to be imminent, among men who still felt, as it were, the physical presence of the mystical Christ, linking the world of reality to the world of faith.

Ever since the day when he had been miraculously commanded to undertake the succession of Christ, whom, in his former Phari-saism he had come to look upon as destructive of the oldest and most sacred ideals of Israel, Paul had dedicated himself to rebirth in expectation of the spiritual kingdom; he had combined his apocalyptic experience, the intuition of a mystical Christ, with the concept of a religious community and the practical precept of an all-embracing brotherly love.

At that time the "kingdom" was in a sense anticipated, because men expected it and yearned for it so fervently, and Paul strove in his "church" to create a common bond in grace which would be an anticipation and pledge of its beatific peace. But what unexpected and painful vicissitudes were to assail this vast plan in the course of his stormy apostolate! The supreme principles of the Pauline ecclesiology are laid down in the epistles to the converts of Corinth. Corinth! Paul had made his first appearance among the Galatians after a grave attack of the disease which periodically numbed all his energies and distorted his features; and he appeared for the first time in Corinth after the worst failure of his apostolic career, which occurred in Athens. Accustomed to learn quickly from the harshest experiences of his propagandist career and to take countermeasures, Paul decided to leave the hypersophisticated indifference of Athens for the seething vulgarity of Corinth, the "city of the two seas," this cosmopolitan Babel, whose situation made it a meeting place for all the mariners of the Mediterranean and which the cult of Aphro-dite Pandemos made into a city of proverbial vice.

Here Paul followed in the footsteps of Christ. After the arrogance and hostility of Pharisee officialdom, Christ had turned to the publicans and sinners, who, he said, would enter the kingdom before the scribes and Pharisees. Paul left the Areopagus to its intellectu-alistic self-conceit and sought support among the harbor porters and

148

the temple prostitutes. And from these diseased members he began to recreate the immaculate body of Christ in Corinth.

The greatness of a soul can be measured by the boldness of its hopes and the immensity of its disappointments. On the day when Paul in the house of Chloe in Ephesus received the news that the young congregation of Corinth was rent with dissension fomented by the crafty sermons of an Alexandrian schooled in all the subtleties of Platonic speculation and allegoristic exegesis, and that repulsive perversion was widespread, his heart suffered a grievous blow, which was more deeply wounding and damaging than the shocks occasionally inflicted on him by his ailing body. Was this the vengeance of philosophy which had despised him in Athens and which he in turn had despised in Corinth, when he sought his proselytes among the lowest classes of the population? (Had Christ not taught that the glory of this world is an abomination and the abomination of this world a glory?) Were the converts of this Greek city striving to sully the body of Christ with incurable corruption?

Paul's epistles to the Corinthians are an outburst of pain and bitterness; they are a noble and high-minded expression of mystical wisdom as opposed to dialectical wisdom; they are a shrewd defense of threatened missionary positions; and, above all, they are a wonderful celebration of communion in Christ, begun in baptism, nurtured in the eucharist, raised in grace, practiced in love, fulfilled in resurrection.

Christ had summoned his converts to an inner renewal which would consume their old instincts and judgments, preaching in an atmosphere of feverish expectancy and hope which fulfilled the kingdom; and Paul instinctively saw his mission in bringing the faithful to the spirit which is the resurrected Christ: for in him and through him was fulfilled the law which would one day govern the kingdom, the law of love. To his mind the fusion of Moses and Christ, advocated by the emissaries from Jerusalem and their new adherents in Galatia, meant a retreat into the rule of the law and the cosmic elements which the cross of Christ had annulled and destroyed; it meant the grafting of diseased limbs on the body of Christ. It was an ignominious concession to the flesh, which could not but impede the "church," the intermediary between world and "kingdom," in carrying out its spiritual mission and—by anticipation, symbols, and precepts—conferring its glorious and eternal gifts of peace, justice, and joy.

Paul was incapable of thinking in distinctions of race and caste; he spoke always to the concrete man and not to abstractions of nation or class. He needed concrete symbols, visible images and fantasies, tangible comparisons and confrontations. The body of man is the seat of desire, sickness, and death. (Paul speaks of the "thorn in the flesh"—the disease which torments man unremittingly —and of his "corpse"—the place in which the "law of sin" has the upper hand.) But this is a collective body, the hypostasized and personified product of all men's passions and lusts. It is an anonymous, supraindividual body, the sum of those human decisions defined in the laws and embodied in the official relations between men and groups of men.

He who subordinates himself to codified laws, who indulges in moral license under the protection of social institutions, who allows himself to be guided by false evaluations, by sentiments of envy, rivalry, revenge, and dissension, is doing the work of the flesh just as much as he who is given to unrestrained lust and profligacy. To the Galatians led astray by Jerusalemitic legalism Paul had solemnly promised the salvation that springs from faith; and now to the faithful of Corinth, who in the name of human wisdom had succumbed to the strife of brother against brother, he proclaimed with the same solemnity that ethic of mystical communion, which knows only one name, one law, one thing that hallows: the body of Christ. Today, after twenty centuries, evangelical revelation admonishes the world to remember the living existence of the mystical Christ and to take the harmony of his sacred body as a model of brotherly communion in him.

There is, then, a carnal body, which is in a sense doubly carnal, which is, as it were, the legal epitome and the millennial extract of all the instincts, all the basest desires of mankind. (The laws are only measures of man's ethical frailty, insatiable accomplices of sin and death.) But since the death and resurrection of the Lord, there has been a spirit-body—it is Paul's unique power that he does not shrink back before this contradiction—which is the triumphant Christ, the spirit and freedom ("The Lord is the Spirit, and wheresoever the spirit of the Lord is, there is liberty"). In him are united, and in him are solemnized all the values of human resurrection, of man's ascent to the ideal world of peace, justice, kindness, and love.

Paul never asks whether this spirit-body, this "body of the Lord," the Church, is visible or invisible. By the mere formulation of such a question, the Christian denominations show that they have all forsaken and betrayed the Pauline ecclesiology. The Lord's body, the organism which Christ continuously builds merely by gathering the novices around him, is for St. Paul a sublime, concrete, and living reality, composed of visible things (the limbs, which are the faithful) and of invisible things (the blood that flows through the limbs). Paul sees it with his eyes, for he knows all the brethren; he feels it with fear and trembling, for each day these brethren are in danger of relapsing beneath the weight of inner temptation and outward blows of fate into the body of the flesh—that body which consists in human practices, social distinctions, doctrinaire constructions. Half in anger and half in impatience, Paul would have laughed in the face of anyone who asked him whether his church was visible or invisible. For who can separate a living organism from the lymph and blood which animate it? And to remove from muscles and tissues the blood that pulses through them—is it not to doom both tissue and blood to decay? That is why for four centuries the organism of the Church has been decaying in our midst: the Curia thought it could induce a hypertrophic development of the muscles and so paralyzed the invisible heart; the Reformers thought they could restore the charismata by cutting through the visible veins, and so drained the flesh of its blood.

Paul had other worries beside the visibility of the Lord's spirit-body, which was, after all, the only thing that his eyes saw in the world. His worries began on the day when the Galatian converts succumbed to the flesh by their submission to the Mosaic laws, this bitterest offense to the life-giving power of Christ. And his torment renewed and was augmented by the unregenerate novices of Corinth who, having been drawn from the dregs of the population and miraculously implanted in the sacred body of the Lord, now sullied the sacred flesh with incest, rent it with rivalry, profaned it with social distinctions, and parched it with lack of love.

The need to admonish them brought about a total change in the principles of Paul's ecclesiology. What was the nature of this change? Paul's ecclesiology is compelling and normative; but it is non-curial, non-liturgical, non-legislative. Barely twenty years later, Rome would destroy the temple of Jerusalem and deprive Israel of its cult site forever. What matter? Paul, an Israelite, had already proclaimed to the children of faith: "Ye are the temple of God and the spirit of God hath made his dwelling among you." Easter would no longer be a festival of all the children of Abraham, to celebrate in the holy city the memory of Yahweh's passing over, warning the people of vengeance and devastation. What matter? Paul, an Israelite, had proclaimed that the Paschal lamb, foreshadowed and symbolized by the age-old sacrificial rite, had been sacrificed for all time and that henceforth it would be the glad mission of the redeemed to solemnize the sacrifice unremittingly with the unleavened bread of transparent truth (unleavened, because leavening with sour dough was looked upon as unclean). Paul, an Israelite, had proclaimed that the old epic tales of Israel, and particularly the glorious flight from Egypt and the dramatic sojourn in the desert, were nothing other than allegorical prefigurations of that sublime reality which is Christ's work of redemption: departure from the empirical and conventional, ministration of the true thirst-slaking water in baptism, the eating of the miraculous manna in the enduring wonder of spiritual communion. For countless centuries men had striven to realize a balance between their awe of the cosmic mystery and the fearful seduction that emanates from the mystery which is in each one of our brothers—or, in other words, between religion and morality. And now Paul had discovered the "prophetic" religion which dissolved all the old mythical constructions in symbol and allegory, and translated the ineffable vibration of the "numinous" into tangible forms, which subordinated every desire for magical power over the elemental forces of nature to a common striving for magical mastery of the relations between brothers.

Paul made religion into an enduring brotherly liturgy and magic into a body of effective charismata. Many others, before and after him, have represented collective life as an expression of mutual aid among the diverse members of a united organism. But this—an instinctive comparison, we might call it—embodied a stupendous vision of sacramental significance and scope. The body of Christ, forever forming but never formed, was the spirit-body of one who conquered death, who by annulling sin gained the power to pledge a beatific resurrection.

This immanent and predominantly mystical-corporate meaning is a constant note in the preaching of St. Paul, and lends a unique character to the rites which he adopted and established in his congregations: baptism and the brotherly supper. Paul felt truly and above all that to be immersed in the water and to issue from it cleansed of all taint and all traditional convention was an actual entrance into the mystical body of the Lord and the spiritual reality of the resurrected Christ. The baptismal bath washed away all the old uncertain rites and at one stroke translated them into that realm of transcendent values which had been prefigured in God's promise to Abraham, and which the seed of Abraham, to which this promise had referred, namely Christ, had introduced into collective life; and this miraculous event was not a delusion or a dream. This was the great new Creation brought about by the coming of Christ. So that those who in Corinth doubted the possibility of a resurrection of the flesh and therefore exchanged the Christian message— that is, the announcement of an imminent, visible kingdom, for an intangible, speculative counterfeit—were lamentably belittling the mighty reality of resurrection through baptism. For baptism is the annunciation of a spiritual body which will be fully manifested in the kingdom to come. Anyone who denies this has lost his feeling for the enduring wonder whose epic unfolding is the cosmos:

> Thou fool! that which thou sowest is not quickened, except it die: and that which sowest, thou sowest not that body that shall be, but bare grain, it may chance of wheat, or of some other grain: But God giveth it a body as it hath pleased him, and to every seed his own body. All flesh is not the same flesh: but there is one kind of flesh of men, another flesh of beasts, another of fishes, and another of birds. There are also celestial bodies, and bodies terrestrial: but the glory of the celestial is one, and the glory of the terrestrial is another. There is one glory of the sun, and another glory of the moon, and another glory of the stars: for one star differeth from another star in glory. So also is the resurrection

of the dead. It is sown in corruption; it is raised in incorruption. It is sown in dishonour; it is raised in glory: it is sown in weakness; it is raised in power. It is sown a natural body; it is raised a spiritual body (I Cor. 15:36–44).

It is twice sown: in the symbolic death of baptism and in the physical death of the grave. And it is twice reborn: in the mystery of consecration through baptism and in the sacred reality of the kingdom of God. And just as no one can doubt the reality of his own bodily constitution and the concreteness of his own living limbs, so no one can doubt the reality of the spiritual body which is constituted by man's embodiment in Christ, who triumphed over death, or of its immortal destiny in the kingdom.

But the sublime power of water in cleansing the ephemeral man on his road to eternity was celebrated by Paul in a way that was still more profound and significant. Baptism is not the only rite by which man has sublimated an empirical (in this case hygienic) function; since the beginnings of history, the banquet has held a solemn, one might say numinous, significance in the eyes of the participants. An unbroken line runs from the primitive rite of atonement through the funeral supper solemnizing the bond between the survivors and the departed who are present in our hearts and in our hopes.

At the Last Supper, on the eve of his tragic temporal death and l•is joyous return to the "kingdom," Christ had announced that he would sup again with his beloved apostles on the day of resurrection, which would usher in the Messianic age. Paul gave to the feast commemorating this last supper which is forever renewed the character of a promise and a fervent entreaty; he made it into a collective prefiguration of the *parousia* (the promised coming of the Lord). But for Paul there is no sacrament which can be divorced from its pragmatic and normative importance for the moral order of the congregation. In each one of his epistles he enjoins the faithful to partake of the mystical body by celebrating the Eucharistic supper in a spirit of peace, harmony, love, understanding, and mutual helpfulness. St. Augustine would one day interpret this to mean: "You eat what you yourselves are: the body of the Lord."

Love! The anonymous and secular yearning of human society

154

for a universal bond to appease the earth, which had been tainted with brother's blood ever since the first day of human society, was now fulfilled. From the vulgar speech of the lowest classes, Paul took the word which was to express the instinctive solidarity of the humble, the disinherited and abused, who hold out a hand to one another in their common misfortune; and he made this word into a sign of recognition for those who were embodied in Christ: *agape,* love! It is not sensual passion; it is not uncertain friendship; it is not the illusory bond of common blood or geographic proximity. It is not the coercive outward discipline of a material organization that is almost always synonymous with oppression and violence. It is the blood that flows in the veins of Christ's body. It is the new blood, which now, flowing in harmony, will redeem and atone for the shedding of brother's blood, by which men's life together has been tainted ever since Cain built the first city. It is a name, a symbol, a program.

The circumstances and the situation which provided the point of departure for Paul's doctrine of charisma and love had in them something grotesque and awkward which did not escape the apostle of Tarsus, that mighty explorer of souls. And for this reason he seasoned his utterances with the slightest trace of irony, which is not the least argument for the authenticity of this Pauline hymn to love. Here, too, Paul is entirely a disciple of Christ.

Strange men they were indeed, these converts of Corinth! The overwhelming majority of them were recruited among the lowest strata of the population. They included neither great spiritual heroes nor political leaders nor aristocrats of exalted birth. Paul told them this to their faces, without softening or embellishment— though of course, as he added at once, this was the most glittering proof that it was God and not any man who had been at work among them.

Forgetful of their humble origin, unconsciously offended at their deficiency in human honors and privileges, the converts of Corinth had hit upon the most unexpected means of satisfying their human thirst for distinction and privilege. Their vanity cloaked itself in the wisdom of Apollos (so far, so good) and in the gifts of the spirit (from here on, it is more serious), for their aim was to make the Lord, "who is the spirit," an accomplice who would justify the most carnal depravity into which a congregation can fall: the depravity of petty jealousies and rivalries.

They shared their faults with the environment from which they sprang—there is no one who has mounted the social ladder too quickly who does not occasionally betray the crudity of his vulgar origins. In their correspondence with Paul, they had committed two breaches of tact, one more incautious and disrespectful than the other: they had asked him to send back to them Apollos, his rival, and they had asked him to draw up a hierarchical scale of the charismata (the spiritual gifts which each of them claimed to possess).

As for Apollos, this was a very delicate point, and it was not without embarrassment that Paul drew himself out of the dilemma. He called to mind the various members of the Corinthian congregation of which he was the organizer and father; he considered how each one of them put forward his own charisma, somewhat in the manner of a charlatan praising his wares. There was first of all Apollos, or his supporters, shamelessly exalting themselves as masters of intuitive and discursive knowledge. There was the wealthy freeman, perhaps the same who brought his own rich fare to the Lord's supper and devoured it before the hungry people of the congregation arrived, who boasted of the alms which he distributed amid drums and trumpets. There were the Christian women and young girls who prided themselves on their gifts of healing and prophecy. There were the poor harbor porters who boasted of speaking in tongues, while others stood by and presumptuously interpreted their babblings. A heathen coming among them on such an occasion would no doubt have thought them drunk.

In realistic terms bordering on the trivial—the childish buffoonery of the Corinthians deserved such treatment—Paul castigated their presumption. He reminded the congregation that the charismata are all members of one body, the body of Christ, and that there can be no hierarchy among members of the same body: this would be distortion.

And, as in the human body, the weakest and least distinguished members require the greatest care, so should these foolish, overweening Corinthians bear in mind that in the hierarchy ordered by Christ, the greatest honour and most loving devotion must be given to the charismata which are seemingly the lowest: "And base things of the world, and things which are despised, hath God chosen" (I Cor. 1:28).

Then Paul pauses and asks ironically: "If you would know which are the best charismata, I will show you the true way" (paraphrase of I Cor. 12:31). At these last words his voice must have vibrated with a special intensity. Tertius, his scribe, must have looked up with emotion from his papyrus scroll and gazed at the shining eyes of the apostle. But quickly, with trembling heart, he lowered them, to capture the inspired words. Since the day when Cleanthus sang his wonderful hymn to Zeus, the Greek language, the noblest and supplest of all human tongues, had not given expression to such profound emotion. Paul said:

> Though I speak with the tongues of men and of angels, and have not charity, I am become as sounding brass, or a tinkling cymbal. And though I have the gift of prophecy and understand all mysteries, and all knowledge; and though I have all faith, so that I could remove mountains, and have not charity, I am nothing (I Cor. 13:1–2).

With this wonderful hymn to communion of spirit—which Paul regarded as the highest charisma, the most sublime gift of the spirit, of that spirit which for him was the living Lord in a congregation of brothers—the apostle made his ecclesiology and his christology one. And it would always have been well for Christians to remember his salutary work whenever there was danger that Christianity, which in its innermost essence is a religion of conversion, might relapse into a religion of initiation.

Indeed, the mystical Christ and the spiritual church issued from the vast hope of the convert of Tarsus. The mystical Christ, which is the true body of Christian believers, is his miraculous doctrine.

Here begins the tragic drama of Christian history. Like a mother whose vitals are torn at the mere suggestion that her child be taken from her, Paul in the midst of the world's treachery and persecutions cried out:

> Who shall separate us from the love of Christ? shall tribulation, or distress, or persecution, or famine, or nakedness, or

157

peril, or sword? As it is written, For thy sake we are killed all the day long; we are accounted as sheep for the slaughter. Nay, in all these things we are more than conquerors through him that loved us. For I am persuaded, that neither death, nor life, nor angels, nor principalities, nor powers, nor things present, nor things to come, nor height, nor depth, not any other creature, shall be able to separate us from the love of God which is in Christ Jesus our Lord (Rom. 8:35–39) .

But Paul had failed to consider the one enemy more ruthless than persecution, more cutting than the sword, colder than nakedness: the sodden inertia of men. For men speak of courage when they risk their lives lurking in wait for a prey which they will seize and tear to pieces, but such courage is proper to the beasts of wood and desert. Men do not love the one form of courage amid neverending danger that deserves the name of human: the courage of him who instinctively, without consideration of greed or desire, exposes his life to the whirlwind of daily renunciation and wholehearted devotion. Such men hang between heaven and earth, between spirit and flesh, between the age to come and the present age. They make their lives a lasting death; it is they who are privileged to find in death the eternal continuation of life.

By creating the mystical Christ from his own blood, Paul provided a meeting place for all those souls who espoused and desired to realize by their actions the essential evangelical doctrine that to gain and preserve life we must destroy it. ("For whosoever will save his life shall lose it, and whosoever will lose his life for my sake shall find it." Matt. 16:25.) He translated the Lord's commandment into an eternal mystical and normative reality. He made life into a supple, dynamic equilibrium of transformed values.

And human inertia, which loves rigid equilibria and secure dikes —the dikes of dogma, hierarchy, discipline, legislation—flung itself upon St. Paul, to tear his creation away from him—or him away from his creation.

This unequal, dramatic struggle has been going on for nineteen centuries. And still no end is in sight. Indeed, we can say that it begins anew in every century, that each age has its new campaigns and new tactical positions. Paul has defended his Christ with the impalpable armament of his epistles and with the passionate tones of his ever-present apology. But human inertia has innumerable weapons; it fought successively with Inquisitorial proofs and with dialectical blandishments. The mystical Christ, the spiritual body of the believers in the Lord, is the eternal core of Christian tradition. Without him, i.e. if we make Christ *flesh* and not a mystical *body* as in St. Paul, Christianity—paradoxical as it may seem— becomes an ill-concealed form of paganism or Pharisaic legalism, that is, it becomes a religion of initiation, a religion operating with rites into which one can be initiated once and for all.

Both Pharisaic legalism and paganism (religion of initiation) have striven for two thousand years to separate Christ from Paul and Paul from Christ, for both felt intuitively that they could only in this way regain their discredited power.

The battle was first joined by Pharisaic legalism. Paul had scarcely passed beyond the borders of Palestine; he had scarcely carried the evangelical message to Anatolia and left the new Galatian congregations to digest their new experience, than the first Jerusalemitic treachery raised its head. Incapable of understanding the sublime doctrine of Christ and translating it into the act which revolutionizes spiritual life, transforming it into a venture beyond all laws and canonized customs; incapable of understanding the teachings which Paul had translated into the mystery of dynamic renewal in the spirit of Christ (and that spirit is his mystical body), the Judaizing Christians of the mother city began, under the aegis of Moses, to reconstruct in their own way the mystical Christ whom Paul had borne and nurtured from out of his innermost faith.

Victorious in this first encounter—can new wine ever be poured into old bottles?—Paul was immediately faced with the assault of an individualistic speculation of slightly pagan cast. For what else did Apollos, the master of Alexandrian-Platonic allegorism, seek in Corinth except to make the rebirth of Christ into a mystery of speculative initiation, a nebulous revelation of a transcendent truth, a privileged communication of esoteric wisdom. But the apostle's mystical Christ was not the bloodless, painstaking creation of an intellectualistic creator. He was the higher organism of those who believed in him; he was the living body of the transfigured; he was the essence of the redeemed, who had become one in hope and in love.

Like a desperate mother who sees the fruit of her womb endangered, Paul hastened back to defend the pure, unadulterable integrity of his message. This battle was harder than the one which preceded it. For what gives greater promise of success? To advocate freedom in grace in opposition to the weary guardians of a crumbling legal order, or to champion the spiritual character of a message of salvation implanted in a loose-knit populace in opposition to the coryphees of speculative philosophy?

Paul did not retreat one hair's breadth in this new, unpopular struggle. Consistent to the extreme, courageous to the point of folly, he made this apparent folly into a bulwark surrounding the *body* of his Christ, to defend it against degradation to the *flesh* of an earthly wisdom. For "wisdom," too, is flesh, unless it can transform itself into molecules and organs in the mystical body of the Lord. After a bitter struggle Paul overcame Apollos; and the congregation of Corinth, for a short time led astray by the spell of Greek dialectics, returned to the true tradition of its founder. Up to the time of his death, Paul's epistles resound with his urgent, entreating polemic against the law and against speculative philosophy.

On the day when the apostle offered up his head to the emperor's sword in the street of a Roman suburb, he could rejoice in having remained true to his oath that nothing would separate him from the love of Christ. For him, a citizen of the kingdom, death was truly a gain. He may have felt in his heart that having defeated Cephas and Apollos, he had assured the triumphant, irresistible growth of his mystical Christ up to the day when God would institute the new heavens and the new earth.

In this he was mistaken. Cephas and Apollos, casuistic moralism and theological sophistication, had by no means been defeated for good; they lurked in ambush. And their intrinsic nature enabled them to profit by Paul's execution to rob him, who now had no other weapon than the voice of his fragmentary epistles, of the mystical Christ which he had made into the ideal gathering place for all those who live in the world with a loving vision of divine justice and peace in the kingdom.

And because God is not a truth that can be measured in terms of time, but an ethical truth—that is to say, the pledge and justice in eternity—because he proclaimed that the kingdom was at hand in order that all life should burn and consume itself in impatience and expectancy, regardless of whether the fact and the visible event were accomplished within the scope of man's limited human vision, and because for this reason the coming of the kingdom remains and will remain an eternal mystery, Cephas and Apollos had no difficulty in renewing and intensifying their fanatical attacks. And these attacks were not without success.

By two related means Cephas and Apollos proceeded to confiscate Paul's wonderful discovery. The laws which are valid for the flesh, visible discipline, i.e. the hierarchical bureaucracy, immediately resumed the work of the Judaizing emissaries from Jerusalem. They aimed at investiture with salvation through Christ, and to this end adopted Mosaic practices. Paul had situated the secret of rebirth in a flexible spiritual edifice, whose bricks were the believers and whose mortar was the Lord's gifts, the charismata. His was a conception full of dynamic power, animated by a spirituality which resists all taint of codification, which rebels against any rational schematization or ritualistic atonement—Paul had freed Christ from the fetters of conceptuality, to make him an everlasting mystical being, the fruit of *metanoia* (inner conversion) and rebirth. To become part of Christ, to become the members and molecules of his organism, was to join a host which is in readiness day and night to fulfill a mission of painful renunciation and arduous conquest. Was it not more comfortable to turn Christ back to flesh within a system of hierarchical institutions, to cast him into the chains of visible discipline? What a gain that would be for the instinctive inertia of man, who likes to rest easy on the couch of official customs and to entrust the magical work of his salvation to others. Every progress in the regime of the Curia diminishes the freedom and hence responsibility of those who believe in the spirit of their totality, which is the Lord. And this is a day-to-day historical process.

For centuries Cephas despised the collaboration of Apollos—of heathen, so-called philosophical culture; as long as he was zealously engaged in robbing Paul of his mystical Christ and reducing the Christ of the gospels and of history to the flat plane of hierarchical disciplines and organized, casuistical ecclesiasticism, Cephas distrusted Apollos. The gray, unformed, inert masses strive instinctively toward bureaucratic systematization. The hierarchy exploited man's yearning for effortless atonement through visible discipline, and so transformed the ecclesiastical community, which Paul had conceived as an organism based on a purely charismatic bond, into a visible militia, tamed and controlled by the sanctions of a temporal regime. The hierarchy believed it could accomplish this without the support of abstract speculation, which for its part attempted to reverse those suprarational values on which the apostle had built his edifice of communion in love, and transform them into artificial abstractions. In normal times a bureaucrat can do without culture. It was not until later that Cephas went in search of Apollos. For centuries speculation was synonymous with heresy—as Origen bears witness.

But with the disintegration of the feudal Middle Ages, which had fashioned the ecclesiastical bureaucracy from the raw material supplied by barbarian invaders and the wreckage of the Roman Empire, the monastic traditions produced a new generation of the sons of Abraham, of men saved by faith—of dreamers who followed in the footsteps of Paul and dreamed of the freedom of the spirit. Now Cephas needed Apollos. And Aristotle provided the Curia with weapons. Paul was robbed irrevocably of his mystical Christ. The Church ceased definitively to be the consciousness of the common bond of charismata and hope and congealed into a theological formalism guarded by the Inquisition; it became a bureaucratic hierarchy striving avidly for that ephemeral, material power which Christ and Paul had cursed as an expression of the Evil One, the sovereign of their age. And the reaction came, spewing rage and devastation. Through it the family of European Christendom was divided and impoverished. This reaction should have been a re-creation of the Pauline mystical Christ. It should, as the mystics of the first Italian Reformation, Waldo, Joachim, and St. Francis dreamed, have re-created the invisible organism of values, in the name of the Lord, who is spirit and freedom. And instead, it was a violent break, not with Paul's mystical Christ but with the Paul of the mystical Christ; it failed to understand Paul or see him through the whole of his rich and varied experience.

It was Paul's belief that, despite their worthless social and religious institutions, all men could be redeemed through embodiment in a mystical reality which, though non-hierarchical and extralegal, was absolutely concrete; and in the hands of the Reformers, with their hatred of the Curia, this belief became an assurance of personal justification, which made the mystical Christ into a chaos of atoms scattered in the void. They worshiped Christ and his wonderful saving power that was victorious over death and sin; but they no longer saw him, as Paul had seen him, in the act of building his new body, of taking into himself those who believed in his kingdom. They saw him instead in the act of giving immediately and personally, to each sinner who professed his own incurable inclination to sin and his own functional need of forgiveness, the cloak of an external and false justification.

They thought they had found in Paul the Christ of their own justification. But instead they had created a Christ who is a pledge of redemption and thus in no way distinguished from the mythological figures of the old mystery religions of initiation; in so doing they departed entirely from Paul's conception of a Christ built upon the mystical union of the faithful—the apostle's unalterable accomplishment.

Thus, once again Paul was separated from Christ, in the very moment when men believed that he had been called forth from oblivion and given back to his Lord. The Pauline odyssey continued its dramatic, sorrowful progress.

The Reformers were not entirely to blame for this renewed martyrdom, bitterer than that which the apostle had suffered at the hands of Rome. Their one-sided, paradoxical reaction was understandable and, up to a certain point, justified. The tradition of the Roman Curia had thrown Christ into the fetters of a resurrected Pharisaic legalism, and abstract speculation had reduced the mystery of inner redemption to the puns of scholastic discussion. It had become necessary to revive man's consciousness of unconquerable sin and his confidence in his immediate reinstatement in the justice of the Savior. But in their unchecked fury at the visible administration of invisible zealots, in their angry revolt against the hierarchy of the Curia, with its venality and unrestrained lust for power, the Reformers surpassed the limits which they should have observed if they really intended to restore St. Paul's living, mystical Christ. The fundamental Christian vision of a world immersed in evil and redeemed on the cross had been watered down and distorted by the diligent labors of scholastic metaphysicians; canonical discipline had reduced the ineffable mystery of inner rebirth to something empirical, carnal, materialistic; in answer to all this, the Reformers once again demanded of Paul a schematic statement regarding our death in Adam and justification in Christ. But in their desperate revulsion against any tangible control of man's inner purification, they failed to perceive that according to St. Paul the justification which is acquired through Christ's redeeming act on the cross is accomplished in the survival of Christ's body, spirit, and life in space and time. Christ twice made himself our mediator before God: when he suffered in the flesh and when he was resurrected in the spirit. The mystical body of Christ is in space and time the vehicle of our reborn nature and its bond with the Father.

And now that the Reformers had created an arbitrary split among the harmonious and complementary elements which made up the Pauline doctrine, the strangest and most astonishing situation in all Christian history occurred. For Paul had fought passionately to separate salvation in the resurrected Christ from any legalistic administration; but he did not make salvation an individual mystery of initiation or a miracle of personal justification. Christ Savior was for him not a mythical person shrouded in the mists of a sacrifice and resurrection outside of space and time. In Paul's eyes the specific historicity of his manifestation in the world was not necessary or fundamental. As we have said, he attached no importance to any perceptible physical encounter with Christ. The complete reality of Christ which was important to Paul was not the reality of his manifestation in the flesh. It was the reality of his corporeal survival in the spirit, in the faithful who are his members and partake of him. So that the Christian ethic, which Paul boldly and resolutely had freed from every codified norm, from the letter of the law, from the arrogant and overweening evaluations of casuistic justice, was firmly and imperatively reconstituted in the sanctions and prohibitions of men's common conscience rejoined in Christ. The mystical Christ, the body of those who believed in him, was the supreme arbiter, the absolute guarantor of good and evil, of life and death, of righteousness and guilt. From Christ's maxim—"whosoever will lose his life for my sake shall find it"—he made a miraculous normative discipline, free from visible discipline and visible norms, and precisely for that reason infinitely rich in disciplinary power.

By re-creating Christ in the matrix of his own faith and his own mission, he made of him a product of his own soul and of the new congregations. Thus the names of Christ and Paul became inseparable in the religious experience of those congregations which had sprung from his apostolate. The "kingdom" and the "church" were fused into one. If this had not been so, the religion of Christ, distorted and imprisoned in visible institutions, would have become an amoral faith and an individualistic initiation. In order to regain this flexible balance, which had been impaired by the legalism of the Curia, the Reformers pursued the vision of an individualistic (extrasocial) doctrine of "justification by faith." They saw only the Christ who had redeemed the world from the unbearable burden of original sin. And they obscured the corporative element which Paul had made the indispensable instrument of our elevation in the spirit.

This disturbance of the subtle harmony of antithetical coefficients which Paul had united in the miraculous and delicate balance of his apostolic faith was catastrophic. Eccentric and paradoxical as it may seem, it remains nonetheless true that, in the field of collective morality, the repercussions and consequences of the justification by faith proclaimed by the Reformers were identical with those following from the Jesuitical abuse of indulgences and justification by good works. The bitter consequences of this undermining of the sublime and delicate foundations upon which Paul built his edifice of common evangelical experience are felt to this day.

The domination of the Curia and of theological speculation had robbed Paul of his mystical Christ, whom it reduced to a carnal being, subordinated to laws and codices and to the oratorical sophistry of that day. The Reformers wished to reconquer Christ, the pledge of justification by faith, but they did not see him as embodied in Paul and his converts.

First the twofold wiles of Cephas and Apollos, then the fleshless and boneless "personalistic" perversion of the doctrine of justification, led lay exegetes to conclude that there was no bond between Christ and Paul, but that Paul's message was a fundamental dis-

tortion of Christ's gospel. This error was fraught with dire consequence. The deeply ingrained cynical insensibility of the men of
those days to those collective moral values, the definition of which
constitutes the true and miraculous originality of the first Christianity, led to two divergent positions among the radical critics of
our own time: the one denies the historical reality of Jesus, the
other makes the message of Christ and the message of Paul two
conflicting and incompatible sources of Christian tradition.

Perhaps the first, despite all appearance, is easier to discuss and
to confute than the second. For the historical manifestation of
Christ can be demonstrated and discussed by historical exegesis and
pure historical research. But an understanding of the complex
process by which the experience of Christ was embodied in the
experience of St. Paul cannot result from any critical induction or
mere comparison of texts. It must rather result from a painful and
arduous immersion in those living antitheses, which, it would seem,
must be boldly explored by a religious vocation which desires, in
defiance of the world, to enact the stormy drama of its profoundest,
predestined dialectic.

For nineteen centuries St. Paul has lain in his tomb at the
Ostian Gate of Rome. He has seen millions of pilgrims and travel-
ers pass by on their way to his basilica. Cephas has not ceased to
invoke him from his chair. He has connected Paul's name with his
own. But there are homages which conceal treachery, and there are
conciliations whose purpose it is to conceal incurable and radical
conflicts from the people.

It would seem as though Cephas had never forgotten his defeat
at the first synod in Jerusalem or his humiliation at Antioch; and
among the pilgrims of Cephas there are no doubt many—we do not
know how many—who in accordance with the creed are prepared
to repeat in their heart of hearts Paul's irresistible castigations of
the law, which is the flesh.

And yet there, on the Ostian Way, Paul has heard the footsteps
of his great supporters. He must have trembled on the day when a
master of rhetoric from Africa strode past him on his way to Rome.
But when Augustine came to Rome, he had not yet discovered
St. Paul. Neither on his way to nor from Rome does he seem to
have felt the need of praying at the apostle's tomb for a special

revelation. Paul once called his doctrine food for children. But one must have white hair and a disillusioned soul in order to bite into his heavy bread and make it part of oneself. Many centuries later, there came from distant Sila the monk who had made his watchword St. Paul's prophetic saying: "Now the Lord is that spirit and where the spirit of the Lord is, there is liberty" (II Cor. 3:17). This was Joachim of Floris.

And three centuries later, there came to visit the shrine of St. Paul that German monk who was to stir up the greatest storm that ever rose in Christendom. But then Cephas was riding more arrogant than ever along his highroad of secular-pagan pomp; he had harnessed Paul firmly to his chariot. So great was the monk's indignation over Cephas that the revolt he unleashed in the name of Paul tore those invisible chains with which Paul had bound together the living cells of Christ's organism.

Today a Babylonian confusion and fragmentation prevails. And yet the new hour of Paul is approaching. For when the desperate violence of the world will have made every man a Cain, the words of St. Paul will resound once more—those words which alone are sacred and eternal: peace, love, mercy, justice—in the spirit which is the Lord.

Ernesto Buonaiuti

Symbols and Rites in the Religious Life of
Certain Monastic Orders*

1. The Symbols

The *Medea,* one of Euripides' most powerful tragedies, dealing with
the conflict between the roles of mother and wife in a woman's soul,
contains a brief and cruel scene of leave-taking: Jason, intoxicated
with the prospect of a new, royal marriage and unaware of the
lengths to which a woman spurned in love will go, takes leave of
the "barbarian" Medea, whom he has condemned to return home:
"I don't propose to go into this any further. But if you'd like to
take along some of my money into exile, for your own need and
that of the children, please say so. I am prepared to be generous on
this point, and even to give you [symbols for]¹ friends of mine
abroad who will treat you well. It would be madness for you to
refuse this offer." But Medea is not afraid of appearing mad.
Jealousy and rancor do not operate with the syllogisms of reason:
"I will never accept favors from friends of yours; and I'll accept
nothing from you, so please don't offer it. Gifts from a coward
bring luck to no one."

A great poet and a true precursor of the Greek tragic poets, the
Yahwist author of Genesis, begins the history of human civilization
with two dramatic scenes of leave-taking. His mythical narrative
forms the foundation of the theological tradition of Christianity.
At the gates of the lost paradise, God (a Jason who is not guilty
but offended) gives to man (a Medea who is not betrayed but sinful) "symbols," in order that his wanderings through the world

---

* [Two lectures from the year following have been added, pp. 187 ff.—Ed.]

1 [The English translation is by Frederic Prokosch in *Greek Plays in Modern
Translation,* ed. Dudley Fitts (New York, 1947), p. 216. I have substituted the
words "symbols for" for "letters to" to stress Buonaiuti's point.—Tr.]

168

under the constant curse of labor and suffering may not lead him to destruction; He gives him "symbols" to exchange with his companions in wandering and suffering. And when, his hands bathed in his brother's blood, Cain, the murderer of the *wandering* shepherd, who lived in confidence and expectation, girds himself to build a city as a bulwark between his soul and God, to gain a respite in his fearful flight, God imprints upon him too the "symbolic" marks whereby to save his life.

Mankind is a vast army of wanderers in time and space who, when their paths cross, exchange the perfectly corresponding (συμβάλλω) fragments of their common heritage. They recognize one another by showing fragments of bone (ἀστράγαλος) which they have exchanged at the last meeting and which fit together exactly. Thus it is given to men to preserve the relations of mutual hospitality and brotherhood, in the certainty that in the end they all will find one another in God's eternal peace.

Every instrument of mutual communication devised by man is a symbol. Language is symbolic; it is a composition of specific sounds, modulated by man's instinct of community for the communication of desires and states of feeling. Symbolic are the forms of art, designed to evoke corresponding emotions by representation and intelligible transformation of objects characteristic for their beauty or their magical meaning. Symbolic are the formulas of science, which aim at surprising the rhythm and forces of nature and expressing them in numbers. And religion above all is enmeshed in symbols, which are its means of introducing men into the world of transcendent reality, whose guardian, and in a sense whose life, it is on earth.

All this raises a question and presupposes certain postulates. The question is: What is the order of rank between the different forms of symbolic expression which men use to recognize one another as friends and brothers?

Beyond a doubt the first symbols which men exchanged were religious symbols—that is to say, corresponding fragments of a common experience of terror and pain, desire and dream, symbols which could even dispense with spoken words and perceptible gestures. Does the eye not speak before the lips; do not the tremors of love and horror possess a vocabulary of their own, independent of any audible utterance? Later, other symbols came into being, and sometimes they sought to repress the first kind. In vain! The symbols of art and speculation remain symbols—that is, they serve for fraternal understanding among men—only in so far as they adhere strictly to their function as auxiliaries to religious symbolism. And, on the other hand, religious symbolism can exert its comprehensive and distributing function only if the auxiliary symbolic media are jealously subordinated and the religious symbol's birthright and purity is respected at all times.

The creations of the spirit as a whole, from religion to language, work then through symbolic instruments toward mutual recognition and mutual aid among men. But this presupposes that the world of sensory experience conceals a profounder and wider world, to which mere empiricism cannot attain; and it presupposes the possibility of error in the way of the world. For this reason, we must be vigilant and hold firmly to the symbols which will come to our help in the moment of need and make salutary recognitions possible. And to this end we must observe a dualistic view of the cosmos, differentiating between the sensuous world and the realm of the supersensory, of God.

This gift we have of coming into contact with transcendent realities through an inner harmony and kinship (of which language, art, and science are merely the symbols and in a sense the seeds) is the generative force of religious life. The dissemination of this force proceeds according to a logic of its own, which is eminently exemplified by the development of symbols in Christian society.

The symbolism of Christ is to be found in his parables, which reveal a perfect correspondence between the life of cosmic realities (heaven, stars, earth, plants) and the duties of life in the spirit. Christ accepts purification in water by the Baptist, he recommends anointing with oil for the vigilant expectation of the bridegroom, and with bread and wine he symbolizes his own mystic survival in the community of the faithful. For the water which purifies physically is only the symbolic *fragment* of a continuous purification which the Father effects in the soul. Oil is produced by the penetration of the olive roots into the rock and by the merciless pruning of the tree's branches, just as the joy and triumph of the Christian are born of the testimony known as martyrdom, of man's own mutilation of his selfish lusts. Bread and wine represent the harvest and fermentation of the grain and the grapes that are spread without limit over the whole earth.

Water, oil, bread, and wine are the elements of the Christian sacraments; they are the symbols which have been created and maintained by the spiritual bond of the community appointed to proclaim the kingdom of God, that community which St. Paul called the living and true body of Christ, and which Tertullian designated as the true, the real, the eternal "militia" of God.

> The Christian can never be anything other than a Christian. For the Gospel is one and Christ is always the same, prepared to deny all who deny him and to profess all who profess him, and to recognize all those who recognize God. He has promised to save every soul sacrificed for him and, conversely, to doom every soul which saves itself by denying his name. For before Jesus the believing civilian is a soldier, while the soldier who heeds only his uniform is a mere civilian.[2]

The entire doctrine and sacramental practice of the old Church are permeated by this profound feeling for the symbolic relationship between the reality of the charismatic mystery and the communal life of the brethren. "The word joins the element and thus the sacrament is created,"[3] wrote St. Augustine, and at the same time he reminded the faithful about to partake of the Eucharistic supper: "You receive what you are."[4]

But in a vulgarized Christian society, such as that of the post-Constantinian period, the consciousness of a mystical bond based on common participation in transcendent realities was in grave danger of being weakened and lost. Organized monasticism represented the instinctive will of the community born of the Gospel to save itself from this danger. And indeed, the most essential accom-

---

2 Tertullian, *De corona*, XI, 5 (Migne, *PL*, II, 93) : "Nusquam christianus aliud est. Unum evangelium, et idem Jesus, negaturus omnem negatorem, et confessurus omnem confessorem Dei, et salvam facturus animam pro nomine eius amissam, perditurus autem de contrario adversus nomen eius lucri habitam. Apud hunc tam miles est paganus fidelis, quam paganus est miles fidelis."

3 Augustine, *Tract. LXXX in Joannem* (Migne, *PL*, XXXV, 1840) : "Accedit verbum ad elementum et fit sacramentum."

4 "Vos accipitis quod estis."

plishment of the monks was to preserve and develop the symbolic
and sacramental forms of early Christianity, and to add new symbols of a kind that would help to mold a community living from
alms in the bosom of the Church.

The most perfect symbolic rites of medieval Christianity passed
through the artistic and ritual stylization of the monasteries. What
pedagogic force emanated from the Easter *Exultet* sung from the
pulpit of the Benedictine abbeys in the Middle Ages! And if our
present-day liturgy perpetuates the old Christian symbols, this is in
large part due to the anonymous labors of monasticism over a
period of many centuries. In the Maundy Thursday Mass, the
celebrant sings in praise of the symbolic oil:

> Eternal God, in the beginning, with other gifts of thy good-
> ness, thou badest the earth to bring forth fruit-bearing trees,
> among them the olive tree, bestower of this rich liquor, that
> its fruits might serve for this holy charisma. For when
> David in the spirit of prophecy foresaw the sacraments of
> thy grace, he also proclaimed that our countenance would
> be brightened by oil. And when the waters of the flood
> atoned for the sins of the world, the dove represented an
> image of future gifts, announcing the return of peace to the
> earth by an olive branch. And in more recent times, these
> promises have been fulfilled by manifest works, for the
> waters of baptism wipe out all offenses and anointing with
> this oil makes our faces joyful and serene.[5]

But to the sacramental symbols of the early Church the monks
added others, in order to distinguish more sharply and publicly
the army which carries on the renunciation of the world embodied
in Christian μετάνοια. First of all, they adopted the black cuculla,
the περιβόλαιον of Eustasius of Sebaste, the old pallium of the
philosophers.

This black garment was not unknown to the mystery religions.

---

5 "Aeterne Deus, qui in principio, inter cetera bonitatis tuae munera, terram
producere fructifera ligna jussisti, inter quae huius pinguissimi liquoris
ministrae olivae nascerentur, quarum fructus scaro charismati deserviret. Nam
et David prophetico spiritu gratiae tuae sacramenta praenoscens, vultus nostros
in oleo exhilarandos esse cantavit. Et cum mundi crimina diluvio quondam
expiarentur effuso, similitudinem futuri muneris columba demonstrans per
olivae ramum, pacem terris redditam nuntiavit. Quod in novissimis temporibus
manifestis est effectibus declaratum, cum baptismatis aquis omnium criminum
commissa delentibus, haec olei unctio vultus nostros jucundos efficit ac
serenos."

Several inscriptions on tombs in the Serapeum at Delos—the religion of Serapis is a typical funeral cult—attest the existence of a collegium of black-clad men. And Pausanias tells us that up to the Roman conquest the young men of Corinth were shorn and clothed in black to atone for the murder of the children of Medea. The earliest manifestations of Egyptian monasticism did not commend the cuculla to the respect of the late representatives of Hellenistic culture. In his *Life of Hedesius,* Eunapius tells us that after burning down the Serapeum in Alexandria, the Christians lodged a number of monks in the ruins. He adds, "because in that period everything was permitted to those who donned a black garment and thus openly renounced all respectability."[6]

In Tertullian's day the wearing of the pallium as a sign of Christian faith had appeared eccentric, but now, though this uniform of the Christian "militia" might offend the survivors of "paganism," that is, the cultural bourgeoisie, it seemed perfectly reasonable to the majority of official Christians. And this may be taken as tacit admission of the general departure from the evangelical concept of μετάνοια. But the outward uniform did not suffice as a perceptible mark of the monastic calling. It was held needful to imprint a visible symbol upon the body itself. And since in certain pagan cults the hair of the head was sacrificed to appease an angry god, the tonsure became the outward sacrament of Christian monasticism. As to the form which this sacrifice of the hair should take, an agreement was not easily reached between Celtic monasticism, the heir presumptive of the Druidic organization, and the monks of the mainland. The Celtic monks permitted tufts of hair on the back of the head, but shaved the front of the head from ear to ear. The continental monks left a symbolic wreath, the wreath of the soldiers of Christ, for the day called *Donatorium,* and shaved their heads within it. This was not the only point of controversy between the two forms of monasticism.

The Benedictine form was destined to triumph. In the *Consuetudines monasticae,* that valuable supplement which the great abbeys, in exercising their autonomy, found it necessary to add to the terse but meaningful rule of St. Benedict, we find a number

---

6 "τυραννικὴν γὰρ εἶχεν ἐξουσίαν τότε πᾶς ἄνθρωπος μέλαιναν φορῶν ἐσθῆτα καὶ δημοσίᾳ βουλόμενος ἀσχημονεῖν."

of symbolic gestures and attitudes which disclose similarities to
the ancient traditions of the mystery cults.

The novice, for example, whom his parent dedicated to God
through the cloister, was expected to offer up the mass and come
forth with the seal of his consecration on his hands. Just as in a
mystery papyrus recently found and published by the *Società
filosofica Italiana*,[7] it is enjoined that two seals be scratched on the
hands of the novice with a sharp thorn.

The same *Consuetudines* as well as the memoirs of Benedict of
Aniane, the great monastic disciplinarian of the Carolingian period,
show us how every development of discipline, whether in ritual or
in communal life, must be inspired by a lively awareness of the
symbolic values attaching to every moment of monastic life. In
the architectural or liturgical development of the cloister there was
no detail that did not embody symbolic significance and educational purpose.

Yet precisely this infinite wealth of symbolism in monastic life
confronts its interpreters with a grave danger, the danger of suffo-
cating beneath a plethora of detail.

In the middle of the twelfth century Odo praised the cuculla as
the symbol of the fourth testament, the fourth concluded by God
with the human race.

> O miraculous mystery, O miraculous sacrament! The first
> testament which God gave to the hearts of men is called
> the *natural law;* if they had kept it, they would not have
> needed a second. But since men are lovers of novelty, he
> gave them a second testament because of the neglect into
> which the first had fallen; this was *circumcision,* which some
> readily accepted because of its novelty. But when this in
> turn became obsolete and was neglected, he gave a third
> in *baptism,* which was predestined to endure for all eternity.
> But when it grew old with long use and little by little men
> began to neglect it, he gave a fourth in the cuculla, to which
> the whole world is now thronging in its love of novelty.
> After this there will be no fifth, because in this one the
> blessings of all peoples are wonderfully contained. For all
> the religion and sanctity embodied in the three testaments
> are fully summed up in the testament of Benedict.[8]

7 T.X. No. 1162. "κέντροις ὀξέσιν χαραχθήσονται εἰς χεῖρας δύο σφραγεῖδες."
8 "Epistula Domini Odonis Monachi Cantuariensis ad fratrem suum novitium
Oldanum," in Mabillon, *Veterum Analectorum nova editio* (Paris, 1723), p.
447: "O admirabile mysterium et admirabile sacramentum! Primum Testa-

And yet—strange paradox—while Odo was uttering these sublime words in praise of the Benedictine cuculla, the grandiose historical epoch of monastic symbolism was drawing to a close. For fifty years the Cistercian reform had carried the spirit of the old rule outside the walls of the abbeys and made it into an instrument of incalculable economic change. As though the black scapular were no longer timely now that a new Messianic age was approaching, the Cistercians replaced it by a white one. At this very moment Joachim of Floris was concluding the youthful monastic experiences which impelled him to announce that the era of the Holy Ghost was at hand. After the eras of the Father and the Son, he declared, the third and last era, that of the Holy Ghost would dissolve all sacramental and disciplinary bonds by ushering in the day of perfect *reality*. "The first era brought forth water, the second wine, the third will press out the oil."

By immersing itself in the atmosphere of joyous expectation aroused by Joachim's message, the Franciscan "religio" soared to a realm transcending all material symbols. For the Franciscans of that day a visit to the *Portiuncula* in quest of plenary indulgence was equivalent to a crusade. As in early Christian times, they made religion a pure and humble invitation to a joyful life. "Let the brothers take guard against manifesting a gloomy, woebegone piety; let them appear as rejoicing in God, as merry, pleasant and beseemingly gracious."[9] This admonition of the first Franciscan rule is attested by Thomas of Celano, but has vanished from the text approved by the Curia.

---

mentum dedit Deus in cordibus hominum, quod vocatum est *lex naturalis,* quod si servassent, secundo non indigerent. Sed quia novitatum amatores sunt homines, per inveterationem primo testamento neglecto secundum dedit in *circumcisione,* quod propter sui novitatem paulo libentius amplexati sunt quidam. Sed hoc interdum inveterato atque neglecto tertium dedit in *baptismo,* quod praedestinatum est ut stet in aeternum. Sed quia longa consuetudine inveteratum coepit ab hominibus paulatim in negligentiam duci quartum dedit in *cuculla,* ad cuius novitatem amator novitatum paene totus iam confluit mundus. Post hoc quintum non erit, quia in hoc et mirabili modo omnium gentium benedictiones continentur. Quidquid enim religionis et sanctitatis in tribus testamentis continetur, totum in testamento Benedicti constringitur."

9 "Caveant fratres ne se ostendant extrinsecus nubilosos et hypocritas tristes, sed ostendant se gaudentes in Domino, hilares et jucundos et convenienter gratiosos."

Obviously the Church, as bureaucratized by Innocent III, could not accept the idea that the Gospel history was beginning again, and that the Church need only abdicate. It resisted, clinging more than ever to the symbols of medieval Christianity. But in attempting to turn them into simple instruments of salvation to be administered (and I use the word in its literal sense) solely by the clerical bureaucracy, it robbed those treasures of the unconscious corporate content which, during the golden age of early Christianity and monasticism, had made them into instruments by which men could find one another in a common city of God, built of charismata and mysteries. Thus the papacy of the waning Middle Ages inflicted upon the spiritual body of monasticism the same taint which Constantine had inflicted upon the spiritual body of early Christianity when he destroyed its atmosphere of initiation and mystery. By generalizing the use of sacramental symbols in space and time and so destroying their corporate aim, the papacy diminished their constructive force and transformed them into purely magical instruments by which to silence the individual's fears concerning the afterlife.

The first masters of Scholastic speculation abetted this process. If, for example, we read the theological theory of the sacraments put forward by Hugh of St. Victor (in the Augustinian cloister founded by William of Champeaux), and note the importance it imputes to the formulas of the priest, who now performs the miracle of realizing and communicating the charisma, we see that the mystical horizon of the Church is no longer the same as in the era of the great creations of monasticism. No longer is the symbol a sign of *mutual* recognition or of *communal* illumination in God. It is an insurance against the perils of the afterlife.

It is understandable that the Reformation should have striven to shatter a sacramental order which had become an arsenal for the great *condottiere* in Rome and his agents. But it should also be understood that this schism robbed modern man of the *symbols* by which to make himself known to his fellow, and deprived him of the vision of what lies beyond experience and beyond political exigencies. Since then our journey through the world has become an atomized and planless wandering of fugitives, without aim, without friends to receive us. Now that we have lost all receptivity to the solemn, intangible norms of the transcendent, we have arrived at the belief that the only possible life discipline is the discipline which is maintained by the rod and ordained by human priesthoods.

2. *The Rites*

In the epilogue to his little treatise on the Lord's Prayer—one of the oldest ecclesiastical commentaries on the Pater Noster—Tertullian bursts into a song of praise on the universality of prayer:

> All the angels pray, all that is created in the world prays, the wild beasts in the desert pray, bending their knees earthward. And when in the dawn they emerge from their dens and lairs, they look up to heaven and break the silence with prayer and tremble after their manner. When the birds rise in flight from their nest, they turn upwards to heaven and spread their wings in the form of a cross, and their voices swell into melodies which are songs of prayer.[10]

Without having heard of Tertullian, Whitehead, a philosopher of our day, has said something very similar. He has proved that ritual extends far beyond history—indeed, far beyond the confines of human life. Do we not indeed discover it among the animals, in the habits of the individual, and, to a still higher degree, in the development of the species? If ritual is nothing other than the habitual performance of actions having no bearing whatever on the preservation of the physiological organism, the first rite was born in the skies on the day when a flock of birds began to execute rhythmic movements which served solely for the jubilant expression of an energy that existed only for its own sake. When man for his part discovered how feelings can be called forth and how the faculties for feeling can be sharpened independently of the satisfaction of any physical need, under the sole impetus of joy in the exercise of energy and intoxication with the outcome—in that moment liturgy and the dramatic art were born. Both are forms of the psychic drunkenness by which man enters into contact with the good and the beautiful, for such movements and tones stand in no relation whatsoever to the empirical requirements of daily, corporeal life.

10 *De oratione*, XXIX, 4 (Migne, *PL*, II, 1196) .

Athenaeus (X, 434e) relates that once a year, on the occasion of a certain feast of Mithra, the Persian king was obliged to enter the temple in a state of utter drunkenness. This is not without profound significance. For is the rite not related to ecstasy? And is ecstasy not a dissolution of all clear discourse and rational thought?

A missionary in Gabon relates that when the natives set out on a journey in their little canoes, they strike up a song which is always the same. With a loud voice the leader sings the word *mabango* on a single note. The syllable *go* is held as long as the singer's breath permits, and the man with the most powerful lungs is chosen for this function. Then all the paddlers emit three times a short *va*. The leader now resumes his *mabango* two tones lower, but does not hold the *go* as long as before. Doubtless the rite represents an invocation to the spirit of the water.

When man for the first time set sail in the vessel of his consciousness and found himself caught in the shoreless current of communal life, we cannot doubt that he emitted a sound, which was meant to be a cry of entreaty and propitiation. Music and religion were born as twins. In two different languages, rhythm (ῥυθμός) and rite (*ritus, mos*) betray a surprising kinship and a remarkable accord. Similarly, a comparison of the words *ṛtam* and *assni,* which mean "order" in Sanskrit and Avestan, with the Greek ἀριθμός (number), the Irish *rim,* and the Welsh *rhif* shows a significant relationship between the Indo-Iranian and the Italo-Celtic religious vocabulary. It is no metaphoric manner of speaking when we assert that the historical religions are mighty symphonies woven of motifs which rise up from the spirit of suffering, imploring mankind, while the supreme manifestations of music are religious voices of hope and beatitude. In like form, these motifs are taken from both spheres of sacred human experience, to achieve their most harmonious mixture and profoundest magic in the highest forms of religion. And when their power to show man the way is in danger of being stifled and exhausted by the sterile purifications of a mythologizing theology, the motifs are reborn in art, more elemental and powerful than ever. When, on the other hand, art loses its freshness of inspiration amid the weary decadence of bad taste, the task of modulating the original motifs of our common experience of the sacred returns to religion. Religion must shatter theologies and rebel against Pharisaic disciplinary exercises, to strike up, on a single tone, the eternal motif of faith and hope.

The original rite of Jesus is fully contained in his prayer, the Pater Noster. Jesus taught it to his disciples to prevent their entreaties to the Father from degenerating, like the prayers of the heathen, into idle loquacity (πολυλογία) or a cold stammering (βατταλογεῖν) of fixed formulas. The astounding, incomparable uniqueness of this prayer resides in two characteristics: First, it contains the first person not in the singular but only in the plural: *Our* Father, *our* daily bread, give *us*, forgive *us* our debts as *we* forgive *our* debtors, deliver *us* from evil. And second, it has only one dominant note, entreaty for the swift coming of the Messianic kingdom, in the prospect of which all the burdensome debts of the past are cheerfully remitted. Even those words which seem farthest removed from future hopes, which seem merely to express anxious concern for the preservation of physical life, the "Give us this day our daily bread" of all current Bibles, assume a different meaning in the original text: τὸν ἄρτον ἡμῶν τὸν ἐπιούσιον δὸς ἡμῖν σήμερον in Matthew 6:11 and τὸν ἄρτον ἡμῶν τὸν ἐπιούσιον δίδου ἡμῖν τὸ καθ' ἡμέραν in Luke 11:3. When we compare the puzzling ἐπιούσιος with fragments from the Gospel of the Hebrews, preserved by St. Jerome, these words take on a purely eschatological color: *"Panem nostrum crastinum da nobis hodie"* (Give us today tomorrow's bread) —that is to say: Give us today the kingdom thou hast promised for tomorrow, or, Hasten thy coming, O Lord![11]

We see, then, that the prayer service which Christ handed down to his successors consisted wholly in an impatient entreaty for the coming of the kingdom. And since, as Philo said, hope is the seed which germinates most quickly in the earth of the human soul, it is understandable that this vision of the kingdom should have aroused the state of mind embodied in the watchword: The Lord is at hand (μαραναθα) and expressed in the hymns of praise mentioned by St. Paul.

However, a religious community which unceasingly extends its conquests, which spreads victorious from land to land while each day the ultimate goal of its pilgrimage recedes farther into the

---

11 See M. R. James, *The Apocryphal New Testament* (Oxford, 1924), p. 4.

distance, cannot survive unless it finds suitable outlets and nourishment for the devotional fervor of the masses. This is all the more
true when the new faith must compete with pre-existing religious
traditions, which possess organically developed and sumptuous rituals. In such cases, mutual rivalry leads to mutual assimilations.

We are not yet, and perhaps never will be, in a position to
follow the growth of the Christian liturgical order step by step.
A number of circumstances make this task uncommonly difficult,
if not absolutely impossible. First of all, this development proceeded by leaps and bounds, differed from one church to another,
and only became unified at a later date. Second, we have inadequate
knowledge of those rituals and liturgies which competed with Christianity and whose example the Christians had to imitate in order
to supplant them, namely those of the mysteries and the synagogue.
The fragments of mystery liturgies recorded in papyri which are
occasionally brought to light are indeed useful objects of comparison and may be looked upon as paralleling Gnostic and ecclesiastical liturgies, but extant rules governing the synagogue service must
be consulted with great caution, since in large part they were
codified in a period succeeding early Christianity. In fact, the
Church liturgy is sometimes cited in documentation of a synagogue
liturgy older than that which is now in force.

In any event, the influence of the Jewish devotional forms of
the New Testament period on the rites and prayers of early Christianity cannot be denied. We can argue as to whether the Lord's
Supper as related by St. Paul in the First Epistle to the Corinthians
is descended from the Jewish Passover supper, or at least from the
great *Hallel* sung on this occasion, as Bickell believes, or whether,
as Baumstark assumes, it is derived from the synagogue service of
the Sabbath morning or, in a more general sense, from the prayers
accompanying each Jewish supper. But of the dependence of the
Eucharistic rite on Jewish models there can be no doubt.

The Διδαχή replaces the Jewish eighteen blessings with the three
daily Pater Nosters. But, on the other hand, we learn from the
Talmudic treatise Berakoth (IX, 5) that the Jewish prayers ended
with formulas which correspond exactly to the Greek concluding
words εἰς τοὺς αἰῶνας or εἰς τοὺς αἰῶνας τῶν αἰώνων. These concluding
formulas have entirely vanished from the synagogue liturgy but

have been preserved in the Christian liturgy. A whole section of the seventh book of the so-called *Apostolic Constitutions* (chs. 33 to 38) preserves a complete Jewish-Hellenistic ritual for the Sabbath and matins service beneath a patina of superficial assimilation.

The influence of the mystery religions on the prayer and liturgy of early Christianity is of an entirely different nature. Here, in truth, there was danger of a relapse into the βατταλογεῖν and the πολυλογία τῶν ἐθνικῶν, in opposition to which Jesus had given *his* prayer. And true πολυλογίαι characterize the prayers and formulas of invocation cited in the great Gnostic works of the third century, such as the *Pistis Sophia,* or in the magico-Christian papyri. Prayers from the *Poimandres* have been detected in Christian prayers, e.g. those of Berlin Papyrus No. 9794. And while the litanies to Isis provided a model for the Christian litanies, a large part of the liturgical material in the apocryphal Acts has been shown to derive from mystery sources sifted through the experience of the Gnostic communities. It is no accident that the first master of ceremonies of whose work the ecclesiastical literature preserves an exact description should be Marcus, a Gnostic.

After the conversion of Constantine, Christian prayer was threatened by the same process of "secularization" as we have seen undermining the concept of mystical Christian community formed by the message of Christ. In reverting to a barren, stereotyped πολυλογία, concerned solely with begging for individual advantages, it was in danger of losing all Christian character. Here again salvation came from the reaction within the monastic orders. Viollet le Duc, the great historian of architecture, once called the rule of St. Benedict the most outstanding monument of the Middle Ages. And yet this succinct, practical rule, in its original terseness, is the most unassuming thing in the world; it embodies a very limited program, far removed from any striving for wider influence. It is merely an organization of communal prayer, a regulation of liturgical song and communal ritual. In the Greece of Aeschylus and Sophocles, as it sprang forth from the imponderable contacts between Hellas and the "barbarians," the χορηγός was the λειτουργ῀ς who defrayed the costs of the choruses for that part of the official cult which consisted in dramatic performances. Soon after the contact between the Latin spirit and the "barbarian" world, Benedict was the liturgist who organized and trained the choruses for the new drama of the West. Nowhere has the term *liturgist* ever been more fitting. Even in outward arrangement, the chorus of monks, with their antiphonal singing of the Lord's praises, recalls the Greek chorus.

Of course we must not imagine that the magnificent Benedictine organization was conjured up out of nothing by the hermit of Subiaco and continued in its original form, unchanged. His rule was only a wise and well-considered adaptation of already existing forms of Eastern monasticism, and the Benedictine liturgy is only the organic and definitive conclusion of a development which had passed through its preparatory phases in the East.

From Eusebius of Caesarea to the *Institutiones* of Cassian and the *Peregrinatio Aetheriae,* a number of Church documents permit us to follow the enrichment and progressive development of the liturgy and the heortological calendar in the East. Both grew out of primitive beginnings, which in turn have their origin in the euchology of the synagogue. An example is the daily recitation of the three last Psalms of the Psalter, which are called αἶνοι in the Greek rite and *laudes* in the West. This practice, which was abolished by the earth-shaking event of Pius X's reform of the Breviary in 1911, goes back to the Sabbath morning prayer conducted by the Jews up to New Testament times.

We can be certain that lauds and vespers were publicly celebrated each day after the conversion of Constantine. The Easter festival was preceded by a nocturnal vigil, the παννυχία, which recalls the sleepless nights of the Dionysian "orgies," mentioned by Euripides. The remaining *Horae,* whose main elements were likewise Bible readings and recitations of Psalms, were given up to private devotions. The monks completed the organization of the liturgy. St. Benedict busied himself exclusively with this *Opus Dei.*

Far more important than the appraisal of similarities between the prayers of Eastern and Western monasticism is an understanding of the meaning and value of the communal celebration of the liturgy, as it passed from the cells of the Eastern monks to the order of St. Benedict.

Pachomius divided his monks, according to their daily occupations, into as many groups as there are letters in the alphabet, thus assuring a continuous observance of prayer. Evagrius of Pontus, the great master of asceticism, interpreted the common life of the contemplants as a great "orchestra" directed by the incarnate Logos and unceasingly executing the "symphony" of universal faith in the Father. "The soul which is animated and stirred by the sacred injunctions of Christ," he wrote, "is like a cither touched by the Holy Ghost. The pure spirit, which sets out to gain spiritual knowledge, is a David's harp with many strings, over which glides the skillful hand of the divine artist." St. Benedict took up this mystical vision of the monastic life as an orchestra and proceeded to instill the greatest possible harmony into it.

And yet, when he left Rome in the year 500 and set out for the imposing and forbidding caverns of the Anio, he dreamed only of a lonely life as a hermit and of perfecting himself. Much later, a nameless monk of Subiaco asked him, with words full of meaning: "If it is light you seek, O Benedict, why do you crawl off into a cave? Will you really find the light you are seeking in a cave? But no, you are right. Go, go and seek the light in the darkness. To fill us with profound emotion, the flickering light of the stars requires the night, cloaked in impenetrable darkness."[12] In Euripides' tragedy, Dionysus had proclaimed that "there is something about the darkness that fills us with awe."[13]

Monasticism is the most magnificent example of that heterogeneity of aims and consequences which governs the historical development of Christianity. St. Benedict fled into the wilderness to withdraw from a disintegrating world, and in so doing he created the germ cells of a corporate life from which the spiritual organism of all medieval culture would arise. His only aim was the *Opus Dei*, the polyphonic song which would rise from the gigantic orchestra of his order. According to his conception, which was to animate all medieval mysticism and which was to be explicitly formulated in St. Anselm of Canterbury's *Cur Deus homo*, it was the monks who would fill the gaps which Lucifer and his followers had created in the ranks of the angels. Even the manual and literary labors of

12 Lumina si quaeris, Benedicte, quid pergis ad antra?
　 Quaesiti luminis serviant antra nihil.
　 Sed perge in tenebris radiorum quaerere lucem.
　 Nonnisi in obscura sidera nocte micant.
13 *Bacchae,* 486.

the monks were a secondary point in the program of monastic life, though today this truth is usually passed over in silence. These labors may have been necessary to the independent existence of the abbeys. But the primary mission of the monk was one: to sing the holy praises of the Lord in antiphonal groups. It was from these choruses, drunk with song and dramatic action, that the Middle Ages, in their moments of spiritual crisis, summoned their great "coryphaei." And the world was filled with the echoes of these songs, which poured forth from the hosts of monks living on the fringe of society and persevering in prayer. And thus Christianity taught the world the manifest truth of the Evangelical paradox: "Only in the striving for the kingdom of God do justice and peace descend on the world."

The order of Benedictine prayer rests on certain essential principles which go back to earlier devotional usages. In the course of a week, the Psalter must be recited *in toto*. By Psalter is meant all the 150 Psalms, plus the antiphons and collects which belong to them, as well as the customary Biblical canticles (*cantica scripturae*). In the course of a year, the whole Old and New Testament must be read with suitable commentaries taken from the Fathers (*Homiliae* or *Sermones*). In night prayer, the sacred number of twelve Psalms must neither be exceeded nor reduced. Similarly in the daytime office, twelve Psalms are to be recited, three at each of the "little hours." Of course the material requirements of monastic life and the changes of the seasons had their effect on the schedule of choral prayer. It was necessary to assign short Psalms to the little hours. And in summer, when it grows light so much earlier, the long readings were omitted (*propter brevitatem noctium*) from the matins service, sung at about two o'clock in the morning (the praise of the Lord shall fill day and night without interruption), in order that the early morning hours might be devoted to work. Thus the order of the office reveals the principal characteristic distinguishing the Benedictine rule from that of the Eastern and insular orders, namely moderation. Vespers, occurring as it did at the end of the day, after hours of hard work, was conceived as a brief and not too strenuous service. The lucernarium (evening service) was even divided into two parts, vespers and compline. Thus the number eight, a favorite symbol of Patristic mysticism, was applied to the canonical hours of prayer: *In octava perfectio, in octava summa virtutem* (In eight is perfection, in eight is the sum of virtue). Finally, each hour of the canonical prayer service was calculated to form an organic unit composed in well-considered proportions of Psalms and hymns, readings and maxims. As Cassiodorus said, the singing of Psalms is the *consolatio piae devotionis monachorum* (the consolation of the monks' pious devotion).

We may throw further light on the profound though unintentional analogy between the tragic chorus in the Dionysian liturgy of Greece and the choral liturgy of the Western monasteries by saying that the Benedictine prayer service created the Christian hymn just as the tragedy created Greek music. Moreover, the monks accompanied their choral recitation with gestures and attitudes which can well be described as a stylization of the old sacral dances. Among all attitudes of prayer, the raising of the hands to heaven is unquestionably the oldest—Jews and pagans made equal use of it, though with this insignificant difference: the pagans turned their palms upward (*manibus supinis*). But since the time of Macarius the Egyptian, the arms outstretched to form a cross constituted the favored attitude of monastic prayer. It grew, no doubt, from the orant's sense of total immersion in Christ, since it patently calls to mind Christ on the Cross, praying as he offered up his supreme sacrifice. This position was particularly favored by the Irish penitents. The Old Irish even has a special term for it, *crossfigele,* "Cross vigil." The Irish ascetics favored the severest mortifications. As penance for certain offenses, *De arreis,* an eighth-century penitential, prescribes the alternation of a hundred verses of the Psalms with a *crossfigele* sustained to the point of pain. Yet the arms outstretched in the form of a cross did not merely signify the penitent's solidarity with the divine sacrifice of Golgotha. The monks represent an army. And the ancestral chieftain of the penitents, praying for a favorable outcome of the battle waged in the world between good and evil, is Moses, praying on Mount Sinai with outstretched arms, while the battle between the Hebrews and the Amalekites surged back and forth beneath him.

The monastic liturgy is, then, a choral prayer, a work of penance and sacrifice, serving to safeguard the spiritual life of mankind as a whole, deaf as it is to the most sublime calling of the reasoning creature. It strives to articulate the human voice with the symphony of prayer which rises unceasingly from the world of nature to the Father who is in heaven. Nothing personal, no selfish desires are contained in the ritual. Into tones and gestures of fervent entreaty the monastic chorus translates the essence of Jesus' prayer: a world transfigured by the duskless light of the kingdom of God.

But, once again, the process we have observed in connection with the sacramental symbols is repeated. When, in view of its vast conquests, contemplative monasticism thought itself on the point of absorbing all Christianity, it was in reality approaching its decline. While Joachim of Floris, confident that the era of the Holy Ghost was at hand, proclaimed the end of symbols and the universality of the contemplative calling, the Franciscans, who thought they were already living in the new era, shortened the Benedictine prayer service. The feeling for the sanctity of the common liturgy as dramatic act and as choral praise of God began to be lost. And that common prayer which had grown out of a deep-seated consciousness of the corporate character of ascetic striving toward the kingdom of God became transformed into a personal duty and obligation, into a cold, mechanical, private recitation, differing in no way from the heathen πολυλογία which Jesus had so sternly condemned.

The Society of Jesus, that organization typical of Tridentine and post-Tridentine Catholicism, after whose model all modern religious congregations have been fashioned, knows no common prayer—that is to say, it lacks the specific element of a *religious order*. And, indeed, the Society of Jesus is not a religious order. It is a far-flung corporation of producers and consumers functioning for the benefit of ecclesiastical hegemony and nourishing ill-concealed aims of world conquest.

In the Benedictine monasteries the daily praise of the Lord is still celebrated with all the imposing beauty of the old Gregorian melodies. But between the spiritual life of the Benedictine tradition and the official life of the Curia, which in former days derived strength and counsel from the Benedictines, the Jesuits, with their proselytizing zeal, have thrust the barrier of their spirit and organization. Ecclesiastical Christianity no longer has any means of exercising its original method and charismatic discipline, which presuppose the denial and contempt of the world. From the Counterreformation until our day, Catholicism bears the chief responsibility for the total profanation of corporate religious life.

As we wait in fear and torment for Catholicism to find the way to a new and radical μετάνοια, and as we search for something equal in rank to the liturgy of the Greek drama or the psalmodizing liturgy of Benedictine mysticism, it would seem as though we must turn to the unexcelled modern master of symphonic music, who has made the old religious motifs of destiny and freedom resound for all men.

It can be no accident that when Ludwig van Beethoven wished to communicate to a beloved fellow creature the mystical intoxication which had seized him in the night when he completed the most "mysteriously" sublime of his compositions, he had recourse to the language of those old mystery religions which are the forerunners of the Benedictine sacraments. He wrote: "I have come from an orgy."

3. The Exercitia of St. Ignatius Loyola

It is the night of March 24, 1522. We are standing in the doorway of the shrine of Our Lady of Montserrat, some thirty miles northwest of Barcelona, watching the pilgrims who have gathered to celebrate the feast of the Annunciation. Like the ancient pilgrims in the holy temples of Isis, they are sleeping on the floor, awaiting the dreams that will bring them revelation. Among these pilgrims there is one whose aristocratic bearing, despite the poverty of his raiment, betrays the nobility of his origin and calling. It is Iñigo Lopez de Recalde, born in 1491 in the castle of Loyola.

A year before, a rebellious monk in Worms had risen against the commands of the Spanish emperor Charles V. At almost this very same time Iñigo had been gravely wounded in the leg, while commanding the garrison of Pamplona, which the troops of Francis I were besieging in order to avenge the consequences of the treaty of Noyon. A protracted convalescence and the tedious immobility to which Iñigo was condemned had driven him to seek distraction in the books of the library of Loyola. Two works particularly impressed themselves on the mind of this wounded man impatiently awaiting his recovery: the *Life of Jesus Christ* by Ludolf of Saxony and the *Flos Sanctorum* of an unknown author. Crippled by his wounds, Ignatius had seen himself compelled to renounce the soldier's trade. From this moment on, he poured all his warlike zeal and adventurous spirit into his new religious experience. As soon as he could leave his bed, he journeyed to the Benedictine cloister of Montserrat, which had long been known for its cult of the Virgin and in recent years had acquired great fame, largely through its illustrious abbot, Don Garzia de Cisneros. After a stay in Montserrat Ignatius went on to Manresa, where, as the Jesuit legend relates, he was favored by a number of supernatural revelations, which he recorded in his *Exercitia spiritualia* and perpetuated in the rule of the Society of Jesus.

In 1625 the Jesuits transformed the room inhabited by Ignatius in the hospice of Manresa into a chapel, which they adorned with the following inscription:

> As St. Ignatius was praying in this chapel, he was rapt in ecstasy and fell down on these same stones which we now see and venerate. Carried to heaven in spirit, he beheld the great order which he was to found in the name of Jesus: its blazon, its aim, its rule, its propagation over both continents, its initiatives, its conquests, its victories, its scientific achievements, its sanctity, and its martyrdoms. The vision endured for eight days. This site is memorable because of the ecstasy of St. Ignatius and because of his revelations concerning the Society of Jesus.

Father Bartoli, the saint's official Jesuit biographer, cites further details: One of the most significant favors conferred upon Ignatius, which may be regarded as unique, was the ecstatic trance which lasted for eight days, during which all the saint's sensory functions were suspended. From the hour of compline, on Saturday evening, to the same hour on the following Saturday, Ignatius seemed to be dead. Those about him wondered whether they should not bury him. But, fortunately, someone noticed that his heart was still beating. The saint, Bartoli continues, awakened from his long ecstasy as from a sweet sleep, crying with a soft, muffled voice, "O my Jesus." In conclusion, Bartoli writes: "The most distinguished men of the Order . . . have always believed that God then revealed to him the rules for which He had chosen him, manifesting to him what He destined him to do in the service of the Church, and traced for him the plan of that Order, of which he was afterwards to be the Founder."[14] On awaking from his protracted ecstasy, Ignatius is said

---

14 Daniel Bartoli, *History of the Life and Institute of St. Ignatius de Loyola*, tr. F. C. de la Barca (2 vols., New York, 1856), I, 60.

to have written the *Exercitia,* though it is not known whether God himself or Mary had dictated them.

The official tradition of the "Fathers of the Society" does not, however, agree with the historical reports of the most significant and unbiased witnesses. Dom Antonio de Yepez (1536–1608) tells us that Garzia de Cisneros, abbot of Montserrat, had written several religious manuals, among them an *Exercitatorium Spirituale,* which was printed at Montserrat in 1500 in Castilian and Latin. In his *General Chronicle of the Order of St. Benedict,* Dom Antonio adds: "According to the testimony of all the monks of Montserrat, Father Juan Chemones imparted to his son in Christ Ignatius the manner of the exercises conducted in Montserrat by Father Garzia de Cisneros. Ignatius took his notes with him to Manresa, where, full of zeal, he showed them to certain men, until he himself having perfected himself and become conversant with every science, abridged the book of Fr. Cisneros, changed it, completed it, and finally lent it the form of his *Exercitia,* suitable for his own Society." This by no means detracts from the fame of St. Ignatius, any more than the glory of St. Thomas Aquinas is lessened by the fact that in composing his *Summa* he made use of the *Summa* of his teacher Alexander of Hales; St. Ignatius' *Exercitia* will always be highly valued, even if he derived their first outline from the cloister of Montserrat during the first stages of his conversion.

A heated controversy arose in the seventeenth century between the Benedictines and Jesuits regarding the date of the *Exercitia* and their dependence on Cisneros' spiritual method. This was not the only point of controversy between the venerable religious order which had molded the soul of medieval Christianity and the great Society which was the soul of the Counterreformation. On the contrary! But whereas in other differences of opinion, both of a theoretical and of a disciplinary nature, the new society clearly triumphed over the Benedictine tradition, in this particular question of the dependence of the *Exercitia* on the mystical and devotional works of the Spanish Benedictine, the Jesuits, though victorious in the seventeenth century, have had to capitulate in the face of the clear historical documentation brought forward by modern criticism. Perhaps they have done so the more willingly in the opinion that if Ignatius drew heavily on the *Exercitatorium* of Cisneros, this showed the methods by which the Jesuits had contaminated and

distorted the whole of Catholic intellectual life to be older than
their Society itself. And, indeed, that system of imitation which the
Exercitia perfected and introduced into the whole of Catholic devotional life had begun at an earlier date.

Today the Jesuits expressly admit that the *Exercitatorium* of
Cisneros formed the foundation of Ignatius' *Exercitia*. In fact, it is
to a Jesuit, Father Watrigant, that we owe the most meticulous and
conscientious inquiry into the sources, not only of the *Exercitia*,
but also of the *Exercitatorium*.[15]

Let us sum up his findings: St. Ignatius derived both the title and
the framework of his work from Cisneros. From Cisneros he derived
the unusually protracted period of withdrawal, thirty to forty days,
and the division of these days into intervals which he designates as
"weeks" and which correspond to the "ways" of certain mystics: the
way of *purification,* the way of *illumination,* the way of *mysticism,*
and the way of *contemplation;* similarly, he derived from Cisneros
the organization of the various subjects of meditation, based on the
life and death of Christ. Father Watrigant goes into further details.
He admits that the second, fourth, thirteenth, and perhaps the
twentieth of the "Adnotationes" which stand at the beginning of
the *Exercitia* contain obvious analogies with the instructions of
Cisneros. He owns that the second, fourth, and fifth of the "Addi-
tiones" are to be found not only in the *Exercitatorium* but also in
the same author's *Directorio de los Horos Canonicos.* It is from this
work, still according to Watrigant, that Ignatius took the first week's
"Meditationes" on sin and hell.

Not content with this, Watrigant, seemingly fearful of under-
estimating the relationship between St. Ignatius and Cisneros,
broadens his horizon of inquiry by speculating on the relations between St. Ignatius and the "Brothers of the Common Life," whom
he must have met and whose teachings he no doubt heard in Paris
if not previously in Spain. Here again Watrigant is honest and
objective.

The fundamental ideas which the *Exercitia* and the *Exercitatorium* have in common are also to be found in the *Rosetum exerci-*

15 See I. Diertins, *Historia exercitium spiritualium S. P. Ignatii de Loyola,* ed.
P. Watrigant (Freiburg i.B., 1887) ; Watrigant, *La Genèse des Exercises de S.
Ignace de Loyola* (1897).

tiorum spiritualium of Johannes Mombaer (Mauburnus), whose ideas in turn were taken directly from Gerard Zerbolt of Zutphen's two treatises, *De Reformatione virium animae* and *De spiritualibus ascensionibus*. Thus by the admission of a Jesuit the treatise which, according to the old legend of his order, was miraculously dictated to the "lonely man" by God and the Blessed Virgin in Manresa reveals an ample genealogy.

> It is not only possible but probable that St. Ignatius had heard speak of the Brothers of the Common Life, at least after his arrival in Paris in the year 1528, and that he then felt a desire to know their works more closely. We may even assume that Ignatius knew members of the congregation and must have questioned them on certain matters in the course of his annual visits to Flanders, whither he went to collect the alms necessary for the maintenance of his order among the Spanish merchants.

So much for Father Watrigant.

Nolte, who edited the letters of Gerard de Groot and a pamphlet of Radewin, writes: "In Paris St. Ignatius lived among the 'Brothers of the Common Life,' and the role which Johannes Standonek, doctor of the University of Paris and a zealous supporter of the Brothers of the Common Life, established in the house which he built for them, presumably gave Ignatius the idea of founding his Society."

One writer carried his malicious intent so far as to seek parallels for the *Exercitia* in a field into which neither Father Watrigant nor Dr. Nolte of the *Zeitschrift für katholische Theologie* would have ventured, namely that of Islamic mysticism. And the results of his researches were positively astounding. Under the name of Hermann Müller, this zealous and malicious scholar wrote a rather paradoxical and deplorably biased dissertation, certain particulars of which are nevertheless worthy of our attention.[16]

In accord with Watrigant, Müller states that the originality of St. Ignatius' idea in comparison with that of Cisneros lies in its emphasis on the personality of the director of the exercises, to whom the exercitants, both priests and laymen, must submit in blind obedience. He then goes on to examine the organization of the Islamic

16 Hermann Müller, *Les Origines de la Compagnie de Jésus: Ignace et Lainez* (1898).

congregations, particularly those founded by Chadely in Sid-Abu-Midian, which bears, however, the name of Sid-Abu-Hassan-el-Chadely, the third sheikh. This sect was widespread among the Moors to whom Ferdinand had granted the free observance of their cult. Müller comes to the conclusion that particularly those characteristic features of the Society which the Jesuits represent as its fundamental principles are most reminiscent of the Arabic traditions. These are: its disciplinary form and the obedience required of its adepts, the method of initiation and training to which the novices are subjected, the hierarchy of the members of the community, and the esoteric occultism of its doctrines—in a word, its extreme amalgamation of spiritual and temporal order.

But this fleeting glance at Christian and extra-Christian precedents for the mystical doctrine and spiritual discipline contained in the *Exercitia* and in the Jesuit *Constitutiones* is far from accounting for the influence of Jesuit institutions and pedagogic methods on the development and crystallization of modern Catholicism. To what cause shall we attribute the astounding success of St. Ignatius' work? It is possible that a glance into the past, a study of the organization of the Islamic mystical communities in a period when Islam had consolidated its culture and taken on set forms—that is, at the time of the fullest flowering of Scholastic apologetics—might help us to identify the specific characteristics of that spiritual technique and to understand how the Society of Jesus gained unlimited and uncontested domination over the collective spiritual attitude of Catholicism.

Consider, if you please, that the priests of the Catholic Church may not be consecrated or exercise their priesthood before they have performed the Jesuit exercises three times, each over a period of ten days. Through this compulsory training of the clergy, the Jesuit initiation is passed on to every Catholic believer. And on top of this, the Jesuits everywhere build and maintain houses which serve for the performance of their exercises for laymen. We may say without exaggeration that all Catholic religious life is dominated by the Jesuits, and that the whole mystical and devotional life of the Church bears the stamp of St. Ignatius' *Exercitia*. Hence an accurate estimate of the initiation which the *Exercitia* of St. Ignatius offer

192

the Catholic soul is of the utmost importance for a sound evaluation of the present state and future prospects of Catholicism.

First of all, it must frankly be stated that the *Exercitia,* as even a cursory reading reveals, are an exceedingly pedestrian, not to say banal product. In them we find none of those great, sublime visions, none of those unexcelled flights of spirit, none of the almost supernatural grandeur which characterize not only the original Christian literature based on the New Testament but also the great mystical-monastic literature of the Middle Ages, for example the *Cur Deus Homo* of St. Anselm or the *Sermones in Cantica* of St. Bernard. The *Exercitia* offer a practical guidance, suited for those shapeless, average masses who let themselves be governed by elementary, tangible conceptions, who submit readily to a military organization in which obedience and mechanical adaptation to a bureaucratic discipline are looked upon as the principal virtues. It may well be that in the period following the Reformation, when the Catholic Church was governed by a peremptory and desperate striving to preserve a congealed, crystallized past, such banal and spiritually impoverished methods of initiation represented a force. But it was a force of inertia and obsolescence, not of conquest, growth, renewal.

The four weeks, or decades, into which the time of the *Exercitia* is divided are assigned to the contemplation of sin, of the life of our Lord Jesus Christ up to and including Palm Sunday, of the Passion of our Lord Jesus Christ, and finally of the Lord's resurrection and ascension. The "Consideratio et Contemplatio" of the first week, or decade, begins with the solemn words: "Man was created to praise, do reverence to and serve God our Lord, and thereby to save his soul. And the other things on the face of the earth were created for man's sake, and to help him in the following of the end for which he was created." Then the text goes on to say that man should use them when they serve him to achieve the goal, and not use them when they obstruct him in the attainment of his aim.

> Wherefore it is necessary to make ourselves detached in regard of all created things,—in all that is left to the liberty of our free will, and is not forbidden it,—so that we on our part should not wish for health rather than sickness, for riches rather than poverty, for honor rather than ignominy,

193

for a long life rather than a short life, and so in all other matters, solely desiring and choosing those things which may better lead us to the end for which we were created.[17]

At first sight this might seem to be a satisfactory formulation of the transcendent last things for which any man worthy of a spiritual calling must strive. But it is a formulation full of trickery and traps. Does this view of the universe as an "empirical world created for man" accord with the healthy, religious pedagogy of the Gospel? Is this the view of our world which St. Paul advocates, which he puts forward in his Epistle to the Romans, when he hears the lament of things awaiting that revelation of the son of God, which will bring them all freedom from the yoke of servitude and error? Does this "indifference" to all the things of life not stand in open opposition to those words of the Bible which speak of life as a battle and to the heroic injunction of the Gospel, which promises the kingdom of God to him who battles "with all his might"? Finally (and this is the most important and far-reaching objection to the *Exercitia*), what is the purpose of a "contemplation" of sin, when a doctrine of initiation should be concerned with the transfiguration of life?

This is the crucial point: even in their introductory "Annotationes," the *Exercitia* of St. Ignatius reveal their novelty, their basic sin toward the traditional and specific teachings of Christian spiritual life, or we might say in more general terms, toward the whole dualistic tradition of religious spirituality.

It is generally known that the principal ingredient of the spiritual pedagogy practiced in the *Exercitia* of St. Ignatius is merely a *compositio loci;* in other words, the substance of contemplation is projected by imagination as well as in sensually perceptible form onto a screen. And since a large share in these spiritual exercises falls to the spiritual guide or preacher (the faithful are enjoined to attend four sermons daily), one can easily imagine the harrowing scenes evoked by the diseased or overstimulated imagination of inexperienced or insensitive spiritual guides.

Ignatius himself, we might add, was far from being moderate or endowed with good taste. After indicating the principles to be fol-

17 Joseph Rickaby, ed. and tr., *The Spiritual Exercises of St. Ignatius Loyola* (2nd edn., London, 1923), pp. 18ff.

lowed in the examination of conscience, and recommending the
deadliest, the most ruinous, and depressing mnemonic technique for
the recollection of minutiae, Ignatius sums up the fifth exercise of
the first week in the following terms:

> . . . to see with the eye of the imagination the length,
> breadth, and depth of hell; . . . to see with the eye of the
> imagination those great fires, and those souls as it were in
> bodies of fire; . . . to hear with the ears lamentations,
> howlings, cries, blasphemies against Christ our Lord and
> against all his Saints; . . . with the sense of smell to smell
> smoke, brimstone, refuse, and rottenness; . . . to taste with
> the taste bitter things, as tears, sadness, and the worm of
> conscience; . . . to feel with the sense of touch how those
> fires do touch and burn souls.[18]

Ignatius addresses the same terrifying appeal to the fantasy and imagination of the exercitants in the celebrated meditations on the two
kings and the two banners. Such instructions, which lash the minds
of the exercitants into hallucination and frenzied horror, represent
a deception: they create an illusion of wealth and fullness where in
reality only a hideous and perilous emptiness prevails. Often Ignatius carries these instructions so far as to mingle the grotesque with
the blasphemous. As an example, we may cite the words of the
second week with which he introduces the first meditation on the
Incarnation:

> The first prelude is to bring up the history of the thing
> which I have to contemplate, which is here how the three
> Divine Persons were looking down upon the whole flat or
> round of the whole world, full of men; and how, seeing that
> all were going down to hell, it was decreed in their eternity
> that the Second Person should become man to save the
> human race. And so it was done, when the fullness of time
> came, by sending the angel Saint Gabriel to our Lady.[19]

I doubt whether all religious literature contains another page to
equal this one in vulgar anthropomorphism. The whole concept
of the *Exercitia* places an almost pathological emphasis on the
sensuous and empirical, in obvious conflict with the venerable doctrine of medieval, mystical initiation, which commands us to close

18 Ibid., p. 41.
19 Ibid., p. 85.

our eyes hermetically to the vision of the senses and to amplify the soul's view of the transcendent truths. Throughout his work, Ignatius speaks of "the infinite fragrance and sweetness of the Godhead,"[20] which can be smelled with the sense of smell and tasted with the sense of taste. This sickly, decadent sensuality constitutes four fifths of the charm which present-day Catholic devotional life exerts on weary, disoriented souls. In applying the *compositio loci* to the Holy Trinity and the eternal decision of the Incarnation, St. Ignatius introduced a sacrilegious anthropomorphism; and in conjuring up the most significant scenes of Christ's life on earth to the vision of the senses, he falls into a crude and childish banality. For example, he prescribes the Passion of Jesus as subject of the first meditation of the third week, starting with Jesus' journey from Bethany to Jerusalem, where he was to celebrate his Last Supper with his disciples, and he makes the following recommendation: "Seeing the place . . . consider the road from Bethany to Jerusalem, whether it is wide, whether it is narrow, whether it is flat, and the rest. In like manner the place of the supper, whether large, whether small, whether in one style, or in another."[21] Has anyone ever conceived of so colorless and futile a method for the conduct of spiritual life? A French writer, who knew the spiritual pedagogy of the Jesuits from experience, has rightly likened it to the movement of a squirrel shut up in a moving cage, for it is only an illusory and fruitless movement.

If we now ask whence came this spiritual technique of the *Exercitia* of Ignatius, which consists primarily in attempting to concentrate the spirit by overstimulating the imagination, we shall, I believe, easily find an answer.

The *compositio loci*, that specific characteristic of Ignatius' pedagogy, is a mechanical and uninspired application to mystical doctrine and devotional practice of the Aristotelian-Scholastic gnosiology. What distinguishes the gnosiology of Aristotle from every other gnosiological doctrine is precisely its fundamental assumption that all our knowledge, all our concepts, all of our universal ideas originate in tangible experience and empirical perception. The active intellect works with the "raw material" of particular percep-

20 Ibid., p. 94.
21 Ibid., p. 169.

tions; by differentiating special characteristics it obtains knowledge of the genera and species. Scholastic philosophy did indeed adopt this Aristotelian assumption. But in its golden age, Scholasticism, led by St. Thomas Aquinas, preserved its feeling for the abyss between pure empirical perception and the transcendent world of revealed truths. The Pelagian spirit of the Jesuits annulled this fundamental distinction; it made the frenzied exercise of sensory perception and sensory fantasy a preparation for the pure mystical contemplation to which man cannot rise without absolutely annihilating the world of the senses.

I am far from denying that the spiritual method on which St. Ignatius based the spiritual initiation of his *Exercitia* is a logical evolution from Scholasticism and its Aristotelian gnosiology. I say merely that this inevitable evolution brought about a profound and irreparable disturbance of the equilibrium between the realistic cognition and the mystical idealism which was the very foundation of the spiritual life of the Christian Middle Ages and, for that matter, of the original Aristotelianism, and that the consequences were inestimable, not only for the structure and orientation of Catholicism after the Reformation, but for the whole cultural and spiritual life of modern times.

St. Bonaventure has masterfully shown us the possibility of a mysticism which—though sprung from a realistic doctrine—sought the traces of God in the universe with great discretion and moderation, which retained grace and revelation in its approach to the sphere of supernatural mystery. It must never be forgotten that with Alexander of Hales the Franciscans, before the Dominicans, had admitted Aristotle into the realm of Christian striving for supernatural knowledge. And that, although they retained many elements of the patristic tradition, they nevertheless zealously applied the concepts of Aristotelian doctrine in the first half of the thirteenth century. St. Bonaventure's *Itinerarium mentis in Deum* is a compendious work of mystical syncretism. After pointing to the possibilities of an ascent to God through the contemplation of his acts in the physical and human world, St. Bonaventure, echoing the Augustinian mysticism of the Victorines, strikes the chords of the highest religious lyricism when (in the seventh chapter) he writes that if man would attain in Christ "to the sacrament and the mystery which temporality conceals," he must not only transcend the perceptible world but also transcend himself (St. Augustine had said the same in the same words in his memorable last dialogue with Monica). To attain to God, we must accomplish the superhuman and transcend ourselves, leaving all perceptible *contemplatio* behind.

Paradoxical as it may seem, it is, as I have intimated, untrue to Aristotle to attempt a "realistic" ascent to God through supratraditional spiritual exercises.

As is irrefutably shown by the excellent researches of W. Jaeger and more recently of J. Croissant on the extant fragments of $\pi\epsilon\rho\grave{\iota}$ $\phi\iota\lambda o\sigma o\phi\acute{\iota}\alpha s$, that programmatic work par excellence, Aristotle, more than any other thinker, explored the psychological sources of faith in God. Aristotle knew that neither the most potent dialectic nor the boldest imagination can ever produce that irresistible force of conviction which dwells in the soul's power of surmise. "He who receives the initiation, need learn ($\mu\alpha\theta\epsilon\hat{\iota}\nu$) nothing with his intellect, but must suffer ($\pi\alpha\theta\epsilon\hat{\iota}\nu$) an inner experience and so achieve a certain readiness of the soul, provided that he is capable of such readiness."

But a lesson so rich and complex as that of Aristotle, the unexcelled teacher, cannot be taken over and experienced at all times; it is the precious heritage of the great creative periods. The epochs of conservation and decay use only its inferior by-products. Since the end of the Middle Ages, and even more since the Reformation, the tradition of Catholicism has become a tradition of conservation and decay. From the magnificent complex of the Aristotelian synthesis, it has merely adopted his receptivity to empirical cognition, to which it has lent a paradoxical development, and this emphasis on empirical cognition is best suited to the renewal of an unbending ecclesiastical dogma, to the conservation of a gigantic bureaucratic apparatus.

But if religion consists primarily in the free and personal transformation of finite existence into infinite life, we can today only recommend an infusion of religion into those spiritual exercises which have been utterly vitiated by the method of St. Ignatius' *Exercitia*.

In contrast to the intransigent Plato, who condemned the use of "Phrygian" music in the education of youth, Aristotle recognized the beneficent effects of the mystery religions on the elevation and "catharsis" of the soul.

In place of such spiritual pedagogy as that of the Jesuits, which stuffs its disciples full of conventional phantasmagorias, which crushes them, stifles them, and bends them to an external, servile discipline, I can only recommend a transformation of the spirit, an appeal, above all, to the forces of the unconscious, to the hypersensitive forces of our transcendental calling.

4. Gnostic Initiation and Christian Antiquity

The teachings of Jesus differed from those of John the Baptist, of which they were the continuation and fulfillment, in placing less stress on the law and on works of asceticism and more on inner conversion and spiritual rebirth (μετάνοια). Jesus himself had gone down into the waters of Jordan to be baptized by John. But he did not exact material baptism of his disciples. He promised immediate remission of sins and expectation of the kingdom to all those who bore witness that they had renewed and transformed their soul. He demanded no other test. The only baptism by which he wished to be consecrated as their leader was the baptism of suffering and martyrdom: the baptism of fire and the baptism of the spirit. That his disciples should be prepared to follow him blindly in this baptism was his wish.

But the first Christian congregation lived in rivalry with the supporters of the Baptist (we find traces of this rivalry in the fourth Gospel). Inevitably the Christians were driven to imitate the rite of initiation by water, practiced by their rivals. And to lend authority to a custom thus acquired they alleged that the resurrected Christ had empowered the apostles to preach his doctrine to the whole world and to administer baptism.

Impelled by his mystical conception of the Church, which for him was synonymous with the mystical body of Christ, which lived in the Father and would one day reappear to institute the "kingdom," St. Paul invested the communal supper—at which the congregation of the faithful gathered to taste of the tangible prototype of the imminent kingdom—with sacramental significance and a character of initiation.

199

Toward the end of the first century, the Christian congregations which spread with extraordinary rapidity along the shores of the Mediterranean in the traces of the Jewish Diaspora knew only two rites: purification by baptism, which was the traditional symbol of inner renewal, and the Eucharistic banquet of love (*agape*), which was the pledge of brotherly love and Messianic beatitude.

But the power of a religion to develop and proselytize always depends to a certain degree on its ideological wealth and ritual splendor. The masses must always be guided by systematic ideas and liturgical gestures. Christianity could not have triumphed so quickly and accomplished its spiritual conquest if it had not gone beyond the rudimentary ritual and the meager, embryonic means of its beginnings, for example, such rites as are reported, in the *Didache* or the epistles of Ignatius. It was necessary to amplify Christian dogma and liturgy very considerably if the Christian message was to meet the requirements of the educated circles in which it was principally to develop and at the same time spread to other sections of the population. This fundamental need was fulfilled by Gnosticism.

Our view of the Gnostic phenomenon has radically changed in the last fifty years. The rediscovery of old Gnostic texts which had been believed lost, close analysis of the Gnostic sources at our disposal, the comparative study of the diverse forms of Hellenistic-Roman religion prevailing in early Christian times—all have led to a complete revaluation of Gnosticism and its influence on the spiritual life and discipline of second-century Christianity. Whether with Harnack we regard Gnosticism as a consequence of the Hellenization of Christianity, or with Reitzenstein as a product of its Orientalization, Gnosticism remains the principal factor in the history of pre-Constantinian Christianity. It marks the transformation of the Christian-Messianic apocalypse into a dogmatic and liturgical church. From the very first, it was heretics who saved the Church and gave it its dogma and its liturgy, the two indispensable instruments of every religious conquest. The disciples of Valentinus, most significant of the Christian Gnostics, were the founders of that sacramental doctrine upon which the Catholic road of initiation developed.

According to Irenaeus of Lyons,[22] that indefatigable adversary of heretical Gnosticism, the teachings of Valentinus gave rise to two schools, one Italian, the other Oriental. The leader of the Italian school was Marcus, whose liturgical cycle represented a complete Gnostic liturgy. A leading member of the second was Theodotus, many of whose liturgical regulations and suggestions are cited in the *Stromateis* of Clement of Alexandria.

Irenaeus paints a curious and impressive picture of Marcus, whom he describes as conversant with the arts of magic, a seducer, a forerunner of the Antichrist, "like Anasilaos the conjurer." Marcus' teachings had spread from Asia Minor to the banks of the Rhone, where his Anatolian adherents settled. Irenaeus had before him his liturgical textbook, from which he quoted a number of sacramental formulas.

The six rites practiced by the disciples of Marcus were as follows: baptism as remission of sins, baptism as initiation into Gnosis, confirmation, the Eucharistic rite, the rite of the bridal chamber, and extreme unction—in other words, the sacraments of the Catholic church. In Chapters 13 to 22 of the first book of his great polemic, Irenaeus describes them in detail, beginning with the Eucharistic rite. Over the cups filled with wine and water Marcus recited his words of invocation, declaring that the grace (*charis*) which rests upon all things had poured its blood into the wine. Then those present drank the wine, in order that they too might partake of the grace he had invoked. Thereupon Marcus extended the cup full of mixed wine to the congregation, consisting for the most part of women, and bade them give thanks. After the thanksgiving, he took a cup larger than that for which the multitude had given thanks, and poured into it a part of the wine from the smaller, women's cup, which was then filled to overflowing, while he uttered magic formulas over it. After this action, he presented the cup to those present. Here, beyond any doubt, we find the first intimations of the doctrine of transubstantiation. After the consecration and eating of the Eucharist, Marcus summoned the women to prophesy, for they had been filled with grace.

But this was not the only interesting rite of initiation performed

---

22 *Adversus haereses*, I, 1.

by Marcus. Far more characteristic is another which Irenaeus designates as the rite of the bridal chamber.[23] Marcus, he tells us, prepared a bridal chamber and presided over the initiation of the
aspirants, uttering very special formulas, in which, for example,
he declared that this rite was the symbol of a spiritual marriage
modeled on the mystical marriage in the pleroma between Sophia,
the last suffering Aeon, and the Redeemer. Most probably the
ceremony described by Irenaeus is the only real consecration of
the spiritual marriage between two believers.

Irenaeus goes on to describe the liturgical cycle of Marcus[24] and
speaks of the redemption which the adherents of Marcus regarded
as invisible and intangible.

According to the doctrine of Marcus, there are two kinds of
baptism: that of Jesus, manifesting himself for the forgiveness of
sins, and another practiced in the name of the spirit which descended on Jesus and serving for the perfection of man. The first
baptism is of a psychic, the second of a spiritual nature. Even
though baptism had been initiated by John, redemption had been
effected only by Christ. The first baptism is the simple baptism of
water, the baptism of initiation, which contains the threefold Christian invocation. The triune formula recorded in Matthew 28:19 is
replaced by the threefold invocation of the unknowable Father, of
Truth, and the Spirit. The meaning, however, is the same. Through
initiation by baptism, the novice declares himself to be a part of
Him in whose name the baptism is administered.

This rite is followed by the rite of "redemption," in which the
"eternally hidden" name taken by Christ, the name of "the living
Christ," is invoked. In this "redemption" we can recognize the
sacrament of confirmation. Water and oil are poured on the initiate; he is anointed with balsam, and the following formula is
uttered: "I will separate one from the other neither the heart, nor
the spirit, nor the superabundant, merciful power that stands over
the heavens, that I may partake in Thy name, O redeemer of
truth." And the initiate answers: "I am sustained and redeemed,
and I detach my soul from this Aeon and from everything that is
of it, in the name of Iao, who redeemed his soul for redemption in

23 Ibid., 21, 3.
24 Ibid., ch. 21.

the living Christ." Irenaeus adds that the disciples of Marcus administered extreme unction to the dying by pouring water and oil on their heads. They commanded them to utter, after death, the following formula to the powers: "I am a son of the Father, the Father who was before all being, a son in the pre-existent. I came to see all, what was foreign and what was my own; and it was not entirely foreign to me; for it belongs to Achamoth; for I trace my lineage to the pre-existent, and I return to my own, whence I came." Standing in the presence of those who surround the demiurge, the dead must utter the following formula: "I am a vessel, more precious than the woman who made you. Your mother does not know your origin, but I know myself and know whence I came and I invoke the imperishable Sophia, who rests in the Father, the mother of your mother, who has no father or husband; born malefemale of woman, she bore you, without knowing her mother and in the belief that she alone was; but I invoke her mother." By uttering this formula the souls become invisible and immune to the attacks of hostile powers in the spirit world. This was the extreme unction administered by the disciples of Marcus.

Thus the liturgy of the Gnostic Marcus presents a complete prototype of the sacramentals of the Catholic church.

Another great master of Gnosticism, who devoted a large part of his doctrine to ritual and liturgy, was Theodotus. In the Laurentian Codex we find the *Excerpta ex Theodoto*[25] at the end of the eighth book of Clement of Alexandria's *Stromateis*. These *Excerpta*, numbering eighty-six, can be accepted, almost with certainty, as notes taken by Clement from the works of Theodotus and used as a basis for his *Stromateis*.

Theodotus, an Eastern disciple of Valentinus, gave an entirely new turn to Gnostic thought. He recognized the concept of "fate" and man's need to liberate himself from it. He ascribed great importance to the astral elements because of their influence on human destiny. Certain of these *Excerpta* are of a very special importance for the history of the Gnostic liturgy. First of all, Theodotus distinguished two kinds of baptism, baptism by water and baptism by fire: the former is accessible to sensory perception; the latter is

25 Robert Pierce Casey, ed. and tr., *Excerpta ex Theodoto* (London and Cambridge, Mass., 1934).

perceptible in the manner of the celestial fire, which is of a twofold nature. Baptism by water quenches the fire that is perceptible to the senses; baptism by fire protects us by means of the spirit from the fire of the mind.

According to Theodotus, the power of the water derives from the name of the godhead which is spoken over it. It is this name which gives the water its healing power. Theodotus also refers to anointing with oil and to transubstantiation. Oil and bread are hallowed "by the power of the name" which is uttered over the sacramental elements.

In Fragment 86, Theodotus cites Christ's famous reply to those who show him the talent of silver ("Render unto Caesar," etc.) and continues: "Through the power of Christ, the believer also bears within him the seal of the name of God and the spirit in His image. Like the unreasoning beast, who shows by the brand he bears to which flock he belongs, the believing soul is marked with the seal of truth and bears within it the divine emblems of Christ." Theodotus also professes a theory of marriage. In Fragment 63, he comments on the history of the creation of man as found in Genesis and explains the "calling" as the female element and the "election" as the male element. According to Theodotus, the male element is angelic; the female element is the Gnostics, who must unite with the male element in order to enter into the pleroma.

In this fragment there is a clearly recognizable reference to the marriage rite. Marriage is necessary to those who are elected for salvation. The wise virgins follow the call, while the foolish virgins remain excluded, far from their own angels. All the elect, says Theodotus, will take part in the marriage feast, and each will be joined with the heavenly angel, his bridegroom. But this spiritual union with the angels in the pleroma will be fulfilled only in connection with the union entered into on earth. Marriage is a condition necessary to those who live on earth but are not of this earth: woman is transformed in man, as the Church has transformed itself in the angels.

Finally, the fragments of Theodotus contain detailed and precise references to baptism, which is a purification preparatory to rebirth; to extreme unction, which is a spiritual confirmation; to the Eucharist, which is the bread of life; to marriage, which is the symbol of the heavenly marriage in the spirit.

Those passages, however, which reveal the Gnostic liturgy in its fullest and truest aspect are contained in two Gnostic works that have come down to us in Coptic renditions, the second of the two *Books of Jeu* (the guardian of the great light) and the *Pistis Sophia*.[26] The *Books of Jeu* belong to the second half of the second century; the *Pistis Sophia* was written before the end of the third century.

The scene in the second *Book of Jeu* is characteristic. Twelve years have passed since the resurrection of Christ; he is dwelling in Judaea with his disciples. He is preparing to disclose to them the great, ineffable, unsurmised secrets which have the power to efface the sin in man. All those who will share in these secrets will be deified and immortalized; after death they will enter into the kingdom of light and themselves become light.

Not all men can share in these secrets. A man must previously have renounced the world, must have turned all his thoughts toward eternal life, and must have received three baptisms: the baptism of water, the baptism of fire, and the baptism of the spirit—that mystery which protects us against the attacks of the Archons —and, finally, spiritual unction.

Jesus describes the three rites of baptism:

> Then it came to pass that Jesus summoned his disciples and spake to them: "Come all and receive the three baptisms before I speak to you of the mystery of the Archons." All the disciples, both male and female, came then to Jesus, and all together gathered round him. Jesus spake to them and said: "Go up towards Galilee and ye will meet a man and a woman in whom wickedness is nearly extinguished— the man does not hold intercourse and the woman is a virgin; from the hands of these two ye will receive two pitchers of wine; bring them here to me; and then bring vine shoots from that place."
>
> The disciples brought two pitchers of wine and the vine shoots from the appointed place. And Jesus laid an offering upon it; to the left of the offering he placed one pitcher of

26 Both the *Pistis Sophia* and the *Books of Jeu* are found in *Koptische-gnostische Schriften*, I, ed. Karl Schmidt (GCS 13, 2nd edn., Berlin, 1954).

wine, to the right of the offering he placed the other pitcher of wine, and upon it he strewed juniper berries and spikenard; he caused the disciples to be clad in linen raiment; he laid psyllium on their mouths and set upon their hands the sign of the seven voices, which is 9879, and in their hands placed sunweed and bade his disciples stand before the offering; to one side he laid out cloths of linen, and outside he set a pitcher of wine, over which he placed loaves to the number of the disciples. On the place where the offering rested he laid olive branches and on the heads of the disciples he set olive wreaths. And Jesus placed this sign upon his disciples.

His name is σαζαφαρας; and its interpretation is as follows: Oηζωζαζ. Jesus went with his disciples to the four corners of the world and commanded each one of them to set his feet close together and utter this prayer: "Hear me, my Father, Thou Father of all fathers, Thou infinite Light, which dwellest in the realm of light. Let the fifteen guardians come, who hold out the light to the seven virgins, and let them bestow the baptism of life. Their imperishable names are: Astrapa, Tesphoiode, Ontonius, Sinetos, Lachon, Poditanios, Opackis, Phaedros, Odontuchos, Diaktios, Knesion, Dromos, Euidetos, Polypaidos, Entropon. Let them come and baptize my disciples with the water of life of the seven virgins of light and efface their sins and cleanse them of their wickedness, and cause them to enter among the inheritors of the kingdom of light, and when Thou hast effaced their sins and taken away their wickedness, let a miracle occur and let ζοροκοθορα come and divide the water of life from the wine and make it spring up from one of these pitchers full of wine."

And in the very same moment the miracle occurred for which Jesus had prayed, and the wine to the right of the offering became water, and the disciples went in to Jesus and he baptized them, gave them of the offering and signed them with this seal. And the disciples were filled with great joy, for their sins had been forgiven them, and their wickedness was cloaked, and they were received among the number of the inheritors of the light and marked with the holy seal.

And it came to pass that Jesus resumed his sermon and spake to his disciples: "Bring me branches of vine, that ye may receive the baptism of fire." And the disciples brought him branches of vine and he laid incense upon them and also juniper berries, myrrh, cedar, gum from the mastix tree, spikenard, terebinth, and balsam from the cinnamon tree, and in the place of the offering set out cloths of linen, and outside he placed pitchers of wine, and upon them laid loaves to the number of the disciples. He bade all the disciples don linen raiment and wreathed them with verbena and laid psyllium on their mouths and commanded them to set the sign of the seven voices on their hands, and he himself laid flowers between their two hands and meadow-grass beneath their feet and placed them before the incense he had strewn, and bade them set their feet close together. And Jesus trampled the incense he had strewn and signed them with this seal.

Jesus went with his disciples toward the four corners of the world and with a loud voice spake the following prayer:

"Hear me, my Father, Father of all Fathers, thou infinite Light, make my disciples worthy to receive the baptism of fire, and worthy that thou mayest forgive them their sins."

The description of the rite, which by now included a great number of magical sacramental elements, is continued at great length. In the course of its development, Gnosticism became increasingly rich in religious concepts and liturgical usages. In order to combat it, the orthodox Church was compelled to adopt as many Gnostic elements as it could assimilate without disturbing the balance and justness that constitute the law of religious catholicity.

Gnosticism itself culminated in the ultramystical forms recorded in those apocryphal Acts that relate how the resurrected Jesus revealed the highest truths to his disciples. As late as the fourth and fifth centuries, the faithful who attended secret Gnostic conclaves still celebrated esoteric rites modeled on those which, according to the apocryphal Acts, were taught by Christ before or after the Passion and Resurrection.

In the Acts of John, Leucius Charinus describes the cult dance as follows:

Now before he was taken by the lawless Jews, . . . he gathered all of us together and said: Before I am delivered up unto them let us sing an hymn to the Father, and so go forth to that which lieth before us. He bade us therefore make as it were a ring, holding one another's hands, and himself standing in the midst he said: Answer Amen unto me. He began, then, to sing an hymn and to say:
Glory be to thee, Father.

207

And we, going about in a ring, answered him: Amen.

    Glory be to thee, Word; Glory be to thee, Grace. Amen.

    Glory be to thee, Spirit; Glory be to thee, Holy One:

    Glory be to thy glory. Amen.

    We praise thee, O Father; we give thanks to thee, O Light, wherein darkness dwelleth not. Amen.

Now wherefore we give thanks, I say:

    I would be saved, and I would save. Amen.

    I would be loosed, and I would loose. Amen.

    I would be wounded, and I would wound. Amen.

    I would be born, and I would bear. Amen.

    I would eat, and I would be eaten. Amen.

    I would hear, and I would be heard. Amen.

    I would be thought, being wholly thought. Amen.

    I would be washed, and I would wash. Amen.

    Grace danceth. I would pipe; dance ye all. Amen.

    I would mourn: lament ye all. Amen.

    The number Eight singeth praise with us. Amen.

    The number Twelve danceth on high. Amen.

    The Whole on high hath part in our dancing. Amen.

    Whoso danceth not, knoweth not what cometh to pass. Amen.

    I would flee, and I would stay. Amen.

    I would adorn, and I would be adorned. Amen.

    I would be united, and I would unite. Amen.

    A house I have not, and I have houses. Amen.

    A place I have not, and I have places. Amen.

    A temple I have not, and I have temples. Amen.

    A lamp am I to thee that beholdest me. Amen.

    A mirror am I to thee that perceivest me. Amen.

    A door am I to thee that knockest at me. Amen.

    A way am I to thee a wayfarer. Amen.

Now answer thou unto my dancing.

Behold thyself in me who speak, and seeing what I do, keep silence about my mysteries.

Thou that dancest, perceive what I do, for thine is this passion of the manhood, which I am about to suffer. For thou couldest not at all have understood what thou sufferest if I had not been sent unto thee, as the word of the Father. Thou that sawest what I suffer sawest me as suffering, and seeing it thou didst not abide but wert wholly moved. Thou hast me as a bed, rest upon me. Who I am, thou shalt know when I depart. What now I am seen to be, that I am not. Thou shalt see when thou comest. If thou hadst known how to suffer, thou wouldest have been able not to suffer. Learn thou to suffer, and thou shalt be able not to suffer. What thou knowest not, I myself will teach thee. Thy God am I, not the God of the traitor. I would keep tune with holy souls. In me know thou the word of wisdom. Again with me say thou: Glory be to thee, Father; glory to thee, Word; glory to thee, Holy Ghost. And if thou wouldst know concerning me, what I was, know that with a word did I deceive all things and I was no whit deceived. I have leaped: but do thou understand the whole, and having understood it, say: Glory be to thee, Father. Amen.

Thus, my beloved, having danced with us the Lord went forth. And we as men gone astray or dazed with sleep went this way and that. I, then, when I saw him suffering, did not even abide by his suffering, but fled unto the Mount of Olives, weeping at that which had befallen. And when he was crucified on the Friday, at the sixth hour of the day, darkness came upon all the earth. And my Lord standing in the midst of the cave and enlightening it, said: John, unto the multitude below in Jerusalem I am being crucified and pierced with lances and reeds, and gall and vinegar is given me to drink. But unto to thee I speak, and what I speak hear thou. I put it into thy mind to come up into this mountain, that thou mightest hear those things which it behoveth a disciple to learn from his teacher and a man from his God.[27]

This wonderful song is truly the acme and epitome of esoteric Gnosticism.

27 James, *Apocryphal New Testament*, pp. 253ff.

Gilles Quispel

Gnostic Man: The Doctrine of Basilides

1. Introduction

The great Christian Gnostics, Valentinus, Basilides, et al., were mystics: they seem to have had an inner experience which we must assume to have been, I shall not say true, but sincere and authentic. If even in our most meticulous researches we keep in mind this fundamental truth, Christian Gnosticism will appear to us in a new and unexpected light. For the mysticism of all times and all nations has its source in the same spiritual attitude and reveals the same trends. And that is why it often arrives at similar conclusions. Hence it should not surprise us to hear of a scholar who was able to find striking analogies between Basilides, for example, and the Buddhist religion of distant India.[1] This scholar, writing in the first years of the present century, tried to explain these parallelisms on the basis of a dependence: according to his hypothesis, Basilides, living in Alexandria in the second century A.D., borrowed his conceptions from a Buddhism propagated by Indian merchants visiting the great city at the crossroads of the world. The arguments on which this theory is based are none too substantial. We hope, indeed, to show in the course of this essay that Basilides was not influenced by the religions of the Far East. But that makes the problem all the more interesting, for we must then conclude that within the Greek world of the second century, within the Christian church of Alexandria, a mysticism comparable to the religions of India was born of an original and living inspiration which was the very foundation of the Gnostic doctrine.

When we consider the documents concerning Basilides in this perspective, which is that of the phenomenology of religions, we

---

1 J. Kennedy, "Buddhist Gnosticism, the System of Basilides," *Journal of the Royal Asiatic Society* (London, 1902), 377–415.

soon perceive that these texts have not always been studied with the respect due to all religious phenomena. And disrespect is indeed the offense with which we might reproach certain scholars who have concerned themselves in their way with the Gnosis of Basilides: having discovered that certain phrases of Basilides quoted by Hippolytus showed some resemblance to passages from other Gnostics transmitted by the same author, they presumed that all these texts were mere forgeries, ephemeral and fantastic inventions of a Roman Gnostic determined to make a little money and deceive the good Hippolytus. This would make a forgery of Hippolytus' whole collection, which contains the most varied documents, sometimes bearing the distinct imprint of a personal and individual experience.[2] What the proponents of this thesis forget is that such a forger would have had to be a religious genius. Hypotheses of this sort merely demonstrate the dullness of their author and clearly show that in philology, as in other fields, *akribeia* for its own sake is fatal.

However, the critical study of our sources for the doctrine of Basilides is not a simple matter. Clement of Alexandria has transmitted a number of fragments revealing a subtle mind, attentive to the message of the Gospel and concerned with the radical character of original sin; and Irenaeus gives an account of his system, representing it unmistakably as a theory of emanation. Hence it was a great surprise when in 1852 a young Greek discovered in a monastery on Mount Athos a book hitherto unknown, the *Elenchos* (*Refutatio*) of Hippolytus, which created a sensation among scholars and contains among other things a so-called Basilidian system irreconcilable with that described by Irenaeus, because it is clearly monist and evolutionist. Finally, we find in a Latin manuscript a fragment of Basilides in which he speaks of two eternal principles, light and darkness, and which can only be called dualistic.

Emanation, evolution, monism, dualism: what confusion, what contradiction! It is understandable that certain critics should have presumed that the doctrine transmitted by Hippolytus was not that of Basilides. What is less understandable is that these same scholars should have failed to recognize the importance of this document

---

2 H. Stählin, *Die gnostischen Quellen Hippolyts* (Leipzig, 1890).

for the knowledge of Christian gnosis. Actually, it is a matter of relative indifference whether the *Elenchos* reflects the original doctrine of Basilides himself or of an unknown Gnostic master. Even in anonymity, greatness remains greatness. De Faye, however, believes that the author of this document, which he believes to be of much later date than the era of the great Gnostics, was a man of little originality, whose sole merit was to take up again the ideas of the old masters and compound them into a new system foreshadowing the decadence and degenerescence of gnosis as embodied in the *Pistis Sophia* and the *Books of Jeu*.[3] But if, as is becoming increasingly evident, Hippolytus' note is authentic and reflects the original doctrine of Basilides, and if on the other hand, as recent discoveries demonstrate, the distance between the vulgar gnosis represented by such works as the *Apokryphon Johannis* and learned gnosis is much smaller than a de Faye or a Harnack would like to admit, why have these adherents of the school of the history of dogmas, who considered the Christian Gnostics as philosophers and theologians—why, I say, have these scholars fallen into such radical error? Is it perhaps because they approached the texts with a preconceived idea, which led them to reject and misunderstand everything that did not suit them? Is it because they wished to find their own rational, enlightened idealism in texts of an entirely different character?

And certain adepts of the school of the history of religions can also be reproached with disrespect for the texts. Bousset would like at all costs to find Iranian dualism in the Gnostic texts.[4] In a fragment of Basilides he finds the following words:

> Let us renounce this vain and curious eclecticism and rather examine the questions which the barbarians themselves propounded concerning goods and evils, and the opinions at which they arrived on all these matters. For there are some who have said that the principles of all things are two, to which goods and evils attach, and that these principles themselves are without principle and unengendered. That is to say, there was at the beginning light and dark-

---

3 Eugène de Faye, *Gnostiques et Gnosticisme* (Paris, 1913) , p. 215.
4 W. Bousset, *Hauptprobleme der Gnosis* (Göttingen, 1907) , pp. 93–96, based on a passage in Hegemonius's *Acta Archelai*, LXVII, ed. C. H. Beeson (Leipzig, 1906) , p. 95.

ness, which issued only from themselves and from nothing other. When each of these principles was in itself, each one led its own life, the life it wished and the life which was appropriate to it. For each thing loves that which is appropriate to it and nothing appears evil to itself. But after each principle had attained knowledge of the other, after darkness had contemplated light and recognized it as a better thing, it coveted the light and pursued it, desiring to join and participate in it. Such was the action of darkness. As for the light, it accepted nothing from darkness, nor desired it, but it did also feel impelled to contemplate it. And so it regarded darkness as in a mirror. And thus a reflection, that is to say, a certain color of light, arose in the darkness; but the light itself merely looked and withdrew, having taken no particle of darkness. The darkness, on the contrary, seized the regard of the light and the reflection or color that matter had received from it in the moment when it inspired horror in the light. As the most evil beings had taken from the best not the true light, but a certain appearance and reflection of it, it acquired a certain good by a rape which changed the nature of that good. This is why there is no perfect good in this world and why what good there is is exceedingly weak, since that which was conceived in the beginning was already weak. Nevertheless, thanks to this little light, or rather thanks to this appearance of light, creatures have had the strength to engender a semblance of this mixture of light that they had received. And that is the creature which we see.[5]

According to Bousset there is no doubt that this fragment reveals the true thinking of Basilides, that it shows the influence of Persian religion, and that it is one of the most important documents of Gnosticism. The notes of Hippolytus and Irenaeus (still according to Bousset) merely represent later developments and are not authentic.

But what does a rigorous analysis of this text in its context show? The author of the *Acta Archelai* wished to consider Basilides as a precursor and teacher of Mani. Accordingly, he wishes us to believe that Basilides taught the same dualism as the Persian Mani, and that he preached in Persia, not that he was influenced by Persian religion. Of this the *Acta Archelai* do not say a word. On

5 *Acta Archelai*, LXVII, 7–11; ed. Beeson, pp. 96–97.

the contrary, they tell us that Basilides borrowed the principle of dualism from a certain Scythianus, an apprentice in Egyptian and Pythagorean wisdom, who invented dualism in the course of his sojourn in Egypt.

We need not say that these fantasies are without historic value. It may seem curious, however, that the author, like modern scholars, believes that Manichaeism grew out of a Christianized gnosis. What is important, however, is that he nowhere mentions an Iranian influence.

If in this fragment Basilides cites the authority of certain barbarian writings, this does not mean that the content of these writings was Iranian. We know from other sources that the same Gnostic referred to the prophets Barcabbas and Barcoph and other more or less imaginary barbarians (Eusebius, *Historia Ecclesiastica,* IV, 7, 7, Mommsen) with names which do not seem particularly Persian. The syncretist writers of this period often affect exotic and mysterious pseudonyms, but in general they reflect the eclectic and vulgar philosophy of the Greek world. And this seems to be the case with the work which Basilides has quoted in this passage.

Here are the principal motifs of the text: the light is desired, the light is curious, hence it must be a woman, the Virgin of Light or a similar personage; this woman becomes a victim of her curiosity, like Psyche, who in the learned allegory of Apuleius wished to see the face of Eros. Basilides' contemporaries would surely have recognized this motif: the woman whose curiosity causes her to fall into the darkness of matter, they would have said, is a Platonic myth on the fall of the human soul. And indeed, Clement of Alexandria remarks that a certain Gnostic supposes, like a true Platonist, that the divine soul descended from on high into the world of generation and corruption because of its amorous desire (*Stromateis,* III, 13). The consequence of this catastrophe is that the visible world is an image of the luminous world, a conception close to that of Plato. Our fragment would seem, then, to reflect the pleasant, fragrant atmosphere of the syncretism then in vogue. But, to continue: darkness, the power which later created the world, is quite hostile to the light. Repelled by the darkness, the light departs. This reminds us of the Gnostic myths of the creation, of the hostile angels and Wisdom's disgust in the system of Valentinus

(*Excerpta ex Theodoto*, 33, 4) and in the *Apokryphon Johannis*. Finally, the absolute dualism of matter-darkness and spiritual world-light is found in various Gnostic documents. If we compare the fragment cited by Basilides with the oldest Gnostic document known up to now, Chapters I, 29–30 of Irenaeus, we find almost the same motifs. It would seem, then, that this exotic book, the authority of which is cited by Basilides, is merely a product of an early, pre-Christian gnosis.

But this fragment does not contain the Basilidian doctrine in the stricter sense. It is clear that the Gnostic quotes these lines with a certain sympathy: doubtless because they contain the doctrine of an original confusion, a chaotic state in which all things were intermingled. We know through Clement of Alexandria that Basilides accepted this conception (*Strom.* 2, 20), which, moreover, recurs in the account of Hippolytus. But, as we shall see, he modified it in a highly original way. Thus, the most we can say is that Basilides cited a Gnostic document and Hellenized and Christianized its content. In this case Bousset's hypothesis becomes highly improbable.

After this orientation we see clearly with what attitude a seeker after truth will approach these texts. He will have but one aim: to seize the original inspiration which animates the doctrine, whose depth and authenticity he recognizes. However, his method will be rigorously inductive: he will seek patiently to discover and determine the elements borrowed from the tradition, because he knows that there is no other means of distilling the original emotion. For this reason we have divided our essay into three parts, the first of which, rather technical in character, is an attempt to determine the Platonist influence, while the second stresses the Christian elements of the doctrine. These preliminary investigations will at length enable us to penetrate to the core of Basilidian gnosis.

2. The Frame: Platonist Philosophy

Basilides is the oldest Gnostic thinker known to us. Consequently, students of the origins of Christian Gnosticism have given very special attention to his doctrine. Some scholars have thought it to be of Oriental origin. Hilgenfeld and Bousset believed the

Basilidian theory to be an offshoot of Iranian dualism. Kennedy, on the other hand, asserted that Basilides borrowed most of his ideas from Buddhism. But these interpretations assuredly go too far. Basilides was an Alexandrian Christian living in the second century A.D. We may be justified in presuming a priori that he was primarily influenced by the spiritual currents of his era and of his native city. Recent studies and discoveries make it increasingly clear that the main currents to be considered are Egyptian Christianity, vulgar gnosis, and contemporary Platonism.

True, the orthodox church of Egypt has left us no literary documents, but the polemics of Valentinus and Clement of Alexandria against the *simpliciores* prove that such a church existed. Next, we may presume that the vulgar, or, if you prefer, pure, gnosis, which seems to have been imported to Egypt from the Near East and which in the course of the years assimilated certain Christian elements, goes further back than Basilides and Valentinus. Finally, the Platonism of the period, whose initiator is held to have been Antiochus of Ascalon, was in vogue in Alexandria, and it is this Platonism which contributed more than any other school to the philosophical formation of the great heresiarchs.

If I stress the influence of the *schools* on the Alexandrian Gnostics, it is in order to make it clear that in my opinion the Gnostics did not, as the "historians of dogma" like to believe, have a profound knowledge of classical philosophy. The period in which they lived owed most of its rather superficial philosophical notions to little manuals and arid doxographies. This is also true of Valentinus and Basilides. It even seems to me that Hippolytus' thesis that Basilides was inspired by Aristotelian doctrine rests upon rather dubious arguments. It is true that this hypothesis, energetically defended by a highly suspect witness, has been accepted by several modern scholars and has led them to doubt the authenticity of the account transmitted by Hippolytus, our principal source for the Basilidian gnosis.[6] But on close inspection we perceive that this presentation of the matter is schematic, artificial, and inexact. If we disregard certain conceptions which were accepted in that period by the most divergent schools and which had long been current in

6 C. Schmidt, *Religion in Geschichte und Gegenwart*, I, 790.

certain semi-civilized circles, the doctrine of Basilides, as transmitted by Hippolytus, shows no influence of the esoteric writings of the great Stagirite.

Nor can we consider the Gnostics as direct disciples of Plato, even if they had read some of his better-known works. For, considered as a whole, the eclectic Platonism of the epoch, and particularly its conception of the spiritual world, was far removed from the original doctrine of Plato. The truth is that this late Platonism taught certain opinions which are not to be found in the books of the master. The most important of these are the following:

a) The ideas are God's ideas but they serve as patterns solely for the things of nature.[7]

b) The spiritual world has been divided into two parts: on the one hand we have ideas residing as patterns in the mind of God; these are designated by the technical term "paradigmatic" (τὸ παραδειγματικόν) ; and on the other hand we have the ideas which served as an instrument for the creation of the world; these are called "organic" (τὸ ὀργανικόν) ; this conception is already found in the early works of Philo Judaeus of Alexandria.[8]

These Platonist concepts occur in all the texts of the Valentinian gnosis and are exceedingly important for their interpretation. Thus, for example, the relation between the Savior, who descends from the pleroma, and the Aeons becomes infinitely clearer if it is studied against the background of late Platonism: the Aeons are in certain respects ideas remaining in the consciousness of God (our sources tell us so quite categorically and no one has yet denied it) ; these ideas are the patterns for the things of nature; the demiurge (without knowing it) fashions the heavens after the ideal heavens, man after the archetypal man, and the earth after the ideal earth (Irenaeus, *Adversus haereses*, I, 5, 3) . The influence of Platonism is evident.[9] And it is tempting to give the same explanation of the conception of the Savior, formed by the union of all the Aeons and sent down from the pleroma to show the ideas to Wisdom and in-

---

7 Willy Theiler, *Die Vorbereitung des Neuplatonismus* (Berlin, 1930) , pp. 10, 15–19; Tertullian, *De anima*, xviii, 3 (Migne, *PL*, II, 678) . It does not seem to have been observed thus far that this rather important modification of original Platonism is also found in Tertullian.

8 Theiler, pp. 19ff.

9 See Pseudo-Justin, *Cohortatio ad Graeco*, 30 (Migne, *PL*, VI, 295–98) .

duce it to create the visible world. Beneath its mythological appearance does not this division of the ideas reflect the Platonist distinction between the "paradigmatic" and the "organic" which we have just noted? Are not the Aeons contained in the Νοῦς, the archetypal ideas, and does not the descending Savior represent in certain respects the instrumental ideas? It must indeed be admitted that the Valentinian notions, which at first sight seemed so complicated and confused, become quite simple and limpid when examined in the perspective of the Platonism of their time.

What is truly astonishing—and we frankly own that we did not expect this result from our researches—is that the same division of ideas recurs in the doctrine of Basilides as transmitted by Hippolytus. This is all the more surprising when we consider that the general view of things is quite different from that which we find in the documents of the Valentinian school. This would seem to exclude a mutual influence and suggest a common source.

Actually the two men lived at approximately the same time in the same city, Alexandria, where they received a Greek education; they must have been familiar with the same brand of Platonism, from which they both seem to have borrowed this conception of a division of ideas. To prove this thesis we shall have to outline the Basilidian conception of the world as we find it in the account of Hippolytus, *Elenchos*, VII, 20–27.

We know that according to Basilides the universal seed produced in the beginning by God contained a triple filiality which was in all things consubstantial with God. The first of these, as soon as it was produced, detached itself from the cosmic seed and rose up to God. Then the second was raised and placed below the first. It was only the third filiality, the spiritual man, who remained here below in the great mound of the universal seed.

Basilides, then, conceived the spiritual world as a hierarchy, composed of a God, two filialities, and the human spirit.

Though his conception of the spiritual world is quite remarkable, his view of the external world is rather simplistic. The visible world includes a zone of pneuma, a zone of ether, and finally a zone of air, beneath which is the earth. The origin of these zones is described in mythological images. This second filiality, we are told, was raised up by the "intermediate pneuma" (μεθόριον πνεῦμα). But

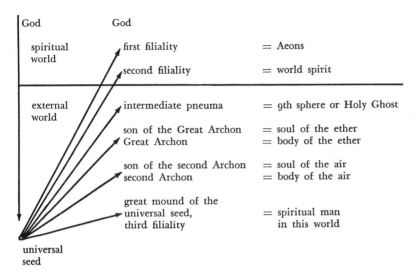

God	God	
spiritual world	first filiality	= Aeons
	second filiality	= world spirit
external world	intermediate pneuma	= 9th sphere or Holy Ghost
	son of the Great Archon	= soul of the ether
	Great Archon	= body of the ether
	son of the second Archon	= soul of the air
	second Archon	= body of the air
	great mound of the universal seed, third filiality	= spiritual man in this world

universal seed

BASILIDES' WORLD CONCEPTION

when these two reached the second filiality and God, the intermediate pneuma was compelled to remain behind, because it was not
of the same substance and nature as the transcendent entities. That
is why the intermediate pneuma is in the immediate vicinity, but
not within the confines of this blessed zone; it is the firmament
(στερέωμα) between the visible world and the transcendent world
and is situated beyond the sky (ὑπεράνω τοῦ οὐρανοῦ).

It is clear that this demarcation line, this iron curtain, as it were,
between the two worlds, designates the sphere outside the visible
world. Like a true syncretist thinker, Basilides identified this entity
with the Holy Ghost of the Christians. All this is comprehensible.
But how shall we conceive of an "intermediate pneuma" which,
though belonging to the perceptible world, is beyond the heavens?
For by heavens the Gnostic seems to mean the Ogdoad, the heaven
of the fixed stars, which is the dwelling of another entity and is
below the demarcation line (Hippolytus, *Elenchos*, VII, 23, 7).
There is, then, according to Basilides, still another region beyond
the fixed stars. Greek astronomy knew the conception of a ninth
sphere. We might then suppose that the intermediate pneuma,
which is at the same time the Holy Ghost, was localized by Basilides
in the ninth sphere, posited by the Greek astronomy of that time

219

and adopted by Ptolemy the Alexandrian astronomer in his geocentric system. Be that as it may, the intermediate pneuma constitutes the highest part of the perceptible world.

After the ascent of the Holy Ghost, the Great Archon rises from
the formless mound of the universal seed to the demarcation line.
He then produces a son far wiser and better than himself, whom he
places at his right hand. After this, inspired by his son, he forms
the region of the ether (23).

It is evident that in certain respects this Archon is the Jewish God;
the son whom he sets at his right hand is the pre-existent Messiah.
But why is this son wiser and better than his father? Why is the
father subordinated to his son? Hippolytus believed that he knew.
This son, he said, "is the entelechy of an organic physical body, he
is the soul acting upon the body. . . . Basilides conceived the relation between the Great Archon and his son as Aristotle before him
conceived the relation between body and soul" (24, 1).

Hippolytus cannot be said to have found all this in his source.
However, it is possible that the heretic conceived the relation between son and father as that between soul and body. For Hippolytus seems to be rendering the doctrine of Basilides and not his own
invention when he describes the action of the Son on his Father in
these words: "as the entelechy directs the body, so does the son,
according to Basilides, direct the God who is more ineffable than all
ineffable things. But all ethereal things as far as the moon are
animated and directed by the entelechy of the Great Archon" (24,
2, 3).

It is possible that a philosophical conception is concealed beneath
this mythologem. For we do in that period encounter the belief
that according to Aristotle God was the soul and body of the ether.

> Aristotle and his disciples, introducing a being analogous
> to a composite living creature, say that God is constituted
> by a soul and a body. They think that *his body* is the *ether*
> with the planets and fixed stars, all of which revolves; that
> his soul is the reason presiding over the movement of the
> body, being itself motionless and the cause of this move-
> ment.[10]

It is not impossible that Basilides combined this philosophical
conception, which he may have found in any doxography, with

10 Athenagoras, *Supplicatio,* VI. French tr. by G. Bardy (Paris, 1943), p. 85.

mythologems having nothing to do with Greek wisdom: for in his version the Ogdoad, the dwelling place of the Great Archon and the son who inspires him, includes the ethereal region of the fixed stars and planets. Nevertheless, the opinion of Hippolytus is erroneous. For the doctrine described in the *Supplicatio* of Athenagoras is not, as Hippolytus would have us believe, to be found in the preserved writings of Aristotle, but presumably goes back to the young Aristotle of the lost dialogues.[11]

After the intermediate pneuma and the Great Archon of the ether another Archon rises from the great mound and also produces a son: this lower Archon reigns over the sublunar world: his domain is the air (24). It is not certain that this lower Archon should be identified with the devil.

If we disregard certain mythological amplifications and certain philosophical emendations, it would seem that fundamentally this conception of the external world is a variation on a well-known theme: the sensory world includes a pneumatic region, an ethereal region, and an aerial region which surround the earth; in this there is nothing astonishing. Moreover, the philosophers and syncretists of that period liked to describe how the elements, one after another, detached themselves from brute, chaotic matter and rose up to occupy the place befitting their greater or lesser subtlety. Accordingly, this conception of Basilides, which perhaps reveals a Stoic or Peripatetic influence, might be that of an eclectic Platonist. On the other hand, the Stoics and Peripatetics would never have recognized the existence of a spiritual world composed of God, two filialities, and man. It is not the Portico or the Academy which could have inspired this doctrine, for the simple reason that those schools did not know of a transcendent world. Moreover, though it is probable that Christianity suggested the term "filiality," since the pre-existent Christ is the son of God and the elect are the sons of God, it is impossible to see how this Christian conception could have led to the doubling of the transcendent filiality. Finally, the vulgar gnosis preceding Basilides knows of a pleroma populated by innumerable entities such as Aeons, Ogdoads, lights, angels, and powers, but not this relatively simple conception of a double, transcendent filiality.

What then can be the significance of the triple filiality? In the

11 Luigi Alfonsi, "Traces du jeune Aristote dans la *Cohortatio ad Gentiles*," *Virgiliae Christianae* (Amsterdam), II (1948), 8off.

literature on Basilides, and even in the monograph of Hendrix,[12] we search in vain for a serious interpretation of this mythologem. De Faye even goes so far as to say that it is "indubitably a most curious conception, but an absurd one even for a speculative thinker of that time." We shall see, however, that this conception cannot have been invented by Basilides because several texts of the imperial period show striking analogies to it. And what shall we say of Kennedy's theory of a Buddhist Basilides? In the triple filiality he finds the three *guṇas,* i.e. *sattva* (the intellectual, light principle), *rajas* (the emotional principle), and *tamas* (the heavy, dark principle); his interpretation would place the second filiality in the region of the passions—*rajas.* But it is hardly sound methodology to elucidate an obscure conception by a very remote analogy, and we are not justified in ignoring the facts of the text even in order to obtain such alluring conclusions. And this is just what Kennedy does when he situates the second filiality in the region of the passions, when the texts place it in the transcendent world above the line of demarcation dividing it from the visible world.

Such adventurous and unsubtle interpretations cannot be sustained in the presence of the facts: the conception of a triple filiality is neither absurd nor exotic, but finds exact parallels in the texts of Hellenic syncretism.

In this connection we must extend our researches to a passage in Arnobius which has hitherto escaped the attention of students of Basilides. It is true that editors of Arnobius have wished to correct the transmitted text. But it has long been recognized that the manuscript is excellent and requires no conjectures. On the subject of the human soul, the Christian rhetorician questions his adversaries: "Is this, then, the soul which you call learned, immortal, perfect, divine, which after God is the cause of things and after the twin Intellects occupies fourth place?"[13]

This passage presents a striking analogy with the conception of Basilides. The God who is the "cause of things" can be regarded as a parallel to the God whom Basilides names αἴτιος τῶν πάντων. The

---

12 P. J. G. A. Hendrix, *De alexandrijnsche Haeresiarch Basilides* (Amsterdam, 1926).

13 Arnobius, II, 25: "Haecine est anima docta illa quam dicitis, immortalis perfecta divina, post deum principem rerum et post mentes geminas locum optinens quartum et affluens en craterilas vivis?"

"learned, immortal, divine soul" is none other than the spiritual man (the third filiality) : and the "twin intellects," *mentes geminae,* correspond to the two filialities situated between God and man. One question arises, however: in what period did the conception mentioned by Arnobius originate, and what is its significance? The adversaries of Arnobius seem to have been Gnostics of various schools and sects, who invoked the authority of Plato among others and lived in the third century A.D.[14] It seems certain, however, that the doctrine of a double divine mind goes further back than Porphyry and even Plotinus, because it occurs in two documents which do not seem to have undergone the influence of Neoplatonism, namely the Hermetic book of *Asclepius* and the *Chaldaean Oracles.*

The *Asclepius* contains a passage whose meaning has been well brought out by Father Festugière's translation:

> The total intellect (*omnis sensus,* ὁ πᾶς νοῦς) which resembles the godhead, is without motion of its own but moves in its stability: it is holy, incorruptible, eternal, and possessed of any superior attribute there may be, since it is the eternity of the supreme God, subsisting in absolute truth. It is infinitely filled with all sensible forms (*sensibilium,* or, better: νοητῶν = intelligible things) ; it is universal, coexistent, as it were, with God. The intellect of the world (*sensus mundanus,* ὁ ἐγκόσμιος νοῦς) is the receptacle of all sensible forms and particular orders. Finally, the human intellect depends on the retentive power proper to the memory, thanks to which it preserves the recollection of all its past experiences. The divine intellect does not descend beyond the human animal.[15]

In this passage the author distinguishes four divine intellectual entities: the godhead, the total intellect, the intellect of the world, and the intellect of man. Clearly this presents a striking analogy to the passage in Arnobius quoted above. And it is only on the basis of the Hermetic work that we can understand the meaning of the *mentes geminae* of Arnobius. These are the introspective intuition of the godhead and the intellect of the world, which is directed

---

14 See A.-J. Festugière, "La Doctrine des *Viri novi* . . . d'après Arnobe," *Mémorial Lagrange,* ed. L. H. Vincent (Paris, 1940) , pp. 97–132.

15 *Asclepius,* 32. French tr. by Festugière in A. D. Nock and A.-J. Festugière, *Hermès Trismégiste* (Paris, 1945) , II, 340. [Cf. W. Scott, ed., *Hermetica* (4 vols., Oxford, 1924–36) , I, 355.]

largely toward externals. If our hypothesis that the *sensibilia* of which this passage speaks should be identified with the νοητά, or ideas, is sound, we may conclude that the conception is Platonic.

These two divine intellects, immediately followed by the soul, seem to occur also in the *Chaldaean Oracles,* which mention a Heavenly Father, a paternal intellect, and a second intellect. Kroll supposes God and the paternal intellect to be identical.[16]

It would seem, however, that the excellent author of the *Oracles* was more skeptical in this respect. For Pletho tells us categorically that the *Oracles* designate the paternal intellect as a second God (δεύτερος θεός).[17]

This explains the following verses (Kroll, p. 14) :

> δυὰς παρὰ τῷδε κάθηται·
> ἀμφότερον γὰρ ἔχει, νῷ μὲν κατέχειν τὰ νοητά
> αἴσθησιν δ᾽ ἐπάγειν κόσμοις·

(A dyad is seated before him;
for he has this double aspect: he contains the ideas
in his mind and brings perception to the worlds.)

Our surprise becomes still greater when we read (Kroll, p. 28) :

> μετὰ δὴ πατρικὰς διανοίας
> ψυχὴ ἐγὼ ναίω θέρμῃ ψυχοῦσα τὰ πάντα.

(After the paternal intellects
I, the soul, remain, animating the universe with my warmth.)

We believe, then, that we are justified in saying that the *Chaldaean Oracles,* which seem to date from the second century A.D. and reveal a Platonist influence, presuppose a triad consisting of a supreme God and two intellects and followed by the soul.[18] We may presume the Gnostics of Arnobius to have held the same conceptions as we find in the *Asclepius.* All these passages contain indications

16 W. Kroll, "Die Oraculis Chaldaicis," *Breslauer Philologische Abhandlungen,* VII (1894), 14.
17 Quoted by W. Theiler, *Die Chaldäischen Orakel und die Hymnen des Synezius,* Schriften der Königsberger Gelehrten Gesellschaft, 18, 1 (Halle, 1942), p. 7.
18 See E. R. Dodds, "Theurgy and Its Relation to Neoplatonism," *Journal of Roman Studies* (London), XXXVII (1947), 55ff.

that these two divine intellects signify on the one hand the introspective intuition of the godhead (or else the archetypes in the mind of God) and on the other hand the "extraverted" mind of God, turned principally toward the outward world. Basilides' doctrine of the triple filiality shows an unmistakable analogy to these speculations. Furthermore, the atmosphere of the Basilidian gnosis is much closer to Hermeticism and the Chaldaean system than to the pedantic and arid Platonism of the first centuries of the Roman empire. We might then be tempted to suppose that Basilides borrowed his conception from the syncretistic systems of Hellenistic gnosis. Alluring as it is, this hypothesis encounters an objection which is more than a matter of detail. For we do not know whether these Hellenistic systems, or at least the conception we have been discussing, existed at the time of Basilides. All the documents we have just quoted are of a later date. The most that can be said today is that the documents of the vulgar Egyptian gnosis, which have preserved a number of doctrines anterior to Basilides, do not mention any conception analogous to that of the triple filiality. Hence it is more prudent to assume that the pagan Gnostics and the Christian Gnostic drew on a common source. Seen in this perspective, the speculation on God's two intellects as well as the mythologem of the triple filiality would be merely an adaptation and mystical development of the Platonic doctrine which distinguished the archetypal (paradigmatic) ideas from the instrumental (organic) ideas. Since this doctrine was accepted by Philo of Alexandria and Valentinus of Alexandria, it seems quite possible that Basilides should also have adopted it.

But was Basilides a Platonist?

The fragments preserved by Clement as well as the account of Hippolytus show that Basilides was influenced by Platonism. True, the fundamental experience of gnosis in general and of the Basilidian gnosis in particular is far from being either Christian or Platonist; it is nonetheless true that Basilides expressed this experience in Platonic terms and more than once modified the conceptions he found in the Gnostic tradition in a manner consonant with his philosophical education. Platonist influence can be found both in the fragments and in the system.

A. D. Nock was therefore right in saying: "An explanation in

terms of Platonism and independent thought fits the general accusation against Basilides and Valentinus, that they followed Greek
philosophy rather than revealed truth."[19]

Consequently, the Platonist conception of a division of ideas can
help us to explain the doctrine of the triple filiality in Basilides.
Hippolytus' account declares: Basilides divides being (τὰ ὄντα)
into two main, contiguous parts, one of which he calls the world
(κόσμος) and the other the transcendent world (τὰ ὑπερκόσμια;
Elenchos, 23, 2). It is quite possible that these terms refer to the
sensory world and the spiritual world of the Platonists. In this
same document there is an allusion to a time before the creation of
the world, when there were as yet neither sensory nor spiritual
things (δι' αἰσθήσεως λαμβανομένων ἢ νοητῶν πραγμάτων; 21, 1);
this seems to indicate that after the creation there were νοητά,
ideas, as well as perceptible things. Finally, we read—and this is
especially significant—of the "ideas of the filiality" (τὰ νοήματα τῆς
υἱότητος), which are communicated to us in the visible world
(25, 7). These passages permit us to conclude that the two filialities
must be conceived as τὸ παραδειγματικόν, the introspective intuition
of God and the seat of the ideas, and τὸ ὀργανικόν, the "extraverted"
mind of God, in the sense employed by the syncretist authors we
have quoted.

True, these "ideas of the filiality" in Basilides are not exactly
Platonic ideas. This we must conclude from a fragment transmitted
to us by Clement. This fragment speaks of two "hypostases," Justice
and her daughter Peace, which remained in the Ogdoad. The context of this fragment in Clement (Strom., IV, 25, 162) suggests that
this Ogdoad is not situated in the sensible world but is the superior
Ogdoad.[20]

If this is true, the brief fragment on "Justice and her daughter
Peace" is extremely important. For it then shows that Basilides
conceived these "ideas of the filiality," these archetypes remaining
in the mind of God, not as ulterior objects of rational thought, but

---

19 Arthur Darby Nock in *Classical Philology* (Chicago), XXXVII:4 (1942),
450, n. 12 (review of Konstantin Vilhelmson, *Laktanz und die Kosmogonie des
spätantiken Synkretismus*, Tartu, 1940).
20 Actually, Basilides did not deprecate justice as did Marcion and Valentinus:
according to him the supreme God is just (*Strom.*, IV, 11, 83: δίκαιον δὲ τὸν
θεόν).

as Aeons, powers, and hypostatic personifications revealed by initiation.

3. Christian Influence

Platonist philosophy provides the frame of Basilides' thought. But the movement of his thinking is not in the least Platonist. To appreciate this contrast we need only compare those sublime pages of the *Phaedrus* or *Symposium* in which the noble Athenian describes with inspired enthusiasm the ascent of the human soul, raised by the love of beauty to the spiritual heights where it rediscovers its home and contemplates the pure ideas of eternal being. This theme was developed by the Platonists of the second century (Maximus of Tyre 143, 11 Th. 57). We may reasonably presume that Basilides was familiar with it. Yet, what a contrast! For Basilides, it is not man who rises up to seek God, but God who descends to reveal himself to man. Revelation moves downward from on high, ἄνωθεν κάτω, to use his own words. For him this descent was not a metaphor without content, as it is for a modern man who can no longer accept the geocentric conception of the world. Basilides visualizes this descent in a striking image: the strange new light spreads through the dark, ignorant worlds, illumining all the terrifying demoniacal powers which people this universe, and finally descends on Jesus at the moment of his baptism. The conception concealed beneath mythological details is a simple one: only Christ reveals the unknown God. Yet this is the fundamental experience of the great heretics of the second century. And this is not the subjective impression of a modern student: it is the explicit testimony of the sources themselves. The conception is found in Marcion as well as in Basilides and Valentinus. Their sole preoccupation was salvation, their only hope, Christ. Despite differences in detail, all three believed, each in his own way, that man by himself cannot know God (and it should be stressed that, according to Basilides and Valentinus, even the spiritual man could not know God before the coming of Christ), that Christ was alone in revealing him, that man receives the gnosis of an unknown, transcendent God through Christ, i.e. indirectly.

Each of these heretics expressed these conceptions in his own way. Basilides expresses them as follows: Before the coming of

Christ everything was veiled in a mysterious silence. This was the mystery which, in the words of the apostle, was not made known to the sons of men in other ages (*Elenchos*, VII, 25, 3). For "God is so great and such is His nature, that creation cannot express Him or conceive Him in thought" (22, 1). Consequently "the third filiality, spiritual man, is abandoned like an abortion in the formlessness [of our sublunar world]. The mystery which in other ages was not made known to the sons of men must be revealed to him" in accordance with the words of Scripture: "How that by revelation he made known to me the mystery" and "I heard unspeakable words which it is not lawful for a man to utter."

This ardent aspiration, this unquenched thirst of the spiritual man assumes cosmic dimensions: the entire universe suffers with him, suffers because of him. And here Basilides invokes St. Paul, alluding to the profound words of the Epistle to the Romans: "When it was needful that we be manifested, we the children of God, for whom the creature sighed in the pangs of childbirth while awaiting revelation, then it was that the Gospel came into the world and entered into every principle and every power and every thing that can be named" (25, 5).

"This light of the Gospel descended upon Jesus, son of Mary, and he was illumined, set aflame by the light that cast its brightness upon him" (26, 8). This Jesus, who must be distinguished from the divine Christ which descended on him, was the spiritual man *par excellence*. "He is the inner spiritual man in the natural man (ψυχικός) according to their conception," who was predestined from all eternity (προλελογισμένος) to receive the Christ (27, 6, 7).

This union of the Christ and Jesus determines the course of history. For now the spiritual power of the sons of God is confirmed according to their nature by this light which has projected its brightness downward from on high (26, 10); the third filiality has been purified by the Christ (27, 11).

For Basilides, as for the other heretics, the coming of Christ was the decisive moment in human history, the moment in which eternity traverses and intersects all the *"Seinsschichten die sich überlagern."* And this "revelation of transcendent things" is the goal of all human history.

Less radical than the other heretics, Basilides could not accept the notion that history is meaningless and has fallen into absurdity. To him God is the absolute and transcendent cause of all things ($\alpha\H{\iota}\tau\iota os \pi\acute{\alpha}\nu\tau\omega\nu$; 27, 7) ; his plan is carried out in the course of time. Before the beginning of the cosmic process, God established in his mind which things should happen when and how (24, 5). It may seem, to be sure, that a great Archon, a god of this world, has put himself forward to dominate the visible world: all this is necessary, everything in its time, nothing is unforeseen: "for all these events were predestined by God," the transcendent, unknown God who acts behind the scenes and carries out his plan conceived in the beginning. God's plan, however, the goal of history, is the salvation of man, who must be manifested and then restored to the spiritual world when the time has come (25, 1). And the salvation of man does not signify primarily the personal salvation of any individual, but rather the deliverance of the entire human race. It might be argued that according to Basilides not all the living creatures called men are saved. But these men without spirit, who feel so thoroughly at home in the immanent world and know no transcendental nostalgia—are they men in the true sense of the word? Basilides categorically denies this: "We are men," he declares, "all the others are pigs and dogs."[21] Man is purely and simply the spiritual man. In this perspective, the coming of Christ, prepared for by all preceding history according to God's plan, is the spiritual freedom of all humanity.

If the descent of Christ is the center of history, toward which the preceding development moves and which determines the subsequent development, history must have a beginning and an end. Thus the strictly Christocentric conception implies a true philosophy of history which is quite remarkable and in certain respects suggests that of Hegel. Basilides applies the notion of evolution to the history of the universe and finds instructive comparisons to elucidate his thought. Let us, he tells us, observe the development of a human being: the teeth appear only several months after birth; the spermatic vein does not function before the fourteenth year;[22] the intelligence develops only after a certain number of years—in short the growing man gradually becomes what he was not before:

21 Epiphanius, *Panarion*, 24, 5, 2; ed. Holl, *GCS*, I, 262.
22 This is my interpretation of the enigmatic words on the child's $\pi\alpha\tau\rho\iota\kappa\H{\eta}$ $o\dot{\upsilon}\sigma\iota\alpha$.

however, all his faculties were virtually present in the newborn babe. The same is true of the universe: "All the things which we can enumerate and all the things of which we can say nothing because they have not yet been discovered, which were to belong to the future universe that has been developed progressively, all in its appointed time, by God . . . were heaped up within the original germ" (*Elenchos*, VII, 22, 1). This germ is a potential world, comparable to a mustard seed which contains a whole plant, a world in which everything was present in an undifferentiated state.

In the beginning, then, there was confusion. From this great mound issued one after another the personifications representing the strata of the universe: the ideal world, the world spirit, the pneuma, the ether, the air. The invisible and external world were formed in successive stages. Everything is perfect: nothing is missing. However, "the third filiality still remains in the great mound of the universal seed." This is man, who is in this world but does not belong to it; from the very beginning he is consubstantial with God, because he is spiritual, but he does not yet know this. The aim of history, the *raison d'être* of the universe, is to "manifest man and to restore him" to his spiritual home (25, 1). True, history requires centuries to arrive at this aim: for hundreds of years the Archons reign, who are quite different from God and do not know God. But without knowing it they carry out the pre-established plan of God, who directs the historical process.

If it is permissible to transpose the mythological terminology of Basilides into better-known categories and to interpret so obscure a text with a certain boldness, we may divide the history of the world into three periods: that of paganism, dominated by the devil; that of Judaism, in which Yahweh ruled; and that of Christianity, inaugurated by Jesus. Thus the history of religions, represented by the gods men worship, culminates in Christianity, which is the absolute religion. The Gospel, which is nothing other than the revelation of the transcendent world, has spoken through the mouth of Jesus. This was the decisive moment in the history of the universe: for it was then that, thanks to revelation, man for the first time became aware of his kinship with God. And this determines the whole subsequent course of history: like Jesus, the elect among men can remember their divine essence and return to God. Through Christ, the spiritual man is freed from matter and purified, the spiritual element is released from the great and formless mound of the immanent world, the great differentiation begins. And that is why Jesus is called "the initiator of the differentiation of confounded things."

Ever since the decisive moment of Christ's coming, the last period of history has been in progress: the spirit can take form, now that "its total power has been confirmed according to its nature by the light that has descended from on high." The spirit returns to its proper dwelling place. This process will be continued until the filiality has fully purified itself and has crossed the limit of the spiritual world. That is the moment of restitution, when everything finds the place assigned to it by nature. Then there will be no more nostalgia, no more tears, but absolute repose, the consummation of the historic process. "And such will be the restitution of all the things that were heaped up in the germ of the universe at the beginning; at the proper moment they will be restored to the place befitting them."

This conception of history is both simple and grandiose: history has a beginning, confusion or σύγχυσις; a center, the φυλοκρίνησις, or election of the chosen people; and an end, the restitution or ἀποκατάστασις. "Their whole doctrine is summed up in the confusion of the universal germ, and in the selection and restitution to their proper place of the things that are now confounded" (27, 11). This historic process is determined by God's pre-established plan, which is progressively carried out in the course of the centuries. This plan, it goes without saying, does not change in accordance with the arbitrary will of this God. It is an unalterable law, fixed and eternal, given in the beginning of the world as an immanent force which directs evolution. "Do not seek to know whence have issued the things of which I say that they appeared later, after the planting of the cosmic seed. For [this cosmic germ] contains piled up within it all the [particular] seeds, not yet existing and destined to come into being by a God who is not" (22, 6). This doctrine, so original and characteristic, is found in a fragment preserved by Clement (irrefutably proving the authenticity of Hippolytus' account): "Providence was inseminated in the substances by the God of man's salvation at the very moment of their genesis [in the universal germ] by the God of all things" (*Strom.*, IV, 13, 90). The purpose of this plan is man's salvation; history is the history of salvation which is accomplished when Jesus teaches men that God is their Father. Now man can be free; the elect can purify themselves and leave the world to regain the spiritual dwelling places to which they were destined.

It is clear that this conception of history cannot be of Greek origin, for the simple reason that the Greeks conceived no philosophy of history, excepting for Poseidonius, whose idea of it was very different. True, Basilides expresses himself as a learned man and sometimes uses philosophical terms, but the meaning he ascribes to them is new and original. In this connection it is interesting to consider one of the terms he borrowed: the "restitution of all things" (ἀποκατάστασις τῶν πάντων) was of Stoic origin. But how changed is its content! For the Stoics, the apocatastasis was the return of things to their primitive state in the course of the successive and aimless cycles of the cosmic process. For Basilides, on the other hand, the apocatastasis is the realization of the aim of history; in it things regain the place which was appointed to them by nature but which they never occupied before. The same term designates two very different conceptions.

The same is true of the term "original confusion." Basilides seems to have found this expression in the work (a Gnostic work, in our opinion) which he quotes in his commentary on the Gospel. It is interesting to note how he modified this conception. In the Gnostic work the confusion of things, the chaotic state at the beginning of the world, was the consequence of a fall. The Virgin of Light fell into pre-existing matter. Basilides does not accept these ideas. These conceptions, dear to gnosis, are not adopted in his system and are not to be found in his fragments: "Basilides absolutely avoids, and fears to speak of, an *emanation*. For how would it be possible for God to require an emanation or a pre-existing matter to make the cosmos, in the manner of a spider spinning its web or of a mortal man taking copper or wood or any other material to fashion it" (22, 2). Even the primitive germ from which the universe issued is not an emanation; indeed, it is nothing other than the creative word God uttered when he said: "Let there be light." There is no emanation and no pre-existing matter: "He spoke and it came to pass." We find—and this is absolutely startling —that Basilides attempted to introduce into gnosis the conception of a *creatio ex nihilo,* and that for this reason he eliminated the mythologems of a fallen Wisdom or of an archetypal man.

It seems that it was also Christian influence which gave the system of Basilides an eschatological tendency. The early Christians awaited the end of the world and believed that it would come as soon as the number of the elect was complete. These believers had been elected before the creation of the world, and all history, the entire universe in fact, awaited their deliverance. Basilides' account of the genesis of the world is not very unusual. Quite a number of philosophical and syncretist documents of the time offer similar cosmogonies. What is truly extraordinary is his idea of historical evolution, culminating in the coming of Christ and the end of the historic process. I shall not go so far to say that this idea is to be found in the Bible, but it is certain that in reading the Bible the ancient Christians formed the idea of a historic evolution, beginning with creation, having as its center the coming of Christ, and culminating in the liberation of the elect from the *massa perditionis.* I think it safe to say that Basilides' conception is a development, though a very free one, of these Christian conceptions. It is certain that the clearly predestinationist theology of St. Paul made a profound impression on him: the idea of election, fundamental in Basilides as well as Valentinus, was borrowed from the apostle, though the Gnostics assuredly distorted it.[23]

All in all, the Gnostic election is, as it were, a *mystification* of the Biblical conception. It remains none the less true that the mere adoption of this doctrine shows the enormous influence of Christianity on Basilides.[24]

This Christian influence is not a matter of detail, but gives an

23 When the apostle speaks of the chosen people, he has in mind the historic people of Israel, of which the Christian Church is a continuation, while Basilides applies this term to the transcendent, i.e. nonhistorical, spirit. Furthermore, St. Paul would never have identified God's predestination with astrological fatality in the manner of the Gnostic master.
24 It should not be forgotten that this man wished most of all to be a Christian. He wrote innumerable commentaries on the Bible. It is even probable that he was a member of the Church: we have no indication that he was excommunicated. Egyptian Christianity seems to have been rather peculiar and extremely

eschatological perspective to the entire system. If Basilides saw the history of the world from an evolutionist point of view, it is because the historical process is directed toward an end. "All things below strive upward."

This trait becomes particularly important when we recall that Gnosticism tends to be retrospective.

The recently discovered *Gospel of the Egyptians,* "a document of high gnosis, swarming with cabalistic formulas," lists Aeons, powers, Ogloads without number. The external world, the course of history are scarcely mentioned. Such works must have been known to Basilides, but how different is the atmosphere in his doctrine, which is not a regression to the origin but an anticipation of the end (*nicht Nacherleben des Ursprungs, sondern Vorwegnahme des Endes*); it is oriented strictly toward future events, toward the supreme moment which will bring the restitution of all things; it is dominated by an eschatological tendency.

True, this eschatology is different from that of primitive Christianity, which liked to paint the end of the world in the most garish colors. For Basilides the end of the historic process is the end of the impulse which animates the universe: everything is in its place, imbalance has been done away with, disorder has ceased. The regions of being succeed one another in perfect harmony. The spirit has arrived at its end. "When the entire filiality has come together and risen beyond the limit, then the world will find mercy. For up until now it sighs and suffers and awaits the manifestation of the sons of God, in order that all men belonging to the filiality may rise from this world. When that occurs, God will bring *the great ignorance* over the whole world in order that all things may remain in their place and nothing may desire anything contrary to its nature" (*Elenchos,* VII, 27, 3). These are words of infinite melancholy; imagine, if you will, this great merciful ob-

---

tolerant. It was in Rome that bold, unsubmissive thinkers were excommunicated.

Let us add that this conception of history cannot have been borrowed from Gnosticism. For gnosis is essentially a revolt against time; it aspires to an eternity which negates and annuls the flow of time. *Time must have a stop.* If a Gnostic recognizes that historical evolution is necessary for salvation, he does so in spite of himself, because Christianity has opened his eyes to this truth.

livion descending upon the earth and covering all things like snow.

And those who have remained here below must not attempt to pass the limit imposed on them. They cannot attain to the things of the spirit. The psychic man does not accept the things of the spirit. A time will come when no knowledge of the spiritual world will be left in this world. No one will know that there is a beyond; all men will content themselves with the given world. Happily so, for if they aspired to the impossible they would be as ridiculous as a fish wishing to graze on the mountainside along with the sheep. "For all the things that remain in their place are incorruptible, but they can perish when they seek to surpass the natural order."

Thus the great ignorance will spread through the universe and its being. There will be no more pain or suffering; there will be no more desire, but neither will there be any spirit. It would be hard to say which prophecy is more frightening and more timely: the destruction of the universe announced by primitive Christianity, or the heretic's vision of a world in eternal repose, without nostalgia.

4. The Inspiration of the System: The Gnostic Experience

We have attempted to show that the Basilidian conception of the world, hidden beneath its Christian aspect and very personal terminology, is essentially Platonist: the framework is Greek. The central place occupied by Christ in the system, the ideas of pre-destination and election, the conceptions of a *creatio ex nihilo,* of cosmic salvation, eschatology, and evolution reveal the influence of the New Testament and particularly of St. Paul: the movement of thought is Christian. These analyses may help us to understand the mythologems of Basilides. But when we read and reread the account of Hippolytus and find ourselves still baffled by its rich, strange content, we cannot help feeling that our investigations, whose findings, it must be owned, remain more or less uncertain, have not led us to the true essence of the doctrine. These bold, profound speculations, these furtive flights of the imagination, this remarkable combination of the most abstract thought with an authentic mythology cannot be explained on the basis of Christianity alone. We must go farther and penetrate to the true core of the theory: the Gnostic experience which animates the whole and gives it its characteristic imprint.

It seems to me that for Basilides the world and history were merely symbols referring to an inner process. I am well aware that in putting forward this point of view a writer must exercise the greatest circumspection to avoid being confused with those simpletons who seek to explain the phenomena of religion without recognizing the autonomy of religious experience.

For this reason I shall call upon a witness who is above all suspicion, Father J. Daniélou, a subtle critic, who remarks in connection with the mysticism of St. Gregory of Nyssa:

> All cosmological expressions are allegorical in Gregory. They are the symbols of the stages in an inner ascent that is profoundly real, that leads the soul through distinct, objective worlds which however cannot be localized in space. In this sense we have in Gregory the same interiorization of the concept of the soul's return through the cosmic spheres as in Plotinus or Augustine.[25]

What is highly remarkable is that St. Augustine was perfectly well aware that this return of the soul to God is not a voyage through the spheres of the external world. This is revealed by the words with which he described the experience he had in common with Monica, his mother, at Ostia:

> We, raising ourselves with a more glowing affection toward the "self-same," did by degrees pass through all things bodily, even the heaven whence sun and moon and stars shine upon the earth; yea, we were soaring higher yet, by inward musing, and discourse, and admiring of Thy works; and we came to our own minds, and went beyond them, that we might arrive at that region of never-failing plenty, where Thou feedest Israel for ever. . . .[26]

I own that I am struck by the great profundity of these words: "et ad hoc *ascendebamus* interius cogitando et loquendo et mirando opera tua et *venimus in mentes nostras et transcendimus eas.*"

But what Daniélou says is true also of the Gnostics. The center of their doctrine is man with his anxieties, his wretchedness, his transports, and his joy. The Valentinian myth, as I have said before, merely states in images and symbols the encounter between man and

25 Jean Daniélou, *Platonisme et théologie mystique* (Paris, 1944), p. 157.
26 *Confessions*, IX, 25; tr. William Benham (New York, 1909).

Christ. Father Sagnard has remarked in speaking of Valentinianism: "The point of departure is always *man:* it is of man that we must think unremittingly. The center of gravity of this system is *our salvation*."[27]

But the mythologems of Basilides also reflect the Gnostic's states of mind rather than objective contemplations.[28] Accordingly, we

27 F. M. M. Sagnard, *La Gnose valentinienne et le témoignage de St. Irénée* (Paris, 1947), p. 591.
28 This is clearly brought out by a passage on the Great Archon: This Archon, the God of the world, persisted, like a true Gnostic demiurge, in believing that he was the sole existing God in this world; he knew nothing of the spiritual things above him. We have seen that this Great Archon represented the ether and that he was identified with the Jewish God. However, the following words show that he had still another aspect which might well have been the most important of all. When the Gospel descended into the world, the Archon understood that he was not the God of all things but that he had been engendered and had above him the treasure set in place by the nonexistent "God" who is ineffable and unnamable, and by the filiality. And he repented and was afraid, understanding in what ignorance he had been: and therefore it is written: "The beginning of wisdom is the fear of the Lord"; for he began to be wise when he was catechized by the Christ (the Messiah) who was seated beside him, when he learned who was the nonexistent "God," who the filiality, who the Holy Ghost, and what had been the disposition of the universe to which these things will be restored. This is wisdom spoken in a mystery, of which the Bible says, "not in words taught by human wisdom but in 'words' taught by the spirit." When the Archon had been catechized and instructed, and when he had grown afraid, he confessed the sin he had committed in glorifying himself (*Elenchos,* 26, 1, 2).
This passage, absurd from the philosophical point of view and blasphemous from a Christian point of view, reveals the heart of Basilides' thinking. The Gnostic would never have opposed the human wisdom of the Archon to the spiritual wisdom of the Gospel if this Archon had not been the symbol of man, that is to say, of that short-sighted man who contents himself with the visible world. Light and gnosis are revealed to him. A student of mysticism might suppose that Basilides is here alluding to illumination as an indispensable phase in mystical life. Though I have no wish to oppose this hypothesis, I believe we can go into greater detail. The light that is diffused through the world is the Gospel, the gnosis of transcendent things which illumines the man Jesus at the time of his baptism in the Jordan. What relation is there between this light and baptism? An old interpolation in the Gospel's account of the baptism declares: "Et cum baptizaretur, lumen ingens circumfulsit de aqua, ita ut timerent omnes qui advenerunt" (When he was baptized, a vast light arose from the water and shone round him). But still more important for our subject is the circumstance that the baptism of the faithful in the Christian Church was called φωτισμός, illumination. This ceremony was preceded by the confession of sins, instruction in the form of catechism, and the *traditio symboli,* the communication of the rule of the faith. A passage from the *Excerpts from Theodotus* tells us that the Gnostic catechism dealt with important questions of esoteric gnosis: "But it is not only the wishing that

shall venture to reconstruct, after the account of Hippolytus, the various stages of mystical life as Basilides saw it: the origin in ignorance, the illumination which marks the beginning of the ascension, and the final return to God.

The Origin in Ignorance

The spiritual man's life begins in ignorance and despair. It is in himself that the Gnostic finds this confusion, this disorder, this primitive chaos. The human spirit is not pure and simple but weighed down by passions, possessed by demons, obsessed by evil. Why? Because man is in this world but does not belong to it. This is the fundamental experience of the Gnostic, who knows that he is an alien in this world and that the world is alien to him; who cannot content himself with the immanent world, because he feels at the very bottom of his being a yearning for eternity. "The elect are strangers in this world, because they are transcendent by nature" (*Strom.*, IV, 26). Thus there is a kind of original guilt (*Urschuld*), which is the immediate consequence of being in the world. "Anguish and misery accompany existence as rust covers iron" (*Strom.*, IV, 12).

This human experience of being a stranger in the world is readily expressed in Platonist conceptions. Confusion and disorder, according to Basilides, have enabled the passions, which in essence are spirits (demons) to fasten on to the rational soul. The passions are "appendates" (ἀπαρτήματα). Later, probably in the course of successive reincarnations, other components of the human beast were added: the natures of the wolf, the monkey, the lion, and the ram. Diverse reincarnations have left the characteristics of animals in the lower strata of the soul; they appear to the soul and inspire it with bestial desires (*Strom.*, II, 20, 112).

---

is liberating but the knowledge of who we were and what we have become, where we were or where we were placed, whither we hasten, from what we are redeemed, what birth is and what rebirth" (*Excerpta ex Theodoto*, 78; ed. and tr. R. P. Casey, 1934, pp. 88–89).

It is plain that the passage on the catechizing of the Archon reflects the impression made on the neophyte by the Gnostic baptism. Basilides has projected this inner experience into space and time. Such details give us an indication of how we should interpret the Gnostic myths, which are above all human documents.

Clement of Alexandria ridicules this conception, declaring that this Basilidian man, who takes a horde of diverse demons into his body, rather resembles the famous Trojan Horse. But does not this charming pleasantry of a learned, well-balanced man conceal an inability to sound the depths of man's miserable condition? The Gospel says that the name of the demons is Legion, and the heretic would seem to have understood this better than certain lovers of gilded mediocrity.

Thus it should not surprise us that Basilides prized the Christian doctrine of original sin. He echoes the words of Scripture: "No one is pure of taint." Even if a man has not committed a sin, he remains inclined toward sin, because the sins exist in him virtually. Such a man resembles a child who has not yet found occasion to sin but carries within him the disposition to sin.[29] "Thus the perfect man, who has never sinned in effect, still carries within him the disposition to sin, but he has not yet found the material to sin upon: it is for this reason alone that he has not committed sin. Hence it is not permissible to call him impeccable" (*Strom.*, IV, 82).

No doubt the Gnostic conception of man's alien condition in this world, the Platonist conception of the passions as appendages to the rational soul, and the Christian doctrine of original sin are confounded in Basilides. Actually, they resemble one another considerably, and we must take care not to place the accent on their divergences by an excess of intellectualism. Beyond any doubt, the very Gnostic antithesis between spirit and soul lies at the base of all these speculations. The transcendent pneuma is attached to an immanent psyche; there is a $\psi v\chi\grave{\eta}\ \pi\rho o\sigma\phi\acute{v}\eta s$ and an $\dot{a}\nu\tau\acute{\iota}\mu\iota\mu o\nu\ \pi\nu\epsilon\hat{v}\mu a$.

This antithesis was not invented by Basilides: it is characteristic of all gnosis and cannot be mechanically identified with the banal dualism of good and evil, or of spirit and matter.

The pneuma feels nostalgia for the transcendent world; the psyche remains by nature in this world (Hippolytus, *Elenchos*, VII, 27, 6).

> Two souls, alas, are housed within my breast,
> And each will wrestle for the mastery there,
> The one has passion's craving crude for love,
> And hugs a world where sweet the senses rage;

[29] We see, then, that Basilides, like St. Augustine and the psychologists of our time, did not look upon the child as innocent.

> The other longs for pastures fair above,
> Leaving the murk for lofty heritage.[30]

Consequently, the aim of the mystical life can be none other than that of the historic process: purification, catharsis. The third filiality which has remained in the great mound of this world, requires purification (ἀποκαθάρσεως δεόμενον; 22, 7).

But why does the spirit find itself in these tragic circumstances? Why is the spirit attached to this soul? Not because it was exiled from the heavens, as Plato believed: indeed, Basilides does not mention any fall into matter. Nor are these passions which darken the spirit a consequence of the first man's sin. In this Basilides differs from Tertullian. The essential difference between their two conceptions is that according to Tertullian the union of a divine soul with another nature results from a moral transgression on the part of the first man. Basilides makes no mention of this conception. True, men expiate the crimes they have committed in their earlier existences; but from the very beginning the spirit is bound to the passions. Why then was man placed in the world, to which he does not belong, if he did not fall into matter and did not commit this original sin?

Basilides reflected on this central problem. He declares that "the filiality is abandoned in formlessness in order that it may perfect (εὐεργετεῖν) the souls and be perfect itself" (26, 9). In short, the task of the spirit is to work upon the soul: "and the sons of God," he says, "are ourselves, the spiritual men, who have been abandoned here that they may order, form, correct and perfect the souls which have a natural tendency to remain in this region of the world" (25, 2).

But how does the spirit, or, as it is called, "the internal man in his psychic envelopment" (27, 6), profit from its association with the soul? It is intimated that the spirit needs the soul (27, 6 and 22, 11): just as a bird cannot rise without wings, so does the spirit ascend, thanks to the soul. In less figurative language, this means that the spiritual ascent to God is not possible unless the soul frees itself from matter by submitting to an ascetic regime and abstaining from marriage.[31]

---

30 Goethe, *Faust, Part One*, tr. Philip Wayne (Harmondsworth and Baltimore, 1960), p. 67.

31 The libertinism of which Irenaeus accuses the Basilidians is unknown to

Illumination

This spiritual life is, of course, unknown before the coming of Christ. Man is in a state of unconsciousness and his spirit still slumbers; it is an abortion (ἔκτρωμα) without form; the phantom self obscures the true self; man is already the son of God, but he does not yet know it. That is why the universe groans and suffers, awaiting the deliverance of the sons of God. But when Christ enters into the existence of the elect he reveals to them their real self and makes them aware of their consubstantiality with God. This event, as we might suppose, takes place at the moment of baptism. It is then that "the filiality which is abandoned in formlessness to perfect the souls and be made perfect is formed; it follows Jesus and rises up and is purified and subtilized to the point where it can rise by itself: for it has confirmed all its power in accordance with nature by virtue of the light which casts its beams downward from on high." The initiation of the elect is only the beginning of this process; the selection of the spiritual people begins with the coming of Christ. Illumination is the first stage in the mystical ascension. At this moment Christ reveals the gnosis of transcendent things. And the initiate discovers that he is sensible to the grandeur of the unprecedented words which are addressed to him and which respond to his most profound aspirations. For "it is by an essential disposition (φύσει) that we know God" (*Strom.*, V, 1, 3) : the faith of the elect finds insights through a spiritual intuition (καταλήψει νοητικῇ; *Strom.*, II, 3, 10) .

From the moment of his initiation man knows that he is "believing and elect by virtue of his essential disposition"; he seeks to overcome the passions which trouble the purity of his spirit and to expiate the faults he has committed. In this connection Basilides is particularly severe: "Not all sins can be pardoned, but only those that have been committed involuntarily and from ignorance"

Basilides. He advises abstention from the marriage tie not because it is bad but because of the numerous cares it involves. And his son Isidore declares: "Beware of a passionate woman." This accent on ἐγκράτεια does not suggest a pedantic, pitiless moralism. "But a man is young or poor or sensual and he does not wish to marry in accordance with reason. He does not leave his brothers. Let him say to himself: 'I have entered into the sanctuary; nothing can happen to me' " (*Strom.*, III,1, 2) . Nevertheless, the mores of the Basilidians were strict and austere.

(*Strom.*, IV, 24, 135). But God's goodness has given the elect the means of expiating this original sin, of purifying themselves from their hereditary guilt. God has given man the grace of suffering.

Basilides' strange speculations on human suffering have their origin in the problem which martyrdom presented to Christians. The Christian martyrs were condemned by Roman judges for merely confessing to the name of Christians. It is true that in the popular faith these martyrs rose immediately to heaven, while the other dead had to await the Last Judgment. Nevertheless, the problem of the martyr was vexatious: did God permit innocent men to be tortured? To this Basilides could not assent: "I shall say anything rather than admit the malice of providence." There are no innocent men. All have sinned even if no one knew it. Accordingly, martyrdom is a grace, a good (ἀγαθόν), granted by the goodness of God who directs the historical process (τοῦ περιάγοντος), who enables the elect to expiate their crimes and rise to their celestial dwelling place.

> I maintain that all those who become victims of persecution are led to this good by the goodness of Him who directs the world, because, though no one is aware of it, they have sinned through other transgressions; they are accused of offenses other than those which they have committed in reality, in order that they may not suffer for confessed crimes or be covered with opprobrium for such offenses as adultery and murder, but for the sole fact that they are Christians, which so comforts them that they do not believe that they are suffering at all (*Strom.*, IV, 81, 1).

The same is stated in similar terms in another fragment: "The soul, having sinned in another, previous existence, suffers punishment here below; the elect soul is privileged by martyrdom, while the other is purified by his own punishment" (*Strom.*, IV, 12, 83). This process is called an "economy of catharsis." Through martyrdom the elect soul is totally purified of its sins.[32]

32 On the one hand, this reflects the Christian conception according to which the martyr rises immediately to God. But, on the other hand, we are given to understand that martyrdom is a good, because it expiates transgressions and purifies the soul. This is almost word for word what Basilides may have found in a Platonist doxography: "For to suffer a punishment is not an evil but a good (ἀγαθόν) because it will be a purification from crimes committed" (Hippolytus, *Elenchos*, I, 19, 22: τὸ γὰρ κόλασιν ὑποσχεῖν οὐ κακὸν εἶναι ἀλλὰ ἀγαθόν, εἴπερ μέλλει κάθαρσις τῶν κακῶν γίνεσθαι).

Not only martyrdom, but suffering in general is a grace: "If the child, not having previously sinned or having effectively sinned, but having sin within him, is subjected to pain, he benefits, drawing profit from his numerous sufferings" (IV, 82).

Here we begin to see how the elect benefits by his sojourn in the world. Suffering is a good because it purifies the spirit, liberates the soul from matter, and accelerates the rise of the inner man: suffering leads man to God.

The Final Return

The documents tell us that the life of the initiate is characterized by severe asceticism and acceptance of suffering. But when the spirit has been freed from matter by asceticism and suffering, it will rise upward. It will leave behind it the soul that has enveloped it and traverse the "real but interior spheres," it will traverse the Limit that separates the visible world from the spiritual world and will arrive at the summit of happiness, because it will be close to God. The mystic ascent, which is at the same time the most radical internalization, has reached its end. The spirit is close to God.

Though this motif is discernible in the account of Hippolytus, it might pass unnoticed if it were not confirmed by a passage in Clement—a passage of paramount importance which has scarcely been mentioned in studies on Basilides.

> For if a man knows God by essential disposition (φύσει), as is believed by Basilides, who regards the faith of the elect as an "intuition" (νόησις) as well as a "royal dignity," a "beautiful creature," and an "essence worthy of being with its creator," then he will call faith an "essence," but not a freedom, he will call it a nature and a substance, an "infinite beauty of the most sublime creature," but not the logical adherence of a soul gifted with free will (*Strom.*, V, 1, 3).

The human spirit, Basilides means to say, is a substance worthy of being with its creator. And Hippolytus' account tells us that the third filiality is situated close to the other filialities, above the Limit (*Elenchos*, VII, 27, 11 and 27, 1). The spirit, Clement's fragment continues, is "an infinite beauty of the highest creature." And Hippolytus explains this by recording that the spirit has become "the most subtle of things, so subtle that it can rise of itself, like the first filiality" (26, 10). The spirit is, in the terms employed by Basilides, "an intuition," "a royal dignity." However, it is not confused with God. Why not? Because it is a creature—true, a beautiful creature (καλὴ κτίσις), but still a "creature." These words, it might be said in passing, prove the authenticity of Hippolytus' account, which declares that the germ was not an emanation but a creation out of nothingness, and that the filiality, though in all things consubstantial with God, had issued from nothingness (22, 7). And it might also be remarked that the conception of a creation of the spiritual world reveals a profound Christian influence. What is more important is that for Basilides there is always this difference between God and the spirit: God is unengendered, while the spirit is engendered. And that is why the spirit is not confused with God and is not dissolved into the absolute being but keeps a certain distance.

All this is highly significant, for the same conception is found in Valentinus, who condemns the striving of the spirit to penetrate to the very depths of God and taste his sweetness. Thus the Christian gnosis is a mystique of Christ and not a mystique of God. Though on the one hand it stresses the consubstantiality of man with God, on the other hand it does not forget that God is "entirely different," and it describes God in purely negative terms. Valentinus says that God is "abyss and silence." Basilides is more eloquent in this respect. In striking paradoxes and with a sobriety betraying the profoundest emotion he makes it clear that God escapes all human definition.

His passage about God before the creation of the world is rightly famous and merits the greatest attention because it shows the nature of the God whom Basilides encountered in the profoundest depths of his being.

> Once upon a time there was nothing, nor was that nothing any kind of entity, but in plain, unequivocal, and unsophisticated language there was nothing at all. When I say "was" I don't assert that "there was," but merely to indicate my intention I declare that there was nothing at all. For if we would call that about which I am speaking "transcendent" (ἄρρητος, uneffable), it would not be absolutely transcendent, because we give it this name. But it is

beyond transcendency: for what is beyond transcendency cannot be predicated, not even as transcendent, but is above every possible name. That this must be true appears from the fact that there are not even names enough to predicate the things of the visible world, so complicated this is. And I don't undertake to find proper names for everything, but one must grasp the properties of the things not by spoken words, but by silent intuition. . . .

Now when there was nothing, neither matter, nor substance, nor nonentity, nor simple nor compound, nor perceptible nor imperceptible, nor man nor angel nor god, nor anything that can be named or perceived by sense or by thought, but when in this and in a still more subtle way everything was simply designed, then not being God, without consciousness or perception, without plan, without purpose, without affection, without desire, willed to make a world. I only say "willed" to express my feeling, but I mean an act involuntary, irrational, unconscious. Likewise, by "the world" I don't mean the world of time and space, which came into being afterwards, but the germ of a world. And this seed of the world contained all things within itself, just as a grain of mustard-seed collects into the smallest body all things at once (potentially), the roots, the trunk, the numberless leaves, the seeds begotten by the plant, that are cast off as germs of innumerable other plants in an endless process. Thus not being God made a not being world out of nothing (*Elenchos,* VII, 20, 2–21, 4).

This God whom Basilides encountered in his most secret heart is the Gnostic God, a nothingness beyond thought and will, unconscious, and containing within it the future universe in a state of unconsciousness. God is transcendence of transcendence.

It is clear that this passage reflects a personal experience of Basilides. However, it would be a mistake to suppose that such descriptions of God are an exception in Gnostic literature and unknown to the Gnostic masters who preceded Valentinus and Basilides. This is, indeed, the great error of the adherents of the history-of-dogmas school, who believed that a gulf separated learned gnosis from vulgar gnosis. Now it is true that Irenaeus does not breathe a word about any such description of God in his account of the Gnostic system of the predecessors of Valentinus, who were also the predecessors of Basilides, i.e. representatives of the vulgar gnosis of Egypt: he merely says a few words about a "certain un-namable Father" (*patrem quendam innominabilem;* Iren., *Adv. haer.,* I, 29, 1). But, thanks to a discovery of Carl Schmidt, we know today that Irenaeus, in his extract from the *Apokryphon Johannis,* his source for this chapter, omitted a highly remarkable description of a God transcending transcendence—a description worthy to be considered on a plane with that of Basilides.[33]

Thus, we can say that the conceptions of God in learned gnosis and vulgar gnosis were fundamentally the same. We can even go further and declare that, in the phenomenological sense at least, the God of Basilides, this God who is actually nothing and po-tentially everything, is the God of mysticism pure and simple. For the phenomenology of religion has very well demonstrated that the conception of God in ontological mysticism is everywhere the same, in all times and in all religions.

The problem then arises: Is this Gnostic God, this mystical God different from the God of the Bible? Is he another God? This problem is delicate, terrifying in fact, but it does not belong to the field of philological research. All we can say is that the Gnostic conception differs from the Biblical conception. It is most signifi-cant, for example, that Valentinus and Basilides, who wished to be Christians, who were well acquainted with the Bible and in par-ticular with the Gospel of St. John, never said that God is love. The Valentinians themselves noticed this later and attempted to introduce the notion of love into their conception of God. This is the best proof that Christian Gnosis was a premature attempt to Christianize a pre-Christian mysticism and did not succeed in adopting the characteristic trait of the Christian religion. Later, Gregory of Nyssa, though recognizing the Neoplatonic conception of divine transcendence, made it clear that the very essence of God is love. This he did because he was a mystic more penetrated by grace than Basilides, knowing not only the night of the senses but also the night of the spirit in the ecstasy of love. *Hoc nemo novit nisi expertus.*

33 See Sagnard, *La gnose valentinienne,* p. 588.

Henri-Charles Puech

The Concept of Redemption in Manichaeism

1. The Gnostic and Manichaean Notions of Redemption: The Problem of Evil in Manichaeism

It will be difficult, even in the space of this paper, to give a clear exposition of our present subject. The difficulties lie partly in the nature of the vast source material, originating in widely divergent times and places. We have, on the one hand, countless secondary records of greater and lesser value, for the most part stemming from opponents of Manichaeism: Greek, Latin, Syriac, Iranian, Islamic, Armenian, and Chinese.[1] And, on the other hand, we now possess important direct sources, in addition to the passages from Manichaean works cited by non-Manichaean assailants or expositors of the doctrine—particularly Titus of Bostra, St. Augustine, Theodor bar Khouni, En-Nedîm, and Al-Bîrûnî. Since 1904 we have had at our disposal fragments, hymns, and dissertations in three Iranian dialects (Persian, Parthian, Sogdian), in Uigur (Old Turkish), and in Chinese, discovered in the northwest of Chinese Turkistan, in Turfan, and in the caves of Tun-huang.[2] In 1933 a collection of Manichaean works translated into Subakhmimic Coptic was found in the southwestern Fayum, in central Egypt.[3] Our greatest diffi-

---

1 On all this source material, see Prosper Alfaric, *Les Écritures manichéennes*, I, *Vue générale;* II, *Étude analytique* (Paris, 1918).

2 A. V. Williams Jackson, *Researches in Manichaeism* (New York, 1932), pp. xxiv–xxvi, gives a bibliography of the texts published up to 1930 in *Abhandlungen der preussischen Akademie der Wissenschaften,* Berlin (*ABA*); *Sitzungsberichte* of the same Academy (*SBA*); *Mémoires* or *Bulletin de l'Académie Impériale de St.-Pétersbourg;* and *Journal Asiatique* (*JA*). Since 1930 other Turfan texts have been published in *SBA* 1932, pp. 175–222; 1933, pp. 294–363 and 480–608; 1934, pp. 27–35 and 848–912. Also in the *Nachrichten von der Gesellschaft der Wissenschaften zu Göttingen* (*NGG*), 1932, pp. 214–28; 1933, pp. 306–18.

3 Carl Schmidt and Hans Jacob Polotsky, "Ein Mani-Fund in Ägypten," *SBA* 1933, pp. 4–90. Publications on this discovery: *Manichäische Homilien,* ed. H. J. Polotsky (Stuttgart, 1934), and 147 pages of *Kephalaia* (Lieferungen

culties, however, lie in the nature of the subject itself. Of all the religions of redemption Manichaeism is the most comprehensive and complete. To paraphrase the 154th chapter of the *Kephalaia*,[4] one of the texts recently discovered in the Fayum: this third-century Gnosticism gathers into a mighty stream, unites, and gives finished form and system to all the revelations, all the gospels of redemption contained in the religions, philosophies, and gnoses which went before it. Above all, the whole of Manichaeism is redemption. Redemption is the one aim of this system. The universe is interpreted as a machine for producing and safeguarding redemption. Every cog in the cosmic mechanism, every episode in the history of the world has a bearing on redemption; man's life has only one meaning and only one determinant: redemption. The Manichaean religion itself is primarily an apostolate: a religion of missionaries who journey through the world and proclaim the glad tidings of redemption,[5] preaching the complete and definitive revelation, to which men must give themselves on pain of irrevocable damnation. To speak of the Manichaean theory of redemption is therefore to speak of Manichaeism as a whole. Such an undertaking cannot even be considered here. And yet it seems to me that we can gain an over-all picture of Manichaeism if we consider the central idea of redemption and its implications for the system as a whole. Assuredly such a picture will accord in the main with the existing expositions of Manichaeism,[6] but it will not coincide with them.

The organization of our essay follows from the foregoing. If everything in Manichaeism is related to redemption, we must first determine whence and how this orientation toward redemption arose. Accordingly, we must first demonstrate the similarity between

---

1–6, Stuttgart, 1935–36). On the literature inspired by the discovery, see J. Simon, "L'Édition des textes manichéens coptes," *Orientalia* (Rome), V (1936), 269–77.

4 *SBA* 1933, p. 42, and cf. the parallel Turfan text T II D 126, ibid., pp. 295ff.

5 See H. H. Schaeder, "Urform und Fortbildungen des manichäischen Systems," *Vorträge der Bibliothek Warburg, 1924–1925* (Leipzig, 1927), pp. 127–35.

6 See Schaeder's fine article already mentioned and Christian Baur's by no means obsolete *Das manichäische Religionssystem* (Tübingen, 1831). A good recent account of Manichaeism is provided by H. J. Polotsky, *Abriss des manichäischen Systems* (Stuttgart, 1934 [= Pauly-Wissowa, *Real-Encyclopädie,* supplementary vol. VI, cols. 241–71]), in which the reader may find documents and proofs which lack of space prevents me from citing here. See also my book, *Le manichéisme. Son fondateur, sa doctrine* (Paris, 1949).

the Gnostic and Manichaean conceptions of redemption and elucidate the purely psychological experience of evil which gave rise to
the desire for redemption and the idea of redemption. We shall
see that the need for redemption was expressed and explained in
a—mythological—metaphysic which may be formulated as follows:
(1) By its structure and history the world proves the necessity of
redemption and the possibility of its realization; (2) man's origin
and nature make him capable of being redeemed. I shall deal with
this twofold, cosmological and anthropological, myth in the second
section of this paper. It will thus be concerned with the theoretical
aspect of the problem and its solution as envisaged by Manichaean
dogmatism. The third section will show the actual process of redemption, the moral and religious behavior prescribed by the myth,
the role played by the redeemers, the organization of redemption
by the church, the ultimate purpose of redemption—in short, the
realization of redemption in Manichaeism. In other words, this
last section will concern itself with the practical aspect of the
problem, which, however, cannot be separated from the dogma,
since it merely represents its application.

There are direct links connecting Manichaeism with older Gnostic doctrines; moreover, it is in every way a Gnostic type of religion.
For a sound understanding of it, we must therefore inquire into
the specific Gnostic approach to the problem of redemption. I
shall undertake this inquiry on the basis of documents belonging
to the systems of the late second and third centuries, some of
which may have been known to Mani.

Gnosis in its full significance may be defined as an insight encompassing immediate redemption.[7] This insight, which is both
consciousness and knowledge, is an indispensable instrument of
redemption, since it reveals the secrets of the road to salvation.[8]
But, more than this, it redeems by itself, by the fact that one
possesses it, whether through revelation or initiation. For gnosis
is more than an insight, in the usual sense of the word. It is not

---

7 For the following points I take the liberty of referring to my article "Où en
est le problème du Gnosticisme?" *Revue de l'Université de Bruxelles*, année
39 (1933–34), pp. 137–58, 295–314.

8 Τὰ κεκρυμμένα τῆς ἀγίας ὁδοῦ, γνῶσιν καλέσας, παραδώσω. Hymn of the Naassenes
in Hippolytus, *Elenchos*, V, 10, 2 (ed. P. Wendland, *GCS*, p. 104, lines 2–3).

only a complete knowledge, laying claim to absoluteness and universality: it goes farther; it does not content itself with perceiving its objects from without: it unites them and identifies itself with them by an act of encompassing, ἔνωσις. In gnosis, moreover, the subject not only achieves self-awareness; he undergoes a fundamental transformation through this self-awareness. Thus gnosis can be redemption: it causes the knowing subject to be dissolved in the known object—i.e., causes it to participate in the transcendent realities, in their supreme knowledge, and in their power. It reveals the world of the gods, the system and the history of these gods, of the cosmos, and of man, and it articulates the knowing subject with the whole of this human, cosmic, and divine destiny by linking his fate and substance with the myth of the divine entities or of a supernatural savior. And in its achievement of self-awareness the act of gnosis carries self-awareness back to its true source, revealing to the subject that in substance he is one with the divine world. Through this world, he is reborn and redeemed in a complete inner metamorphosis, regaining his true identity, his divine and true self, which he had temporarily lost through his life in this base world and through ignorance. In Gnosticism this rebirth, this second, celestial and spiritual birth, is designated by a number of terms: *secunda* or *divina nativitas;* παλιγγενεσία; μεταμορφοῦσθαι; μεταβάλλεσθαι; μετασχηματίζεσθαι; μεταγεννᾶσθαι or ἀναγεννᾶσθαι; *renasci, reformari, transfigurari.* As a whole, gnosis can be defined as a mysticism of transformation, in which knowledge brings not only a theoretical solution to the problems raised by the need for redemption but an actual solution which results in the immediate and definitive liberation of the knower. Gnosis, *conditio sine qua non* of redemption, beginning, middle, and end of redemption, is theoretically sufficient to itself. For practical purposes, particularly in the Christian Gnosticism of the late second and third centuries, it surrounds itself with outward instruments, with such sacraments as baptism, the laying on of hands, anointing, mystical marriage— these ceremonies representing initiation into gnosis or confirming the possession of gnosis. But such rites, whether directly effective or merely symbolic, are secondary; they are meaningful only in reference to gnosis, which remains the core of revelation. This is made clear by the controversies concerning the sacrament of ἀπολύτρωσις[9] (literally, ransom; redemption) in the Valentinian school. Some Valentinians maintained that without this sacrament those in full possession of gnosis could not be reborn in the power that is over all things. Others maintained, on the contrary, that all those having knowledge of the mystery of the ineffable and invisible power, having insights regarding supersensory realities transcending the intelligible, required no practical exercises or tangible symbols. Τελεία γνῶσις, the complete insight, which is ἐπίγνωσις, re-cognition of the ineffable, is itself τελεία ἀπολύτρωσις, the perfect resurrection. The *Pistis Sophia* states, on the other hand: "Without mysteries no one will enter into the realm of light, whether he be a just man or a sinner."[10]

What then is the source of this need for redemption? The Christian adversaries often find the basis of the Gnostic heresy in excessive concern with the origin and significance of evil. Because they have reflected too long on these troublesome questions: Πόθεν τὸ κακόν; *Unde Malum et quare?* they themselves have succumbed to evil.[11] It is indeed probable that preoccupation with the question of why evil exists in the world; despair at all that is evil and base in human life; the difficulties that arise when one imputes a meaning to the presence of evil, attributing it to God's will and so attempting to justify it—that all this is the fundamental religious experience at the root of the Gnostic idea of redemption. The Gnostic feels himself beset on all sides by the tyrannical pressure of fate (εἱμαρμένη), encompassed by the limitations of time, body, matter, and all the temptations and humiliations they bring with them. This sense of servitude and inferiority can only be explained by a fall. The mere fact that man has this feeling proves that he is essentially—and that he must have been—something other than what he is in this world, where he feels alien and rejected. Hence revolt against the world, refusal to accept it, refusal to accept himself. Hence also a striving for transcendence, nostalgia for a previous existence, where his substance was pure and he was infinitely

9 Cf. Irenaeus, *Adversus haereses*, I, 21, 1 and 4 (ed. Harvey, I, 180–82, 185–86).
10 *Pistis Sophia*, ch. 133 (ed. C. Schmidt, *GCS*, p. 226, lines 36–38 and cf. p. 227, lines 20–21).
11 Tertullian, *De praescriptione haereticorum*, 7 (Migne, *PL*, II, 19–20) and *Adversus Marcionem*, 1, 2 (*PL*, II, 248–49); Eusebius of Caesarea, *Historia ecclesiastica*, V, 27; Epiphanius, *Panarion*, XXIV, 6 (ed. K. Holl, *GCS*, I, 263).

free—nostalgia for a lost paradise which he will regain through gnosis.[12] The Gnostic knows his present fallen state is only accidental and temporary; he becomes conscious of an innate superiority which this temporal existence, this body, this matter which confront him have been powerless to destroy. To the extent that his temporal existence is unacceptable to his feeling it shocks his reason. The emotional need for redemption raises intellectual problems which—theoretically at least—must be susceptible of solution by intellection and self-knowledge. The experience of evil is formulated on the plane of knowledge and demands explanation and solution on this plane. Thus in the consciousness of the Gnostic there is, side by side with the experience and dread of evil, a desire—which turns to arrogant certainty, a certainty that is more than hope and faith—for the possession of absolute truth, for an omniscience which will resolve all the pangs and problems of evil.

One of the most complete definitions of gnosis is given in Excerpt 78 from the works of the Valentinian Theodotus. Here the function of gnosis is to answer the following questions: "Who are we? What has become of us? Where are we?—i.e. whither have we been cast down? Whither are we going? What is our birth ($\gamma \acute{\epsilon} \nu \nu \eta \sigma \iota s$)? What is our rebirth ($\dot{\alpha} \nu \alpha \gamma \acute{\epsilon} \nu \nu \eta \sigma \iota s$)?"[13] This definition shows that gnosis is primarily concerned with our present situation, which is unacceptable to our feeling and absurd to our reason. It seeks an explanation of our situation which will at the same time annul it. This solution is found by situating ourselves within a vast system having our present condition as its center. It is twofold, presupposing a twofold revelation: the revelation of our origins and the revelation of our destiny. What was before our present situation (who are we)?; and what will be afterward (whither are we going)? The first revelation takes the form of a cosmic myth, culminating in a history of mankind and of our time. This myth has the function of explaining to the Gnostic that God did not will evil but that either evil is a substance in itself, which has always existed in opposition to good (dualistic solution), or that evil comes into being through gradual diminution of the divine essence

12 This Gnostic attitude has been analyzed by Hans Jonas in *Gnosis und spätantiker Geist,* I (Göttingen, 1934), 94–225.
13 *Excerpta ex Theodoto,* 78, 2 (ed. R. P. Casey, London, 1934, p. 88, lines 677–79).

(emanatistic solution) or through the fall of a transcendent being, which, having offended against peace and the divine pleroma, created an imperfect world outside of the light, in which man is compelled to exist at the mercy of fate and sin. The second revelation contains a soteriological myth, different from the cosmological myth but closely connected with it. This myth of redemption serves to assure us that even though we are at present in a fallen state, we have our source in a transcendent world, with which we remain joined through our inner being, or that we are connected with the fallen being who will in the end be redeemed and whose fate is therefore our own. Thus the divine in us remains unharmed in our accidental association with the evil and the matter which constitute our life on this base earth. It therefore suffices to awaken the divine spark ($\sigma\pi\iota\nu\theta\eta\rho$), which is always present in us or is given to us by the $\Pi\nu\epsilon\tilde{\upsilon}\mu\alpha$ or the $No\tilde{\upsilon}\varsigma$; and we shall be one again with the being with whom we are consubstantial and whose ultimate destiny is revealed to us by the myth. We shall then depart from the world and find ourselves again in our pristine, perfect, eternal, and enduring truth. Thus the self-knowledge contained in the knowledge of our present situation encompasses in turn a knowledge of the divine beings and of the history and structure of the cosmos. Actually—and this may be seen, for example, from the vast knowledge which Chapters 92 and 93 of the *Pistis Sophia* adduce as the content of the revealed mystery[14]—gnosis embraces all knowledge: theogony, cosmogony, astronomy, geology, botany, history, etc. But it must be stressed that this body of knowledge, which purports to be scientific and even rational, actually dissolves into a system of myths; that even though emotional experience is expressed in the form of intellectual problems, these problems receive purely mythical solutions; and, moreover, that this exhaustive knowledge and the myths in which it is stated are solely and exclusively concerned with the "pneumatic" man. Their purpose is not only to explain to man his situation here and now, but also, by revealing to him his origin and true nature, to give him the certainty of redemption as his eternal condition which he need only rediscover. Self-knowledge is self-redemption, just as world knowledge is world redemption and domination.

14 Ed. Schmidt, pp. 135, line 27–139, line 10.

The redemption which is conferred by illumination through gnosis is essentially liberation and rebirth. But it is liberation in the strongest sense: ἐλευθερία is not only a negative release or liberation from the tyranny of fate and enslavement by the body and by matter; it is also a positive freedom, ἐξουσία, an absolute power, the right to do anything one pleases (hence the amorality of all Gnosticism, sometimes expressed in acts), independence in both this and the other world from the laws and the lords of this earth and from the lower or demonic godhead, which is the creator and judge of the cosmos. This redemption is rebirth in the sense that it is a re-collection (συλλέγειν) [15] of one's own luminous and divine substance, recovery of the true self, return to an original nature and place. Thus redemption removes the Gnostic from time and sets him in a place that is transcendent in relation to the limited, enslaved existence that was his, an existence perceived by the senses, hence an illusion. Redemption operates in time, but the act of cognition on which it is based is timeless. The knowledge which it reveals is all-embracing, absolute, immutable in its utter perfection, self-contained; the rebirth it occasions produces a state which is also all-embracing and immutable in its pristine perfection. This does not mean that the Gnostic conception of redemption entirely disregards time. To be sure, Gnosticism has a tendency to look upon time as a phantom, an illusory travesty (ψεῦδος) of eternity,[16] but it does not succeed in denying it altogether. The attitude of the Gnostics toward time is rather one of impatience: they seek to outdistance time, as, for example, when they declare that "the resurrection is already accomplished" by spiritual rebirth,[17] or when their sacraments anticipate a situation which will indeed occur only at the end of the world.[18] But this again shows that Gnosticism is not lacking in the eschatological vision, which, after all, presup-

15 Cf. Leonard Fendt, *Gnostische Mysterien* (Munich, 1922), pp. 4–12, 77; and H. Jonas, *Gnosis*, pp. 139–40.
16 Cf. Irenaeus, I, 17, 2 (ed. Harvey, I, 168) and the Mandaean Hymn, III, 1 of Ginzā L. (ed. M. Lidzbarski, Göttingen and Leipzig, 1925, p. 508, lines 22–29).
17 II Tim. 2:18. As late as the 13th century this thesis was attributed by Bar Hebraeus to the Audians; R. Graffin and F. Nau, eds., *Patrologia Orientalis* (Paris, 1919), XIII, 259: "There is no resurrection and even now the souls are going to judgment."
18 This eschatological implication of the Gnostic sacraments can be seen by comparing the Marcosian rites described by Irenaeus in chs. 13 and 21 of the first book of *Adversus haereses* and the Valentinian myths summed up by the

poses the reality of the world. And, moreover, the Gnostics must admit that certain "psychic" men—i.e., those who are not, like the "pneumatic" men, redeemed by nature regardless of their acts, and who are not irremediably damned like the "hylic" men—can achieve redemption by training, endeavor, and good works in the temporal world.[19] Finally, and this is the main point, the Gnostic myth bursts through and transcends pure intemporality; it takes the form of history and so gives value and meaning to time. Redemption is accomplished in the dramatic course of a world process in which supraterrestrial beings intervene with their saving revelation.

I should now like to add one last trait to the Gnostic picture of redemption. As we have seen, the content of redemption is that we become aware of our true self, so releasing it from the world in which it is imprisoned and guiding it back to its heavenly home. But this is possible only because the πνεῦμα or the luminous νοῦς is consubstantial with the transcendent world or with a divine being to whose fall and redemption the myth links its fate. This mystical being can in turn be looked upon as the prototype of the men who redeem themselves, and it redeems itself in the same measure as "pneumatic" men are redeemed. These pneumatic men represent the sum of its fallen luminous substance, dispersed in matter, and their rediscovery of their true self is equivalent to the progressive reconstitution of the "members" or parcels of this being, which in this way return to their body and place of origin. In redeeming pneumatic men, this mythical being redeems itself, just as the pneumatic men, by redeeming themselves, contribute to the redemption of this being, whose parts they are. Thus the Gnostic drama of redemption can ultimately be reduced to a single theme: the Redeemed Redeemer. The mythical being whose history is fall and redemption may assume the form of Anthropos, man as such, whose parts are individual men. Richard Reitzenstein attempted to reduce all Gnostic trends and their common source, the "Iranian

---

same author in ch. 7, p. 1, or by examining, *Excerpta ex Theodoto*, 63–65. Furthermore, there is a close connection between the terms τελειότης (τέλειος) συντέλεια, ἀποκατάστασις, *consummatio*. I incline to attribute the same eschatological significance to the Manichaean festival of the *Bēma* as a prefiguration of the Resurrection following the Last Judgment.

19 Cf. Irenaeus, I, 6, 1 (ed. Harvey, I, 51–55, 64–67); *Exc. Theod.*, 56, 3 (ed. Casey, p. 76, lines 529–78), 53, 2 and 54, 1–3 (ibid., lines 510–18).

myth of redemption," to this figure and to this thus simplified myth. This, no doubt, is an unwarranted simplification, an arbitrary, artificial construction. There is, however, a Gnostic document in which the myth of the Redeemed Redeemer stands out clearly: the Apocalypse of Nikotheos, a work dating back at least to the beginning of the third century. This work was known to Porphyry and the author of the anonymous Coptic Bruce Codex, and I believe that its influence is discernible in Book Ω of the alchemist Zosimos.[20] The sole hero of this myth is a being whose name may not be uttered and who is called light (by means of the pun: $\phi\tilde{\omega}s = \phi\omega s$). Lured by evil powers who take him prisoner, he falls into matter. Here he becomes Adam. The history of the world consists in nothing other than the regathering of Adam's luminous substance, which survives in "pneumatic" men, whose personal redemption consists precisely in recapturing their luminous self, their $\pi\nu\epsilon\tilde{\nu}\mu\alpha$ or their $\nu o\tilde{\nu}s$, which makes them lords over the world and destiny. When the luminous form of Adam-Phōs is restored, when all the pneumatic men are redeemed, the original man, reconstituted in all his parts, will rise up again to the realm of light. This redemption is made possible by successive revelations of one and the same savior, who manifests himself in various forms; its first embodiment was Adam himself, its last is Christ. Jesus shows us in the Passion (which is mere illusion) the way to free ourselves from the world and the body by radical rejection and renunciation.[21] Here again this redeemer, who is always the same and manifests himself at various intervals in time, is the being who fell at the beginning of time. Here we have assuredly to do with the Redeemed Redeemer. We must bear this point in mind for the following. It will help us to understand the Manichaean myth of redemption, and moreover it seems likely that Mani owed this basic myth in part to the Apocalypse of Nikotheos. We now know from Turfan Fragment M 299[22] that the Manichaeans counted

---

20 Berthelot and Ruelle, *Collection des anciens alchimistes grecs* (Paris, 1888), *Textes*, pp. 228–33; R. Reitzenstein, *Poimandres* (Leipzig, 1904), pp. 102–06.
21 In my opinion, the docetic character of this section 8, which Reitzenstein regards as an interpolation, proves, on the contrary, that it is an integral part of the Gnostic development summed up by Zosimos.
22 *SBA* 1934, pp. 27–28, Henning.

Nikotheos among the prophets of mankind, along with those men —Šēm, Sēm, Enōš, Enoch—who were the vehicles of the true revelation down through the ages.

We shall find all these characteristic traits of the Gnostic conception of redemption in the Manichaean conception.

It would be tempting to seek to reconstitute the history of this conception, to discover Mani's personal expression of the need for redemption, to determine what part of his theory originated in his own experience, and what part was the heritage of earlier Gnostic systems. But this would be a venturesome undertaking. What little information we have on Mani's youth is presumably very much distorted by legend, and in attempting to disclose a real emotional experience beneath the imaged language of the Manichaean texts we must never forget that these significant images may themselves have been stereotypes borrowed elsewhere and far removed from any immediate experience.

Once we have made these reservations, we may consult two documents dealing with Mani's calling: a passage in the *Fihrist* of En-Nedīm, doubtless copied from a Manichaean hagiography, and *Kephalaion* 1, which gives the impression of an autobiographical fragment. In the first it is reported that Fatak, Mani's father, thrice received this warning in the temple at Ctesiphon: "O Fatak, eat no flesh, drink no wine, and abstain from women." This revelation led him to settle in Lower Babylonia and adopt the religion of the Mughtasila, "those who wash themselves" or "those who purify themselves," presumably a community of baptists related to the Mandaeans or pre-Mandaeans. In this community, saturated with Gnostic influence, Mani received in his twelfth and twenty-fourth years a revelation from an angel of God, at-Taum, "The Twin": "Leave this congregation. Thou art not one of its believers, thy task is ethical purity and the negation of desires. But because of thy youth, it is not yet time for thee to manifest thyself." And later: "The time has now come for thee to manifest thyself and proclaim thy doctrine aloud." And further: "Greetings, O Mani, from me and from the Lord who has sent me to thee and has chosen thee for thy mission. He commands thee to gird thyself for

257

thine apostolate and proclaim the glad tidings of the truth that comes from him, and spend all thy zeal upon it."[23]

And in *Kephalaion* 1, Mani himself speaks:

> In this year, when Ardashīr the King [?] [was about to?] [receive] the throne, the living Paraclete came down [to me and] spoke with me. He revealed the living mystery that is hidden before the worlds and the generations, the mystery of the depths and heights. He revealed to me the mystery of light and of darkness, the mystery of battle and of war [?] and of the great war. . . . [Afterwards?] he also revealed to me how the light has . . . darkness in consequence of its mixture and how this world was established. He also enlightened me as to how the ships were made fast in order that [the gods] of light might descend upon them, to purify the light from Creation, [to cast] the dregs and the waste [?] [into the] abyss; the mystery of the creation of Adam, the first man. He also taught me the mystery of the tree of knowledge, of which Adam ate, [whereby] his eyes became seeing. And the mystery of the apostles, who were sent into the world [in order that they] might choose the churches; the mystery of the Elect [and their] commandments; the mystery of the Catechumens, their helpers, and [their] commandments; the mystery of the sinners and their works and the punishment which lies ahead [?] of them. In this way, everything that has happened and everything that will happen was revealed to me by the Paraclete. . . . Everything that the eye sees and the ear hears and the mind thinks . . . I have know through him. I have seen the universe through him, and became one body and one spirit.[24]

These documents, which may be presumed to reflect a real experience, reveal the two constant aspects of the Manichaean conception of redemption— (1) negative: horror of life, accompanied by the categorical commandment to abstain from the things that are regarded as evil, rejection, renunciation, severance; (2) positive: the presumption to total knowledge, the certainty of a gnosis which is of divine origin, which brings redemption and calls for the immediate dissemination of the gospel of redemption.

We find these two aspects more amply developed in the Mani-

---

23 Translation from Gustav Flügel, *Mani, seine Lehre und seine Schriften* (Leipzig, 1862), pp. 83–84.
24 *Kephalaion* 1 (ed. Polotsky, pp. 14, line 31–15, line 24).

chaean texts, where they constitute, as it were, the two poles of religious consciousness. Here, as in Gnosticism, the need for redemption seems to stem from the experience of evil. But—though in almost all other religious experience the experience of evil consists in a feeling of severance, alienation, or duality, and redemption is understood as a process which will make the consciousness one with itself and reunite the split existence—the Manichaean attitude is the exact opposite: here cleavage, duality is looked upon as the highest good. The Manichaean strives for redemption because man's present state is intolerable and absurd, because he is a mixture or—to use an image current in Manichaeism—an "amalgam" of mutually exclusive substances,[25] an artificial and violent fusion of good and evil, of the divine and the demonic, of spirit and matter—in short, of light and darkness. This mixture constitutes our temporal and ephemeral existence, and it is sustained, prolonged, aggravated by the law of existence. For if man does not free himself from the mixture, he is condemned to pass through a whole series of lives, in each one of which he encounters suffering and sin. This is the "eternal transfusion" ($\mu\epsilon\tau\alpha\gamma\gamma\iota\sigma\mu\acute{o}s$)—the term is of Gnostic origin[26]—in the Turfan texts often compared to the Buddhist *saṃsāra,* a "death in birth,"[27] to which each new birth takes us back. But transient, recurrent existence not only brings us into contact with evil; it immerses us in evil and makes it an integral part of our present being. We shall see that evil has positive reality for Manichaeism, that the world is not a zone between light and darkness but lies entirely in the darkness, from which it has emerged only through the ever-feebler admixture of the fallen light particles. If there is a world, if there is development, it is because there is matter and body: living matter, living body beyond a doubt, because they are bound up with light and soul, but—as the Manichaeans say—world and body, which are poisoned by this

---

25 Cf. M 9 II V (ed. Andreas and Henning, *SBA* 1933, p. 300); É. Chavannes and P. Pelliot, "Un Traité manichéen retrouvé en Chine," *JA* 1911, p. 537; *Fihrist,* in Flügel, *Mani,* p. 88; al-Murtaḍā in K. Kessler, *Mani* (Berlin, 1889), I, 353.

26 The most important references are Epiphanius, *Panarion,* 66, 28, 1 (ed. Holl, III, 62, line 14). On the term, see *Pistis Sophia,* ch. 100 (ed. Schmidt, p. 160, lines 6, 13; p. 161, line 33).

27 Cf. e.g., M 38 V (in F. W. K. Müller, "Handschriften-Reste in Estrangelo-Schrift aus Turfan," *ABA* 1904, p. 77).

mixture and which, just as an unclean vessel spoils its contents, poison the light and the soul which they hold imprisoned.[28] Hence the profound, concrete experience of evil incurred by the man who is immersed in this mixture, which finds its expression in images of horror: a world composed of corpses and the excrement of demons,[29] the abysses of evil—this "empested earth," which is smoke, consuming fire, wild wind, muddy water, dense darkness—each with its own peculiar taste: salty, sour, acrid, insipid, bitter, and each inhabited by its stupid monsters.[30] Matter is eternal dis-ordered motion,[31] revolt and struggle, dissolving and consuming itself, a self-devouring scab.[32] This cruel immersion in evil fills man with horror at his existence and a sense of the strangeness of his situation. And this very feeling of horror proves that man has an origin and destination outside his present enslavement.

To give you a living sense of this experience, I should like to read to you from Turfan Fragment M 7 the dialogue between Zoroaster—the redeemer, who here symbolizes the νοῦς—and the soul, i.e. the part of himself which is imprisoned in matter and which is also the human soul in need of redemption:

> [Zoroaster:] "Heavy is the drunkenness in which thou sleep-est, awaken and look upon me. May salvation [come to] thee from the world of peace whence I was sent for thy sake." And he [the soul] answered: "I am the tender unsuf-fering son of Srōshār, I am in a state of mixture and know

28 On the image of poisoning, see Titus of Bostra, *Contra Manichaeos*, I, 17 (ed. P. A. de Lagarde, p. 9, line 39); Theodor bar Khouni, in Franz Cumont, *Recherches sur le Manichéisme*, I, *La Cosmogonie manichéenne d'après Théodore bar Khôni* (Brussels, 1908), p. 18; Chavannes and Pelliot, "Traité," pp. 530–31. For the comparison with the unclean vessel, Alexander of Lycopo-lis, *Contra Manichaeorum opiniones*, ed. August Brinkmann (Leipzig, 1895), p. 6, line 3.
29 Cf. Cumont, *Recherches*, I, 27 and *škand gumānīy Vižār*, XVI, 8–15 (tr. A. V. W. Jackson, *Researches*, p. 177).
30 Cf. Polotsky, *Abriss*, cols. 249–50, and particularly *Kephalaia* 6 and 27 (ed. Polotsky, I, 30–34, 77–79).
31 Ἄτακτος κίνησις (Alexander of Lycopolis, ed. Brinkmann, p. 5, line 8). Cf. Titus, I, 16–20, 27, 31; Epiphanius, 66, 19, 1 (ed. Holl, III, 42–43); M 33 (*SBA* 1934, p. 31); Shahrastāni, in Theodor Haarbrücker, tr., *Abu'l-Fath' Muhammad asch-Schahrastâni's Religionsparteien und Philosophen-Schulen* (Halle, 1850–51), I, 286.
32 On this image and on the self-destruction and self-consumption of matter, see Severus of Antioch, *Homily* CXXIII, in F. Cumont and M.-A. Kugener, *Recherches sur le Manichéisme*, II, *Fragments syriaques d'ouvrages mani-chéens* (Brussels, 1912), pp. 117–18, 127.

suffering. Lead me out of the embrace of death." Bringing salvation, Zoroaster questioned her with these primeval words: "[Art thou] my member? May the salvation of the living force and the supreme worlds [come] over thee from thine home. Follow me, son of gentleness, and set a wreath of light on thy head. Thou son of the mighty, who hast been made so poor that thou must beg in all places. . . ."[33]

And later on in the same fragment we find this "hymn to the living soul":

> I come from the light and the gods, I have become home-less, parted from them; my enemies fell upon me, they led me among the dead. Blessed and redeemed be he who re-deems my soul from torment. I am a god, born of gods, glittering, sparkling, fragrant and beautiful—but now I have fallen upon misery. Devils without number have seized me, hideous evils that made me powerless, they raped me, bit me, flayed me and devoured me. Dêvs, Yakshas, and Peris, sinister dragons hard to repulse [?], ugly, stinking, black—I suffered much pain and death from them. They roar, attack, pursue, they assail me. . . .[34]

These outpourings express the whole desperate situation of man-kind and its hope for liberation, but amid all the horrors and perils of life, they reveal the certainty of redemption. In one voice the creature in need of redemption cries out his misery and invokes his transcendent origin. This "son of God," this prince, this "mem-ber" of the redeemer, knows himself to be exalted by right of birth above the amalgam into which he has entered with demonic matter. He feels himself to be essentially alien on earth, different from his present illusory existence. His present situation seems to him an accidental and absurd contamination. To evoke a number of images which are classical themes of all Gnosticism,[35] this existence is slavery, exile, oblivion, ignorance, drunkenness, sleep—in contrast to freedom, the original home, memory, knowledge, untroubled radiance, wakefulness—i.e., to a previous state which can be re-discovered and redeemed through the renunciation of corporeal ties and awareness of the strange and unnatural situation.

33 SBA 1934, p. 872, Andreas and Henning.
34 Ibid., pp. 874–75.
35 Cf. Jonas, Gnosis, I, 105–20.

What are the concrete consequences of this experience of evil, i.e., of mixture? First of all, a negative attitude: rejection of this unworthy contact with matter, break with the amalgam, renunciation of the world. Only this self-withdrawal, this inner separation, enables us to avoid contamination and sin and the unconsciousness arising from the entrance of the dark element into the soul. Sin—of which we shall have more to say—is interpreted by the Manichaeans primarily as desire and temptation. Darkness is essentially pleasure, ἡδονή, and the evil at its root, ἐπιθυμία, *concupiscentia,* a wild impulse that strives stubbornly for propagation and enjoyment, comparable and ultimately identical with the sexual urge. The restless, harrowing horror of evil actually culminates in carnal desire and in the sexual act; matter is sexuality. The division into sexes, and generation, are the work of demons. Only the cessation of generation and absolute segregation of the sexes can put a definitive end to darkness. This obsession with sexuality in the Manichaeans survives its inhibition to such a degree that we often encounter it in images and myths sharply contrasting with the ascetic severity of Manichaean life. In opposition to such images the Manichaean consciousness projects the idea of untainted purity, and nothing can give us a better idea of the spiritual climate of Manichaeism than the miniatures preserved in Turfan, with their clearly delineated forms, their fine features, their clear and pure colors, or those symbols which the Chinese Chavannes-Pelliot treatise finds for piety:[36] salt, the precious pearl, which bears the name of "clear moon," colorless lacquer, surfaces evenly whitewashed, or finally that love of flowers which was carried to the point of abuse in the cosmogony and cult of the Manichaeans.[37] An ideal of delicate tones, clear outlines, self-contained visions, soft fragrance. An ideal of purity, consonant with the refined taste of men who feel repelled by all grossness and confusion and who have removed themselves completely from the things of the world and the flesh.

Now we shall consider the *positive* attitude to which the experience of evil leads. Awareness of the duality and irrationality in our present situation presupposes that the Manichaean has awakened

36 Chavannes and Pelliot, "Traité," *JA* 1911, pp. 563–64.
37 Cf. Augustine, *Contra Faustum,* XV, 5 (ed. J. Zycha, *CSEL* 25, p. 425, lines 4–18).

to consciousness and that this consciousness includes the memory of a perfect state preceding the mixture and surviving in spite of it. This experience, then, constitutes both the need and the certainty of redemption; or, in other terms, it both raises and solves the problem of redemption. Consciousness is indeed the illuminating presence of the spirit, the Νοῦς—the redeeming element in the soul in need of redemption. It gives to the soul knowledge (gnosis) and the intellectual faculties, just as in Gnosticism *conscientia* is *scientia*. It enables man to understand his special situation by revealing to him every particular of the divine, cosmic, and historic events that led to his downfall, by explaining to him the structure of the world in which he finds himself, and by showing him the instrumentalities provided by the godhead for his redemption. And again, as in Gnosticism, this gnosis is epignosis, this cognition is re-cognition. "The soul awakened by this knowledge and given back to the memory of its origins *(scientia admonita anima et pristinae memoriae reddita)* ," says the Manichaean Fortunatus in his disputation with St. Augustine, "recognizes *(recognoscet)* whence it comes, in what an evil condition it finds itself, and through what good, which wipes out the sins it has committed against its will, it can—by the purging of its errors and the performance of good works—acquire the reward of a reconciliation with God."[38] These words are in a sense an echo of the definition of gnosis that we found in Theodotus. Thus consciousness, i.e. the νοῦς, along with the gnosis which it embraces, is prerequisite to redemption. "The soul cannot be saved, unless it partakes of gnosis" (πάλιν δὲ ψυχὴν οὐκέτι σῴζεσθαι, εἰ μή τι ἂν τῆς γνώσεως τῆς αὐτῆς μετάσχοι) , we read in Epiphanius.[39] Now to what does this indispensable knowledge primarily refer? To this axiom of Manichaean thought: If there is mixture, it presupposes a duality of two irreducible substances: light and darkness, good and evil, spiritual and carnal. The function of consciousness is to transform this perception into a clear statement and express it in conceptual language. "If we did not see the limited and transient good and evil in the world and the mixture of the one with the other," says M 9, "the injunction to abstain from evil and attain to the good could not enter into the thinking

38 Augustine, *Contra Fortunatum*, 20, 21 (ed. Zycha, pp. 99, 100) .
39 *Panarion*, 66, 9, 9 (ed. Holl, III, 30, lines 25–26) .

263

of any man."[40] Thus we must arrive at this indubitable insight, "that the soul is of different substance from the body and that it is in the body mixed, mingled, bound up with the spirit of the body—i.e., anger, lust, and sensuality." Or, in the Pelliot Fragment we read: "He who wishes to partake of religion must know that the two principles of light and darkness are of a fundamentally different nature: if he does not distinguish them, how can he put theory into practice?"[41] This consciousness of duality makes it possible to distinguish what the Manichaeans sometimes call the "two paths," that of light and that of darkness,[42] and the separation of the mixture—i.e., the separation that the Manichaean effects within himself, his release from the dark aspect in himself, and that makes it possible for him to give preference to the good path. It virtually embraces the whole of Manichaean lore, the whole system which both justifies and satisfies the need for redemption. If our actual existence is a mixture and if light and darkness are a fundamental duality, then we must assume that prior to the mixture there was an original state in which the two substances were distinct, and we must assume the possibility if not the reality that the mixture will be followed by an ultimate state in which the substances will again be absolutely separate. Their present abnormal union in the world is only an episode interpolated between two states of complete natural duality. And so the doctrine of the "two principles" leads immediately to another doctrine essential to the structure of the whole Manichaean system: the doctrine of the "three epochs."[43]

This concludes our analysis of what we presume to have been the religious experience of Manichaeism. The experience of evil and the emotional need for redemption have been transformed into concepts, demanding a solution on the plane of the intellect. This they

40 M 9 I R and II R (SBA 1933, pp. 297, 300).
41 JA 1913, p. 114.
42 Cf. Homily II (ed. Polotsky, p. 29, line 8).
43 Homily II (ibid., p. 7, lines 11–13); Chinese documents published by Chavannes and Pelliot, JA 1913, pp. 135–45 and cf. p. 335; Khuastuanift, VIII, tr. W. Bang, "Manichäische Laien-Beichtspiegel," Le Muséon (Louvain), XXXVI (1923), 157, and cf. Augustine, Contra Felicem, I, 9–10, 12; Contra Faustum, XIII, 6 and XXVIII, 5 (ed. Zycha, pp. 383–84, 742–43); Škand gumānīy Vičār, XVI, 4–7 (tr. Jackson, Researches, p. 177); Pelliot Fragment, JA 1913, pp. 114–16.

find in a knowledge which explains to man his position and at the same time redeems him from it, a knowledge which (as Strophe 172 of the Chinese Hymn Book[44] indicates) is an initiation into all the mysteries, into "the two principles, the three epochs, the meaning of nature and glory"—a vast program, for it embraces insight into the origin and destiny of man, a whole cosmogony and a divine prehistory of the cosmos. "Behold first," writes Mani in the *Epistle of the Foundation*, "what was before the creation of the world and how the struggle [between good and evil] began, in order that thou mayst distinguish the nature of light from that of matter."[45] This doctrine—as we have seen from the revelation carried to Mani by the angel at-Taum—is held to be a total knowledge, exhaustive and certain; it encompasses theology and theogony, cosmology, astronomy, geology, botany, anthropology, and history, and offers both an eschatology and a theory of redemption. This, no doubt, is the nature of all gnosis, but only in Manichaeism does it appear so rational and positive. A number of passages in St. Augustine[46] actually indicate that the Manichaeans, unlike the Catholic Church, claim that their doctrine is based on an authentic science, on reason pure and simple (*mera et simplici ratione*)[47] and not on authority and faith. St. Augustine himself admits that he adhered to Manichaeism for nine years because he believed that it offered the true philosophy.[48] And here we have a basic element in the Manichaean conception of redemption. Manichaeism is a religion of the Νοῦς. Redemption is a problem of insight, solved "objectively" by an act of the intellect. Redemption is knowledge and knowledge is redemption. Assuredly Manichaeism is Gnosticism, but Gnosticism of an intellectual type. Can we, then, go so far as to compare Manichaeism with rationalism or with any other system seeking to liberate man through positive science? Can we make a philosophy of enlightenment out of the theology of light? By no means. And in

---

44 *SBA* 1933, p. 491, Ernst Waldschmidt and Wolfgang Lentz.

45 Augustine, *Contra Epistulam quam vocant Fundamenti*, 12 (ed. Zycha, p. 208, lines 23–26).

46 E.g. *De moribus ecclesiae catholicae*, 3 (Migne, *PL*, XXXII, 122); *De utilitate credendi*, 2 and 21. Cf. the title of *Kephalaion* 142 (*SBA* 1933, p. 22): "Man must not believe unless he sees with his own eyes."

47 *De utilitate credendi*, 2.

48 See *Confessiones*, III, 10–12; IV, 24–27.

my opinion it is only in a certain sense permissible to compare the Manichaean system with the Hellenistic philosophy of the time. For, like all Gnosis, Mani's system is only seemingly rational and positive; it merely claims to be so. His concepts dissolve into images that are often exceedingly material and realistic; cosmology and anthropology are expressed in a myth, through their association with the doctrine of redemption. Both the Manichaeans and Mani himself may have looked on this myth as a science because it provided an answer to all questions and above all because it offered to the mind the purely formal satisfaction of a self-contained, symmetrical, and unshakable system.[49] We remain, however, in the realm of revelation and imagination, of mysticism and myth—in short, of Gnosticism. Even if the Manichaean concept of redemption is rational in principle, in its formulation, and in its claims, its implications and its solutions are anything but rational.

2. The Theoretical Foundations of Redemption: The Cosmological and the Anthropological Myth

Let us now turn our attention to this mythology itself, which responds to intellectual demands and represents the theoretical answer of Manichaean dogma to the problem of redemption.

In a certain sense the myth is here an ultimate expression of the need for redemption, of an experience amplified into a cosmogony; but, above all, it is a system and composition of cosmic and historical perspectives in which our present being can find its place, a system of the universe and of human nature, capable of explaining, justifying, and finally of satisfying the need for redemption. Here cosmology and anthropology are, almost in a physical sense, the foundations of redemption. The myth of redemption fuses, as it were, with the cosmogonic and anthropological myth, joining world, man, and redemption into a close-knit structure which may seem complicated but is exceedingly simple in its broad outlines. (1) Each stage in the genesis and development of the world contains an element of redemption. Every increase of evil brings with it a new possibility of resistance. There is a thorough going parallelism —Waldschmidt and Lentz undertook to represent it as a diptych[50]

49 Cf. Polotsky, *Abriss*, cols. 246–47 and 271.
50 *ABA* 1926, pp. 16–17.

—between the cosmic incarceration and liberation of light in their successive phases. Cosmogony is soteriology. (2) We find the same parallelism between the incarceration and liberation of light in man: anthropology is also soteriology. (3) Anthropology corresponds to cosmogony in the sense that the creation and history of man repeat and epitomize the creation and development of the world; macrocosm and microcosm are closely connected and correspond to one another. Man and cosmos, cosmos and godhead are consubstantial. One and the same substance—light, which is God himself—is mixed with the matter of the world and of the body, and consequently the liberation of this light from the universe and its redemption from the human organism are the same process. Ultimately, it is always and everywhere God himself who is ensnared in the darkness and who frees himself from it; it is one and the same entity which, on the cosmological as on the anthropological plane, is to be redeemed and redeems. Here we find—in complete form— the central but not the only figure of Gnosticism: the Redeemed Redeemer. This explains why throughout the Manichaean myth we encounter one and the same hero and a single, eternally recurring situation. Nearly all the figures who appear in the Manichaean cosmogony and soteriology under the most diverse names are essentially incarnations or successive aspects of this same being, who remains eternally the same, or hypostasized functions of the divine action. The successive emanations of the godhead do not constitute a descending hierarchy or imply progressive imperfection of the supreme deity. The deity issues a call (Syr.: *qerā*), which evokes a being that is merely the personification or mythical vehicle of the call.[51] Thus we have everywhere and always the same being in the most diverse aspects imposed by its activity, adventures, and vicissitudes: the same luminous substance which must be redeemed and which redeems itself.

These few remarks will enable us to disengage from a welter of confusing detail the broad outlines of the mythical picture which the Manichaeans formed of the cosmos and of man. We shall limit our present investigation to those episodes which are of crucial importance for our problem.

51 Cf. Polotsky, *Abriss*, col. 248, lines 29–57 and the remarks of F. C. Burkitt, *The Religion of the Manichees* (Cambridge, 1925), pp. 22–24.

At the beginning of the cosmological myth, in the earliest time, there was a complete and unimpaired duality of the two natures or substances or roots: light and darkness, good and evil, God and matter. Both are original principles, eternal and unengendered. The two have equal value and equal power. They have nothing in common and are opposed in all things.[52] Thus, from the outset, the problem of evil is solved in the most realistic and extreme way; evil cannot be denied, since it has existed since all eternity, and it cannot be attenuated, since it is not in any way descended from good and does not depend on good. Certain texts do indeed say that light is "superior" ($\kappa\rho\epsilon\iota\tau\tau\omega\nu$) [53] to darkness, but it is superior only through its inherent qualities of kindness, beauty, and intelligence, which contrast it—as a king to a pig[54]—to the malice, ugliness, and stupidity of matter and which cause the Manichaeans to accord the title of God only to the light.[55] And in another sense, as well, light is "superior": the lust of matter is directed toward light; dazzled by its radiance, it seeks to engulf the light, whereas the light feels neither curiosity nor desire for the darkness. The fact nevertheless remains that this natural superiority implies no inequality between the two substances, or even the optimistic certainty that the good by its very nature must necessarily triumph over evil. It might even be asserted that the pacific gentleness of light puts it at a disadvantage in its conflict with the warlike violence of the darkness.[56] Considered statically, the two principles are construed as two distinct realms, separated by a border line and symmetrically opposed; the realm of the good in the north and the realm of evil in the south, each ruled by a king—in the one case the "Father of Greatness," in the other the "Prince of Darkness," who is sometimes a personification, some-

---

52 In order to simplify our account, I refer the reader here to Hans Jonas, *Gnosis*, pp. 287–93. On the image of the two trees, which often serves to express this dualism, see *Kephalaion* 2 (ed. Polotsky, pp. 16, line 33–23, line 13); for a description of hell, *Kephalaion* 6 (ibid., pp. 30, line 13–34, line 12) and 27 (pp. 77, line 23–79, line 12).

53 Titus of Bostra, I (ed. de Lagarde, p. 12, lines 26, 28). See also Alexander of Lycopolis (ed. Brinkmann, p. 5, lines 2–3): and Severus of Antioch (Cumont and Kugener, *Recherches*, II, 124, 132–33).

54 Severus (Cumont and Kugener, II, 97).

55 Cf. Augustine, *Contra Faustum*, XXI, 1 (ed. Zycha, p. 568, lines 14–15).

56 Alexander of Lycopolis (ed. Brinkmann, p. 5, lines 20–21); also Augustine, *De vera religione*, 9 (Migne, *PL*, XXXIV, 129–30); Theodoret, *Haereticorum fabularum compendium*, I, 26 (Migne, *PG*, LXXXIII, 377–82); Severus (Cumont and Kugener, II, 127–28).

times an outgrowth of matter. Each realm consists of five elements: νοῦς, ἔννοια, φρόνησις, ἐνθύμησις, λογισμός, which are the "dwellings" or "members" of the Father of Greatness; smoke, fire, wind, water (or mud), and darkness, which are those of the king of the dark realm. The one is inhabited by aeons, the other by unnumbered demons.[57] But this antithesis must also be construed dynamically: light and darkness are more than substances, areas, persons, and, it goes without saying, more than concepts; they are primarily forces, each with its own field and moving in a direction determined by its nature. The good strives upward and can extend infinitely to north, east, and west. Evil strives downward and can extend infinitely only to the south. Both tending to extend infinitely, the one in three directions, the other in only one, the two bar each other's paths and delimit each other wherever they meet, from which it follows that the light is delimited below and the darkness above. The darkness juts like a wedge into the light, which embraces it on three sides.[58]

Unless we conceive of good and evil in this way, we cannot explain the event with which the cosmological drama begins: the catastrophe which ushers in the "middle epoch," the bursting of the original duality and the mingling of the two natures. Matter is force, striving to invade and engulf the realm of light, which lies above it and repels it. It is "un-co-ordinated" motion,[59] half unconscious. In the imagination of the Manichaeans, this state of affairs is represented by the endless battles of the demons, flaying and devouring one another; matter is continually consuming and destroying itself. An accidental jolt within this disordered, aimless motion raises the Prince of Darkness to the uppermost limit of his realm. Here he beholds the radiance of light and conceives the desire to

57 See Polotsky, *Abriss*, cols. 249–50.
58 Alexander (ed. Brinkmann, p. 5, lines 11–13); Titus, I, 9–11; Augustine, *Contra Epist. Fund.*, 18–20, 23–25; *Contra Faustum*, IV, 2; *Confessiones*, V, 10; Severus (Cumont and Kugener, II, 96, 100–02, 105); Simplicius, *In Enchiridion Epicteti*, 27 (ed. F. Dübner, p. 71, lines 15–17); "Histoire Nestorienne," in Graffin and Nau, eds., *Patrologia Orientalia*, IV (1908), 227; Bar Hebraeus (Kessler, *Mani*, I, 356); En-Nedîm (Flügel, *Mani*, p. 86); Shahrastāni, tr. Haarbrücker (above, n. 31), I, 286.
59 Alexander (ed. Brinkmann, p. 5, line 8 and p. 10, lines 5, 24) and cf. Titus, IV, 19 (Syr.); Titus, I, 15–20, 27, 31; Serapion of Thmuis, *Against the Manichees*, XXXI (ed. R. P. Casey, Cambridge, Mass., 1931, p. 47, lines 8–9); Shahrastāni, tr. Haarbrücker, I, 286; M 33 (ed. Andreas and Henning, *SBA* 1934, p. 876).

conquer this strange realm with his demons and to make it his own by devouring it. This myth may well correspond to a psychological experience which would lend it profound meaning. The essence of matter is ἐπιθυμία, *concupiscentia,* and the essence of evil is lust for pleasure (ἡδονή), comparable if not identical with the sexual urge, the libido. This violent, devastating urge strives darkly for satisfaction. It develops freely in the unconscious or semiconscious, which for the Manichaeans is matter, but is inhibited by consciousness, which is the good and the light. Encounter with consciousness corresponds exactly to the emergence of an inhibited urge. A smoke cloud of evil strives to expand; desire seeks to occupy and submerge the field of clear thinking. I am very much inclined to interpret this myth—the assault of darkness on the realm of light—as a projection of the Manichaean experience of sin. We shall see that in the texts temptation is represented in accordance with a similar schema.

In the face of the threatening peril, the Father of Greatness, who precisely because of his goodness is without weapons, decides not to call upon one of the aeons forming his entourage, but to defend himself. He sends forth a first emanation: the "Great Spirit" or the "Mother of Life," who in turn projects the "First Man" (Syr.: *nāšā qadmāyā;* Gr.: Πρῶτος Ἄνθρωπος; Lat.: *Primus Homo;* Parth.: *mardōhm naxvēn;* Arab.: *al-insān al-qadīm;* in certain of the Turfan texts assimilated to the god Ōhrmizd). The First Man ascends to the border with his five sons (air, wind, light, water, fire), who form his "armament." Here he is defeated by the darkness, and his sons are devoured by the demons. We must dwell for a moment on this defeat, for here lies the origin of the mixture, hence of the problem of redemption. First of all, we must bear in mind that the First Man is merely a hypostasis of the Father of Greatness, of God himself. In the Manichaean cosmogony, recorded by Theodor bar Khouni, the Father says literally:

> Of those [var.: my aeons, the] five škīnās,
> I shall send none to the battle,
> For I made them for peace [and blessing].
> But I myself will go
> And wage war against him.[60]

60 Tr. H. H. Schaeder in Schaeder and R. Reitzenstein, *Studien zum antiken Synkretismus aus Iran und Griechenland* (Leipzig, 1926); see also Polotsky, *Abriss,* col. 251, lines 11–13.

That is, I my*self* will fight (Syr.: *b-napš;* literally "with my soul"). Thus the First Man is identical with this soul, or, as the Manichaean Faustus says in St. Augustine, "He is made of the substance of God, he is the same as God" (*De substantia Dei, idipsum existentem quod Deus est*).[61] And the five sons of man who constitute his "armament" are his soul (Syr.: *napšā*). They represent—to use a term borrowed from St. Paul—the "living soul" ($\psi v \chi \dot{\eta} \, \zeta \tilde{\omega} \sigma a$), the *substantia vitalis*, which is *pars Dei*. It is a part of the Father, which combats matter and is devoured by it.[62] The hero who went out to battle and was defeated is the luminous substance of God himself, which saves and requires salvation. Here we have a profoundly pessimistic view of the genesis, since both the world and man came into being through a defeat of good and a victory of evil. Nevertheless, a plan of redemption is discernible. The devouring of the soul by the demons, i.e. the mixture of light and darkness, can be regarded as a voluntary sacrifice on the part of God, or as a stratagem which will later redound to the benefit of man, which limits the devastations of evil and prepares the final defeat of matter. Like a general who, to save his main army, throws his advance guard against the enemy, or like a shepherd who, to preserve his flock, leaves a single lamb to the wolf, the First Man conceives the plan of sacrificing his soul to the Darkness.[63] For the moment, matter's lust is appeased, and, moreover, the sacrifice of the light becomes a baited hook which holds the darkness fast, placing it at the mercy of the divine.[64] Life proves a food unsuitable to matter: the divine soul poisons the demons. True, the devoured light is sullied and

61 *Contra Faustum,* XI (ed. Zycha, p. 316, lines 22–23).

62 Cf. Epiphanius, 66, 9, 6 (ed. Holl, III, 30); Augustine, *Contra Faustum,* XI, 3 (ed. Zycha, p. 316); *De vera religione,* 9 (Migne, *PL,* XXXIV, 129–30); *De natura boni,* 44 (ed. Zycha, pp. 881–84); *Confessiones,* VI, 20; Theodoret, *Haer. fab. comp.,* I, 26; Severus (Cumont and Kugener, II, 126, 128, 143–44); Simplicius, *In Enchir. Epict.,* 27 (ed. Dübner, p. 70, lines 39–42). On the armament of the First Man, which is the soul and above all the universal soul, cf. Titus, I, 36 (ed. de Lagarde, p. 23, lines 8–9) and Epiphanius, 66, 25, 6 (ed. Holl, III, 55, lines 4–5). See also Baur, *Das Manichäische Religionssystem,* pp. 63–64; Cumont, *Recherches,* I, 18, n. 4; Schaeder, "Urform und Fortbildungen des manichäischen Systems" (above, n. 5), p. 111.

63 Cf. Hegemonius, *Acta Archelai,* 28, 2–3 (ed. Beeson, *GCS,* pp. 40, line 33–41, line 7); Augustine, *Contra Fortunatum,* 22 (ed. Zycha, pp. 106, line 23–107, line 8); Simplicius, *In Enchir. Epict.,* 27 (ed. Dübner, p. 70, lines 42–45); and perhaps T M 282 verso (*ABA* 1911, p. 18, von Le Coq).

64 Titus, I, 17; Theodoret, I, 26; Severus (Cumont and Kugener, II, 1); Chavannes and Pelliot, "Traité," p. 514.

poisoned by the darkness, but the darkness is no less poisoned by the light. It can no longer subsist without the life that has been infused into it; it knows that it would be doomed to definitive death if this life were to be withheld.[65] Thus God must save his own soul, which is mingled with the demons; but at the same time he has gained a weapon which will enable him to defeat them and free the engulfed light.[66]

The first redemption must be that of original man. This is a new, highly important action, the pledge and prototype of all future redemption. If we piece together the accounts of the *Acta Archelai*,[67] of the *Fihrist*,[68] of Turfan Fragment M 10,[69] and particularly of Theodor bar Khouni,[70] we arrive at the following version:

> The First Man regained consciousness [imprisoned in the darkness he had lost soul and consciousness] and seven times prayed to the Father of Greatness. [The Father heard his prayer.] And he called forth the second creation [evocation],[71] the "Friend of Lights," and the Friend of Lights called forth the "Great Demiurge," and the Great Demiurge called forth the "Living Spirit." And the Living Spirit called forth his five sons. [I omit their mythological names.] And they went to the land of darkness and found the First Man engulfed in the darkness, him and his five sons. Then the Living Spirit called with his voice; and the voice of the Living Spirit became like unto a sharp sword and [he] revealed his form to the First Man. And he spoke to him:
>
> Hail to thee, who art good in the midst of the evil ones,
> Light in the midst of darkness,

65 On the poisoning of the soul by matter, Alexander of Lycopolis, ed. Brinkmann, p. 6, lines 2–6; Titus, I, 17; Theodor bar Khouni (Cumont, *Recherches*, I, 18) ; Chavannes and Pelliot, "Traité," pp. 530–31. On light of different nature, hence unassimilable by matter, cf. Titus, I, 17; Augustine, *De moribus manichaeorum*, 36 (Migne, *PL*, XXXII) ; *Contra Faustum*, XX, 17; Theodor bar Khouni (Cumont, I, 18) ; John Damascene, "Disputatio cum Manichaeo" (Migne, *PG*, XCVI, 1320) . The soul becomes a poison that weakens the demon: Augustine, *Contra Faustum*, XXXI, 13; Theodor (Cumont, I, 18) . But the removal of the light would mean death for matter: Alexander, ed. Brinkmann, p. 5, lines 23–25; Titus, I, 39 and III, 5.
66 Cf. *Contra Fortunatum*, 22 (ed. Zycha, p. 107, lines 6–8) .
67 VII, 4–5 (ed. Beeson, pp. 10, line 24–11, line 16) .
68 Flügel, *Mani*, p. 88.
69 Tr. W. Henning, *NGG* 1933, pp. 306–18.
70 Tr. H. H. Schaeder, *Studien*, pp. 343–44.
71 On the second evocation, see Jackson, *Researches*, pp. 271–95, which also deals (pp. 255–70) with the liberation of the First Man.

> [God,] who dwellest amid the beasts of wrath,
> Who do not know his Glory.

Then the First Man answered him and said:

> Come with blessing, bringing
> The cargo [message? letter?] of peace and salvation.

And he spoke to him further:

> How fare our fathers,
> The Sons of Light in their city?

And the Call spoke to him: They fare well. And the Call and the Answer rose up to the Mother of Life and to the Living Spirit, and the Living Spirit donned the Call [as a cloak], and the Mother of Life donned the Answer, her beloved son. And they went down to the land of darkness where the First Man and his sons were.

The Living Spirit stretched out his right hand to the First Man to raise him out of the darkness, and "the Man was freed from dark matter and became God again." But he left behind him his soul, the five luminous elements of his armament.

This account of the first redemption provides a prototype for all redemption. Here—as we see from M 10[72]— the First Man is not only a hero who annuls death, defeats his enemies and reveals the paradise of light; he is primarily the prototype of the redeemed creature, of the redeemer who redeems himself. Redemption is first and foremost the awakening of a consciousness which had been lost for a time through the forgetfulness and ignorance induced by the flesh ("The First Man regains consciousness"); it culminates in his deification, i.e. return to his divine origin ("And the Man became God again"). This spiritual resurrection is the work of the Νοῦς—the redeeming element—which becomes flesh and blood in the First Man, while his "armament," which remains imprisoned in darkness, represents the element that must be saved: the psyche. The awakening of the Νοῦς is brought about or symbolized by the intervention of the Living Spirit, which, as we discover elsewhere,[73] brings to the soul "the Power of Life," the pneuma with its five gifts (life, force, luminosity, beauty, fragrance), and these in turn enable the divine substance to recognize itself and to be reborn.

72 *NGG* 1933, pp. 313–14.
73 Cf. Polotsky, *Abriss*, col. 253, lines 51–68.

Nowhere has the need and will for redemption been expressed with such moving symbolism. Man's prayer to the Father is followed by a piercing cry from the Living Spirit, which finds an echo in the Man's answer. Call and Answer are embodied in two figures (Syr.: *qaryā* and *'anyā;* N. Iran.: *Xrōštaγ* and *Paδvāχtaγ*), two deities whose names are usually translated as Caller and Answerer, but which actually—since the Syriac participles are passive and not active—mean "that which is called" and "that which is answered."[74] The Call goes forth from the Living Spirit and returns to it; it is the call for redemption, the voice which comes mysteriously from above, permeates the soul, and awakens in it the hope and the will to be redeemed. The soul gives answer to this call by an act of yearning, confidence, and assent, which here goes forth from the Man, or, more exactly—for it is almost a gift of grace—from the "Mother," who is the First Man's mother and the "Mother of the Living," i.e., of all future believers. The dialogue of the divine pair ends with the union of Call and Answer, which, like the redeemed Man, rise up to the realm of light. These circumstances are exceedingly important; the drama of world redemption will always consist in this dialogue. To the call of revelation, perpetuated by the apostles of light, preached by Mani and his missionaries, published abroad by all those who, like Xrōštaγ, awaken consciousness and proclaim the truth[75]—to this call the souls give, or decline, an answer. As M 4 puts its,[76] the redeemed soul will be "the afflicted soul which has given answer." Thus united, Call and Answer will form what the Manichaeans call the ἐνθύμησις of life, which opposes the ἐνθύμησις of death and matter and enables the soul to answer the call of the Νοῦς and of revelation. This union, designated as the "Great Idea," endures up to the final annihilation of the world; then, gathering all the lost particles, it becomes the "Last Statue" and returns to heaven.[77] Everything, even the gesture with which the Living Spirit draws the First Man from the darkness, has a soteriological significance: as we see from *Kephalaion* 9,[78] this ges-

---

74 Cf. Schaeder, *Studien,* pp. 263–70; Waldschmidt and Lentz, *SBA* 1933, pp. 513–15; F. C. Burkitt, "Xrōštaγ and Paδvāχταγ, Call and Answer," *Journal of Theological Studies* (Oxford), XXXVI (1935), 180–81.
75 See Waldschmidt and Lentz, *ABA* 1926, p. 36.
76 *ABA* 1904, p. 54, line 13, Müller.
77 See Schmidt and Polotsky, *SBA* 1933, pp. 75–79.
78 Ed. Polotsky, pp. 19–24; cf. also pp. 40, lines 30–33 and 41, lines 3–10.

ture, this stretching forth of the hand, makes the First Man the Lord of all creatures to be saved in the future and forms the basis of the Manichaean ritual usage of the δεξιά, the sign by which those who have been redeemed may recognize one another and attest their liberation from darkness, their membership in the community of truth, and their descent from the Mother of the Living, who, as we have seen in our account, accepts the answer of the Man, her beloved son, and clothes herself in it. In conclusion, we should like to add that in another version of our tale,[79] the First Man, before returning to the paradise of light, descends to the very bottom of darkness and there cuts the roots from the tree of evil, whose crown forms the kingdom of hell. Severed from the sources of its power, matter is gradually dominated by the light.

The history of the First Man's salvation is not merely a symbolic myth of redemption or a prototype of the experience of redemption; it provides an instrumentality and assurance for future redemption.

We have seen that the First Man left his soul in the darkness. This luminous substance gave life to matter and so poisoned it by mingling with it in varying degrees, and at the same time the light was sullied, weakened, shrouded in forgetfulness, suffering, and unconsciousness. To save the light becomes the motive and purpose of Creation, which I shall briefly describe.[80]

Supported by its five sons, the Demiurge—who is the Living Spirit—passes judgment on the demonic Archons; they are flayed and the heavens are made from their skins, the earth from their flesh; he crucifies them in the firmament and makes the first move toward the liberation of the light by dividing the mixed substance into three parts: the part which has remained pure despite the mixture becomes sun and moon; that which has suffered only a little becomes the stars; the release of the third, most sullied part proves more difficult and time-consuming. At the entreaty of the Mother of Life, the First Man, and the Living Spirit, the Father of Greatness proceeds to the third evocation, that of the strictly

---

79 En-Nedīm (Flügel, *Mani*, p. 89) ; see also Chavannes and Pelliot, "Traité," pp. 536, 559–61.

80 On the following see the account of Theodor bar Khouni and F. Cumont's commentary, *Recherches*, I, 25–41; on the seduction of the Archons, ibid., I, 54–68, or Polotsky, *Abriss*, cols. 254–56.

soteriological deities, comprising chiefly the Third Envoy, or cosmic redeemer,[81] and Jesus, the individual redeemer. The Third Envoy redeems the world by organizing it into a machine—one might say, a factory—for gathering, refining, and sublimating the buried light. Its mechanism consists of the sun and moon and the "wheels" of wind, water, and fire, which one of the Living Spirit's sons sets in motion. During the first fifteen days of every month the liberated substance rises in a pillar of light—"the Perfect Man" —to the moon, which, as this charge of light increases, slowly becomes a full moon. During the latter fifteen days of the month, the charge is transferred or transfused to the sun, whence it is restored to its heavenly home. But the Third Envoy also employs less mechanical means: in his glittering nakedness he appears in the sun as a Virgin of Light—a figure borrowed from Gnosticism[82] —now in feminine form before the male Archons, now in masculine form before the female Archons. He arouses their desire, and the light they have devoured is mixed with the seed which they pour forth. Their sin falls to the earth where it grows into vegetation, while the female demons, nauseated by the turning of the zodiac to which they are bound, give birth to abortions, who fall to earth and eat the blossoms from the trees, so assimilating both the diffused seed and the light. Overcome with desire, they interbreed, and bring forth a swarm of demons. This is the origin of the animal kingdom. The part of the light which remains to be redeemed is united on earth but dispersed and poisoned in the marrow of plants and the bodies of demons. But a new danger threatens: the appearance of the Third Envoy leads Matter to fear that its prisoner may escape. To secure it more firmly, Matter resolves to assemble most of the light in a personal creation, which will be the antithesis of the divine creation. To this end, two demons—a male, Ašaqlūn, and a female, Nemraël—devour all their children with a view to concentrating in themselves all the light they can hold. Then they copulate and engender the first two human beings: Adam and Eve.[83]

81 Cf. Waldschmidt and Lantz, *ABA* 1926, pp. 50ff. and *SBA* 1932, p. 180, nn. 2, 4. The action of the Third Envoy is summed up in *Kephalaia* 34 and 35 (ed. Polotsky, pp. 86, line 32–87, line 29) and XLVI (pp. 117, line 11–118, line 12).

82 Cf. W. Bousset, *Hauptprobleme der Gnosis* (Göttingen, 1907), pp. 61–63 and 76–77.

83 Cf. Cumont, *Recherches*, I, 42–46 and T III 260, *SBA* 1932, pp. 191–201, Andreas and Henning; p. 194, n. 6 contains a bibliography on the question. The

Thus the human race owes its origin to a series of revolting acts of cannibalism and sexuality. And it has retained the stigma in its body which preserves the bestial form of the Archons[84] and in the libido, which drives man himself to copulate and procreate—i.e., to further the plan of matter to hold the luminous substance in captivity forever. But, just as the fall of the First Man was followed by an act of redemption and was transformed into an instrument of creation, Adam's disgrace calls forth a new act of redemption. Since the main part of the light is concentrated in him, it is Adam —and through him the race of his descendants—who now becomes the central object of redemption.

We must therefore accord special emphasis to the story of Adam's redemption. It is available in several versions, the most important of which are to be found in Theodor bar Khouni[85] and in Turfan Fragment S 9.

> She [Āz, the demon of matter] makes him [the first man, perhaps his soul] as though blind and deaf, unconscious and confused, in order that he may not know his origin and his lineage [lit., family]. She has created his body and prison; she has chained his soul, which has lost its insight.—I am a prisoner, cruel to me are the demons, demonesses and witches!—She [Āz] has firmly chained the soul to the accursed body; she has made it ugly [?] and evil, angry and vengeful.[86]

In T III 260[87] the first pair torments and ignores the five elements of light that are within them. They are without fear of the gods. They wish to rule the earth and, like the demons, fill it with their fury and their vileness. According to the *Fihrist*,[88] when the five angels—a celestial repetition of the imprisoned five elements—see the light of God in this fallen state, they entreat the Bringer of Glad Tidings (the Third Envoy), the Mother of Life, the First Man, and the Living Spirit to send someone to this creature, whose true origin is so lofty, to free it and redeem it, to give it knowledge

---

first two humans are named Gêhmurd and Murdiyânay. Today we can add *Kephalaia* 55, 56, and 57 (ed. Polotsky, pp. 133ff.).

84 See Epiphanius 66, 76, 1 (ed. Holl, III, 117, lines 23–24) and Hegemonius, *Acta Archelai*, XVI, 10 (ed. Beeson, p. 27, lines 16–19).

85 Tr. Schaeder, *Studien*, pp. 346–47.

86 Tr. Henning, *NGG* 1933, pp. 214–24.

87 *SBA* 1932, pp. 200–01, Andreas and Henning.

88 Flügel, *Mani*, p. 91.

and rectitude and snatch it away from the demons. These divinities send Jesus, who is here the transcendent Jesus of Manichaeism, Jesus-the-Radiant, Yišoʻ Zīvā, the individual redeemer, distinguished from the cosmic redeemer, the Third Envoy. In S 9 it is the redeemer Ōhrmizd, the First Man, with whom Jesus sometimes merges, for both are the son of God to whom the *Acta Archelai*[89] impute the redemption of Adam. The redeemer descends to earth in human form, punishes the two Creator-Archons, Passion and Lust, and approaches Adam. We read in Theodor bar Khouni:

> The luminous Jesus approached the unknowing Adam; he awakened him from the sleep of death, in order to free him from many spirits. And as a righteous man who finds another possessed of a terrible demon and soothes him by his art—so was it with Adam when that friend found him immersed in deep sleep, awakened him, shook him till he stirred, drove the seducing demon from him, and took the mighty Archoness prisoner. Then Adam examined himself and knew who he was. He [Jesus] showed him the Fathers on high and his own self [Syr.: *napšeh,* i.e. Adam's soul],[90] cast down before the teeth of the panthers and the teeth of the elephants, devoured by the devourers, consumed by the consumers, eaten by the dogs, mixed and chained in everything that is, captive in the stench of darkness. . . . He raised him up and caused him to eat of the tree of life. Then Adam cried and wept: he raised his voice terribly like a roaring lion, tore his hair, beat [his breast] and spake: "Woe, woe to the maker of my body, the chainer of my soul, and to the rebels who have reduced me to servitude!"

According to S 9:

> Then Ōhrmizd the Lord [the First Man] took pity on the souls, and in human form he descended to the earth. He blasted the wicked Āz; he made manifest and clearly showed [him] everything that was and will be. Quickly he revealed [to him] that Ōhrmizd the Lord had not created this carnal body and that he had not chained the soul. Gifted with insight, the happy man's soul was resurrected. It believed the wisdom of Ōhrmizd the good Lord. Like a valiant hero

---

89 VIII, 4 (ed. Beeson, p. 12, lines 21–26) and Epiphanius, 66, 26, 4–5 (ed. Holl, III, 59, lines 2–8).

90 See Polotsky, *Abriss,* col. 258, lines 57–63.

it received all the commands, injunctions, and seals of blessing. It cast off the body of death and was redeemed forever and was raised up to paradise, to the realm of the blessed.

These few passages suffice to show the significance of this narrative and its parallelism with the story of the First Man's redemption. S 9 expressly states that "the good soul, from which Āz formed luminous elements of Ōhrmizd's [the First Man's] armor." The Adam and which it chained within his body, consists of the five same theme recurs constantly: the element which must be saved is consubstantial with God: Adam's redeemer redeems himself, and there is no more striking version of the myth of the redeemed redeemer than that in which the redeemer is designated as the First Man himself. Whether as the First Man or as Jesus, the redeemer is here an incarnation of the Noũs. In other accounts, Jesus is called "the God of the Noũs," and Alexander of Lycopolis calls him simply the Noũs.[91] This redemption is always a redemption of the soul by insight; insight awakens the soul—i.e., awakens the soul to itself and to universal knowledge. The symbols are highly impressive: Adam has sunk into the death-sleep of the body, which signifies contamination and captivity; he has become an instrument of the unconscious and has forgotten his divine origin. He is physically and mentally weak, blind, and deaf. The redeemer reveals him to himself ("Then Adam inquired into himself and recognized who he was"). With his consciousness, his eyes open. Elsewhere it is expressly stated that as soon as he had eaten of the fruits of the tree of life and of evil he could see. This tree is also the tree of knowledge, which the *Acta Archelai* equate with Jesus in paradise, which is the world.[92] Adam is now enabled to recognize the mixture of his suffering soul, diffused through all matter, and the diabolical origin of his body, which he curses as he curses his

---

91 Cf. M 473 I R 4–6, quoted by Andreas and Henning, *SBA* 1932, p. 197, n. 2, and Alexander, ed. Brinkmann, p. 7, lines 14–46. On Jesus as Noũs, Xradê-šahr, or Xradêšahryazd see Baur, *Religionssystem*, pp. 209ff.; Waldschmidt and Lentz, *ABA* 1926, pp. 21–22, 39–40, 43, and 72; Schaeder, *Studien*, pp. 283–86 and "Urform," p. 112; Schmidt and Polotsky, *SBA* 1933, pp. 68–69.

92 XI, 1 (ed. Beeson, p. 18, lines 12–19) and Epiphanius, 66, 29, 1 (ed. Holl, III, 66, lines 8–10, with his note). Agapius in Photius, *Bibliotheca*, Cod. CLXXIX (Migne, *PG*, CIII, 521). On the opening of Adam's eyes, *Kephalaion* 1 (ed. Polotsky, p. 15, lines 12–13).

creator—and which the Manichaeans, as we see from *Homily* I,[93] likewise learned to curse—and finally he recognizes the fundamental duality of his situation. This revelation of self-consciousness is accompanied by a revelation of cosmic knowledge: The redeemer, the Νοῦς, gives the soul gnosis, the perfect knowledge encompassed in the revelation of Adam's origin and destination and applying to all things past and future, or, as the *Fihrist* says, "paradise and the gods, hell and the devil, earth and heaven, the sun and the moon."[94] The practical consequence of this cosmological and soteriological wisdom, this science of good and evil, is the renunciation of the flesh and, specifically, to cite the *Fihrist* once again, the injunction never again to touch Eve, the terrible embodiment of the sin of sexuality and the principle of procreation, which prolong suffering and evil. Finally, Adam's redemption, in principle an awakening and in essence an insight, is a rebirth—it is called "resurrection" in S 9—i.e., in its perfect form an ascent to the realm of light, a restoration of the luminous substance to its original home. At the beginning of human history the myth of Adam's redemption, a repetition of the First Man's redemption, is—like the redemption of the First Man at the beginning of the world—a pledge of redemption to future mankind and the most typical example we could wish of what the Manichaeans meant by redemption.

The development of the myth, the history of the cosmos and of man, are nothing other than the progressive fulfillment of redemption. The myth is based on the interaction of a twofold power present in the universe: an active δύναμις—creating, protecting, revealing—and a δύναμις παθητική—passive and suffering—which is the soul in the world and hence also the world soul.[95] This ingredient, which is consubstantial with God and present in all bodies, but which is imprisoned particularly in herbs and in seeds, in the trunks and fruits of trees, and smothered in flesh, this "Living Soul" is often, in a magnificent symbol, equated with the person of Jesus Patibilis. It is the "pathetic aspect" of the transcendent

93 Ed. Polotsky, p. 6, lines 1–9.
94 Flügel, *Mani*, p. 91.
95 Cf. Alexander, ed. Brinkmann, p. 27, lines 7–9, and Baur, pp. 71–77; Schaeder, "Urform," pp. 151–55.

Jesus, the suffering and salvation-hungry part of Jesus Zīvā, who, in so far as he is Pure Light, represents the redeemer.[96] This cosmic and timeless Jesus is crucified on the matter with which his luminous soul is mixed. The whole world is the "Cross of Light."[97] Especially the trees, in which a large part of the divine substance is concentrated, must stand in judgment over Christ. As the Manichaean Faustus says in St. Augustine, "Jesus, life and salvation of men, is crucified on all wood" (*Patibilis Jesus, qui est vita et salus hominis, omni suspensus ex ligno*).[98] The suffering and crucifixion of the historical Jesus assume the dimensions of the universal and eternal; they become doctrine and prototype. "We see everywhere," says Faustus, "the mystical nailing of Christ to his cross (*crucis eius mystica fixio*). Through it are made manifest the wounds of the passion which our soul suffers."[99] The history of the world becomes the history of a god who is his own redeemer, and the history of mankind is the drama of our passion and our redemption, which are an essential part of this mythical process. It is this interrelation which gives the world aim and meaning. To cite the Chavannes-Pelliot Treatise,[100] it is the "prison," where dark demons throw the light into chains, but it is also a prison for the powers of darkness, who are thus held in check and, as it were, defeated from the start. In another, essential aspect, "the cosmos is a pharmacy where luminous bodies radiate cure," a place of redemption, where poison and medicine lie side by side, where wounds can open and close—a hospital, if you will, with its affliction but also its promise of health and joy. The vast cosmic machine revolves, and unremittingly the gigantic wheel with its twelve buckets, built by Jesus for the redemption of souls, draws forth the luminous souls of the dead and forms them into a pillar of light, whose mystical cargo is

96 On Jesus Patibilis—aside from the reference above—see Waldschmidt and Lentz, *ABA* 1926, pp. 26–27, 74, with which we can perhaps associate M 42, *SBA* 1934, p. 881. On Jesus Zīvā or Φέγγος see Waldschmidt and Lentz, *ABA* 1926, p. 36, and Schmidt and Polotsky, *SBA* 1933, pp. 67–68.

97 Augustine, *Enarratio in Psalm. CXL*, 12 (Migne, *PL*, XXXVII, 1823). The Cross of Light is found also in *Acta Johannis* 98 and in *Acta Philippi* 138 and 140 (ed. M. R. James, *Apocryphal New Testament*, pp. 254, 450).

98 *Contra Faustum*, XX, 2 (ed. Zycha, p. 536, lines 20–21).

99 Ibid., XXXII, 7 (ed. Zycha, p. 766, lines 20–22).

100 *JA* 1911, p. 515.

borne on the ships of the sun and moon to the glittering paradise of its origin.[101] In the course of the months, years, and centuries, the devoured divine substance is liberated, and gradually life and matter are exhausted. This slow physical process of liberation is accompanied and facilitated by a progressive revelation which runs parallel to the history of mankind. The human race has propagated itself and will continue to do so until men adopt the sexual abstinence that signifies the ultimate liberation and end of the cosmos. But the First Man has received the revelation of a perfect wisdom; its guardians are a line of perfect men: Seth, Noah, Abraham, Shem, Enosh, Nikotheos, Enoch—and after them the envoys of the light, the founders of the true religions, Buddha, Zoroaster, Jesus, and Mani, who in his supreme and perfect revelation unites all preceding revelations and makes them into a universal and ultimate religion.[102] Man can redeem himself by accepting the gospel of truth, or he can remain in damnation and mixture by rejecting it. Gnosis opens to his insight the two roads of good and evil, of truth and error, of light and darkness.

This rhythmic progress of redemption by the rotation of the cosmic machine and the advance of revelation in the course of human history is accelerated and concluded by the coming of Mani. Mani, "the seal of the prophets,"[103] is the herald of the whole, immediate truth; his revelation is followed by the end of the world. This is the "Great War," consisting of a number of events, the details of which are now known to us through *Homily* II, recently found in the Fayum:[104] persecutions crowned by the triumph of Manichaeism; a judgment held by Christ; a conflagration lasting 1468 years; the fall of matter into a great pit hollowed

101 Cf. F. Cumont, "La roue à puiser les âmes du manichéisme," *Revue de l'Histoire des Religions* (Paris), LXXII (1915), 384–88, and Polotsky, *Abriss*, col. 255, lines 27–67.

102 See W. Henning, *SBA* 1934, pp. 27–29. I shall come back to this point in part 3 of this paper.

103 Bīrūnī (Albērūnī), *The Chronology of Ancient Nations* (Athār-al-Bākiya), tr. C. Edward Sachau (London, 1879), p. 190, line 10; al-Murtaḍā in Kessler, *Mani*, I, 355; cf. Shahrastāni, tr. Haarbrücker, I, 290.

104 *Homily* II (ed. Polotsky, pp. 7–42); cf. also the fragments of the *Shâbuhragân*, published by F. W. K. Müller, *ABA* 1904, pp. 11–25, and revised by A. V. W. Jackson, "A Sketch of the Manichaean Doctrine concerning the Future Life," *JAOS*, L (1930), 181–98.

out of the new aeon. We shall pass quickly over these matters and reserve for the third part of this paper a treatment of the points relating to the redemption of the human souls. Here it suffices to state that this eschatological act, which concludes the cosmological drama, this "third epoch" of the myth, consists in the return of the two substances to their original division (ἀποκατάστασις τῶν δύο φύσεων),[105] in the restoration of the radical duality of the "First Epoch." But the situation is no longer the same: the experience of mixture and its ultimate defeat have made evil unable to repeat its incursion ever again. Dualism, the victory of the good, the security and peace of light endure forever.

This prospect of the end proves, theoretically at least, that the cosmos is destined to be redeemed and that within the cosmos man —man in particular—should be mindful of redemption. Everything that the myth discloses concerning the origins, the development, and the destination of the world, its account of the creation of the human race—all this provides men with examples, elements, and, if not with certainty, at least with hopes of redemption. But can man be redeemed? What in his development provides support for his will to redemption, what theoretical foundation is there for the practical rules of conduct which are to bring about redemption? As an answer, let us develop the consequences following from the anthropological myth.

Man is indeed a mixture and by right a duality; he is at present an amalgam of temporally and spatially delimited lightness and darkness. The proportions of this mixture, which the sexual act and the sequence of the generations transfer and perpetuate, vary with the individual: the bond holding the two antithetical substances together is sometimes firm and sometimes loose; the mixture is sometimes complete, sometimes imperfect. From this it follows that the soul varies in mixture and composition, and the intellective faculty varies with it; where the darkness has the firmest hold upon the light, the consequence is almost absolute unconsciousness and ignorance.[106] The natural duality of the two substances does

---

105 Epiphanius, 66, 31, 7 (ed. Holl, III, 72, line 1).
106 Alexander, ed. Brinkmann, p. 6, lines 16–18, and M 9, *SBA* 1933, pp. 297–300, Andreas and Henning.

not imply—as a great number of critics have maintained since St. Augustine[107]—that two souls exist within man, the one good and rational, the other evil and irrational: the soul as such is always good and rational. An evil soul would be just as much of a contradiction as a dark light. There is only one soul, which finds itself in a bad situation; the contradiction is not between two souls, but between two entities: the soul descended from God and light, and the body, an abortion descended from the devil and from darkness. Or, expressed more concretely, the duality of man is that of his ego, pure in origin and substance, and of its present condition, in which the body, alive by virtue of its mixture with the soul, is possessed by evil impulses, which conceal or threaten the true ego. The battle is fought between an I and a Self, or—to invoke a Manichaean theory going back to St. Paul—the battle within us is waged between a "New Man" and an "Old Man," the one inward, celestial, of lofty, hallowing, purely spiritual origin, the other outward, earthly, of the tainted origin common to man and beast.[108] Here we again encounter—side by side with the trichotomy which the Gnostics introduce into the study of man (body, soul, spirit) — the eternal pair which lies at the base of the entire Manichaean myth of redemption: the Νοῦς, the redeeming element, and the psyche, the element which must be redeemed. Actually the "Old Man"—which the *Khuastuanift* calls the "Old I"[109]—is primarily the body (σῶμα) or the flesh (σάρξ), whence we have the outward form of demons, which—in the common terminology—is prison, forgetfulness, drunkenness, unconsciousness, death. But it is the body endowed with all the natural impulses of matter and animated through its association with the soul, hence what the Manichaeans sometimes call "Demonic I," "dull consciousness," "dark insight."[110]

---

107 Texts and discussion in Baur, pp. 162ff.; Prosper Alfaric, *L'Évolution intellectuelle de Saint Augustin* (Paris, 1918), p. 117 and n. 5; W. Bang, "Manichäische Hymnen," *Le Muséon*, XXXVIII (1925), 54–55; Waldschmidt and Lentz, *ABA* 1926, pp. 75ff.

108 See Augustine, *Contra Faustum*, XXIV, 1 (ed. Zycha, pp. 717, line 12–718, line 12).

109 VI B, tr. von Le Coq, p. 288. W. Bang finds fault with this translation in *Le Muséon*, XXXVI (1923), 198–201. On the theory of the "Old Man" and the "New Man" in Manichaeism, see Waldschmidt and Lentz, *ABA* 1926, pp. 31ff., 52ff.

110 Cf. *ABA* 1926, pp. 18–19 and pp. 74ff., and *SBA* 1933, p. 566, n. 2, Waldschmidt and Lentz.

The Old Man represents, then, the soul in its damned and suffering situation. The New Man, on the other hand—which the *Khuastuanift* calls "the I here"—is the soul, considered as active and redeemed, having renewed and regained its original purity, man's true I, to which the Turfan texts give such an abundance of epithets: "Good Soul," "Pure I," "Pristine I," "Subtle I," "Transcendent I," "Luminous I," "Joyous I," "Divine I," "Living I" (*grīv žīvandaγ*, corresponding to St. Augustine's *anima viva*).[111] The New Man is the soul to which has been restored the consciousness that awakens it and releases it from mixture, and, since this consciousness comes from the Noῦs, it is now a soul united with the Noῦs and adorned with spiritual graces. According to the later scholastics,[112] this New Man consists of five substances (the five luminous elements of the First Man); of five members, which are the intellectual faculties; of five gifts, which are the cardinal virtues; of three luminous powers (light, health, radiant body); of twelve dominions; and of four virtues, corresponding to those of the supreme God (paternity, force, light, wisdom). Elsewhere, the gift bestowed on the soul consists in the five members of the Noῦs (νοῦς, ἔννοια, φρόνησις, ἐνθύμησις, λογισμός), from which arise the five virtues (love, law, perfection, patience, wisdom), and the principal element is here the first of the five members, the νοῦς, which is consciousness. The sum of these gifts and virtues with which the Noῦs arms and adorns the psyche, is juxtaposed to the "Sinful Body" or Old Man, as is the luminous I to the dark I. It corresponds also to the Great Idea, which, as we have seen, sometimes intervenes to save the First Man, which is at once a call from deep distress and the active will to redemption, or the pair Call and Answer. It is the ἐνθύμησις of the soul's life, counterpart and antithesis to the ἐνθύμησις of the carnal body's death.[113] This theoretical structure of his nature would in itself enable man to be redeemed, but the myth of his origin, closely connected with the cosmological, or we might say theogonic myth, has much more

---

111 On all these terms, Waldschmidt and Lentz, *ABA* 1926, pp. 13, 18, 25, 29, 31, 33, 35, 63, 77, 100, 102, 104–07, 110, 120, 125. On the "Living I," Schmidt and Polotsky, *SBA* 1933, pp. 71–72.

112 E.g., M 14, *SBA* 1933, pp. 547–48 and the commentary of Waldschmidt and Lentz, pp. 570ff.

113 See Polotsky, *Abriss*, col. 254, lines 1–18.

to contribute. First of all, the creation of Adam has made man into the principal object of the process of redemption; in him the greater part of the fallen light is gathered. Hence cosmic history is concentrated in him, and toward him the redeeming will of the Father of Greatness is directed. Moreover, the devoured light can be liberated only through him and with his help; since he feeds on the divine substance that is dispersed among the plants, it becomes a part of him and can be redeemed. And so man becomes an essential wheel in the machine of redemption. Second and most important, the myth assures man of a twofold consubstantiality: by his origin he is one substance with the cosmos; by his structure he is a microcosm, counterpart of the macrocosm, whose mixture and ingredients are recapitulated in him, whose historical epochs he reflects.[114] Thus he participates supremely and fully in the purpose, organization, and destiny which determine the future of the cosmos and which all serve but one aim, the liberation of the light. Furthermore, in the world and in transcendence, man is one substance with the godhead. The soul of Adam, transmitted to his descendants and dispersed through their bodies, is, as we have seen, the soul of the First Man, which in turn is identical with the soul of the Father of Greatness. Thus our soul is a member, a substantial part of God, or, more precisely: the soul of man, in so far as it suffers and is mixed with darkness, is a fragment of the δύναμις παθητική of the Redeemer, of Jesus Patibilis, whose cosmic crucifixion is repeated, or rather perpetuated. His suffering and his wounds are ours, or rather our suffering and our wounds are incorporated in him, are his. Moreover, Jesus, in so far as he is the Luminous One, Jesus Zīvā, unites within himself all active, free souls. As we see from the Turfan texts,[115] he is also the "Living I," the "Luminous I," the "radiant" and "transcendent I" of men, these "supreme I's" which to quote M 36 V 7 are "the sons of Jesus the Friend."[116] It is the Νοῦς, whence all intellects are descended, to which they

---

114 Cf. *Acta Archelai*, IX, 4 (ed. Beeson, p. 14, lines 26–28) and Epiphanius, 66, 27, 4 (ed. Holl, III, 62, lines 7–9) ; *Epistola Fundamenti* in Augustine, *De natura boni*, 46 (ed. Zycha, p. 886, lines 14–17) ; Chavannes and Pelliot, "Traité," p. 526; *škand gumānīγ Vičār*, XVI, 24 (tr. Jackson, *Researches*, p. 178).

115 *ABA* 1926, pp. 65, 70–77, Waldschmidt and Lentz.

116 *SBA* 1933, p. 325 and n. 5, Andreas and Henning.

return, and by which they are led back and restored to the divine intellect. In the fine phrase of the concluding hymn of the Cha-vannes-Pelliot Treatise, Jesus is "the I in the luminous I of all that lives."[117] By virtue of this consubstantiality, and because he is Living Soul, man is not only—in the Gnostic term revived by M 10[118] —"the first son of the King," i.e. like Jesus and the First Man son and member of God, king of paradise; he is also like God in His manifestations as redeemer; his destiny is linked with the painful and glorious adventures of the redeemer whose soul must be re-deemed and who redeems himself. If his Passion has a divine mean-ing, it is because all his hopes of redemption derive from his par-ticipation in a luminous substance which is God and which God— He cannot do otherwise—must seek to liberate and reunite with himself.

Here we have an explanation of man's paradoxical situation in time: *de facto* tainted but intrinsically pure, a prey to demons and a glittering, invaluable treasure. Let us listen, in Hymn M 95 R, to the "Words of the Living I" which symmetrically expose the contradictions in its situation and in the treatment it receives at the hands of men.

> You buy me from thieves like slaves
> And you fear me and entreat me like lords.
>
> You choose me as pupils from the world [?]
> And you venerate me like masters.
>
> You beat and torment me like enemies
> And you redeem and revive me like friends.
>
> But my fathers are mighty and powerful [enough]
> To requite you many times over.
>
> And as reward for a fast day
> To give you eternal joy.

---

117 *JA* 1911, p. 586.

118 *NGG* 1933, p. 313 (Henning) and M 33, *SBA* 1934, p. 877 (Andreas and Henning), where the term refers to the First Man. The Gnostics called themselves "children of the king" (Clement of Alexandria, *Stromateis*, III, 4, 30, 1; ed. O. Stählin, *GCS*, II, 209, lines 34–210) and "sons of the First God" (ibid., II, 209, line 31).

And to send you the part that [is] yours through me,
They will send the gods before you.

And [they will send you] the part of cares and hardships [?]
That you suffer on my account.[119]

It is this two-faced soul, slave and king, pupil and master, mistreated by men and exalted by them to the heavens, loved and punished by the gods, this greatness and disgrace which must be redeemed, or rather which must redeem itself. This sleeper must awaken, this crucified creature must release itself from the cross in order to return to the light.

3. The Realization and Practical Instruments of Redemption

In this section we shall examine the practical side of the Manichaean problem of redemption—i.e., from the theoretical statements offered by the cosmological and anthropological myths we shall draw their practical consequences for man's actions and determine the moral and religious conduct they impose on the creature striving for redemption.

The theoretical solution to the problem is very simple: the experience of evil, which the myth intensifies and explains, proves that man in his present state is not a duality but that he was so originally and should above all strive to regain his original duality. Redemption is essentially a recovery of self-knowledge, a regathering of the luminous substance, a restoration of the original duality; this process takes place in time but transcends time. The two substances must be restored to their integral state and original separation; man must undertake in himself this ἀποκατάστασις, which the cosmos and the whole of redeemed mankind will achieve at the end of time. This transformation, which is a kind of inner and personal eschatology, must consist in the recovery of a pure substance, which is always present in mixture and which is our essence, our true I. The act of cognition which makes this possible is at once a re-cognition and a rebirth. Its consequence is, first, an absolute purity, free from any taint of matter; second, total restoration of the original situation: that which is God's own is returned

119 *SBA* 1933, pp. 318–19, Andreas and Henning.

to God, as Titus of Bostra[120] says (τὸ ἀποδοθῆναι γε τῷ θεῷ τὸ οἰκεῖον αὐτῷ), i.e. it becomes again part of his own substance; the soul, as one of the Turfan hymns puts it, returns "to the earth where it was at the beginning."[121] Or, to cite Augustinian texts,[122] it returns to its homeland, its original kingdom (sua patria, propria regna, propriae sedes). Peace and rest will follow suffering and conflict, or—for these, too, are Manichaean terms—nirvāṇa will follow saṃsāra. Thus we begin to see that the practice as well as the dogma of redemption revolves around the Noῦς, the Manuhmeš of the Iranian texts, the luminous intelligence, which is consciousness and knowledge, the instrument of awakening, of recollection, of revelation, of judgment and hence of will. The Noῦς is inevitably the principal element in the process of redemption; it is incarnated in the redeemers of mankind; it is the foundation of the Manichaean Church, which is essentially conceived as an organization of redemption; and finally, the soul finds its radiant image in the resurrection which is man's ultimate liberation from death.

And now let us inquire as to how the theoretical solution is transformed into acts.

First we shall examine the practical course of redemption—what the Manichaeans call the "road of redemption."[123] We shall concentrate on three points: the theory of temptation and sin, Manichaean ethics, and the process of rebirth.

Concerning the first point we are fully informed, thanks to Kephalaion 138, discovered in the Fayum, and bearing the title, "Who is it who sins but then repents?" The text answers:

> He who sins is none other than the living soul which [dwells] in the body of sin, since it finds itself in a state of mixture. Another [i.e., another reason for sin] is that the Old Man dwells with it in [. . .]: he causes it to stumble [. . . by not . . .]. But no sooner does he cause it to

---

120 I, 37 (ed. de Lagarde, p. 23, lines 28–30).
121 M 4, ABA 1904, p. 53, line 6, Müller.
122 E.g., De natura boni, 44 (ed. Zycha, p. 883, line 6); De moribus manichaeo-rum, II, 15, 36 (Migne, PL, XXXII, 1361); De haeresibus, 46 (Migne, PL, XLII, 35). Chavannes and Pelliot, "Traité," p. 533, call it "monde" or "domaine primitif."
123 See Bang, "Manichäische Hymnen," Le Muséon, XXXVIII (1925), 41–42.

sin than the Νοῦς reminds it of the sin it has committed.
Thus reminded by the Νοῦς, it turns away from sin, it asks
the luminous Νοῦς for forgiveness and its sins are forgiven.
—Likewise, he who is instructed and [then] forgets, he is
the soul which is instructed by the luminous Νοῦς, who instructs it: he reminds it of its original state [lit., first οὐσία],
and it forgets his teaching, since the Old Man dwells with
it and torments it. Therefore it forgets and goes astray because of its distress. Its master, however, who instructs it
and instills repentance in its [heart] is the luminous Νοῦς,
which comes from above, which is the light of the pure
[sacred] φωστήρ, he comes **and shines before** the soul and
purifies it and illumines it and [leads] it to the land of
light, from which it issued at the beginning of things: and
it will return and [rise] up to its original form of existence.[124]

This text makes it clear that sin originates in the soul's immersion in mixture: existence itself is sin. The soul is not intrinsically sinful, and fundamentally it is not responsible for sin:
it does not succumb to sin from its own impulsion but through its
mixture with the flesh. *"Carnis enim commixtione ducitur, non
propria voluntate,"* says the Manichaean Secundinus.[125] The sole
cause of sin is matter, whose essence and spontaneous function is
evil, or desire, which is not an occasional, but an eternal, vice.
(*"Manichaei,"* says St. Augustine, *"carnis concupiscentiam non
tamquam accidens vitium, sed tamquam naturam ab aeternitate
malam vituperant."*[126]) This evil, which lies in the nature of matter,
has always existed and always will exist: time can only increase and
propagate it but cannot extinguish it. The sin of the soul, however,
has no reality in itself, or at most has an ephemeral reality: it
arises from a momentary and unwilled attraction of the soul by
matter and leaves no trace except in the memory. *"Omne enim
peccatum,"* writes Mani in his letter to Menoch, preserved by
St. Augustine, *"antequam fiat, non est, et post factum memoria sola
ejus operis, non ipsa species manet. Malum autem concupiscentiae,*

---

124 *SBA* 1933, pp. 70–71, Schmidt and Polotsky. Cf. Chavannes and Pelliot,
"Traité," p. 547.
125 *Epistula ad Augustinum* (ed. Zycha, *CSEL* 25, p. 894, lines 17–18) and cf.
Augustine, *Contra Secundinum*, 9 (ibid., p. 917, lines 27–28).
126 *Contra duas epistulas Pelagianorum*, II, 2, 2 (ed. C. F. Urba and J. Zycha,
CSEL 60, p. 461, lines 16–28).

quia naturale, est antequam fiat, est, quum fit, augetur, post factum, et videtur et permanet.[127] For the soul, sin is essentially temptation which can only originate in the body; against this temptation the soul left to its own resources is defenseless because of its mixed state. Only the Noῦs, with the spiritual gifts it confers and the ἐνθύμησις of life, which it opposes to the ἐνθύμησις of death, can enable the soul to resist this hostile penetration which is a repetition of the assault of darkness upon light at the beginning of time. Only the New Man, constituted by the presence of the Noῦs in the soul, can oppose and defeat the unremitting assault of the Old Man. This he does by awakening the soul's memory of its divine essence, which it has temporarily forgotten, and sustaining its consciousness of its true being. He can extinguish sin as soon as the soul has committed it: by causing it to recognize sin as such (in this connection it is characteristic that the Manichaean book of confession, which has been preserved in Uigur, is called *Khuastuanift,* or insight) he induces repentance (μετάνοια); the transgression is effaced by the recollection of the essential purity of the I, so that the sin, as we have seen, survives only in the memory. We do not will sin and we cannot combat it; it arises solely from the forgetfulness in which the body, the Old Man, strives to cloak the soul: temptation is the menace of consciousness, transgression is unconsciousness itself. Thus sin is either made impossible through enduring illumination by the Noῦs, or it thrives through the soul's impenitence, i.e. stubbornness, which makes it persevere in mixture and reject the instruction of the Noῦs. "The soul is not punished," writes Secundinus, "because it has sinned, but because it has not repented of its sin."[128] This means that though the right to redemption is only temporarily suspended in consequence of any particular transgression, it is irrevocably lost through obdurate rejection of the teachings of the Noῦs. Since the knowledge it confers is everything, to thrust it aside or disobey it is tantamount to damnation. In the last analysis, the soul can commit but one sin, but that sin is immeasurable and irreparable: an intellectual sin, which, as the Greek texts put it, consists in failure to recognize the truth (μὴ γνῶναι τὴν ἀλήθειαν) and in denying the universal duality (μὴ λέγειν

127 *Opus imperfectum contra Julianum,* III, 187 (Migne, *PL,* XLV, 1326).
128 *Epist. ad August.,* ed. Zycha, p. 894, lines 21–22.

δύο ἀρχὰς εἶναι τῶν πάντων) —in short, in denying itself to the Νοῦς.[129] Evil is ἀγνωσία, redemption is gnosis.[130]

This gnosis, which is above all the knowledge of the duality in mixture, and this sin, which is the mixture itself, i.e. a taint, imply a definite moral attitude toward evil, and the Manichaean ethic merely develops and codifies this attitude. The entire practice of morality can have no other purpose than to make man an instrument for the liberation of light. Like the macrocosm, the microcosm must sunder the mixture and release the living soul, must restore the original duality. Accordingly, the entire ethic consists in a single commandment: abstain, in order to acquire and preserve purity, a largely negative commandment. It implies a rejection, almost a negation, of this world which oppresses us, of the evil beings which dominate it and our present situation, and might well imply the fundamental attitude of revolt and nihilism that lies in all Gnostic thinking. But here the negation does not, as in Gnosticism, lead to a theoretically and practically unlimited freedom, to license toward both the outside world and the body, with which the "pneumatic man" can deal as he pleases. On the contrary, the break with matter is here renunciation, withdrawal, removal: here it implies only abstinence and continence, not domination and enjoyment. The complete Manichaean forgoes desire and renounces the world. He is detached from the flesh and the world, to which, since he possesses nothing, nothing attaches him. As we can see from the *Khuastuanift* and other records, the purchase or possession of a house, a vineyard, a slave, constitutes an act of violence and a sin.[131] Wealth, even property, are forbidden. The saint is at most entitled to a meal each day and a garment each year.[132] The Elect is not attached to the earth, he is above all a wanderer, and this accords with the Manichaean ideal of mission and struggle. In the Chavannes-Pelliot Treatise we read:

---

129 See on this whole question and for the references Polotsky, *Abriss*, col. 260, lines 5–20.

130 Cf. Epiphanius, 66, 9, 9 (ed. Holl, III, 30, lines 25–26) ; 29, 3 (III, 66, lines 14–15) ; 55, 9–10 (III, 92, lines 4–7).

131 *Khuastuanift*, IX B and XII B, *ABA* 1910, pp. 20, 27 (von Le Coq) ; cf. Bang, *Le Muséon*, XXXVI (1923), 159, 163. On the condemnation of wealth, see Epiphanius, 66, 28, 4 (ed. Holl, III, 64, line 6) and Augustine, *Contra Faustum*, X, 1 (ed. Zycha, p. 310, lines 7–23).

132 References in Chavannes and Pelliot, "Traité," p. 576 and n. 2.

> [The Elect] take no pleasure in remaining always in the same place; like a king who, depending on no one, does not always remain in his residence but sometimes goes forth, taking with him the throng of his soldiers who bear their weapons attentively and are completely armed, like him the Elect can make all wild beasts and hate-filled enemies vanish into their hiding places.[133]

And, a little further on: "[The Elect] do not avoid the crowd and remain alone in a chamber; there are people who act thus, they are called sick men." Bīrūnī informs us that Mani commanded his supporters "continually to wander about in the world, preaching his doctrines and guiding people into the right path."[134] Thus the perfect Manichaean is a monk or priest who goes about begging. This ideal of total detachment includes of course the rejection and condemnation of war, hunting, commerce, agriculture—in short, of all profane activity. These prohibitions are based not only on the fact that these occupations create a contact with matter and hence carry a taint, but also on the mythical conception that they constitute so many assaults upon life, upon the luminous substance that is mixed with all matter: since the entire outside world is more or less animated, the fruit moans when it is plucked, the earth suffers when the plough tears it open, the air cries out when it is cleft, the water is sullied by the bath that is taken in it.[135] Similarly it is a crime to kill an animal or, it goes without saying, a man. But it is not merely his acts but his every movement that may prove a sin. Since the essence and most dangerous expression of matter is concupiscence, we must above all guard ourselves against the temptations of desire. Intrinsically and because of its consequences, the sexual act sullies most of all. As the *Acta Archelai*[136] explain, desire *(incitatio concupiscentiae)* arises spontaneously out of the body, or more specifically, out of the body that is glutted with meat: in the soul that it penetrates, desire destroys all consciousness and all wisdom *(non ex virtute aliqua, non ex philosophia, nec ex alio ullo intellectu, sed ex sola ciborum satie-*

---

133 Ibid., pp. 572–73.
134 *Chronology*, tr. Sachau, p. 190, lines 23–25.
135 On all these points, exposition and references in Alfaric, *Évolution*, pp. 144–59 and notes.
136 XVI (ed. Beeson, p. 27, lines 1–6).

tate et libidine et fornicatione). The fornication which follows is bestial, an imitation of demonic fornication, and, worst of all, it results in the propagation of the race, the perpetuation of the original evil; through it man makes himself an instrument of matter, whose sole aim is to imprison the particles of light in the body, to retain its dominion over them, by prolonging their captivity from generation to generation. Sexuality delays and obstructs the redemption of mankind. From this it follows that the perfect man should abstain from carnal pleasures, from marriage and procreation. ('Ἀπέχεσθαι γάμων καὶ ἀφροδισίων καὶ τεκνοποιίας, ἵνα μὴ ἐπὶ πλεῖον ἡ δύναμις ἐνοικήσῃ τῇ ὕλῃ κατὰ τὴν τοῦ γένους διαδοχήν, as Alexander of Lycopolis aptly sums up the doctrine.[137])

Thus, on the whole, the Manichaean law, the rules it prescribes and the ordinances (ἐντολαί) which codify the ethics of Mani, consists in prohibitions. The most frequent formulation, the theory of the three seals (*tria signacula*) represents a sum of taboos—the term is not quite exact—or prohibitions applying to the mouth, the hands, the breast (*os, manus, sinus*), i.e. sins of thought, word, action, and the carnal sins.[138] And—in greater detail—though the five regulations for the Elect[139] embody the duty of truth, freedom from sin, religious fervor, purity of the mouth, and pleasure in poverty, the ten commandments for Catechumens[140] prescribe observance of the four or seven prayers, but otherwise consist in prohibitions: of idolatry, mendacity, avarice, murder, magic, of the argumentation that leads to doubt, of sloth and negligence in the execution of good works—a very negative decalogue.

In short, the whole Manichaean ethic is based on a complete renunciation whose purpose is a radical separation of the luminous from the dark substance. More than an ethic, it is indeed a system of asceticism with a metaphysical foundation and aim; this is dra-

---

137 *Contra Manichaeorum opiniones*, ed. Brinkmann, p. 7, lines 21–24.
138 See Baur, *Religionssystem*, pp. 248ff.; Flügel, *Mani*, pp. 289–91; Chavannes and Pelliot, "Traité," p. 574, n. 1; Alfaric, *Évolution*, pp. 126ff.; Waldschmidt and Lentz, *SBA* 1933, pp. 588–90.
139 Cf. M 14 V 20–22, *SBA* 1933, p. 548 and the commentary of Waldschmidt and Lentz, pp. 579–81.
140 En-Nedīm in Flügel, *Mani*, pp. 95–96 and cf. ibid., pp. 291–301; al-Murtadā in Kessler, *Mani*, I, 354; Shahrastānī, tr. Haarbrücker, I, 290. Cf. *Khuastuanift*, VI B (Bang [above, n. 43], pp. 152–55) and XI (ibid., pp. 158–59).

matically shown by *Homily* I—"The Lamentation of Salmaios."[141] Strictly speaking—and this was held up to Mani in the course of his trial[142]—the fulfillment of this ideal would mean only death: destruction of man and the world. Theoretically, the saint is permitted no dealings with an evil but animated world in which temptation and demonic guile lurk everywhere in wait; he must renounce his body to the point of absolute withdrawal in order to maintain himself in a state of redemption. Ultimately such total abstinence must imply immobility and suicide; a gruesome refusal to move, to take nourishment, to live, corresponding to the *endura* which the medieval Cathari imposed on those of their brethren who, thanks to the *consolamentum,* had attained to an immutable perfection. But in reality this ideal theory of redemption permitted of a certain alleviation. First of all, there was a double morality, one for the perfect, another for the imperfect. The Catechumens were permitted to work, to pick fruit, to drink wine—the gall of the Archons —to eat meat, to take wives, and even to beget children[143] (this was in part justified by the Church's need for new members[144]), but through such acts the Catechumens lost all right to redemption, at least in this life. The Elect, on the other hand, were forbidden to consume meat or alcoholic drink (replaced by fruit juice), to perform any acts which might harm the plants or elements, and, above all, to engage in sexual intercourse.[145] In them the ethical ideal would thus have been fully realized, except for the need of nourishment.

Here we must seek a proper understanding of the Manichaean casuistry. This nourishment could only be vegetarian, for the beasts are of more strictly demonic origin than the plants, and the light that is imprisoned in them remains in them forever. The myth states that the greater part of the luminous substance susceptible of being saved is distributed among the human bodies and the plants, which, having grown from the seed of the Archons,

141 Ed. Polotsky, esp. pp. 2–4.
142 See the utterances imputed to King Bahram I by Bīrūnī (*Chronology,* tr. Sachau, p. 191, lines 12–13).
143 See Alfaric, *Évolution,* pp. 149–54.
144 Cf. *Homily* II, ed. Polotsky, p. 24, lines 15–16 and p. 31, lines 10–16.
145 Alfaric, *Évolution,* pp. 144–49.

contain it in greater or lesser degree. This leads to a hierarchy of fruits and edible plants according to the quantity of light which they contain—the cucumber and melon were believed to contain the most. It also implies the injunction to eat them raw in order to avoid squandering the light by cooking.[146] But the enjoyment of fruit remained, nevertheless, a danger and a crime: a danger because (according to T II D 173 d verso[147]) sin enters the body with foodstuffs, and, as we have seen in the case of meat—taints the soul and leads to the sexual act; a crime because to pluck a fruit or harvest a vegetable is an attack on life, and to eat them amounts to imprisoning their light in our body in the manner of the demonic abortions or animals. The Manichaeans evaded this difficulty in the following way: on the one hand, they assumed that the digestion of the Elect has the faculty of separating and liberating the light particles contained in the plants,[148] or that these particles, which are combined with the luminous substance of the Elect, are released along with it at his death. Thus the Elect is eminently a machine for purifying and releasing the light devoured in the world. Indeed, he is the one and irreplaceable instrument of liberation in the entire living universe. On the other hand, the Elect did not pluck fruit or harvest vegetables himself: the Catechumens brought them to him and so took on themselves the sin of sowing the seed, of harvesting the grain, of grinding the flour, and of baking the bread. At the moment of accepting his food, the Elect stated explicitly[149] that it was not he who committed this crime and so offended against life, and at the same time he granted the Catechumens forgiveness for a transgression which became an act of piety, since on the one hand it amounted to almsgiving and on the other it led to a liberation of light through the digestion of the Elect.

Thus understood, vegetarianism ceases to be an obstacle to the redemption of the Elect. It represents something less than absolute

146 Ibid., pp. 127–31.
147 *ABA* 1911, pp. 16–17, von Le Coq. Cf. *Acta Archelai,* XVI, 7 (ed. Beeson, p. 27, lines 1–6).
148 Cf. Baur, pp. 283–90 and Chavannes and Pelliot, "Traité," p. 539 and n. 3.
149 *Acta Archelai,* X, 5–7 (ed. Beeson, pp. 16, line 27–17, line 21) and Epiphanius, 66, 28, 7–8 (ed. Holl, III, 65, lines 4–12); Holl quotes the texts of Cyril of Jerusalem and Titus of Bostra in a note.

abstinence, but it is supported by additional prescriptions: the Elect is permitted only one meal a day, and, furthermore, weekly, monthly, and annual fasts are prescribed, one of which, interrupted at sunset, lasts as long as thirty days. The fasts are stricter and more frequent for the Elect than for the Catechumens.[150] Here we find the nature of Manichaean purity reconfirmed in practice. Abstinence, within the limits set by necessity for maintaining life, is the only means to redemption.

We now come to a third question, the form of man's inner redemption. Since the redemption of man has its prototype or projection in the mythical redemption of the First Man and of Adam, the question is easily answered. In principle, redemption consists in an awakening of the living soul, accompanied by an inner illumination; this awakening brings about a state of clear and full consciousness, a recovery of the Noῦs. The New Man revives and replaces the Old Man, or rather the New Man gains dominion after defeating the Old. A second, spiritual birth occurs, a return to an earlier state, a regeneration in the twofold sense of the word. This inner palingenesis corresponds to the transformation which constituted redemption for the Gnostics. To use a term which we find in S 9 and again in Shahrastāni,[151] it is *resurrection*—a purely spiritual resurrection of course, for the body, which is evil, cannot be resurrected. It liberates the soul, reuniting it with the soul substance; the result is a deification, an apotheosis. In a sense, it is a perfect and timeless transformation in time; it in itself is redemption, but though the soul is entitled to this redemption, this redemption by virtue of its luminous nature and the presence of the Noῦs ("*a principio natura sua victoriam dedit animae,*" says Secundinus[152]) can become definite only in death, which the rebirth anticipates. Since the body is unremitting temptation, the Noῦs can indeed be temporarily darkened or, in extreme cases, hopelessly lost. Rebirth does not confer an absolute ἀπάθεια. Even the Elect are obliged to make confession. (A special ritual of this nature has been found in Turfan.[153]) In order to sustain his illumi-

150 See chiefly En-Nedīm in Flügel, *Mani*, pp. 95, 97 and the notes.
151 *NGG* 1932, p. 224, Henning. Cf. Shahrastāni, tr. Haarbrücker, I, 289.
152 *Epist. ad August.*, ed. Zycha, p. 894, line 12.
153 See *SBA* 1935, p. 488, Henning.

nation by the Noῦs or to regain it after a fall, the Elect must live
a life of unremitting vigilance and struggle, from which only death
can redeem him. This brings us to a new problem, discussion of
which will lead to a deeper understanding of the practical Manichaean approach to redemption.

This new problem might be formulated as follows: can man
attain to rebirth by his own efforts? At first glance, it would seem
that—just as in the various episodes of the myth—it is man who
redeems himself: through his Noῦs and his psyche he is both in
one: redeemer and redeemed. The Noῦs contains in itself all possibilities, even to the reality of redemption. Consciousness and the
knowledge it embraces are not merely illuminating, but compelling
as well. In revealing and explaining the duality of light and darkness, consciousness distinguishes good and evil; it is in itself a
choice, for the soul, which by its nature is identical with the good,
can choose only the path of the good, once it has found that path
again. If redemption consists in the release by the intelligence of
the natural inclination and trend of the soul, then man would
seem to have in himself all the means necessary to his redemption.
Since illumination is given by the Noῦs, will and redemption must
follow.

To this, however, two objections can be raised: on the one hand,
there are cases in which the soul *cannot be illuminated* by the Noῦs.
The luminous substance is too profoundly dispersed in mixture,
too much tainted, to regain any consciousness whatsoever. We have
seen that there are varying degrees of admixture with darkness, so
that there is an unalterable, physical, material foundation for the
inequality of human souls with regard to the possibility of redemption. And conversely, to cite M 9: "The degree of the soul's
consciousness is the foundation of the degree of mixture."[154] From
this it follows that at the lower end of the scale of mixtures there
are souls which can never regain consciousness. The Manichaeans
accept the notion that these are damned from the start. But is it
not possible, on the other hand, that the soul which declines illumination by the Noῦs does not wish to be redeemed? Mani would
seem to have envisaged such a situation in a passage of his "Treas-

154 *SBA* 1933, p. 299, Andreas and Henning.

ure of Life" (preserved by St. Augustine). Here he speaks of those *"qui negligentia sua a labe praedictorum spirituum purgari se minime permiserint, mandatisque divinis ex integro parum obtemperaverint, legemque sibi a Deo liberatore datam plenius servare noluerint, neque, ut decebat, sese gubernaverint."*[155] But to interpret the passage in this sense, we should—with St. Augustine and certain critics—have to impute to the Manichaeans a belief in free will and presume that the soul has the faculty of accepting the good revealed by knowledge or of rejecting it. Ferdinand Christian Baur[156] showed the unlikelihood of this interpretation long ago, and we too have seen that it is excluded by the theory of unwilled sin. Indeed, the Manichaeans do not construe freedom as a faculty but as a state, which is given or not—the state of the soul that has been freed from contact with the outside world. And they go much further. For them the soul is not free to choose evil if the Noῦs shows it the good: for such freedom of choice would imply a contradiction within the luminous substance, which being intrinsically good can only incline to the good; and its ultimate consequence would be that God himself can do evil and cause the soul to do evil. But the soul does evil only reluctantly, when it is overpowered by the mixture; given back to its nature, it can only go the way of light. Consequently, the problem of salvation is not a matter of choice and will, but one of weakness or strength: the soul illumined by the Noῦs resists the darkness; without the Noῦs, when its consciousness is darkened or lost, it succumbs to the darkness.

This makes it clear that redemption does not fundamentally depend on man alone, precisely because the will to redemption depends on the presence in the soul of the ἐνθύμησις to life, which is conferred by the Noῦs. Redemption, then, depends entirely on the Noῦs, which is assuredly a part of man, but only of the man who has been illumined by it. This is a question of presence or absence, as it were: redemption is a rightful, natural state, fundamentally a state of grace, a gift of the Living Spirit conferred at the same time as the ἐνθύμησις to life. If redemption is an immediate

---

155 *Contra Felicem*, II, 5 (ed. Zycha, p. 832, lines 22–27).
156 *Das Manichäische Religionssystem*, pp. 184–202 and cf. Polotsky, *Abriss*, col. 257, lines 34–43.

consequence of illumination by the Noῦs, our question can be answered as follows: Man redeems himself through the Noῦs, but the
Noῦs must be continuously awakened and sustained in him. In
other words, since redemption is above all awakening, the practical
problem of redemption raises this question: what means can
awaken the Noῦs in the soul and maintain the soul in a state of
wakefulness?

These means transcend man. They are:

1. For the awakening: revelation and the revealers, who thus
play the role of redeemers.

2. For the maintenance of this state of awakened consciousness:
the Manichaean church, conceived as an organization of redemption.

The myth itself showed the need for the intervention of gods
who are not identical with the being to be redeemed: in the case
of the First Man, they were the Mother of Life, the Living Spirit,
and his sons; in the case of Adam, the Envoy of Joy, the Mother
of Life, the First Man, the Living Spirit, and Jesus. The weakness
and the ignorance of the soul in mixture demand a redeemer. "If
the human soul does not see the benefit," we read in M 9, "which
grows from recognition of eternal and unmingled goodness, it
needs a leader and guide, who will show it the road and the path
leading to redemption from evil and the repose of the soul, that
is, to eternal, unmingled and imperishable goodness."[157]

These guides to redemption are the successive bearers of revelation in the world—enlighteners (φωστῆρες) or apostles (ἀπόστολοι;
Pers.: frēstaγān), the perfect men since Adam: Seth, Abraham,
Shem, Enosh, Nikotheos, Enoch, and particularly the heralds of the
true religion: Buddha, Zoroaster, Jesus, Mani.[158] Each of these revealers—they are all "brothers"[159]—is essentially an incarnation of
the same being. As in the pseudo-Clementinian theory of the "true
prophet," which seems to have been revived here, Adam is the first
of them and Mani the last: he is the *Adam redivivus* who transmits

157 *SBA* 1933, p. 298, Andreas and Henning.
158 References in Henning, *SBA* 1934, pp. 27–29. Also: *Homily* II, ed. Polotsky,
p. 11, lines 20ff.; *Homily* III, ibid., p. 68, lines 17–22 and p. 70, lines 2ff.;
Kephalaia, ed. Polotsky, pp. 7, line 27–8, line 7 and *Kephalaion* 1 (ibid.,
pp. 9–16).
159 See *Homily* II (ed. Polotsky, p. 11, line 9).

the gnosis which Jesus revealed to Adam. At the same time, these envoys constitute human repetitions of the savior in the Manichaean cosmogony. This is the envoy of light, who successively takes the form of the First Man, the Living Spirit, the Third Envoy, Jesus Zīvā and finally of the Noῦs. These envoys of light are, as we see from *Kephalaion* 7,[160] emanations of the Noῦs; they are themselves light and essentially they are its manifestations in the course of time. As "proclaimers of the truth," they embody the cry for redemption personified by the god Xrōštay.

Let us quote from M 42 a dialogue between Jesus Zīvā and Jesus the Child, an offshoot of Jesus, who, banished into this base world, embodies the suffering soul and its hope of life and redemption. This dialogue shows us the successive redeemers in the course of history who—as the first lines remind us—continue the work of the cosmic redeemers of the myth.

(Child)   All eyes have seen the honor and the benefits
        which thou, O God, hast time and time
            again conferred upon me;
        but for this one thing I make plaint, that thou hast
            arisen and left me orphaned.

(Jesus)   Remember the chief of warriors, O prince,
        the father, God Ōhrmizd, who rose from the darkness,
        but left his sons behind in the depths
            because of the great gain [?].

(Child)   Hear my prayer, dear Lord;
        if thou wilt not yet release me now,
        send many gods, that I may attain
            victory over the tormentors.

(Jesus)   I instructed the great Noῦs
        to send the messengers when . . . came;
        reveal thou too thy long-suffering
            for the afflicted lights.

(Child)   The world and its children were concerned [?] for me:
        Zarahusht went down into the kingdom of Pars,
        he revealed the truth, he gathered my members
            from the lights of the seven regions.

---

160 *Kephalaion* 7 (ed. Polotsky, p. 35, lines 21–24 and p. 36, lines 1–6) . Cf. *Kephalaion* 38 (ibid., pp. 82–102) .

(Jesus)   When Satan learned of his descent,
he sent demons of wrath; before help came
pain struck thee, beloved, from their works
and perverted [?] wisdom.

(Child)   Mourning departed from me
when Shakimun But [= Buddha Sakyamuni] . . . me,
he opened the gate of redemption to the happy souls
which he redeemed from among the Indians.

(Jesus)   Because of the arts and wisdom thou receivedst from But
thou wert envied by Dībat, the great virgin;
when he entered into *nirvāṇa*, he commanded thee:
wait here for Mêtrag [= Maitreya].

(Child)   Then Jesus took pity a second time,
he sent the four pure winds to my help,
he bound the three winds, destroyed Orischlem [= Jeru-
salem]
with the battlements of the demons of wrath.

(Jesus)   Poison and death . . . to thee, prince,
monster of ugliness, Iscariot,
with Israel's sons and much other woe,
that came. . . .

(Child)   . . . .
. . . of the messengers . . . slight,
and the two armies that are moving toward me
[are] innumerable.

(Jesus)   Thy great battle is like that of Ōhrmizd, the god,
thy gathering of treasure like that of the companions
of light;
and in flesh and wood thou canst redeem from "Lust"
this Living Soul too.

(Child)   All three gods sheltered this child,
and they sent Mar Mani the Redeemer to me,
who led me from captivity when I was serving my
enemies
against my will and in fear.

(Jesus)   My guardian, I give thee freedom. . . .[161]

161 *SBA* 1934, pp. 878–81, Andreas and Henning. Tr. H. H. Schaeder, in "Der
Manichäismus nach neuen Funden und Forschungen," *Morgenland* (Leipzig), XXVIII (1936), 106–07.

In its obscure language this dialogue sums up the essential points in the Manichaean conception of revelation. The documents that have been discovered in the Fayum throw full light on the question: some passages in the *Homilies*[162] and, above all, the *Kephalaia,* their introduction and chapters 1,[163] 143, and 154,[164] which are complemented by Turfan Fragment T II D 126.[165] Revelation, this indispensable instrument of redemption, is always present in the world. Throughout the history of the world, at great and solemn moments (καιροί), Jesus-the-Radiant sent down revealers from heaven to help save the crucified souls, and each time to choose and liberate some of them. The gnosis brought by them takes on different forms but is always the same. It forms the foundation of the true religion, the religion of δικαιοσύνη. But, as always in Manichaeism, this communication of gnosis is a battle, and, as in the consciousness of man, moments of illumination are followed by darkness. The Demon envies the heralds of light. He hurls himself upon them and, when he has destroyed them, upon their work. Matter creates false religions, the δόγματα, which exist side by side with the religion of truth: idolatry, magic, mantism, and, above all, the cults of baptism and fire—the exact opposite of the revelations of Zoroaster—and Judaism, which killed Jesus.[166] Through the world runs a twofold chain of tradition, that of light and that of darkness, to which the souls adhere.

And another danger threatened the revelation of the apostles of light down to Mani; although the truth it communicates is only one, the forms in which it is cloaked and the languages in which it is proclaimed are different—and this difference brings with it a limitation of the One Message. The work of Zoroaster remained limited to Persia, that of Buddha to India, that of Jesus to Judaea, or at best to the Occident. Moreover, this revelation was not set down by the envoys themselves: neither Zoroaster nor Buddha nor Jesus committed his doctrine to writing. This is the cause of the

162 *Homily* II (ed. Polotsky, pp. 10, line 24–13, line 7). See Augustine, *Contra Faustum*, XX, 4 (ed. Zycha, p. 538, lines 19–23); M 104, *SBA* 1934, pp. 882–83, Andreas and Henning; *Homily* III (ed. Polotsky, p. 74, lines 13–14); *Homily* IV (ibid., p. 91, lines 6–7).

163 *Kephalaion* 1, ed. Polotsky, p. 7, lines 17ff.; pp. 9, line 12–16, line 31.

164 *Kephalaia* 143, 154 (*SBA* 1933, pp. 42, 43, 45, 60).

165 *SBA* 1933, pp. 295–96, Andreas and Henning. ·

166 Cf. esp. *Homily* II (ed. Polotsky, pp. 10, line 24–11, line 25) and *Kephalaion* 6 (ed. Polotsky, pp. 33, line 9–34, line 5).

rapid decline of the religions they founded, particularly of the Christian Church, in which, since St. Paul, the meaning of Jesus' message has been lost, except for two righteous men—presumably Marcion and Bardesanes.[167] Each time it seemed that darkness would be victorious over the light an increasing fear seized the soul and the hope of redemption seemed destroyed. To those who are worthy of it, redemption is finally assured only by the revelation of the last envoy of light, Mani, the "seal of the prophets" and "apostle of the last generation."[168] The message of Mani is ultimate in both senses of the word. It is the last call to redemption; now the world need only be converted and disappear. Refusal to adhere to the Manichaean doctrine is accordingly a transgression which can never be made good. Since this faith is the most dazzling of illuminations, to reject it is tantamount to rejection of knowledge as such. And it seems that at least the first generation of Manichaeans actually did believe that the end of the world was at hand.[169] And Mani's revelation is ultimate in the second sense of the word, because it is the supreme, perfect gnosis. Mani, the last of the prophets, is for this reason the Paraclete.[170] His gnosis—and on this the Manichaeans known to St. Augustine insist[171]—is all-embracing and all-explaining, and moreover it is immediately intelligible and free from contradiction. Mani does not speak in symbols and allegories as his predecessors did, but with logical clarity. He does not cloak his ideas in

---

167 *Kephalaia*, ed. Polotsky, pp. 7, line 18–8, line 19; 1, ibid., pp. 13, line 10–14, line 2; 154, *SBA* 1933, p. 43 and cf. T II D 126, *SBA* 1933, p. 295. From this it can be seen that the Manichaeans looked upon the exact copying of the Scripture as an absolute duty and sacred work. It can further be seen that the canonical books were preserved even in the Last Days; see *Homilies* II and III (ed. Polotsky, pp. 18–20, 24–25, 44–45).

168 Concerning the first invocation, see Bīrūnī, *Chronology*, tr. Sachau, p. 190, line 10; al-Murtaḍā in Kessler, *'Mani*, I, 355; Shahrastāni, *Religionsparteien*, tr. Haarbrücker, I, 290. For the second, see *Kephalaion* 1 (ed. Polotsky, p. 14, line 6) and the beginning of the *Shâbûhragân* in Bīrūnī, tr. Sachau, p. 190, line 7.

169 Cf. *Homily* II (ed. Polotsky, p. 28, lines 4–6 and p. 33) and presumably S 9 verso in Salemann, "Manichaica III," *Bulletin de l'Académie Impériale de Saint-Pétersbourg*, ser. VI, vol. 6 (1912), 13–14 and *Kephalaion* LVII (ed. Polotsky, p. 146, lines 9–10).

170 *Kephalaion* 1 (ed. Polotsky, p. 14, lines 3ff.), and for the older reports see e.g., Alfaric, *Évolution*, p. 212, n. 5. See St. Paul on the type of the Paraclete among the Valentinians, *Excerpta ex Theodoto*, 23, 2 (ed. Casey, p. 58, line 258).

171 E.g., *Contra Faustum*, XV, 6 (ed. Zycha, p. 427, lines 4–12).

riddles; on the contrary, he came to solve difficulties and to say openly what had hitherto been concealed in images. Above all, Mani's religion is the universal religion which has gathered all preceding religions into itself and gone far beyond them. Geographical or linguistic limits are unknown to it. It is destined to spread both to east and west.[172] Finally, it is Mani who had the perspicacity to commit his doctrine to writing and establish an unalterable and unassailable canon. Thus neither the truth nor its church is in danger of being falsified or destroyed. Hence it is evident that if redemption is achieved by a gnosis which has itself the face of a revelation, the revelation of Mani is the *conditio sine qua non* of redemption.

In so far as they are representatives of the Noûs and awakeners of souls, the envoys of light—particularly Jesus and Mani, whose functions correspond—play the role of redeemers. Jesus—the historical Jesus differentiated from the transcendent Jesus—is an emanation of the Noûs which is incarnated in him.[173] In numerous Turfan hymns (particularly those collected by Waldschmidt and Lentz in their article in the *Abhandlungen der Preussischen Akademie,* 1926, in which the role of Jesus as redeemer is exhaustively examined) he is invoked as "The Lord," "The Mighty," as he who has reawakened the Living I, which had been crucified and utterly mixed.[174] He brings gnosis. As Noûs, he is the "Protector," the "Friend," the "Lord"; it is he who has the power to forgive sins and who at the end of time will be the judge of souls. And one more highly significant trait: his Passion has power to save only in so far as it represents an effective teaching for the human intellect, not as a sacrifice, but as an example. For the Manichaeans it was only seemingly a story of suffering. If Jesus had been born of woman, if his body had been like ours, then this God would have partaken of the taint and corruption of the flesh, or his body would

---

172 *Kephalaion* 143, *SBA* 1933, p. 60; *Kephalaion* 154, ibid., p. 45; and T II D 126, ibid., p. 295.

173 On the different Manichaean Christs see Augustine, *Contra Faustum,* XX, 11 (ed. Zycha, pp. 550, line 14–551, line 28).

174 E. Waldschmidt and W. Lentz, "Die Stellung Jesu im Manichäismus," *ABA* 1926, IV. Cf. on the same theme O. Michel, *Zeuge der Wahrheit,* reviewed by E. Peterson in *Theologische Literarzeitung,* LXIII, cols. 249–51, and O. G. von Wesendonk, "Jesus und der Manichäismus," *Orientalistische Literaturzeitung* (Leipzig), XXX (1927), cols. 226–27.

have been sinless, which for Manichaean dualism would be a contradiction in itself.[175] If Christ's sufferings on the cross had been reality, the Passion could not have a divine character: as in the Docetic Gnosis, Jesus, on the contrary, commands the soul to distinguish absolutely between body and Νοῦς, because he himself cannot be touched by suffering. Furthermore, the Passion of Christ is only an image of the cosmic crucifixion of the mythical Jesus Patibilis: a historical event which reflects in striking form the doctrine of the Redeemed Redeemer. Alexander of Lycopolis rightly declares: "In the end, the Νοῦς [which is Jesus] is crucified in order to bring gnosis [ἀνασταυρωθέντα παρασχέσθαι γνῶσιν], that is, the knowledge that the divine substance is in like manner [τοιῷδε τρόπῳ] dispersed and crucified [ἐνηρμόσθαι and ἐνεσταυρῖθαι] in matter."[176] The Manichaean finds redemption not, like the Christian, in a participation in the incarnate and crucified Jesus, but in the example of a fictitious and symbolic Jesus, whose role consists primarily in awakening and illuminating the souls.

Mani, "the apostle of Jesus Christ,"[177] has for the Manichaeans the same characteristics; his functions often merge with those of Jesus. He, too, is an envoy of light, an emanation of the Νοῦς. As "seal of the prophets" and Paraclete, he is the Holy Ghost of the Christians, to which corresponds the Manichaean "Great Spirit," i.e. the Νοῦς.[178] He, too, is often invoked as the awakener, e.g. in the following Uigur fragment:

> When thou foundest beings in need of liberation [redemption], thou liberatedst [redeemedst] them all without exception. To beings like us, who were awakened, thou hast extensively [fully] preached the Gospel, the treasure of the law. Hearing the path of salvation and redemption in that doctrine [sermon], we understand the instrument of salvation [?]. If thou hadst not fully preached the sacred doctrine, would the world not have passed away [met its doom] by now?[179]

175 See Evodius, *De fide*, 24 (ed. Zycha, p. 961, lines 25–33) and cf. on all these points Baur, pp. 398–402, and Polotsky, *Abriss*, cols. 268, line 59–269, line 42.
176 *Contra Manichaeorum opiniones*, ed. Brinkmann, p. 7, lines 16–19.
177 References in *SBA* 1933, pp. 26–27 and Polotsky, *Abriss*, col. 266, lines 6–14.
178 See Polotsky, *Abriss*, cols. 256, line 48–267, line 45.
179 Tr. Bang, *Le Muséon*, XXXVIII (1925), 41–42.

Or, in M 32, if we assume that this passage deals with Mani: "O great caller, who awakenest this my soul from slumber."[180] As we see from other Turfan texts and from *Homily* I, Mani—to whom his worshiper devotes himself entirely, whose slave he is, who replaces everything for him, family, friends, the goods of the earth— is the "new God," the Mighty Enlightener, the Head of the Community, the Lord of Religion, he who has the power to redeem from sin and death, the "Physician of the Soul," the "King of the Law," he who "has revealed everything that is hidden," he who knows our sins, and who at the end of time will be man's advocate before the judgment seat of Christ, which he occupies up until that moment.[181] In a word, Mani is the "redeemer."[182]

Strophe 135 of the Chinese Hymn Book of London sums up these functions as follows:

And [we] invoke: the all-embracing Mani, the Sublime,
   The Leader, the Light of Wisdom, the Sun [or the Day]
      of Enlightenment,
who came from that great light into this world,
proclaimed the right law, and saved the good sons.[183]

And Mani himself has all these redeeming powers from the perfect gnosis which he has brought with him. His own Passion—which the Manichaeans call his σταύρωσις (crucifixion) even though Mani died in prison crushed by heavy chains—plays, no doubt, a certain role in the Manichaean religion, which renews the memory of it

180 *ABA* 1904, p. 62, lines 4–5, Müller.
181 See particularly *Homily* I (ed. Polotsky, pp. 1–7), throughout, a prayer in which Salmaios glorifies Mani and entreats his favor in the hour of his death. —Concerning Mani's titles and the functions he fulfills in the Turfan texts, see, e.g., *ABA* 1904; M 99, p. 44; M 4, pp. 53–54, 58; M 176, pp. 60, 61; M 311, pp. 67–68; M 38, p. 77; M 3, p. 80; M 64, pp. 91–92. Also, *ABA* 1922: T II D 78, pp. 24–28; T M 166, p. 28; London Chinese Hymn Book, 172a, *SBA* 1933, p. 491 and cf. 517. —Concerning Mani's role with respect to sin, see *Homily* I (ed. Polotsky, p. 5, lines 18–26 and p. 7, lines 3–4); cf. M 176 and M 38, *ABA* 1904, pp. 61, 77; T II D 78, *ABA* 1922, pp. 24, 25; prayer to Mani in *Fihrist* (Flügel, *Mani*, p. 96). —On Mani as his followers' advocate at the end of days, Secundinus, *Epist. ad August.* (ed. Zycha, p. 896, lines 5–8), and Augustine, *Contra Secundinum*, 25 (ed. Zycha, p. 943, lines 12–17). —Concerning the gradual merging of Jesus and Mani in the Manichaean movement, see Baur, p. 372, n. 5 and Waldschmidt and Lentz, *ABA* 1926, pp. 30, 59ff.
182 M 4, *ABA* 1904, pp. 53–54; M 501, *SBA* 1933, p. 553; *Homilies* I and II (ed. Polotsky, pp. 6, line 10 and 11, line 24 resp.).
183 *SBA* 1933, p. 487, Waldschmidt and Lentz.

each year at the festival of the *Bēma*.[184] But the symbolism of the
Bēma makes it clear that here, too, the Passion possesses no power
of salvation, except as an example of martyrdom for the faith. What
the faithful praise in this festival is, above all, the *chair* of Mani—
i.e., his doctrine and his judgment,[185] his power to forgive sins and
to prepare men's souls for the Last Judgment, where redemption
awaits the Elect. The accounts of the Turfan and Fayum texts[186]
now in our possession show that the important aspect of this passion
is not Mani's suffering, but his ascent to *nirvāṇa* immediately after
his death in prison. Here again it is made plain that the "Crucifixion
of the Enlightener"—as *Homily* III is characteristically entitled—is
of interest solely as an example of the liberation of the Νοῦς.

But the revelation of the Νοῦς by the Redeemer is not sufficient.
The consciousness it arouses must be maintained with as little interruption as possible, it must be nourished and renewed. This task
falls eminently to the church. And it is noteworthy that here again—
according to *Kephalaion* 7[187]—the church, and the community of the
Elect of which it consists, is an immediate emanation of the luminous Νοῦς. Their principle—the "Glory of Religion" or the "Majesty
of Law" (Pers.: *farrah ī dēn;* Uig.: *nom qutī*)—is designated as the
"unique awakener": "this uniquely awakening *nom qutī*."[188] And
the church, the "religion," or the "law"—as heir and vessel of the
revealed wisdom—also awakens. This is particularly true of the
perfect church established by Mani, which preserves, copies, and
disseminates those writings whose canonical character safeguards
them against any distortion, thereby safeguarding the church itself
against schism. The church, guardian of redemption, is conceived as
an organization of this redemption. Within the congregation, the
tradition of illuminating gnosis is handed down by the unbroken
line of Mani's successors, the ἀρχηγοί, who might be called the popes

184 Cf. Augustine, *Contra Epist. Fund.*, 8 (ed. Zycha, p. 202, line 11–203, line 4)
and *Contra Faustum*, XVIII, 5 (ed. Zycha, p. 494, lines 17–24).
185 See particularly Psalm 222 of the London Coptic Hymn Book (cf. *SBA* 1933,
p. 33, n. 1).
186 *Homily* III (ed. Polotsky, pp. 42–85); *SBA* 1934: T II D 79, pp. 860–62; M 5,
pp. 863–65; M 454, pp. 891–92. Some indications in the historical collection
of Berlin; see *SBA* 1933, pp. 28–30.
187 Ed. Polotsky, p. 35, lines 21–24 and p. 36, lines 1–6.
188 T M 298 R 8–9, *ABA* 1922, p. 9, von Le Coq. I follow the translation by
Bang in *Le Muséon*, XXXVIII (1925), 46.

of the Manichaean church. The missionaries carry to all four winds the call of redemption which the envoys of light have emitted. The congregations—often, as in Central Asia, they are organized as cloisters[189]—make possible a realization of the life of renunciation and piety, which is redemption, and give it form. Here it is not our task to go into the details of this organization and the Manichaean hierarchy. It suffices to state that both are in principle based on a division of the faithful into the Elect and the Catechumens, or listeners. The former are redeemed by virtue of their total asceticism; the others have still to achieve redemption, but cannot do so in this life. Actually the Catechumens must, after their death and until their perfect purification, undergo a more or less protracted cycle of rebirths or transfusions ($\mu\epsilon\tau\alpha\gamma\gamma\iota\sigma\mu o\acute{\iota}$) [190] as a punishment for their imperfection, varying according to the nature and number of the good and bad works they have performed on this earth. Those who are closest to perfection will be reborn in the bodies of the Elect; others, less perfect, may reappear in the form of plants, with the prospect of serving as food for the Elect; those for whom there is no hope will return to life as animals and so lose all prospect of redemption, since the consumption of meat is forbidden to the Elect.[191] The listeners would seem to correspond to the soul and the Elect to the Νοῦς, and in this light the Elect are not only redeemed but, in their relation to the Catechumens, they are also redeemers. Actually redemption is oriented entirely toward them and resides entirely in them. According to the interpretation of Matthew 25:40 in Fayum *Homily* II[192] the "least of my brethren" are the very substance of Jesus Patibilis. It is this naked, starving, suffering, and alien Jesus whom the Catechumens clothe when they give the Elect a garment, whom they feed when they bring him

189 Cf. Pelliot, Fragment, *JA* 1913, pp. 108–10; Bang, *Le Muséon*, XXXVIII (1925), 30–31; M 36, *SBA* 1933, p. 326.
190 See A. V. W. Jackson, "The Doctrine of Metempsychosis in Manichaeism," *JAOS*, XLV (1925), 246–68.
191 Cf. Alfaric, *Évolution*, pp. 153–54, and esp. Augustine, *De haeresibus*, 46 (Migne, *PL*, XLII, 37) and *Homily* II (ed. Polotsky, p. 27, lines 6–18). The correction of line 14 proposed by F. C. Burkitt, "Polotsky's Manichaean Homilies," *Journal of Theological Studies*, XXXV (1934), 358, n. 3, need not be accepted.
192 *Homily* II (ed. Polotsky, p. 38, lines 9–26); M 475 and M 477, *ABA* 1904, pp. 12–13, 13–15. Cf. Augustine, *Contra Faustum*, II, 5 and V, 10 (ed. Zycha, p. 258, lines 16–18 and p. 283, lines 11–23).

plants and fruits, whom they assuage when they bring him drink, whom they shelter when they give him lodging. The works of the Catechumens have no immediate redeeming efficacy: they are only a pledge toward their redemption, and this through the concrete mediation of the Elect. This accounts for the accusation of inhumanity that has often been raised against the Manichaeans, whose charity is directed entirely toward the Elect.[193] They are not only elect in a passive sense, but likewise, in an active sense, it is they who elect and choose, who by their knowledge of good and evil are to distinguish those acts which should be performed and those plants which should be eaten.[194] The Elect contributes to the redemption of the Catechumen by his teaching and in various other ways. First, by his weekly remission of sins. Second, by his acceptance of the alms (*misericordiae*) brought him by the Catechumens. Third, by his digestion, which liberates the fruits and vegetables he eats (this is the redemption by the belly of the Elect, which is ridiculed by St. Augustine).[195] Fourth, and last, by the fact that in the Last Days the Catechumens who have been transformed into plants will in increasing number enter into the seed and the body of the Elect.[196] Thus the Manichaean church is primarily a community of the Elect (ἐκλογή). Only in them and through them can redemption be realized. The Catechumens are a profane element; at best they can become auxiliaries of redemption by serving the Elect.

Does the Manichaean church possess any outward instruments of salvation in addition to this organization centered around the Elect? Does it possess sacraments? We have seen in the first section of this paper that the Gnostics of the second century gave contradictory answers to this question; some believed that gnosis sufficed for redemption, others believed that certain rites must accompany the revelation. Manichaean Gnosis does not seem to have had sacraments. The Manichaeans condemned baptism and permitted only—though even this is not certain—a communion[197] restricted to

193 Cf. Alfaric, *Évolution*, p. 152, n. 5 and p. 153, n. 1.
194 Cf. Chavannes and Pelliot, "Traité," p. 539, n. 3.
195 E.g., Augustine, *De haeresibus*, 36 (Migne, *PL*, XLII, 37) or *Contra Faustum*, II, 5 and V, 10.
196 *Homily* II (ed. Polotsky, p. 27, lines 11–18).
197 The most complete exposé of the Manichaean cult and its rites still remains that of I. de Beausobre, *Histoire de Manichée*, II (Amsterdam, 1739), 582–

the Elect. It is true that our Fayum texts point to the existence of ritual actions: the pressure of the hand, corresponding to the Mandaean *Kušṭā*, the laying on of hands, the kiss of peace,[198] the use of a table ($\tau\rho\acute{\alpha}\pi\epsilon\zeta\alpha$—for communion?),[199] the viaticum for the dying.[200] But none of these usages seems to have had sacramental efficacy in the eyes of the Manichaeans. Manichaeism remained profoundly true to the spirit of Gnosis: it regarded the consciousness and knowledge that transform the inner man as the necessary and adequate conditions for redemption. The entire church cult consists in fasting and prayer accompanied by the singing of hymns. Only in a single point did the Manichaeans seem to make a concession to the need for outward instruments of salvation.[201] We have seen that, logically speaking, the conception of sin implies only an inner, spiritual penance: the recognition of the transgression, followed by repentance. But the Manichaean church recognized both public and individual confession: every Monday the congregation confessed to the Elect: and all confessed publicly to Mani—whose spirit was believed to attend the ceremony—at the end of the thirty days preceding the festival of the *Bēma*.[202]

Only a single problem remains for us to deal with: the ultimate aims which the Manichaeans ascribed to this process of redemption. Obviously there could be no question of a redemption or resurrection of the body, which is inherently damned.[203] As the

---

806. But Beausobre is too much inclined to maintain the existence of sacraments in Manichaeism, and the documents on which he bases his theory must be treated very critically. On the modern attempts to find references to sacraments in the Turfan texts, see the criticisms of H. H. Schaeder in *Iranica, Abhandlungen der Gesellschaft der Wissenschaften zu Göttingen* (Berlin), ser. 3, no. 10 (1934), pp. 19–24.

198 *Kephalaion* 9, ed. Polotsky, pp. 37, line 29–42, line 23.

199 *Homily* II, ed. Polotsky, pp. 16, line 21; 17, line 14; 28, line 11. Should we add M 11 R 3, *SBA* 1933, p. 556, and I B 4974 R I 21, ibid., p. 558? Communion with bread and salt introduced by Mani, *Homily* III (ed. Polotsky, p. 57, line 18)?

200 *Kephalaion* 144, ed. Polotsky, pp. 346ff. (Information kindly supplied by H. A. Böhlig.)

201 Cf. En-Nedīm (Flügel, *Mani,* p. 90) and Chavannes and Pelliot, "Traité," p. 562.

202 Cf. *Khuastuanift*, XII A and XIV A–B (tr. Bang, pp. 162–65, with the commentary on pp. 220, 226–27).

203 Cf. particularly Epiphanius, 66, 86, 1–2 (ed. Holl, III, 129, lines 1–12) and 87, 1 (III, 130, lines 12–15) with the texts cited in Holl's note.

Fihrist[204] tells us, the corpse, which the soul has abandoned, is a last time purified by the sun, the moon, the gods of light, who draw forth its forces—i.e., the water, the fire, and the soft breath—while the rest, which is darkness, is cast into hell.

Death is actually—to use the Manichaean terms—a "departure" from the body and the world, a "renunciation of the world" (ἀποτάσσεσθαι τῷ κόσμῳ)[205] in its fullest sense, liberation of the true I, final separation of the Living Soul from the body of darkness. For the Elect it is the full realization of redemption, which is symbolized by the meeting of the I with his redeemer, the personified form of his redemption. As the last decisive phase in the earthly struggle, death is sometimes conceived as the appearance of the New Man and the Old Man before the "Great Judge" or the "Judge of Truth." As the case may be, the Judge liberates the soul forever and permits it to return to the True Life—the Old Man is then handed over to the angels, who take him into custody up to the last and final chaining; or else the two are sent back into mixture, to be "transfused" anew; or they are damned and sent to death, i.e. hell.[206] In other accounts, the soul of the Elect leaves the body amid a guard of gods and angels, who protect him from a last assault of the demons; he sees coming toward him a "luminous form," his piety embodied in a halo, a kind of projection of his New Man, his "second self," which is an emanation of the luminous Νοῦς and shows all the features of the Redeemer: of Jesus, Mani, or the Νοῦς.[207] Here again, the Νοῦς is the end of redemption, just as it was its beginning and its instrument. The soul receives a garment, a crown of light and a sign of victory, which is both symbol of its triumph and testimony to its recognized innocence. Thence it rises triumphantly to the pillar of glory, to the moon, to the sun, and from there to peace and joy,

204 See Flügel, *Mani*, p. 100.
205 *Kephalaion* 7, ed. Polotsky, p. 36, line 11.
206 The main texts to be compared with these diverse conceptions are: En-Nedīm (Flügel, *Mani*, p. 100) ; T II D 175, 2, *ABA* 1922, von Le Coq, and *Le Muséon*, XXXVI (1923) , 236–38, Bang; Strophes 388–93 of the London Chinese Hymn Book, *ABA* 1926, pp. 123–24, Waldschmidt and Lentz; *Homily* I (ed. Polotsky, p. 6, lines 15–35) ; *Kephalaia* 7, 9 (ed. Polotsky, p. 36, lines 9–11; p. 41, lines 11–21) , and 141, *SBA* 1933, p. 71, with the commentary of Polotsky, pp. 71–72. In *Abriss*, cols. 260, line 26–261, line 18, Polotsky gives a definitive explanation of the double-image system elaborated in these texts.
207 See Polotsky, "Manichäische Studien," *Le Muséon*, XLVI (1933) , 268–71.

to *nirvāṇa*, the eternal realm of light, which is its new-found home. This in broad outlines is the Manichaean eschatology of the individual.

The universal eschatology,[208] whose material aspect we have already described, offers the following picture for mankind as a whole: the persecution of the Manichaean church is followed by its earthly triumph and the conversion of the greater part of mankind to the truth. Then follows the judgment before the tribunal of Jesus established at the center of the cosmos. Here, recalling a constantly recurring theme, Jesus as "King of the Noũs," as Intelligence, appears in his function of judge. The Elect, who are already redeemed, attend the tribunal in the form of angels surrounding Christ. The worthy Catechumens are led to the right, the sinners—the goats—to the left, where they are given over to the demons. After a brief rule of Jesus in the midst of redeemed mankind, Jesus and the Elect, followed by the gods supporting the cosmos, leave the world. The globe collapses, goes up in flames in a last act of purification, and is destroyed. All the light that can still be saved is united in the "Great Idea" (the "Call" and the "Answer") in the form of the "Last Statue," which rises up to heaven, while the damned and the demons, matter with its lust and bisexuality, are cast into a pit sealed over with an immense stone.

It must be remarked that this eschatological vision ends on a pessimistic note: not all the divine light, not all the devoured substance of the First Man, can be fully redeemed. Since the beginning there have been souls who, by the force of circumstances or because of the sins they have committed in the course of the drama, cannot be redeemed and who must for all eternity share the imprisonment of matter.[209] The struggle between good and evil ends in a triumph of the light, but it is not without its dangers, and the ultimate victory of God is not achieved without losses.

We are now in a position to sum up the Manichaean conception of redemption: redemption is a liberation based solely on gnosis, which produces it, determines its course, provides its instruments,

208 Cf. A. V. W. Jackson, "A Sketch of the Manichaean Doctrine concerning the Future Life," *JAOS*, L (1930), 177–98, and the whole of *Homily* II.
209 En-Nedīm (Flügel, *Mani*, p. 90); Simplicius, *In Enchir. Epict.*, 27 (ed. Dübner, pp. 70, line 51–71, line 5 and p. 71, lines 30–33); M 2, *SBA* 1934, pp. 850–51, Andreas and Henning.

and is its goal. In short, knowledge is the beginning, end, and meaning of redemption. Manichaean redemption is a redemption of the intelligence and by the intelligence. But in its manifestations this intelligence includes a revelation, and in its content a mythology. And it is precisely this mystical and metaphysical character which makes a drama of cosmic events and a battle of man's redemption. Both of these seem to be inevitable processes; the return of the soul to the luminous substance, with which it is consubstantial, is predetermined both *de jure* and *de facto*. But the fundamental dualism, the assumption of evil's actual existence and power to act, shapes this prehistory and this mythical history of the world and man into a series of vicissitudes and benevolent interventions, or, seen from the point of view of the soul, into incessant temptation, resurgences, cowardly backslidings. The story begins with a catastrophe and ends with an imperfect victory. This contemplative religion of sages who strive to withdraw from the world is also a religion of missionaries and warriors. Redemption is in theory pure intelligence and purely intellectual: in reality, the theory is a myth and its practice is a hero cult.

Louis Massignon

Nature in Islamic Thought

Last year we examined the notion of "spirit" in Islamic thought.[1] This year I believe it will be worth our while to consider the notion of "nature" in contrast to that of "spirit."

Natura (Greek: φύσις) is traditionally rendered by the Arabic *ṭabī'a*. The first Arabic translators of the Syriac translations of the *Organon* used for the word "nature" the word *kiyān*, copied from the Syriac *kyōnō,* but this term remained rare and was restricted to the innate element in human psychology.

Ṭabī'a comes from the root *ṭb',* to imprint upon a thing, to seal. In the Koran it is used in a rather pejorative sense: a mark of God the Creator's contempt for His creation, which He imprints with a seal of separation, of shadow, if not of damnation. The "name" which God gives to created things separates them from Him as a "veil" separates things from the light. It is in this sense that the Ismā'īlīs, the Nuṣayrīs, and the Drūses call the Prophet Muḥammad *Mīm,* the Name (Arabic: *Ism*) and the Veil (Arabic: *Ḥijāb*).[2] Ḥallāj said: "God has veiled his creatures with the Name, in order that they may live. . . . If He unveiled his energy to them, they would be destroyed."[3]

The words *ṭabī'a* and *ṭibā'* are static, opposed to initiative, movement, will. The first theologians give a negative answer to the question of whether God creates *ṭab'an* that is, "naturally," hence by necessity (which is impossible). It is true that under the influence

---

1 [See the following paper in this volume.]
2 Anonymous Nuṣayrī, MS. Pers. 1934, fol. 81 b.
3 Al-Ḥallāj, *Akhbār al-Ḥallāj, texte ancien relatif à la prédication et au supplice du mystique Musulman al-Ḥosayn b. Manṣour al-Ḥallāj,* ed. and tr. Louis Massignon and Paul Kraus (Paris, 1936), p. 112 (text), p. 50 (introduction).

of the Hellenistic idea of the "immobile prime mover," Muslim theologians ceased to conceive of God's pure act in the form of "movement" (*haraka*), although the profound Semitic tradition of revealed monotheism maintained that God never ceases to act, to recreate His creation—a Jewish idea reformulated by a great Islamic philosopher, Abu'l-Barakāt al-Baghdādī (d. A.H. 547/A.D. 1153), who showed that the only serious proof of God's existence was this constant actualization, this renewal (*tajaddud*) by which he substantially animates his works.[4]

The first Hellenistic Muslim philosophers are divided into two groups: the "spiritualists," who explain the general functioning and the differentiation of the universe by the action of "spirits" (*aṣḥāb al-rūhāniyīn*), and the "naturists" (*aṣḥāb al-ṭabā'i'*), who invoke the action of the four qualities (hot, cold, dry, moist). *Ṭabā'i'*, qualities, also designates by extension the four humors which constitute the living balance of the human body (bile, black bile, blood, phlegm). Under Manichaean influence these qualities and humors came to be considered as "evil," "dark," and the Shīite extremists identified them with the souls who were damned for having opposed the proclamation of 'Alī as the *khalīfa-imām*—hence predestined elements of Evil.

Two philosophical fables conceived in this period aim in the name of "nature" to minimize the orthodox Muslim belief in the sovereign freedom of God: Ibn al-Rāwendi's fable of the "monotheist Brahmans," who profess that the revelation and the holy scriptures are useless; and the romance of the "Sabaeans," alleged disciples of Hermes, who maintain that through ascetic training human nature, by its own strength and without recourse to revelation, can ascend to the godhead. I have spoken of this in the appendix to Festugière's last book on Greek Hermeticism.[5] This "Sabaean" doctrine is important: it is a spiritual, evolutionist naturism, a spiritualist doctrine of progress.[6] It is also believed that

---

4 Abu'l-Barakāt al-Baghdādī, *Al-mu'tabar fi'l-ḥikma* (Hyderabad, Dā'irat al-Ma'ārif, A.H. 1357/A.D. 1938) cites Ibn Taimīya, *Minhāj*, I, 93, 99, 112, 118, and Ibn Abi'l-Hadīd, *Sharḥ al-nahj*, I, 297.

5 André-Jean Festugière, *La Révélation d'Hermès Trismégiste* (4 vols., Paris, 1944–   ), Appendix, I, 384ff.

6 See P. Kraus, *Jābir ibn Ḥayyān al-Tarasūsī. Essai sur l'histoire des idées scientifiques dans l'Islam* (Paris, 1935); idem, *Jābir b. Ḥayyān. Contribution à l'histoire des idées scientifiques dans l'Islam* (2 vols., Cairo, 1942–43); idem in *Rivista degli studi orientali* (Rome), XIV (1934).

man's natural faculties will enable him to fashion robots and breathe a soul into them. This is the theme of Villiers de l'Isle Adam's famous novel *L'Ève future*.

This spiritualist doctrine of "nature" is close to the Stoic maxim "Ζῆν ὁμολογούμενος Τῇ φύσει" in the Arabic Hellenistic texts on natural law, *Nāmūs*. But, by and large, the Muslim thinkers of the third century after the Hijra continued to see a contrast between "nature" and "divine grace." An illustration of this is the title of a famous anonymous manual of Arabic Hellenistic philosophy composed at the time of Caliph Ma'mūn: *Sirr al-khalīqa waṣan'at al-ṭabī'a*,[7] i.e., "The secret of creative grace and the mechanism of nature," in which this mechanism of nature is synthesized by the famous *Emerald Table* (*Tabula smaragdina*) of Hermes, supposedly written by Belinus (Apollonius of Tyana).[8] Another illustration is the first question that Hallāj asks of Junayd: "What enables us to differentiate creative grace (*khalīqa*) from the signs of nature ('*an rusūm al-ṭab'*) ?"[9]

That the spiritualist naturism of that period was a naturism limiting the divine power is proved by the doctrine of talismans bearing astral "signatures." It is a world order, opposed not only to chance (Greek: τυχή) but to the free intervention of God.

While certain Muslim philosophers, and even the theologian Fakhr Rāzī, attempted to amalgamate the two naturisms, the spiritualist (by astrology) and the materialist (by alchemy), the first Muslim mystics saw in "nature" a mark of punishment inflicted by God on his creatures, an ascetic veil, the sublunar law of pain. 'Amr Makkī attempts to explain the formation of the personality as a disintegration of the "veils" covering the heart, where the divine spark resides, as though incarcerated in a threefold wall.[10] In his Nocturnal Ascension the Prophet successively puts aside the various colored veils (of which there are seven) which conceal the ultimate God from him; these are his human veils. Here we are no longer dealing with the Astral Intellect's illumination of the

---

7 MS. Ar. Paris 2302, studied by H. S. Nyberg; see his *Kleinere Schriften des Ibn al-'Arabī* (Leyden, 1919) under A III, pp. 38–44.

8 Julius Ruska, *Tabula Smaragdina. Ein Beitrag zur Geschichte der hermitischen Literatur* (Heidelberg, 1926).

9 See above, n. 3.

10 'Alī b. 'Uthmān al-Hujwīrī, *The Kashf al-Maḥjūb, the Oldest Persian Treatise on Ṣūfiism*, tr. R. A. Nicholson (London and Leyden, 1911), p. 309.

human person, but with a suprarational liberation by a transcendent spirit realizing the *Tawḥīd*.

These mystics react against the old predestinationist tendency of the *ḥadīths*, according to which the Creator, in the very act of creating them, imprints their "nature" upon the two categories of men, the elect and the damned; and the "handful of earth" that contains the elect—*kūnī*, "be!" (using the feminine of *kun*) —is designated as the Light of Muḥammad, origin of all the elect.[11]

One should also examine the "sentiment of nature" in Islamic literature; the dominant tendency is a naturism full of resigned serenity. With increasing comprehension comes greater religious satisfaction; and, as Mutanabbī eloquently put it (contrary to the well-known thought of Pascal), "The most pitiful of wretches is he who feels nothing, not he who suffers."[12]

This brings us to a fundamental problem of Semitic, and particularly Jewish, psychology in its most "Kierkegaardian" aspect: there is a hidden but divine good in suffering, and this is the mystery of anguish, the foundation of human nature. Our nature does not bear the mark of anguish outwardly as a temporary damnation or sanction; it assimilates it inwardly, like a void into which the divine presence rushes in all its glory. Whatever may be said on this matter, many Muslim thinkers have been struck by this notion of the primordial anguish of created nature given to man in his existential, eschatological, finalist actuality—this "adventure," the presentiment of which sublimates the "nature" in us. Some years ago a highly interesting argument on this subject occurred in Cairo between André Gide and the Muslim writer Ṭaha Ḥusayn, in connection with Gide's novel *Strait is the Gate*.[13] The Muslim replied triumphantly that Islam had also known anguish: not only had it contributed to the elaboration of a theory of chivalric love, the love of ideal renunciation, in the Middle Ages, but it had also inspired the pseudo-blasphemies of the great blind poet, Ma'arrī.

---

11 Muṣṭafā Yūsuf Salām al-Shādhilī, *Majmū'at Jawāhir al-ittilā' wa-durar al-intifā' 'alā matn Abī Shujā'* (Cairo, A.H. 1350/A.D. 1931), p. 123 (*qabḍa ma'lūma = kūnī* of the Carmatians).

12 Al-Mutanabbī, *Dīwān* (Beirut, 1900); cf. Blaise Pascal, *Pensées*, ed. Léon Brunschvicg (3 vols., Paris, 1904), No. 399: "On n'est pas misérable sans sentiment: une maison ruinée ne l'est pas; il n'y a que l'homme de misérable: *Ego vir videns*."

13 Ṭaha Ḥusayn, *al-'Uṣūl wa-l-ghāyāt*, in *al-Mahrajān al-alfīya li-dhikr Abi-l-A'lā' al-Ma'arrī (al-Majma' al-'ilmī al-'arabī)*, Damascus, 1945, pp. 19ff.

Louis Massignon

The Idea of the Spirit in Islam

The notion of the spirit in Islam is designated, as in other Semitic languages, by two sharply contrasting words, *nafs* and *rūḥ*.[1] *Nafs* is the breath of the throat: it comes from the entrails, it is "carnal" and bound up with the blood, it causes eructation and spitting and confers the enjoyment of flavor. *Rūḥ* is the breath of the nostrils: it comes from the brain, it causes nasal speech and sneezing (*'aṭs*, the first sneeze of Adam when God breathed life into him), it confers the sense of smell and the discernment of spiritual qualities. Both are discontinuous and rhythmic and are at the origin of our "internal time" (which is oscillating and living) as opposed to "astral, cyclic time" (measured by the sundial) and to "gradual time" (measured by the passage of the sand in the hourglass or by the water clock). *Nafs* is related to *nafth,* to spit, and to *nafkh,* to breathe into; *rūḥ* is associated with *rīḥ,* to blow.

We shall first examine the experience itself and then take up the matter of definitions.

The experience of inspiration begins in Islam with the "internal upheavals" felt by Muḥammad at the beginning of his prophetic mission. According to 'Ā'isha, the Prophet of Islam first had a vision of isolated, luminous letters (several examples are cited at the head of certain chapters in the Koran) and simultaneously an audition of isolated sounds; the letters corresponded to the sounds, as with a child learning to spell. Then the Prophet, having learned

---

1 The basic verses of the Koran on *rūḥ* are Sūrahs XVII, 87 (and XCVII, 4); VI, 98 (*nafs*); XXXII, 8. See L. Massignon, *La Passion d'al-Ḥosayn-ibn-Manṣour al-Ḥallāj* (Paris, 1922), pp. 482, 517, 596, 661, 689, 852. See also Muhammad A'lā ibn 'Alī al-Tahānawī, *Kashshāf iṣṭilāḥāt al-funūn, A Dictionary of the Technical Terms Used in the Sciences of the Musulman,* ed. Aloys Sprenger (Calcutta, 1853–62), pp. 540–49 (*rūḥ*) and 1396–1404 (*nafs*).

to spell, was enabled to recite inspired sentences. They were "breathed" into him by the Spirit, *Rūḥ,* a vague word which can designate the angel as well as God or the Prophet himself.

Beginning with the earliest companions of the Prophet, Muslims made every effort to learn by heart the sacred text of the Koran, which they had heard and read, combining the two breaths *nafs* and *rūḥ* to produce the rhythm of their recitation: vocalizing and nasalizing (*rūḥ*) the consonants (*nafs,* which alone are noted in the manuscripts) in a staccato manner, thus designedly polarizing the ambivalent three-letter roots. They hoped to recapture the initial divine breath which had first dictated the sacred text by means of this insinuating, persuasive collective declamation which pierces to the heart. And this is still done in the *dhikr* gatherings of the Muslim orders. W. Haas has given us an excellent description of the *dhikr* of the Kabyle sect, the Raḥmānīyah.[2] It is made up of four successive quarter hours of recitation. The disciples are huddled in a circle, cross-legged, forming a chain with their hands; the master stands in the center. For the first eight minutes of each session, the group says *"Allāh"* in a series of violent expirations immediately followed by swifter inspirations producing the sound of a saw. In the second part, likewise of eight minutes, there is a brief inspiration preceding a longer expiration, in the rhythm of forty per minute instead of the preceding sixty. In the middle of the third exercise, however, the rhythm becomes extremely rapid, imposed by the master with the index and middle finger of his raised right hand. At the end of the fourth and last exercise, the disciples kneel around the master in a star-shaped figure, pressing their foreheads to the ground; they are nearly all in a state of trance. The master brings them out of the trance, saying *"Allāh akbar"* and clapping his hands three times. Then they stretch, and a serving brother wipes their faces and kisses them on the head.

(Here I must recall the meeting held on March 10, 1944 by the Société Asiatique of Paris, at which I discussed some of the statements made by Haas. Haas asserts that the name of God employed is *Ḥayy* rather than *Allāh* and fails to state whether the expirations were "vomited" from the nose to "empty the brain," or emitted from the pharynx to "empty the entrails.")

2 "Ein Dhikr der Rahmanija," *Der Neue Orient* (Berlin), I (1917), 210–13.

And now let us note the different attitudes maintained in the *dhikr* of other orders. The Naqshabandīya blink their eyes, gnash their teeth, and press their tongues against their palates. Historically, the oldest *dhikr* (Hamā'ilī) appears in the twelfth century: blinking eyes, crossed legs, palms on the knees. The breath is emitted under the left breast (to empty the heart); then the word *"Lā"* is expired from the navel (against the sexual demon); then *"Ilāha"* is pronounced on the right shoulder and *"Illa"* at the navel; finally, *"Allāh"* is powerfully articulated in the empty heart. Simnānī (d. 1336) makes slight changes: he "vomits" *"Ilāha"* from the cartilage of his nose, pronounces *"Illa"* on the left side and *"Allāh"* in the heart, keeping the vertebrae of his back and neck "erected"—a painful and purifying constraint. He also holds his right hand over his left hand, in which he clasps his right leg. Henri Maspero here sees a possible Taoist influence (Simnānī had been a Mongol functionary).[3] Indeed, the attitudes and facial expressions of the *dhikr* are in part borrowed and recall the Hindu *asanas*. Sanūsī, in his *Salsabīl*,[4] does not hesitate to classify among the *dhikr* of the Muslim orders the eighty-four poses of the *Jūjīya*, the Yogis, whom Ghawth Hindī (d. 1562)[5] regarded as "Muslims."

The first author who differentiates the names of God used in order to "enter into ecstasy" is Aḥmad Ghazālī (d. 1123), in his *Kitāb al-Tajrīd*.[6] The first Ṣūfī who dared to take "poses" in his *dhikr* was Aḥmad b. Tarkanshāh Aqsarāyī of Cairo (d. 1330).[7] At the same epoch, mawlawī Aflakī describes a *dhikr*.[8] But, generally speaking, the accounts of poses in the *dhikr* were not intended to be circulated except among the initiate.

---

3 Henri Maspero, *Mélanges posthumes sur les religions et l'histoire de la Chine*, II, *Le Taoisme* (Paris, 1950), pp. 107ff. (practiques respiratoires); see also Massignon, *Recueil de textes inédits concernant l'histoire de la mystique en pays d'Islam* (Paris, 1927), pp. 143–45.

4 Muḥammad b. 'Alī al-Sanūsī, *al-Salsabīl al-mu'īn fī tarā'iq al-arba'īn:* see Massignon, *Passion*, p. 342; *Recueil de textes*, pp. 169ff.

5 I.e. al-Gawth Muḥammad b. Khaṭīr al-Dīn al-Gujrātī; see Massignon, *Recueil de textes*, p. 169, n. 5.

6 *Recueil de textes*, pp. 95ff.

7 Ibn Ḥajar al-Asqalānī, *al-Durar al-kāmina fī a'yān al-m'a al-thāmina* (3 vols., Hyderabad, A.H. 1348–55/A.D. 1929–31), I, 16.

8 Ahmad Shams al-Dīn al-Aflakī, *Études d'hagiographie musulmane: Les Saints des derviches tourneurs*, tr. Clément Huart (2 vols., Paris, 1918–22), I, 224.

In June 1945 I attended a number of *dhikr* sessions of the Afghan order of the Čishtīya, both at Kabul and at Delhi. These sessions were accompanied by flute playing. The Persian verse which induced ecstasy was:

> ču resī bekūh Sīnā "arinī" negofte beguzar
> kih neyarzed īn tamannī bejawāb "lan tarānī"
>
> (If thou mountest to Sinai, say not [to God]
> "show me" [Thy face], but pass—for it is not
> fitting that to such a question thou hearest
> the answer "lan tarānī" [thou shalt not see me].)

This refers to Moses according to the Koran (Sūrah VII, verse 139) .

On the graves of the Turkish sect of the Bayrāmīya, we find engraved the syllable *Lā* surrounding three little *hā*s (no doubt vocalized as *hū, hā, hī,* as in the *qādirī dhikr,* i.e. the divine name *Huwa,* meaning He) .

Let us proceed now to the matter of the definitions. *Nafs* signifies in general the carnal soul or animal vitality. *Rūḥ* is more mysterious: God, angel, immaterial soul, allusion, spiritual meaning (cf. spirit, "essential perfume" of the flower, according to the Chinese and according to Boerhaave) .[9] *Rūḥ* establishes communication between man, angel, and God; according to Baqlī,[10] the angel drinks the tears of penitents and God drinks the tears of lovers. The colors of the "spirits," discerned in ecstasy, indicate a man's degree of "spiritual finish." In the Nocturnal Ascension, the soul of the Prophet, rising from the first to the seventh heaven, divests itself of its seven spiritual coverings, or *laṭā'if,* or *'anāṣir,*[11] as Ishtar cast off her tunics in descending to hell. In mystical Islam the soul is composed of concentric spheres. At first only three were counted: from the outside in, *nafs; qalb,* or *rūḥ,* seat of the wisdom (*ma'rifa*) which is obtained in dreams; and *sirr,* which is visited by the prophetic *'Aql,* and which is the seat of *Tawḥīd,* faith in the One God.

In my *Passion,*[12] I have given a list of definitions of the *rūḥ,*

9 Hermann Boerhaave (1668–1738) wrote extensively on chemistry.
10 Rūzbehān Baqlī: *Recueil de textes,* pp. 113f.
11 'Alī Ḥusayn Mahfūẓ, *Al-ibdā' fī maḍārr al-ibtidā'* (5th edn., Cairo, 1956, *Dār al-kitāb al-'arabī*) , p. 320.
12 Above, n. 1.

according to the canonists and theologians of Islam, from Muqātil and Jahm, Mālik, Shāfi'ī and Ibn Ḥanbal, down to the period when Hellenistic philosophy caused the old thesis that spirits were "subtle bodies" to be abandoned in favor of the belief (held most strongly since Suhrawardī Maqtūl) that the resurrection was only the liberation of the spirit from servitude to a corruptible body destined to nothingness.[13] Thus Muslim writers went from one extreme to the other, from the thesis of the materiality of souls (to explain the torments of the afterlife) to that of the pure immateriality of the human person.

In Islamic literature the soul, symbolically associated with water and blood, is generally represented by green birds (greenfinches) or, more precisely, the souls after death dwell in the gizzards of birds which fly around the throne of God (a very ancient idea).[14] They can be reincarnated without physical copulation if the breath of a saint is breathed into them (the *nefes-oghlu* of the Turkish legends).

And now, in conclusion, I shall cite a list of the chapters of one of the most interesting treatises on the spirit, the *Kitāb al-rūḥ* by Ibn Qayyim al-Jawzīyah (d. 1350),[15] a Ḥanbalite canonist: Is it permitted to visit the dead in their cemeteries? Meetings with the dead. Does the spirit die? Is it a substance or an accident? Is it tormented in the grave by its sins? Is it, while in the tomb, subject to questions asked by the two Angels? Where are the abodes of the spirits, the blessed, the damned? Did souls have existence anterior to bodies? (This the author, contrary to the majority of theologians, denies.) Is the soul threefold (cf. Aristotle) or one? What is the order of the "states" through which it passes in its gradual purification?

13 See also my *Recueil de textes*, p. 131 (Ibn Sab'īn).
14 Cf. the poet al-Tirimmāḥ, *Dīwān* (Beirut, 1900), No. 35, p. 156.
15 Muḥammad b. Abī Bakr, called Ibn Qayyim al-Jawzīyah, *Kitāb al-rūḥ* (3rd edn., Hyderabad, A.H. 1357/A.D. 1938).

Jean de Menasce

The Experience of the Spirit in Christian Mysticism

Noverim Te, noverim me.—St. Augustine

The present paper, representing a mere segment of an immense subject, is essentially theological in attitude. Some of my readers might have preferred a strictly psychological or descriptive (historical or anecdotal) treatment. Yet it seemed preferable to give an audience accustomed to the methods of psychology and familiar with mystical literature a theological analysis, consonant with experience, to which it is always subservient, and very different from purely phenomenological analysis, for which, however, I have the highest respect. In the course of the Congrès de Psychologie Religieuse,[1] held in the last years preceding the war at the convent of the Carmelite Fathers at Avon-Fontainebleau, psychologists of every shade discussed their methods and problems with a body of Christians specially devoted to the practice of the contemplative life and to the great traditions of St. Teresa and St. John of the Cross; theologians and philosophers did not disdain the collaboration of Orientalists eager to establish a synthesis between their points of view. The contact between disciplines differing not only in their object but in their methods as well proved fruitful. The following pages are inspired by certain of the papers read on those occasions and particularly by the communications of Jacques Maritain, Christian philosopher and theologian, a man thoroughly familiar both with psychology and the history of religion, and especially interested in their borderline problems. Since Eranos is eminently concerned with these problems, it seemed worth while to acquaint this audience with Maritain's ideas. Abjuring any super-

---

[1] Reports of the sessions were published in special numbers of the *Études Carmélitaines.*

ficial attempts at integration, I shall present them in their purity, trusting that no one will be misled by the apparent dogmatism of their tone.

For the Christian, any discussion of "spiritual experience" must involve a number of problems far beyond the sphere of psychology. First, the problem of terminology: Of what spirit are we speaking —of the spirit of man, of the divine person the Holy Spirit (Holy Ghost), of the spirit which God supernaturally infuses in man? These are three very distinct realities designated by a single term, scripturally consecrated by Pauline usage, and in its first and third meanings by the Old Testament.[2] But this real distinction cannot be applied automatically to a given scriptural text; and similarly, in speaking of spiritual experience, we cannot state *a priori* which "spirit" is operative. Moreover, since Christian experience consists in a contact with God, with the Triune God of revelation in Christ, under the influence of the Holy Spirit, the spirit of love, upon the highest and most spiritual region of the human soul; the person of the Holy Spirit, and this fruit of the spirit; and the created spirit itself which is the human locus and "subject" of the visitation—all three "spirits" must be embraced in any spiritual experience. Thus our initial distinction, though ontologically ineluctable, may well disappear when confronted by the unity and immediacy of experience.

Thus we shall not immediately seek this distinction in the experience itself. When, however, this experience is reflected in our mind, when it is to be interpreted or at least expressed, the distinction regains its clarity and force.

But what of those thinkers who look on Christian experience from outside and refuse to explain it through the realities which Christian faith considers basic? Then these realities become mere symbols, conceptual trappings, representing—but at the same time

2 On the interpretation of the Pauline *pneuma*, see primarily the voluminous excursus of Father Allo in his *Commentaire de la Première Epître aux Corinthiens* (2nd edn., Paris, 1935), pp. 87–115: "Is there an esoteric wisdom for the perfect? The pneuma and mystical Hellenism," which ends with these words: "Immense is the scope of these pages of the Apostle (I Cor. 1–4). In them is resolved the whole problem of the relations between profane culture and the knowledge of the supreme realities, the problem of intelligence, of grace, of the representative roles of reason and faith in the science of God— of Greek humanism and Christian supernaturalism."

masking—realities of an entirely different order, namely psychological or cosmological; but the value of the religious symbol, the change of register imposed on the object, still remains to be explained.

It is only the spiritual experience itself that will provide the *raison d'être* of this mechanism; it can be explained only by a postulate of an extrapsychological nature. To take the psychological disguise or transmutation as the point of departure or as the object to be investigated is to assume that the experience of the Spirit can be explained just as well without the Spirit as with it, the experience of Grace just as well without Grace as with it, that illusion or falsification is not relative to the truth, but perfectly equivalent to it.

The Christian for his part refuses to explain Christian experience without the reality that his faith reveals to him; he refuses to explain it as though an analysis purporting to be objective and experimental could benefit from a calculated indifference toward its object. Does it follow that, for the Christian, the experience, both in total content and detail, is uniformly and immediately adequate to its object? Does Christian realism deny that there is such a thing as a misleading symbolism?

Christian mystical experience constitutes a rich and complete totality and at the same time is conditioned by the complex mode proper to human knowledge, which, in its intuition of the divine, is encumbered not only with sensory images, usually charged with affectivity, but also with more or less impure judgments and ideas: thus on the road of man's spiritualization mysticism signifies progress accomplished by the purifying and elevating action of the Spirit. Far from demanding indifference to the Spirit in the critic, this sensory and intellectual, noetic and affective human conditioning of mystical experience necessitates a perpetual confrontation with the object perceived in all its nakedness; it necessitates an increasingly constant and immediate contact with the very first and undeniable reality, which is that of faith.

Any attempt to elucidate the symbolism of experience requires a new and more profound immersion in the higher mysteries. The psychologist who denies the reality of God can only do so by applying methods valid in psychology in the strict sense to the realm of the superconsciousness. He, too, must pass beyond the experience itself and, in order to explain it, must have recourse to the reality which it seeks behind the symbols. But seeking it everywhere else than in a sphere which absolutely transcends the human psyche, he must needs find it either in pure biological instinct, or in a social instinct regarded as the quasi-historical dictate of the collective unconscious imposed upon the individual, or in variable mixtures of these two factors. And these elements are far from meaningless in the eyes of the religious psychologist; he integrates them in his critique in the measure in which they correspond to reality—though, to be sure, he sets aside the conceptual implications which they evoke in those who regard them as the sole realities; and this he does all the more readily since, in his thirst for spiritual purity, he is eager to eliminate aberrations.

Thus the believer can judge the part played by this natural element without "reducing" it to something else or falsifying it; no other attitude, even one respectful of faith but not espousing it, can avoid such reduction, if only because its object is "bracketed."

Let us say at the outset that this principle governs the Christian critique of mystical experience outside Christianity: the Christian does not adopt *ad hoc* an astral indifference to the object, nor does he have recourse to psychological "reduction." But for him the object of non-Christian faith is absolute only by analogy; through the operation of the analogy, it is brought close to Christian revelation. Reduction there is, but of a respectful kind, according to "ontological analogy," and hence on the plane of the transcendent.

It must be admitted that a good many Christian writers, endeavoring to treat the history of religions objectively, forget both the exigencies of truth and the possibilities of analogy; such writers limit themselves to a purely descriptive method, which can, it is true, have a subtlety and sensibility of its own. Even the most hotheaded polemicists, in their passion for the truth, often come closer to the heart of the religion they are attacking and give us a more profound insight into it, precisely because, like those religions, they operate in the sphere of truth.

But one might ask whether this reflection on mystical experience is not calculated to falsify it: would it not be better simply to let the subject of divine inspiration speak for himself? Are his words

327

not sufficient unto themselves? But it so happens that "his words" raise the very first problem, that of expression. The manner of stating a mystical experience depends very much on the motive that leads one to speak of it. First of all, let us set aside pathological confession: a desire to speak of an experience in order to draw attention to oneself is one of the surest signs of the dubious character of the experience. Religious narcissism is by no means negligible: even where it is merely an aberration accompanying an authentic experience, it can vitiate the experience. At the other pole we find "prophetism," with which we need not concern ourselves here: a man relates his experience in support of the truth it embodies, in order to point the way to others by praising the wonders of God's work. And, beyond a doubt, every autobiography, every spiritual confession contains a certain element of this apostolic impetus. The profoundly individual and unique character of the experience does not mean that others are excluded from it, and its incommunicability does not prevent it from serving as an appeal. It is conceived then as transcending the individual; not, to be sure, as impersonal, but as charged with a presence which readily communicates itself. Yet the expression of such an experience implies a desire to go beyond it: to the experience itself the apostle prefers the content it embodies. The prophet states this content, and his experience, which he has made no attempt to preserve, escapes us. That is what makes so difficult the interpretation of certain texts, commonly classified among mystical works, in which preaching takes precedence over confession and hems it in with reasons, arguments, and conventions—all leading up to a theological analysis. And sometimes theology, by its very awkwardness, enables us to feel all the more clearly that the work in question is a confession and not a speculative synthesis. Yet it would be wrong to reject the basic inspiration because of the weakness of the discourse; or, conversely, to confirm the system as organically bound up with the experience.

The autobiographical description that concerns us here springs from an entirely different motive: the mystic speaks in order to attain clarity concerning the meaning of his experience. Here it is the content of the experience that interests him, and his own being is a part of it; but because of the immediacy and totality of

his experience and his own frailty, he feels a certain need of veri-
fication, a confirmation of its authenticity. As the Holy Spirit fills
the soul, it creates new capacities in the soul, but at the same
time puts it on its guard against any undue intrusion on the part
of the subject itself. How will this subject test and verify the
spirit with which it is possessed?[3]

The Holy Spirit in the Church acts upon souls both invisibly
and visibly, both from within and without. Not only is all doctrine
submitted to ecclesiastical authority which is preserved and guar-
anteed by a series of charismas culminating in papal infallibility,
but even the individual experience, which usually concerns only
the progress and salvation of a single soul, demands, as it approaches a high degree of intimacy with God, a test, a guarantee,
which is provided by what we might call the prudential wisdom
based on experience that has been entrusted to the Church in the
course of the centuries by the Holy Spirit. This test is obtained
through spiritual guidance, an institution private in character but
grounded in the priestly hierarchy. The autobiographical genre
among Christian mystics was developed in order to make possible
an informed and expert spiritual guidance. The privileged soul
writes at the request of his confessor, who must know the whole
life, every stage of development, all the depths of his penitent's
soul, if he wishes to help him recognize and hear the Holy Spirit
speaking within him.[4]

3 In this connection it would be valuable to reread in its entirety the Fourth
Relatio of St. Teresa of Avila, addressed to Father Rodrigo Alvarez about
1576. But here we may content ourselves with the following characteristic
passage: "She took extremely great care not to submit herself to anyone who
she thought would believe these things to be wholly of God, for she at once
began to fear that, if she did, the devil would deceive them both. When she
saw that any one of her directors had misgivings about her, she spoke to him
about her soul the more readily, although it distressed her when some, in
order to prove her, treated her experiences with scorn. For of these, she
believed, several certainly came from God; and she was no more pleased
when people condemned them out of hand without understanding them
than when they believed them to be wholly of God. She herself fully realized
that there might be delusion in them, for which reason she never felt
completely confident about a matter in which there might be danger" (Complete Works of St. Teresa, London, 1946, I, 324).

4 It should be noted that this need for a check and "proof of the spirits" is
not specifically Christian. It is bound to occur wherever the soul, aspiring
to a gratuitous contact with a transcendent reality—that is, a contact arrived
at without any supposedly infallible technique of a psychophysiological or

This circumstance explains the special character of the mystical writings in the Catholic Church and the psychology of its mystics. We have here a knowledge of the individual, a documentary and historical science, in which both details and general line are important, in which the symbolism is as significant as the vision it translates, the realities of daily action as essential as the sentiments they induce; but it is a science preoccupied with an end that must be realized progressively. This spiritual dynamism makes it a "practical" as well as a speculative science.[5]

Does this mean that this science never transcends the individual case? The works of the great mystics, who were also masters and theoreticians of the spiritual life, show that this is not the case. But, just as in the profane sphere pedagogy and medicine are at the root of our psychological knowledge, here practical preoccupations have provided speculative minds with their abundant materials. Even more than in the natural sciences, where, to be sure, technique was in certain periods the forerunner of pure science, in psychology, since the soul can be grasped only in its vital dynamism, in its activity, practice seems always to dominate theory. This is why some critics believe that Indian science, which is entirely oriented toward the psychic, is not strictly speaking a speculative science. Its concern with salvation excludes theory, proclaim both those who believe in the superiority of Indian over

---

magical character—is on guard against the delusions of the imagination or the artifices of pride; and these delusions and artifices are the more recognized and feared the more the soul is authentically favored from on high and called to spiritual purification. The critical spirit in these domains is not a discovery of modern psychopathology: the American Indian shaman who shuts himself up in his sweat bath and awaits a dream in answer to his question knows that he must not set stock in delusions provoked by an abnormal somatic excitement; similarly the Buddhist monk is on guard against the vanity he might draw from his charismas, which suffices to discredit him. But interesting comparisons might be drawn between the diverse modalities of spiritual guidance in the religions of grace. Yoga exercise also presupposes a guru, but its role is to transmit an infallible method, a technique of internal action, not to guide a subject through the unforeseen adventures to which God summons him.

5 See the nice distinctions made by Jacques Maritain, in discussing St. John of the Cross and the error of attempting to reduce his vocabulary of a "practitioner of contemplation" to that of theology, in *Les Degrés du savoir* (3rd edn., Paris, 1940), ch. VIII and Appendix VII. [Cf. English tr., *The Degrees of Knowledge*, tr. Bernard Wall and Margot R. Adamson, London, 1937.]

Western science and those who regard this attitude as the fundamental flaw in Indian science. The truth is more complex:[6] it is the very object of psychological knowledge that projects it into "centrifugal" modes. An understanding of the soul is achieved not only by scientific psychology but also by affective, sympathetic knowledge and poetic insight, whose expressive language serves to reveal the depths of personality. The knowledge of the lover and the poet is different—both greater and less—from that of the scientific psychologist (who, as a man, must be both poet and lover).[7]

6 See the discussion initiated by Olivier Lacombe in the appendix to *L'Ontologie du Védânta* by Père G. Dandoy (Paris, 1932) and Lacombe's *L'Absolu selon le Védânta* (Paris, 1937).

7 J. Maritain has outlined a classification of knowledge according to connaturality in a study that we shall cite at length further on, "L'Experience mystique naturelle et le vide," in *Quatre Essais sur l'esprit dans sa condition charnelle* (Paris, 1939), pp. 131–77. Let us say briefly that it is possible to distinguish types of knowledge through affective connaturality. For example, at one extreme of human activity, there is the type that is the core of prudential knowledge; at the other extreme there is the knowledge which on the plane of the supernatural connaturalizes the soul to the divinity under the impulse of charity. In this latter instance we have to do with "a supernatural contemplation that attains, through loving union and through a resonance in the subject—a resonance which has itself become a means of knowledge—to the divine reality that cannot be expressed in any created word." On the other hand, we must recognize the existence of a mode of intellectual connaturality which develops in a natural contemplation of God, though without becoming a fruitful experience, or which, on the contrary, by a kind of unnatural reversal culminates in that experience of the void in which the absolute of the Self is grasped. Finally, and still in line with the affective, there is the poetic, or creative knowledge, to which Maritain has devoted a work entitled *Frontières de la poésie* (Paris, 1930; Eng. tr., *Art and Scholasticism and the Frontiers of Poetry*, New York, 1962; see also his *Creative Intuition in Art and Poetry*, New York, Bollingen Series XXXV.1, 1953). The word "connaturality" implies a kind of proportion between subject and object, which influences the soul in its intellectual and affective functions by acting on its nature rather than on any specific faculty, but ultimately affects the latter. For greater clarity we shall quote the classical passage of St. Thomas on the gift of wisdom: "Wisdom denotes a certain rectitude of judgment according to the Eternal Law. Now rectitude of judgment is twofold: first, on account of perfect use of reason; second, on account of a certain connaturality with the matter about which one has to judge. Thus, about matters of chastity, a man after inquiring with his reason forms a right judgment, if he has learnt the science of morals; while he who has the habit of chastity judges of such matters by a kind of connaturality. Accordingly it belongs to the wisdom that it is an intellectual virtue to pronounce right judgment about Divine things after reason has made its inquiry, but it belongs to wisdom as a gift of the Holy Ghost to judge aright about them on account of connaturality with them; thus Dionysius says (*Div. Nom.* ii) that Hierotheus is perfect in Divine things, for he not only learns, but is patient of, Divine things. Now

The same is true in religious psychology: the connaturality of the saints to everything that pertains to the order of saintliness enables them to penetrate the secrets of a soul more surely, but more implicitly, than theory; nevertheless, in order to express this subtle knowledge, they sometimes employ a rustic theology and an awkward vocabulary.[8] Just so the artist, novelist, or poet expresses psychological processes through the images of his world—but also through the conceptions and theories current in his time or according to his own intellectual preferences—and he often may have recourse to a pseudo-science or a quasi-infantile metaphysics.

A man's testimony concerning himself is all the more subject to this imaginative and conceptual infiltration. To pursue the parallel, we may note here the distance that often separates the suggestive and almost creative psychology of the artist in his art, and his falsified view of himself and his neighbors in real life.

Never is this distinction between observation (turned outward) and reflection (turned inward) so manifest as in the life of grace. It accounts for the tension between the ineffable secret in the depth of the mystic's soul and the desperate need for total truth, security and solidity within this experience, which demands that the secret, in order to be pure, must be stated. The autobiographies imposed on them by their confessors are at once a torment and a deliverance: as God draws man into a wholly spiritual and immediate intimacy, man becomes aware that his soul is not as transparent

---

this sympathy or connaturality for Divine things is the result of charity, which unites us to God" (*Summa Theologica*, IIa–IIae q. 45, art. 2; tr. the Fathers of the English Dominican Province, New York, 1947, II, 1380).

8 Here we shall say nothing of expressive symbolism; the inductions of the psychologists who have concerned themselves with dreams and the subconscious can provide a basis for comparison, but a far more radical analysis of individual cases will still be necessary. Concerning the language of the mystics, numerous studies have appeared in the last few years in such magazines as *La Vie spirituelle, La Vida sobranatural, La Revue d'ascétique et de mystique,* and *Die Zeitschrift für Asketik und Mystik.* Especially significant are the brief notes of Louis Massignon, unfortunately scattered through numerous periodicals; for example, "L'Expérience mystique et les modes de stylisation littéraire" in *Chroniques du Roseau d'Or,* IV (Paris, 1927; now collected in *Opera Minora,* vol. 2, Beirut, 1963) and the *Essai sur les origines du lexique technique de la mystique musulmane* (2nd edn., Paris, 1954). See also J. Baruzi, "Introduction à des recherches sur le langage mystique," *Recherches Philosophiques* (Paris), I (1931–32), 66–82.

as he had thought but contains some element of his own mortal nature, of the ego that we are the last to know and to judge.

Is the confessor in a better position? First, he is "another," and thus has the advantage of disinterestedness. Moreover, as a scholar in the principles of a theology that increases in subtlety and sensitivity as it deals with higher things, he has at his disposal the experience of the Church and the tradition of the "practitioners" who have gone before him. No confessor, to be sure, even supported by the teaching and practice of the Church, can invoke total and complete experience, but the confessor can maintain the distance he requires in order to apply his knowledge. Besides, his priesthood has the mandate of the Church, and this is an inestimable source of confidence in him, by virtue of the community of faith that is the first and indispensable factor in connatural knowledge.

Does the question of the "observer" play a decisive role in the description of the mystical phenomenon, which we have taken so long in leading up to? Let us say that mystical experience, being intrinsically ineffable, cannot be described; yet description does take place. Hence the descriptive process requires an explanation of its own, taking into account above all the motives and modalities of the expression, as well as the conditions of observation. Moreover, it must be borne in mind that the mystical life, in its human and terrestrial condition, is essentially a progress. To study it in a person whose history is well known, without taking this law into account, and to draw comparisons between the visions, or descriptions of states of prayer, without taking into account their role in the individual development of the mystical life, is to expose oneself to all the hazards of the antihistorical comparativism from which religious ethnology has so fortunately escaped during the last third of a century. The spiritual life—and this is the opinion of all the masters—follows a general curve, whose objective, modalities, and tempo are governed by the divine will and whose general contours are laid down by the law of the Gospel; but it is conditioned also by the structure of man's being, not only as such but also in its present "wounded" condition. If we eliminate this dynamic factor, it is impossible to do justice either to the phenomenology of Christian mysticism or to its theology.

The mystical life of the Christian is a seizure of the soul by divine love, which dominates its spiritual faculties in accordance with a mode transcending the ordinary human horizon. The Gospel calls the experience of the divine "a life." Thus nothing would be more fallacious than to consider this experience independently of the process both total and progressive which is that of supernatural life, as though it were a "moment" to be captured. The moment has meaning only within the totality of this life, which is essentially a seizure, more and more profound and more and more actual, of the spiritual forces of the soul by the spirit of love.

Max Scheler's old distinction between *Wesensmystik* and *Vitalmystik* is here transcended: it is in the conceptual or imaginative elements, above all in the mode of expression, that these aspects are manifested; essentially, the mystical union by way of grace and the indwelling presence of the Holy Trinity can operate only on the plane of knowledge and love. That in the language of the theologians grace belongs rather to the mode of "nature" than to the mode of the "habitus," that, on the other hand, spiritual movements are in the highest degree vital, since they are under the gratuitous touch which raises them to the supernatural order, changes nothing in the essence of the phenomenon. Thus Scheler's distinction is shown to be superficial. All true mysticism is "vital"; all true mysticism is based upon an inspiration and a contact situated at a level far more profound than that of the faculties and functions. But it is nevertheless true that the key to Christian mysticism is the gift of love and that it is through the exigencies of divine charity that the process culminating in this experience of contact with the Persons of the divinity is realized, by virtue of a purification of the spirit which tends to make it in a sense transparent to itself. Hence it is by pursuing the dialectic of these exigencies that we shall come to know their fruit.

The "totalitarianism" of love requires an ever-increasing actualization: indifference, lethargy, not to mention the rupture of diversion, result more or less directly in spiritual death. The object of this love, being spirit, will require an increasing spiritualization, a fecundation on the plane of light. Finally, the love thus purified and illumined will be consummated in a union, the Beloved will reveal himself more and more in his very gift, as Himself given.

It is this culmination in love that defines the entire process and justifies the traditional classification of the three ways of the spiritual life, the purgative, the illuminative, and the unitive, provided we do not forget that with the very first movement of spiritual attraction love is already at work, pregnant, one might say, with unitive consummation in all the operations of purification and illumination. Here we are not concerned with tracing the first steps of spiritual life. Our precise object is to underline the actualization of the spiritual forces under the influence of the spirit of love.

Classical theology classifies, beside the supernatural habitus of virtue which we call infused virtues—moral and theological—special endowments which are called the gifts of the Holy Spirit.[9] Equally infused, they are distinguished from the virtues not by their object (the infused virtue of fortitude and the gift of fortitude have indeed the same object) but by the modality of action which they command: a gentler and also a surer action, which seems to be measured not by the norms of man, even of the man uplifted by grace, but by those of the Holy Spirit itself. It is as if, in order to enable us to exercise more freely, more connaturally, the infused virtues, and particularly the theological virtues whose object transcends the powers of any creature, the Spirit endowed us with special faculties which adapt us to its own mode, less by a spontaneity of action than by a kind of passivity, of sensitivity to its unforeseen touch, which is translated in our acts.

It is not surprising that, seen from without, the Catholic theology of the gifts of the Holy Spirit seems at first to be a construction arbitrarily built upon a poetic text of Isaiah (11:2–3). What is forgotten is the singular relevance of this text to the very subtle realities whose bearing on supernatural psychology no informed observer of the mystical life can deny. The spiritual "practitioner,"

9 Though we here follow the theological synthesis of St. Thomas Aquinas, we must nevertheless point out that on the one hand the gifts of the Holy Spirit have in the course of Catholic tradition been the object of very diverse syntheses and explanations (a summary of which may be found in the article "Dons du Saint Esprit," by Father A. Gardeil, in the *Dictionnaire de Théologie Catholique* of Vacant and Mangenot) , and on the other hand that St. Thomas himself did not formulate his definitive doctrine at the outset, since he notes a change of opinion between the writing of the *Ia-IIae* and of the *IIa-IIae*.

the confessor or spiritual guide, encounters these realities in their concrete form; the theologian of mysticism endeavors, by the light of revelation, to explicate them. Systematic thought, far from being detrimental to pure description, gives the observer a marvelous instrument of orientation, indispensable for the function entrusted to him by the Church. Hence it was the pressure of the mystical life itself and the need to analyze it better in order to serve it better that gave rise to the theology of the gifts of the Holy Ghost.

The mere notion of theological virtue does not indeed suffice to take into account the specific character of this life, this vital passivity, this service of pure love, formally diversified according to the modalities of human action toward God. It is impossible to penetrate the delicate interplay of the mystical life without noting the difference of modality which separates the gifts from the virtues, the subordination of the gifts to the theological virtues, the specificity of each of the gifts, finally the bond created between them by the gift of wisdom and charity.

With the help of these definitions we shall be able to find, at each stage of the mystical life, the more or less marked predominance of one or another of the gifts of the Holy Spirit—predominance by virtue of the essential bond which we encounter, as it were, at every step, and not exclusive sway.

At the outset we shall find the purgative life dominated by a fear of God, which will be neither a revulsion against the "taint" nor resentment against one's own weakness, nor malaise in the presence of a flaw in the macrocosmic or microcosmic harmony, but rather a vertigo induced by the mere possibility of a breach of the bond of love with God.[10] This fear is purified by the casting off of all temporal interests and all servility, and, like the works of the Spirit, it enlightens us both concerning itself and concerning our own nature. Here it is God in His terrible eminence who, even in His offer of love, exerts the attraction of the abyss; and even hope sharply reveals the fragility of the creature. The specificity of this fear is precisely that it emanates from the gift of love and increases with it: it presents itself as a gratuitous gift, by this

10 Such a notion of fear obviously presupposes on the one hand an exceedingly pure notion of divine transcendence and of the person of God, and on the other a strictly spiritual conception of sin.

fact very distinct from the sentiment of the "numinous," under which Rudolf Otto attempted to subsume very diverse emotional realities.[11] For the soul knows itself to be both infinitely distant from and mysteriously close to God, illumined as it is regarding its nothingness by a light which it does not possess by right or by nature, but by virtue of the love in which it is invited to participate.

In another sphere—our judgment on creatures—it is the function of the gift of knowledge to measure and in a sense to make us aware of the distance between creature and creator, thus supporting the transcendence of supernatural faith. It is in relating created beings to their proper causes, judged according to the spirit of God, that this delectable judgment knows them to be creatures. This is what distinguishes the exercise of the gift of knowledge from the exercise of the gift of wisdom, which sees the object of judgment only in things divine and acclimatizes the sanctified soul to the secrets of divine wisdom.

Is there a strictly ontological purification corresponding to this moral and affective spiritualization? Does the saint, through this loving fear, free himself from the bonds of flesh and blood in order to comprehend himself in the manner of a pure spirit? Is this the meaning of the worship in spirit and in truth that is the law of Christian mysticism?

The danger of "cosmism," which the early Christians incurred and which Christians will always incur in seeking a conceptual expression of their mystical experience, has recently been much discussed, here and elsewhere. Since in the natural order the spirit is superior to the body, will not this superiority, transposed to the plane of the supernatural, be augmented to the point of excluding any participation of the corporeal in the growth of the spiritual? The Beatific Vision, to be sure, will consist in a purely spiritual act, and earthly contemplation as it moves toward the Vision will divest itself of its sensory sheath in order to immerse itself in naked faith illumined only by supernatural charity. But just as

11 Here it may be briefly stated that in withdrawing the category of "the religious" from the ethical order with a view to establishing its specificity, Otto was compelled to integrate it in an order which, whatever his intentions may have been, could only be aesthetic. Thus he does not emerge from the impasse into which Schleiermacher led the philosophy of religion.

337

at the Last Judgment the bodies themselves, by a crowning miracle, will arise and enjoy a kind of overflow of beatitude, participating in a measure in the privileges of the spirit, though without ceasing to be real bodies, likewise, in the stage of preparations and progressions of which this earthly life consists, it is the order of the redeeming Incarnation which imprints its mode upon our Christian spirituality. Grace comes to us by the intercession of Christ and his humanity, which is raised above the angelic orders, as the author of the Epistle to the Hebrews reminds us. It is by virtue of grace that the angels become our brothers, once we, as well as they, are called to see God face to face, according to the degree of our charity and not according to the original nobility of our nature. Finally, just as we must pass through the sacrifice of the Incarnate Word on Calvary before we can penetrate the mysteries of the God of Grace, our own body plays a subordinate but very real role in the work of our spiritualization. Christian asceticism and the practice of the Christian virtues do not serve to liberate the soul from the body, but to purify love and direct it more fully toward God.

Thus there is no Manichaeaism in the Christian conception of the purification of the senses, but neither is there any illusion as to the effort exacted of man or as to the overwhelming character of God's acts. But in order to grasp the specificity of this purification we must note that it almost always induces a process of spiritual introversion and that the soul runs the risk of halting at this stage and delighting in it for its own sake. There is always a danger that the love of contemplation will compete with the love of the Beloved. I am not referring to vulgar satisfaction at having performed a spiritual feat, and even less to the vanity that made the Gnostics feel superior to the "psychics"; at the source of this pride there is the glitter of the soul captivated by its own beauty (since God is reflected in it) —this temptation to contemplate itself which marks both the essential spirituality of the human soul and the auto-opacity imposed upon it here below by its carnal state.[12]

12 "I readily believe that the various formulas of yoga may lead to all sorts of illusions and psychological extrapolations. But even the most blatant travesties can only be travesties of something authentic; and to me it does not seem possible to reduce to a psychological misunderstanding—which remains a misunderstanding, however respectfully one alludes to it—the age-old and

On this plane, the analysis of non-Christian mystics and of their methods has made it possible to explore, more successfully than before, the borderline regions between natural experience and the

---

multiform, yet ultimately concordant testimony of highly intelligent men who have sacrificed everything for a certain deliverance, men whom we have no reason to consider as sick or unbalanced. At least some of the more eminent personalities must have known a real and not illusory experience, regardless of what we may think of the epigoni and their repetitious verbalism or falsifications. I agree that it is good method to adduce causes sparingly, yet on the other hand let us not lightly reject all possible causes lest we neglect some actual data. And it is also a principle of good method not integrally to reject such confessions as we have discussed unless we are absolutely constrained to do so. It would be singularly unreasonable for us to deny to non-Christian mystics the rules of objectivity that we rightly insist on for the study of Christian mystics. What then do these men of whom we have been speaking say? They say that they have had an experience of the absolute. And what do they call this absolute? They call it *ātman,* that is, the *self.* I do not mean that these Hindu ascetics have achieved what I have just said to be metaphysically impossible, that is an actualization, however imperfect and partial, of the radical auto-intellection of the soul by itself. . . . What I am disposed to believe is, on the contrary, that they so divest themselves of all images, of all special perceptions and distinct operations that by an act, to be sure by an act that is negative and supremely silent, they in a measure reduce themselves, their souls and their intellects to that radical auto-intellection, though it is not actualized. In brief, the idea I wish to advance is that they attain not to the *essence* of their soul, but to its existence, the substantial *esse* itself; and how? By drastically purifying and pressing to its limit that ordinary experience of the existence of the self, of which we have just been speaking, which, situated in the realm of operations and acts, remained immersed in the phenomenal and veiled multiplicity of these operations and acts. Risking all for all, the soul, by a persevering exercise reversing the usual course of mental activity, absolutely divests itself of all separate operations and of all multiplicity, and knows negatively, through the void and the annihilation of all acts and all objects of thought coming from without— negatively but laid bare, free from veils—that metaphysical marvel, that absolute, that perfection of all acts and of all perfection that is existence— the substantial existence of the self. But thus to divest oneself of all images, does it not rather lead to the void pure and simple? In many cases, no doubt, when the operation in question fails and some random illusion is taken as a substitute for the authentic result that is lacking. But intrinsically such an operation, by the very fact that it departs from normal activity and the well nigh infinite universe of psychic multiplicity, and by this death exalts to an extraordinary degree the vitality of the soul and the intellect, must, it would seem, end in something very different from nothingness pure and simple, that is, in a negation, a void and an annihilation which are by no means nothingness. We should then have a negative and apophatic experience— I do not mean a dialectical and conceptual *via negationis* as with the philosophers, but a lived, aneidetic paraconceptual or supraconceptual *via negationis* —which no more attains (and if it did, it would not be negative) to an intuitive vision of the essence of the soul than supernatural mystical contemplation attains to the beatific vision, but which makes use of the void and of negation in order to know the unknown substantial existence of the

339

supernatural experience of the spirit.[13] As a historian of religions, I feel certain that we can derive profit from this increasing preoccupation on the part of theologians with these divergent mysticisms, which they ask us to examine with extreme perspicacity and attention to nuances and formal considerations. Thus comparative mysticism may emerge from the confusion which still, only too often, establishes a kind of parity and equivalence between phenomena as diverse as Sufism and the Upanishads, Neoplatonic ecstasy and the Transforming Union.

---

soul (which is the existence of the entire subject, for man exists by the existence of his soul), just as supernatural mystical contemplation makes use of the connaturality of love in order to know the unknown deity—*in finem nostrae cognitionis Deum tanquam ignotum cognoscimus*" (J. Maritain, *Quatre Essais*, pp. 155–58).

13 "What relation shall we establish between the *void* of natural mystic experience and the supernatural night of the spirit? First of all, it seems to me that the distinction made by St. John of the Cross between the night of the senses and the night of the spirit has not only a theological value, but also and even primarily, a philosophical one, I mean to say, a value based on the nature of man and on his twofold disproportion, on the one hand the disproportion between sense (imagination, sensory affectivity, discourse immersed in symbols) and spirit (in the purely metaphysical sense of the word), on the other hand the disproportion between the spirit and things divine (even disregarding the supernatural). But there is no correspondence nor parallel between the two nights of St. John of the Cross, which apply to certain painful phases of the completion and transfiguration of nature by grace, and the void of natural mystical experience, which is the necessary product of a movement contrary to nature. Whatever sufferings and terrors this void may induce, it does not go so far as the night of the spirit, which parches, disorganizes and in a sense 'destroys' the spirit (not physically to be sure, but in all its operative meaures and proportions and in its natural *élan vital*) in order to proportion it to the deity. For the void of natural mystical experience does not proportion the spirit to the supernatural, to God in His intimate life; moreover, it is induced by the spirit itself, by an effort of the spirit, and always remains intellectual, whereas the night is made by operative grace and by love, which can be as rigorous as hell itself. And it is not, like the night of the spirit, a phase of passage towards a better state (transforming union) but the very goal towards which we strive, since it is the formal means of obtaining experience of the self, and deliverance. And this void goes much farther than the night of the senses, for it 'destroys' the sense in order to proportion it to the spirit. It proportions the spirit to itself. It is like an excess and a paroxysm of a natural night of the senses, ordained to pass beyond the purification of the senses to a metaphysical death" (Maritain, *Quatre Essais*, pp. 169–71). In a preceding passage the same author notes that the advantage of distinctions is to permit a more precise analysis of complex cases—cases, for example, in which philosophical or theological contemplation is combined with mystical contemplation—and he very pertinently refers to St. Augustine, Ruysbroeck, and Boehme, to whom we should add Eckhart.

The gift best exercised by passive purification, both of the spirit and the senses, is the gift of fortitude. It enables the subject to resist calmly the devastating power of the Spirit, the spiritual annihilation to which God seems to subject man in the very moment when he most strives toward Him, renouncing the inner world after having renounced the outer world, renouncing his imagination and his own will. It is then that man most strongly feels his inability, known to him through experience, on the one hand to suppress in himself the radical obstacle that seems to separate him from God, to escape from himself, and on the other hand to take refuge in God, who pursues him with a love that is ineluctable and "strong as death."

The "violent" character of Christian asceticism thus reappears in Christian mysticism. But here it is not only reason illumined by charity that represses and dominates the flesh, it is the Spirit of God himself who seems to do violence to the spirit in order to bend it to its own modulations. And while asceticism of the senses has its natural limits in physical endurance varying according to the individual and the times, spiritual purification knows no limits other than those imposed by God himself, which He sometimes deigns to extend almost indefinitely. The trials of hope, even more than those of faith, show us what capacities of endurance and fidelity the Spirit can create within a soul, and how, even in this darkness governed by love, it can leave the marks of its essential gentleness.

The function of the gifts is precisely to adapt the soul to the divine mode which will enable the theological virtues to operate according to their full perfection despite the resistance specifically created by the character of obscurity, of absence, of difficulty, inherent in faith (certainty as to what has not yet been seen) and hope (certainty as to what is not yet possessed). These theological virtues sunder our limits and present something in the nature of a challenge to our intelligence and our love: the eminent but blinding perfection which they contribute makes more evident their nearly mortal exigence. The soul dies because it cannot die. Salvation can come only from Him who kills in order to create life. Thus the Cross drives its roots into the most spiritual regions of the Christian soul. The loving sacrifice of Christ who for us

341

"emptied himself," defines the scope of the Beatitudes; but the law of the Cross is subordinated to the law of the spirit, that is to the liberty of the spirit to take what direction it pleases. It would be naïve to hold rigidly to the itineraries—ways, stages, "mansions" —distinguished and described by the mystical doctors, as though they had meant to indicate a single road uniform in every detail. Abandonment to God, the human response to the divine will, can conform both to the violence and to the patience of God, precisely because it is based on the immense experience of the Christian past and of the ways of God.

We say that the law of the Cross applies even to the highest purification of the spirit. But a distinction must be made if we wish to avoid misunderstandings. Clearly we have here reached a plane on which love not only governs and sets limits to the soul aspiring to perfect union but still dominates it with increasing actuality. The fact that it has attained to a high degree of purification does not indeed exclude either imperfections or venial and unintended sins; but the suffering which then consumes it is no longer strictly and exclusively the suffering of contrition, of sorrow at its own transgressions. It is sin as such, sin in its devastating totality, borne by the one universal mediator, the sin which, though gratuitously, gained for us the redeeming Incarnation, which is at the base of the soul's sorrow. It is in taking upon itself the cross of its master and friend that the soul participates in this sin, in the measure that He permits. This suffering by way of compassion is no less poignant for being more diluted and internalized (but let us not forget the exceptional cases in which compassion goes so far as to imitate the Passion and identify itself with Christ), or for being entirely penetrated by love (but it is a love of "separation," as Louis Chardon[14] so magnificently phrased it).

To this suffering is added that which comes from the absence of the Beloved, that exile which is not the punishment of the sinner but the test of the friend, and which pertains to our present state. Nevertheless it becomes a part of the cross of the Christian,

---

14 *La Croix de Jésus,* by Louis Chardon, a Dominican of the 17th century, had been virtually forgotten until it was praised by Henri Bremond in his *Histoire littéraire du sentiment religieux en France* (6 vols., Paris, 1916–26), which inspired the new edition of P. F. Florand, O.P. (Paris, 1930).

who is never so pure that he can consider himself an innocent exile and who above all never forgets that the one Innocent, in order to redeem our sins, assumed this same state. It cannot be argued that the Muslim mystic[15] knows the sufferings of the forsaken friend, though he rejects the mediation of Calvary, or that Caitanya places at the summit of his dialectic of mystical love the fidelity, without hope of return and without guarantee, of the milkmaids enamored of the fickle Krishna.[16] Abstractly speaking, the suffering of separation and absence is indeed independent of sin. But concretely, whether we know it or not, we exist on the plane of the supernatural, and even for those unaware of the fall of man, the state of innocence no longer exists. Whenever these sufferings are authentically present—that is, when they are experienced and not poetically or theologically reconstructed on the basis of a dialectic of love (the whole charm of courtly love consists in transporting us fictitiously into an atmosphere of innocence)—they cannot be abstracted from the order of wounded nature. Thus they can very well be the effect of a light of grace and are in a measure an indication of this light.

Characteristic, finally, of these purifications and illuminations is the just estimation in which true mystics hold the charismatic touch of God. Faith, a direct but obscure apprehension, comes to us through the veils of language and symbols. As it purifies the soul, the Spirit grants it the power to penetrate these veils; not the Vision or revelation of new mysteries,[17] but the more delectable apprehension of the highest mysteries gives it something in the nature of a secondary light, a kind of illumination. This is the role that

15 See especially the study of Asín Palacios on Ibn Abbad of Ronda, one of the most striking representatives of the Shādilite school, in *Huellas de Islam* (Madrid, 1941), and the posthumous article of the same author, "Shādilíes y alumbrados," *Al Andalus* (Madrid), X (1945), fasc. 1.

16 Cf. Sukumar Chakravarti, *Caitanya et sa théorie de l'amour divin* (Paris, 1934).

17 Thus we do not agree with Father Joseph Maréchal that the experience of the great mystics follows the line of a spiritual seizure such as Christian tradition accords to Moses and St. Paul, which would amount to a fleeting foretaste of the beatific vision. It does not seem to us that the highest experience, despite all the light with which it may be endowed, pierces the vault of faith. Nevertheless, the *Studies in the Psychology of the Mystics* (tr. Alger Thorold, London, 1927) by Father Maréchal, is a mine of information and serious discussion of texts that it would be very wrong to neglect.

we ascribe to the gift of understanding: it does not, like intellectual and imaginative locutions and visions, bring more sensible lights. These subsidiary graces can lead to contemplation or provide an aura for contemplation. But the gifts of the Holy Spirit, and most particularly the intellectual gifts of knowledge and wisdom, serve to put these sensible constructions in their proper place. Estimable in their own right, as the Scriptures attest, these spiritual graces which we call sensible might easily provide the soul with a pretext for allowing itself to be drawn into the orbit of the sensible proper, or for relinquishing that forgetfulness of self necessary to the soul which should know itself only in God. Here spiritual guidance plays an eminent role: it must enable the soul to discern the meaning of these little sensible lights and at the same time safeguard the freedom of love, which concerns itself with the gift only for the sake of the giver. Here we have a touchstone by which impure mysticism is easily rejected, for in such mysticism the secondary tends to assume a disproportionate place and the preternatural takes precedence over the supernatural elements of faith and charity. The judgment of the gift of knowledge, on the other hand, dominates the created world with all the sublimity of divine reason. Thus it prepares the way for the insight of wisdom, which rises to the mysteries of God and then redescends to the expediencies of the divine work, and notably to the highest of them all, the plan of salvation which is the most perfect manifestation of increate love.

It is there that the soul, united with God in a union the stages of which mystical writers designate as spiritual betrothal and spiritual marriage, is fraternally reunited with those men who are included in the same divine *philanthropia*. Contemplation at its height is not distinguished by a nonactivity which immures it in solitude; it carries its cell inwardly. Contemplation and the love it inspires assume the dimensions of the heart of God, and the devouring desire of which St. Augustine speaks so eloquently in his commentary on the First Epistle of St. John shows that the soul, even while it consumes itself in solitude with pure love, is enlisted by the Beloved himself in the service of his friends.

Thus contemplation can overflow into apostolic life. The Church, inspired by the Spirit in the art of testing the very manifestations of the Spirit and preserving their purity, in order that the Spirit may be better known and better obeyed, is here, at the very summit of the perfection of the Christian soul, again the object of the solicitude of the Spirit.[18] For it is the Spirit which impels the soul to espouse its redeeming will and enlists it wholly in the service of the Church. This apostolic thirst which descends from on high to unite the contemplative with the evangelizing soul is a very visible and striking mark of true Christian mysticism. Arrived at the summit of contemplation, at the point where he knows himself least in himself and knows himself most in God, the Christian does not limit himself to training disciples who will continue his work in a quasi-esoteric tradition. To the day of their death the two Teresas retained the missionary aspirations of their childhood, and Mary of the Incarnation[19] after having been elevated to states of prayer (of which she wrote memorable descriptions closely approximating those described by St. Teresa of Avila), was to know the hardships of the missionary in the early Canadian colonies. As they see themselves in God, they see also the place which the Spirit assigns to them in the building of the Church.

Attaining to the very depths of God, the soul delights in the divine perfections and in the ineffable possession of the divine Persons who inhabit it. Beyond symbolic visions and the signs and ideas that serve it as interpreters, the soul feels an immediate contact with the Three Persons in their One Essence. This is at once an amorous and intellectual knowledge, of which a theologian, eminently versed in these matters, tells us that

> although the will does not formally illumine the intellect, nevertheless when the object is united with us by love, it is represented to the intellect in a new function. And in the case of union through love with things divine, the intelligence perceives that that which is experienced through love is higher and more excellent than any consideration of faith or any other cognitive virtue. Such an experience renders the object cognizable in a new way, that is, as united to the subject and experienced by it.[20]

18 It will be recalled that this was the aspect of the Christian mystics that most impressed Bergson in his *The Two Sources of Morality and Religion.*

19 In the course of our paper we have illustrated most of the stages of mystical experience described with passages from this great mystic of the 17th century, whose *Écrits spirituels et historiques* have been republished by Dom A. Jamet (Paris, 1929).

20 John of Saint Thomas (1589–1644), one of the greatest representatives of the

And the same writer, in the beginning of his highly technical treatise on the gifts, reminds us that the Scriptures, inspired by this same Spirit, call these gifts "spirits" because

> when the soul receives the Holy Spirit like the very breath of God, the Holy Spirit endows that soul with his gifts, kisses it like a spouse, and through the kiss of his mouth infuses his spirit in order that all the virtues of the soul should be made more perfect and elevated to a superior mode of operation. *Verbo Domini coeli parati sunt, et spiritu oris ejus omnis virtus eorum.* This breath from the mouth of the Lord, which confirms the virtues, is the spirit of the gifts that God communicates to us by his kiss, which is so efficacious when it is pressed upon a soul avid with celestial desires, that it breathes in and drinks, as it were, the breath of that soul and transports it into God, snatching it away so violently from terrestrial things that corporeal death sometimes results. Such a kiss has been experienced by all the saints who can say with St. Paul: *Sive mente excedimus, Deo, sive sobrii sumus, vobis.* Wherein the sobriety of the saints' actions toward their neighbors is contrasted with the excess and drunkenness of spirit that enabled them to enter into the powers of the Lord. It is here that we must seek the profound meaning of that very closed book of spiritual love, the Song of Solomon, which begins with the Lord's kiss: *Let him kiss me with the kisses of his mouth.* As though the loves of holy Church began where Moses began his life: *mortuus ab osculo Domini.* Indeed, when the Law given to Moses ends, the law of spiritual love begins with the kiss which is the Holy Spirit himself, emanating from the mouth of God, uniting the Father and the Son, and diffusing itself over the Church on the day of Pentecost and throughout the ages. The Church has been adjudged worthy of greater glory than Moses, and

---

Thomist school, whose treatise on the gifts of the Holy Spirit (*Cursus Theologicus in Iam-IIae,* vol. V of the first edn., Madrid, 1645) is authoritative. He has been excellently translated into French by Mme. Raissa Maritain (*Les Dons du Saint-Esprit,* Juvisy, 1930) ; the texts we have cited are on pp. 18–20. It was long meditation on his treatise on Grace that inspired the highly original work of Father A. Gardeil, *La Structure de l'âme et l'expérience mystique* (2 vols., Paris, 1927), opening perspectives which have been extended by Maritain and Oliver Lacombe in their study of non-Christian mystics (see the latter's study on Ramana Maharshi in "La Yogi indienne," *Études Carmélitaines,* Year 22:2 [October 1937], pp. 163–76, and the works mentioned above).

that is why the Lord Jesus sent his Spirit in such abundance that it was made drunk with it; so that, seeing the Apostles, many said mockingly: These men are full of new wine.

Friedrich Heiler

The Madonna as Religious Symbol

I

Of all the Madonnas I have seen, a majolica relief at the entrance to an old Franciscan hermitage near Assisi has left the strongest memory. The Madonna's white face shines out against a sky-blue background. In the evening, at the hour of the lucernarium, when the lights are lit, the Franciscan sisters in their gray habits appear and chant the old antiphonal prayer, *Salve Regina*. Their transfigured faces are turned toward Mary, their spiritual mother: girlish immature faces, grave mature faces, faces of peasants and faces of ladies—all contemplate the image of the Madonna. And as these devout women pray, the relief becomes more lifelike, more radiant and gentle; it ceases to be lifeless stone and becomes the transparency of a higher reality. I have seen many men and women praying to Madonnas, and I have seen many representations of the Blessed Virgin in churches and art galleries; I have heard many songs and hymns, but nowhere has the cult of the Madonna impressed me so forcefully as here. The union of religion and art, poetry and faith, simple humanity and supernal glory was manifested to me in this Madonna.

The cult of the Madonna has an immense power over men. When we enter a German cathedral in the month of May, we see the image of the Madonna wreathed in flowers and plants, ringed with candles. The church seems filled with all the radiance of spring. And out of the mouths of old and young, of men and women, the joyous song resounds: "Mary, queen of the May, we come to greet thee."

Another scene: In a high mountain shrine, a statue of the *Mater dolorosa* surmounts the altar. Before it kneels a poor, tormented peasant woman, praying for the life of her child. She prays to the mother of mercy, who best knows the joys and sufferings of a mother. She entreats her, trusting implicitly that the mother of God will understand her pain and help her: "Succour us in our fear and distress."

Another scene: A mother holds her little girl on her knees and tells her child the first story of the beloved mother of God. And the child's eyes light up as her mother tells her the secret of this mother who is the mother of all mothers. And the child prays after her mother: "Hail Mary, full of grace. . . ."

And still another: A group of hikers stop beside a stone Madonna in a green meadow, and break into the old pilgrims' song:

> Star of the sea, I greet thee,
> O Mary, help me. . . .

And the delicate melody fuses with the ardent love song:

> Beauteous, magnificent,
> Exalted and glorious,
> Lovely and blessed, celestial lady. . . .

In the singing of this song the boy's awe at the mystery of womanhood is mingled with the girl's chaste modesty and tenderness.

We stroll through the largest of the south German cities. Outside many citizens' houses and outside the royal residence as well, we see statues of the Madonna, often with a red lamp burning before them. On the city hall square, a tall column bears a stone statue of the Madonna with the inscription *Patrona Bavariae*.

When we visit the picture galleries of the great cities, her countenance greets us again and again. The greatest of artists have expended all their love and all their power in painting the mother of God as beautifully as they could: Fra Angelico, Fra Filippo Lippi, Raphael, Stephan Lochner, Dürer, Van Eyck, et al. People far removed from the Madonna cult and even from the Christian faith succumb to her spell in the presence of these paintings.

Like the great painters and sculptors, the great musicians have in their own way sung the praises of the mother of God: Durante, Cherubini, Liszt, and others have translated the grandiose hymns of the church into the language of music.

And the artists and musicians are joined by the poets: Syriac,

349

Greek, Latin, German. Among the authors of the innumerable hymns to the Madonna, the princes of poetry stand out: Dante, who at the end of his *Divine Comedy* intones the hymn *Vergine Madre;* Goethe, who in *Faust* puts the stirring prayer to the *Mater dolorosa* into the mouth of Gretchen, who in the end makes Doctor Marianus sing the praises of the *Mater gloriosa,* and who concludes this greatest of his dramas with the words of the *Chorus mysticus: "Das ewig Weibliche zieht uns hinan"* (The eternal womanly draws us upward).

And what the artists strove to express in colors, tones, and words, the greatest Christian theologians have made the object of their thinking and endeavored to formulate through theological concepts: Cyril of Alexandria, Ambrose, Augustine, Thomas Aquinas.

But not only religious life and theology, not only art and poetry —the simple daily life of the people is also saturated with the love of Mary. Countless women's names, names of places, animals, flowers bear witness to the Madonna's universal spell.

Even Protestantism was unable to tear the cult of the Madonna entirely from the hearts of men. Luther himself was one of Mary's greatest bards. In the interpretation of the *Magnificat* which he wrote on his way from Worms to the Wartburg, he advocated Virgin worship and pointed to its Biblical foundations. Year in, year out, he delivered sermons on the feast days of Mary, singing the praises of her who gave the world its Savior. In the evangelical creeds, the mother of God is exalted as *laudatissima, amplissimis honoribus dignissima;* it was in such superlatives that the early Lutherans spoke of the Lord's mother. Even more than Lutheran theologians, Protestant poets—Arndt, Körner, Novalis, Schenkendorf, Uhland, Geibel, et al.—have concerned themselves with the Virgin, a subject generally regarded as the domain of the Catholic church. Erich Bockemühl has compiled an interesting anthology of modern poets who, each in his own way, have sung the praises of Mary. And finally, the advocates of a "German faith" and "German Christianity"—men rooted in Protestantism—have striven to raise the Madonna cult to new honor. First of all Lagarde, who declared that rivers of blessing have flowed upon mankind from the image of the Madonna; and Max Jungnickel, who cried out after the war, "We must bring the German mother Mary back to the Protestant church." Recently Ernst Bergmann has proclaimed a heathen religious ideal, which he goes so far as to call a "mother religion." We may look upon the exaggerated paganism of this modern Madonna cult as a Protestant cry of yearning for the lost Catholic Virgin worship.

The cult of the Madonna is not a peculiarity of Catholic Christianity or of Christianity in general; it is universally human. Even such anti-Christian creeds as Bergmann's retain the Madonna cult. Detached from Christian history and dogma, the Madonna cult is not bound to any specific religion or ethnic group. The book of Acts tells how by his sermon in Ephesus, the center of the cult of Artemis, the Apostle Paul incurred the wrath of the population. Demetrius the silversmith incited the populace with the words: "So that not only this our craft is in danger to be set at nought; but also that the temple of the great goddess Diana should be despised, and her magnificence should be destroyed, whom all Asia and the world worshippeth" (Acts 19:27). The words of this silversmith are confirmed in the whole history of religion: in the Buddhist temples and dwellings of China and Japan we find the mother goddess Kuan-yin (Kwannon) with her child. She is praised in song and prayer as the helper, the savioress, the embodiment of all gentleness and mercy. In India, particularly in Bengal, the faithful call out in the temples to the great mother Śakti, Kālī-Durgā, and whatever other names she may bear. The epithets that we hear in the Chinese and Indian hymns to the Madonna sound like an echo of those known to us from the Western litany of Mary.

Going back into the earliest days of history, to the temples on the Euphrates, the Tigris, the Nile, and in Asia Minor, we encounter everywhere the figure of the mother goddess: among the Sumerians and Babylonians, the Egyptians and Phoenicians, the Phrygians and Greeks: Ninanasīanna, Ishtar, Isis, Atargatis, Rhea, Cybele, Artemis, etc. It was in all probability from the East that the cult of the mother goddess came to the old Germanic pantheon in the form of Woden's wife Frigg. In pre-Hispanic Mexico we find the same cult of Teteoinnan. And if we go back still farther to the primitive religions we find everywhere the mother goddesses, though in the crude, incomplete form of fetishes. *The Madonna belongs not to Christianity, but to all mankind.*

In view of the universality of the Madonna cult in the whole extra-Christian world, we may repeat the words of Tertullian: *Anima naturaliter christiana*—the soul is by nature Christian. Protestant critique expresses this insight conversely: *Anima naturaliter pagana*—the soul is naturally pagan, even in Catholic Christianity. For, indeed, all manner of pre-Christian ideas and motifs have been given new form in the Madonna cult of the Christian church. Comparison with pre-Christian religions reveals the Christian church as *haeres gentium*. The Virgin worshiped in the Christian church is clearly descended from the mother goddesses—*Maria haeres matrum dearum*. It is significant that in the year 431, a council of Christian bishops held in Ephesus, a city which for centuries had been a center of the mother goddess cult, gave Mary's title *Theotokos*, "mother of God," the force of dogma.

The resemblance between the Christian Madonna cult and the pre-Christian cult of the mother goddesses is not limited to concepts, but extends to forms and symbols as well. Consider the sheaf of grain in the hand of Spica Virgo, the starry mantle of Aphrodite Uranios, the dove of Ishtar—all symbols which were later attributed to Mary. Some feasts of Mary are celebrated on days which had formerly been dedicated to the great goddesses of antiquity—the Annunciation, for example, on the day of Cybele, the mother goddess of Asia Minor.

Between the Christian Madonna and the pre-Christian mother goddesses there is the same similarity as between Christ and the savior gods of antiquity. And the same difference. For Christian faith, Christ is infinitely more than all the savior gods of antiquity, and Mary Mother of God is more than all the mother goddesses of antiquity. Everything truly valuable and great in the pre-Christian savior and mother cults was taken over by the cults of Christ and the Madonna. The world-creating power of Śakti, the infinite gentleness and kindness of Kuan-yin, the love of Isis for her divine son Horus, Ishtar's maternal helpfulness—all these qualities reappear in the Christian Madonna cult. But just as the light of the ancient savior gods pales when we compare it with the radiance of the *Sol salutis,* Jesus Christ, so do the ancient mother goddesses pale before the mother of God. All non-Christian madonnas are more or less one-sided, fragmentary, distorted, while the Christian Madonna cult is universal, many-sided, harmonious, well-proportioned.

Another essential difference is that the Christian Madonna is not a mythical, but a historical, figure. True, she is wreathed about with symbolic legends, but her person is just as indubitably historical as that of Jesus of Nazareth. There is no doubt that the New Testament passages dealing with the mother of Jesus rest on eye-witness reports. Matthew's record clearly goes back to utterances of Joseph, Luke's to those of Mary herself, who "kept all these things and pondered them in her heart." But around this historical Mary, as pictured in the New Testament, all sorts of allegories, legends, and tales have been wound. Even the fourth gospel shows Mary as an allegorical figure, both at the marriage of Cana and under the Cross—as a symbolization of the Jewish or Christian congregation. The earliest Christian legends of Mary are recorded in the Protevangelium of James; they deal principally with Mary's childhood and other episodes not mentioned in the New Testament. In the Middle Ages these early Christian legends were amplified by Hroswitha of Gandersheim, Wernher of Tegernsee, Philip the Carthusian, etc. The New Testament's silences concerning Mary's life and the manner of her death were thus filled with miraculous tales.

While the legends sought to answer questions that arose in the Christian soul, Christian theologians logically deduced a mariological system from the idea of the Incarnation. And this image of the Madonna, fashioned of Scripture, legend, and theology, was colorfully presented in art and poetry.

The figure of the Christian Madonna has three different aspects: cosmic, specifically religious, and universally human. It may seem strange at first sight to many Western Christians to impute a cosmic function to the Virgin. Not so in the Christian Orient, where Mary is represented on icons as *Sophia,* celestial wisdom, whose world-creating function is set forth in the Old Testament books of wisdom. And, for that matter, Western Christianity has not quite lost the memory of this cosmic role. The lessons of the Roman church on the feast days of Mary are full of passages from Proverbs: *"Ab initio et ante saecula creata sum"* (I was set up from everlasting, from the beginning, or ever the earth was. Prov. 8:23). These words are spoken by Mary, Mother of God, here identified as wisdom. The theosophy of Jakob Boehme, Paracelsus,

Gichtel, Gottfried Arnold, and Swedenborg, and the new Russian Orthodox theology of Solov'ev, Bulgakov, Florenski, Karsavin, etc. have developed this motif—the world-creating power of Sophia-Mary. The celestial Sophia, the transcendent Mary, becomes the primal universal creature, the ideal personality of the cosmos, the virginity of nature in one undivided person, an all-in-one encompassing the glory and the beauty of the whole universe. This Sophia is brought into relation with the Trinity; sometimes she is even designated as a fourth hypostasis, through which nature partakes of the divine life, but which remains outside of the triune God. The Neoplatonists went so far as to designate Sophia as the "ideal" or "intelligible world." This Sophia is the created cosmic reflection of the eternal divine Logos through which, according to the Gospel of St. John, all things were made. The workings of the Logos-Christ are not limited to the Creation; they run through the whole history of man and particularly of his redemption; Sophia, wisdom, is his created reflection and participates in his action. It was the realization that Sophia participated in the work of the Logos, before the Logos was incarnated by the Virgin Mary, that led Christian theologians to find the Blessed Virgin concealed in the Old Testament. The burning bush, Aaron's rod, Gideon's dewy fleece, the closed gate in Ezekiel—Christian symbolism related all these to Mary. But just as the Logos-Christ was not perfect before his incarnation in the flesh, all these Old Testament references merely foreshadow the redemption of the New Testament. However, Christian faith in Christ is not limited to the incarnate Christ whose life is related in the New Testament; it embraces also the cosmic Christ who created the world and illumines all mankind. Mary-Sophia is in the same sense a universal, cosmic power. The center of Christ's action lies in the New Testament drama of redemption, but the way for this drama is paved by the faith and religious ideas of all pre-Christian mankind.

The Christian Madonna cult—and herein lies the ultimate and crucial difference between it and all non-Christian madonna cults —has its actual center in the mystery of incarnation. All those Christians who have never ceased to affirm the mystery of the Incarnation recognize the need to revere the Lord's mother. In this the Eastern church, the Roman church, and authentic Lutheranism are one. Calvinism has weakened the mystery of the Incarnation, made it more remote, and thus lost all feeling for the Madonna cult. Protestant hostility to the Madonna cult is not of Lutheran, but of Calvinist origin. By rejecting the mystery of the Incarnation as a Hellenistic myth, the neo-Protestants have created new hostility to the Madonna cult.

Incarnation means the becoming flesh, the descent of the infinite God into a human person in space and time, *hic et nunc*. In one man, the son of God become man, the "fullness of the godhead is made corporeal." "God is manifested in the flesh"—therein lies an immense paradox. But the *skandalon*, the stumbling block for human reason lies not so much in the descent of the infinite into the finite—in the Creation, God descended in just this way—what is strange and incomprehensible for modern man is the uniqueness, the "onceness," of the Incarnation, the idea that at one point in history the Godhead in all its fullness should have burst into the world and manifested itself really and corporeally in a finite individual. For Christian faith God's descent into the form of a man is something entirely real. In contrast to all kinds of Docetism, which seek to dissolve it in illusion and mythological fantasy, Christian faith professes with all its strength the reality of God's incarnation in a man. And what makes the Incarnation truly and tangibly real is that a human being, the mother of God, helped to effect it. The son of God did not himself create the body of his manifestation with his own supernatural power—this would have been the Hindu conception—but took his body from a real earthly mother, who conceived him, carried him, and bore him. The representations of the mysteries of Advent and Christmas in Christian art disclose the realism of the Christian conception of the Incarnation. Yet real as it is—this entrance of the infinite God into the finite world of space and time—it is and remains a mystery, intelligible only to the eye of faith.

The human contribution of the mother is purely passive. We may speak of an active passivity, in so far as Mary answers the angel of the Annunciation with her fiat: "Be it unto me according to thy word." But the generative power lies with God. Christ is conceived not of a man's seed but of the divine spirit. *"Et incarnatus est de Spiritu Sancto ex Maria virgine."* The Christian belief

355

in the Incarnation is thus compounded of the fullest realism and the most impenetrable mystery.

The conviction that the incarnate God cannot have been begotten by mortal man is deeply ingrained in the human consciousness. We find it among primitive peoples, where virgins are impregnated by demons. The saviors of the North American Indians were held to have been born of virgins. The Babylonians and Egyptians believed their kings to be the fruit of a queen's union with a god. Greek heroes, such as Heracles, philosophers such as Pythagoras and Plato, rulers such as Alexander and Augustus were looked upon as demigods born of virgins. Gautama Buddha was held to have been conceived without earthly father. Kabir, the Indian saint, was conceived when the God Rāmānanda saluted his mother. Rāmakrishna was conceived while his father was on a pilgrimage. And these are only a few examples of the virgin birth of demigods. For Christian faith all these notions are mythological precursors, types, anticipations of the mystery enacted in Mary's womb at Nazareth and in Bethlehem made manifest to the world. *Theotokos* (she who gave birth to God), the dogmatic title which the Council of Ephesus conferred upon the Virgin, epitomizes the part played in the mystery of the Incarnation by Mary mother of Jesus as created co-author of man's salvation. It also embodies the immense paradox of this mystery, so eloquently expressed by early Christian theologians. "The genetrix bore her begetter, the creature her creator." "He who was from eternity, descended into the Virgin, the creator of the world was conceived by the Virgin; he who is older than creation was born as a child." The mother of God is "the vessel that was found worthy to contain him whom heaven and earth cannot contain because of the vastness of his glory." "She gave the paltry cloak of the flesh to him who clothes all things," "nourishment to him who nourishes all; at her breast sucked he who governs the stars." This idea appears in countless variations, in theological disquisitions as well as simple Marian hymns.

The belief that Mary was found worthy to be the mother of God implies that she was prepared in body and soul to receive and transmit this mystery. The creature from whom the infinite received flesh must have been a special vessel of grace. The holy one could make his dwelling on earth only in a true temple; that is why Mary is considered *gratia plena*. Thomas Aquinas says: "Mary received such a fullness of grace that she was nearest of all to the author of grace."[1]

From the doctrine of the Incarnation the Christian mind derived a number of secondary dogmas or theologoumena. The first of these is the Immaculate Conception, the principle that Mary was conceived free from original sin. If the Old Testament prophets and John the precursor of Christ were "hallowed in the womb," it goes without saying that the mother of God must have been free from all personal as well as hereditary sin. The belief that Mary, while still in the womb, was purified and hallowed by the Holy Ghost goes back to the old Church Fathers. "As in the Lord there was no stain, so in the mother there was no taint." In the Middle Ages, a theological dispute arose on the question. The Dominicans sustained that Mary was cleansed of original sin in her mother's womb, the Franciscans that she was free of it from the very first moment of her existence. Luther followed the Franciscan school when he wrote that "when the soul was infused in her, Mary was at once cleansed of original sin and adorned with God's gifts. . . . From the first moment in which she began to live, she was without sin." The controversy continued for centuries and was ended in 1854 by Pope Pius IX, who made the Franciscan view the official dogma.

The second conception which Christian thinkers derived from Mary's part in the Incarnation is that of her eternal virginity. Mary is ἀειπάρθενος, *semper virgo*. The Christians shared with antiquity the belief that virginity made possible a particular closeness to God. At least temporary, and often permanent, abstinence was required of those who approached God in the sanctuary. In line with the ascetic, monastic ideal of early Christianity, Mary was looked upon as a model of virginal, contemplative life. An early Christian legend has it that before her marriage she was a temple virgin in Jerusalem and that she fed on manna brought her by the angels. In the early Christian view, Mary remained physically a virgin after giving birth. There is even a crude legend about a midwife who, doubting this miracle, stretched forth her

1 *Summa Theologica*, III, q. 27, art. 5, ad. 1.

hand to touch her and was punished for her disbelief with the paralysis of her hand, which, however, was cured by contact with the swaddling clothes of the divine child. Ephraim strove to express the miracle of Mary's virginity in images:

> The nature of the Virgin was not unsealed when Christ was conceived. And consequently it was not opened when he was born. The womb of the woman in childbirth did not tear. . . . Consequently the child did not impair the seal of virginity nor did the Virgin feel pain. She was indeed opened by the physical mass of the child on his way into the world, but she returned to her sealed condition just as the shells of an oyster, after discharging their pearls, return again to their sealed unbroken union.

And Christian symbolism called on a number of Old Testament images to represent the miracle of Mary's virginity. Thus, for example, Mary is the *ianua clausa,* the closed gate of which Ezekiel prophesies: "This gate shall be shut, it shall not be opened, and no man shall enter in by it; because the Lord, the God of Israel, hath entered in by it, therefore it shall be shut" (Ezek. 44:2).

The dignity of the Mother of God required that she remain a virgin after giving birth; this was the doctrine of *virginitas post partum.* After the birth of the divine child, it was not fitting that the bride of the Holy Ghost should give herself to any mortal man. The older tradition, according to which Mary was merely *adhuc virgo,* i.e. remained a virgin up to the birth of Christ and then became Joseph's wife, gave way to the doctrine of her lasting virginity. In her quality of permanent virgin and ascetic, she became the model of the ascetics of the first Christian centuries. Christians saw in her an ideal of virginity free from the harshness that so often accompanies man's struggle against his natural impulses. In the figure of Mary, the celibate ideal was diffused with a womanly mildness, the terrible earnestness of man's battle with the flesh was alleviated, the hard ascetic ideal was made to seem simple and natural. Model of purity and virginity, Mary was also looked upon as prototype of all the virtues, of humility and piety, poverty and self-sacrifice. Her life was seen as a compendium of Christian perfection, an inexhaustible theme of meditation—*"per-*

fecta virtus et abundantia gratiae," perfect virtue and abundance of grace, as Thomas Aquinas said.[2]

According to the Christian theologians, Mary's function as mother of God included a participation in her son's labors of redemption. In this connection some of them gave her the misleading title *co-redemptrix*. This participation is not limited to the birth of her son, but also includes his death on the Cross. She partook of his sufferings and his death, though even more passively than of his conception and birth. As *Mater dolorosa* she stood beneath the Cross, sharing in her son's profound physical and mental pain.

> Stabat mater dolorosa
> iuxta crucem lacrimosa,
>   dum pendebat Filius.
> Cuius animam gementem,
> contristatam et dolentem,
>   pertransivit gladius.

(The sorrowful mother stood weeping by the Cross where hung the Son. She sighed in grief and anguish, and the sword pierced her heart.)

Another conception derived by Christian theologians from the dogma of the Incarnation is that of Mary's Assumption. The body from which the son of God took flesh could not be given over to corruption. If Enoch, Elijah, and the Apostle John rose up to heaven in the flesh, surely the Savior's mother must be taken up bodily to heaven. This theological inference found its symbolic expression in the legend of the *Dormitio*. At Mary's death all the apostles are gathered in her house; they bury her, but when they visit her grave next day, they find it as empty as the holy women had found the Lord's tomb at Jerusalem.

This is the dogmatic picture of the Blessed Virgin, as woven of Biblical tradition, theological inference, and legendary fantasy. However, it is not the whole picture but only a part of the Christian Madonna—the essential part, in so far as the Christian Madonna cult is nothing more than an emanation of the doctrine of the Incarnation. To the Madonna cult these words are essential:

---

[2] *Summa Theologica*, III, q. 27, art. 3, ad. 2.

Per Mariam ad Jesum—through Mary to Jesus, the incarnate son of God, who gives to the Madonna cult its true meaning. The dogma of the Virgin is indissolubly bound up with the dogma of the son of God. Few have expressed this bond so simply and movingly as Francis of Assisi in his invocation to the Virgin:

> Hail, holy Lady! most holy Queen! Mother of God! Mary! thou art ever-Virgin, elected by the most Holy Father of Heaven, consecrated by His most holy and beloved Son, and by the Holy Ghost, the Paraclete; in thee is and was the plenitude of all grace and all good! Hail, palace of God, His tabernacle, His Mother![3]

II

The image of the Christian Madonna, woven of history, theology, legend, and artistic imagination, has two principal aspects: one dogmatic, the other universally human. In her dogmatic aspect, she is the mother of God, as such participating in Christ's world of redemption, the created co-author of redemption; she is known as *gratia plena,* full of grace, the woman conceived without sin, the eternal virgin, who was taken up bodily to heaven, where she reigns as queen of the angels and the saints. This dogmatic aspect of the Madonna cult has attained its clearest expression in liturgy and hymnody. The antiphon in the liturgy of St. John Chrysostom can be regarded as a compendium of this dogmatic view: "Meet indeed it is to bless thee, Mother of God, ever blessed and most sinless Mother of our God. Honored above the Cherubim, infinitely more glorious than the Seraphim, who didst bear God the Word without stain. Mother of God in truth, thee we magnify."[4]

But to Catholics Mary is not merely a religious figure of the past, an object of theological speculation; she is always present in their hearts as *mater misericordiae,* mother of mercy, the universal mother, interceding for mankind, interceding above all for sinners, in the hour of death and judgment. Christ appears as embodiment of God's stern justice, the apocalyptic rider astride a white horse, bearing a sword in his mouth. To this Christ, in the popular

3 *Works of . . . St. Francis of Assisi,* tr. a Religious of the Order (2d edn., London, 1890) , p. 167.
4 *The Divine Liturgy of . . . St. John Chrysostom,* ed. Placid de Meester, tr. the Benedictines of Stanbrook (London, 1926) , p. 69.

Catholic imagination, is opposed his mother Mary as embodiment of gentleness and mercy. She pleads with her son, who has already stretched forth his hand in judgment and condemnation; she points to her maternal breast and entreats him to forgive the sinner. And the son's heart is softened, the sinner attains to grace through her intercession. She is the great *refugium peccatorum*. In late medieval art, the Madonna is often represented with a great blue robe; beneath it she shelters and protects popes and emperors, bishops and monks, nobles and commoners. All feel safe in her care, confident that she will shield them from God's wrath on the day of judgment.

There are countless medieval legends celebrating the miraculous power of Mary's loving intercession. A characteristic example is the story of Theophilus, told by Hroswitha of Gandersheim in Latin verses; it is one of the sources of the Faust legend. Theophilus, the nephew of a Sicilian bishop, is elected bishop, but does not accept. Another bishop cheats him of his office as Vicedominus (acting bishop). In grief and envy Theophilus makes a pact with the devil, renounces Christ and Mary, and makes over his soul to the devil on condition that he may retain his post. On the following morning he is reinstated. But now he is assailed by terrible pangs of conscience. His only refuge seems to be in the Blessed Virgin. For forty days and nights he weeps and fasts in the church of Mary. And then the mother of God appears to him, saying: "The power of my motherly love has led me hither." He confesses his sin, and she promises him forgiveness and help. Three days later he awakens, holding in his hands the text of his pact with the devil. He goes into the church and publicly confesses his sin. The document is solemnly burned; but he himself falls sick and after three days dies in peace. The legend concludes with the words: "Through sin our mortal brother was lost. But being lost, he returned to life through thee, O holy Virgin."[5]

In popular Catholic belief, Mary is the sinner's advocate, succoring man in his last hour; the powers of hell do their utmost to ensnare his soul, but in his torment and anguish he finds peace with her. Peter Rosegger tells a true story from his homeland: A peasant is lying on his deathbed. The prayers of those with him

[5] *Hrotsvithae Opera*, ed. Paul de Winterfeld (Scriptores Rerum Germanicarum, Berlin, 1902), pp. 63ff.

are so full of the terrible severity of God's judgment that they only increase his terror of death. But when the name of Mary is mentioned, a wonderful peace descends on his features; death loses its terrors and hand in hand with the Mother of God he passes through the dark gate to eternity. The medieval prayers to the Virgin gave particular emphasis to her quality of helper in man's hour of death. One of the oldest German Marian songs runs:

Fraue, deinen Händen
befohlen sei mein Ende,
und geruhe mich zu leiten
und mich zu erlösen
aus der grossen Not,
wenn der leidige Tod
bei mir will scheiden
den Leib von der Seele.
In der grossen Angst
komme mir zu Trost
und hilf, dass meine Seele
werde zu Teil
den lieben Engeln Gottes
und nicht den bösen Teufeln,
dass sie mich dorthin bringen,
da ich müsse finden
die ewiglichen Freuden
die da haben im Himmel
die viel seligen Gotteskind,
die dazu erwählet sind.

(Lady, to thy hands I entrust my end; I pray thee guide me and redeem me from deep distress when cruel death comes to part my body from my soul. Comfort me in my great fear and help me, that my soul may be taken by the beloved angels of God and not by the evil devils; that they may bear me heavenward to find the eternal joys which are the part of those blessed children of God who are chosen.—*Arnsteiner Marienlied*)

It is largely against this conception of Mary as the mild and gentle advocate, entreating forgiveness and redemption for sinners, that the protest of the Reformers is directed. Luther thought it a dishonor to Christ to represent him solely as judge and not also as redeemer, and to look upon his mother as the sole embodiment of love and forgiveness. He considered this attitude an offense against the God who is love and who gave himself on the Cross. Such criticism combines the true with the false. It is true that this conception of Mary as advocate would be un-Christian if it negated God's love. But this is not the case, since Mary is nothing other than the created reflection of eternal divine love. Ultimately, the love with which Mary as advocate mollifies the stern judge is God's own love, by which he permits himself to be conquered. The whole conception is merely an anthropomorphic attempt at a popular embodiment of the polarity and coincidence of divine grace and divine judgment. The God proclaimed in the Old and New Testament is the unity of ὀργή and ἀγάπη, justice and mercy. Man can express this unity of opposites only in very imperfect images, only by recourse to a duality. In the New Testament we also have this duality: on the one hand the wrathful God, on the other Christ the Redeemer, who by his death atones for the sins of mankind and by his sacrifice appeases his father's anger. Luther's criticism would equally apply to the New Testament doctrine of Atonement. But if the image of Mary as advocate is not absolutized but is taken for what it is, a childlike attempt to concretize the fundamental Christian mystery of God's wrathful judgment and forgiving love, there can be no objection to it. Just because the language of the Pauline epistles is not intelligible to many of the simple folk, church pedagogy ascribes a particular importance to this double image of Christ the judge and Mary the gentle advocate.

To the popular Catholic mind, Mary as advocate is not only a saver of souls but also a helper in all the big and little trials of the day: poverty, sickness, hunger, childlessness, imprisonment, persecution. The popular Catholic mind has produced its fairest flowers in its simple prayers to Mary as helper. Prayer to the Mother of God is a true outpouring of the heart. She is truly a mother and understands the distress of her children. The places of pilgrimage, with their miraculous images of the Madonna, bear witness to this simple faith. Wax hands, feet, eyes, etc. attest the curative power of the Virgin as advocate; wax animals show that her efficacy extends even to the animal world. Gold and silver hearts suggest that she fulfills the secret desires of lovers. The votive tablets read: Mary has helped us; Mary is helping us; Mary will help us. Votive offerings, candles and other objects, are donated at these shrines; the faithful promise to undertake pilgrimages or to build churches in order that the Mother of God may hear their prayers. An immense power resides in the pilgrim's faith in the Mother of God.

Yet it is not through her own power that Mary helps and cures; it is solely through her interceding prayer, her appeal to the might and love of the eternal God. Because she stands close to God, she can ask anything of him. This is what makes her an "all-powerful advocate" in the eyes of the faithful.

This belief in Mary's helpfulness amplifies her motherhood. She is "the mother of God and men." The early Christians used the father symbol in their invocation of the divine. Other religions prefer the mother symbol. Often the two are combined and the godhead designated as father-mother. It was doubtless one-sided of the Jews and early Christians to designate the divine exclusively by male symbols: king, lord, father. This deficiency was soon made good by the application of the mother symbol to Mary. In a certain sense it is surely more fitting to apply the term "mother" to the person who stands closest to God than to God himself. The father is absolute omnipotence; the mother has the relative omnipotence of the advocate. In prayers to the Virgin we encounter time and time again this invocation of Mary's universal motherhood. "Thou art called mother and mother thou art," says one of the oldest German prayers. And in a widely sung Catholic folk song: "Thou art the mother, I would be thy child, in life and death solely thine."

This universal motherhood of Mary is closely related to the motherhood of the Church. In early Christian art, we often do not know whether a woman in prayer is Mary, the Church, or merely an anonymous woman. Mariology and ecclesiology constantly overlap. And here the cosmic aspect of Maria-Sophia comes to the fore. "The church is nothing other than a Christianized cosmos," says Karsavin, the Russian Orthodox theologian. "Just as Christ was individualized in Jesus, so was the Church individualized in the Virgin Mary, mother of Jesus in her loveliness." The childlike love of Catholics for Mother Church is closely bound up with their love of Mary, Mother of God. Both imply the same feeling of security in the wisdom and love of a great spiritual mother.

But faith in the advocacy and the loving motherhood of Mary is far from exhausting the universally human aspect of the Christian Madonna cult. Mary appears as the prototype not only of succoring love but also of pure love—*Minne*. Here this old German word, referring explicitly to the confluence of *eros* and *agape*, seems most appropriate. Mary is called *Mater pulchri amoris*, Mother of beautiful *Minne*, the source of all pure love. In the *Stabat Mater* she is praised as *fons amoris*, fountain of love. One of the greatest visionaries of the German Middle Ages, Mechtilde of Magdeburg, makes Mary speak as follows in her *Fliessendes Licht der Gottheit* (Flowing Light of the Godhead):

> When our Father's joy was darkened by Adam's fall, so that He was enangered, the everlasting wisdom of Almighty God was provoked. Then the Father chose me as bride that He might have something to love; because His noble bride the soul was dead. Then the son chose me as mother and the Holy Spirit received me as friend. Then was I alone the bride of the Holy Trinity.[6]

Before the fall, the human soul was the bride of God. After Adam's fall from grace, God's only human bride was the immaculate Virgin Sophia-Mary. The lessons for the feast days of Mary are taken from the Song of Songs as well as Proverbs. The glowing sensuous colors and images of this Jewish epithalamium have become symbols of the purely spiritual love between Sophia-Mary and the eternal Godhead. Here again we see the suprahistorical, cosmic character of Mary. Another medieval mystic, Heinrich Suso, says in a prayer to the Virgin: "Thou canst well say: 'My beloved is mine, and I am His!' Ah, thou art God's, and He is thine, and ye two form an eternal, infinite play of love, which no duality can ever separate!"[7]

And Mary is not only a model of pure love; she is also its object. The courtly love poetry of the Middle Ages was closely bound up

---

6 Mechtilde of Magdeburg, *Revelations*, tr. Lucy Menzies (London, 1953), p. 13.
7 Suso, *Little Book of Eternal Wisdom. . .* , tr. James M. Clark (London, 1953), p. 113.

with the Madonna cult. It began as a deification of woman. Woman became the object of a purely spiritual, contemplative love, her lover's *summum bonum,* a symbol of the divine, an incarnate divinity. In this secular deification of women the Church saw a danger, which it sought to avert by directing the spiritual love of woman as vehicle of the divine toward the Mother of God, the Blessed Virgin. Chivalric love was guided into the channel of the Madonna cult; it was hoped that the hymn to Mary would replace the love song. And, indeed, some of the Provençal troubadours, under pressure from the Church, chose Mary as their heavenly beloved in place of an earthly woman.

This spiritual love took on a still stronger religious note in Suso, the courtly mystic. His biographer, Elsbeth Stagel, gives a moving account of Suso's spiritual courtship: It was the custom in his country for the young men to stand outside their beloved's window on New Year's night and sing until she gave them a little wreath. "This custom so appealed to his youthful, loving heart that when he heard of it he went that very same night to his eternal beloved and besought a pledge of love. Before daybreak he went to the statue of the immaculate mother, holding her tender child, beautiful, eternal Wisdom, in her arms and pressing it to her heart; he knelt down and began in sweet, gentle tones to sing a sequence, until the mother granted him a wreath from her child. . . . When summer came and the tender little flowers opened, he picked not a one, before he had dedicated his first flower to his spiritual love, the tender, flowery, rosy maid, God's mother. When it seemed to him that the time had come, he picked the flowers with loving thoughts and carried them to his cell and to the chapel of our Lady and knelt humbly down before our beloved Lady and set the wreath of love upon her statue, in the thought that she would not despise the first flowers offered by her servant, for she herself was the fairest flower of all, the summer's joy of his heart."[8]

This spiritual courtship of the Madonna survives in Catholicism and has found its expression in hymns. One of the most popular of German hymns to the Virgin is an emanation of that metaphysical love:

8 Elsbeth Stagel, *The Life of Blessed Heinrich Suso by Himself,* tr. Thomas Francis Knox (2d edn., London, 1913), pp. 29ff.

> Wunderschön prächtige
> Hohe und Mächtige,
> Liebreich holdselige,
> himmlische Frau,
> welcher ich ewiglich
> kindlich verbinde mich,
> ja, auch mit Leib und Seel
> gänzlich vertrau.
> Billig mein Leben,
> alles daneben,
> alles, ja alles, was immer ich bin,
> geb ich, Maria, mit Freuden dir hin.

(Splendid and beautiful, exalted and mighty, loving and gracious, heavenly Lady, to whom childlike I pledge myself forever, to whom I entrust myself wholly, with body and soul. Worthless my life, all else, yea all else, whatever I may be, I joyfully give thee, Mary.)

And the Catholic poet Friedrich Wilhelm Weber sings:

> O du eine, o du reine,
> die ich minne, die ich meine,
> Königin in Himmelssaal,
> hochgebenedeite Fraue,
> der ich ganz mein Herz vertraue:
> sei gegrüsset tausendmal.

(O thou unique, thou pure one, whom I love, queen in the heavenly halls, most blessed lady, to whom I entrust my heart: Hail and a thousand times hail.)

Mary is mother and beloved of the human soul as of the eternal God. She does not remain sublimely distant, to be approached only with trepidation; she comes close to the believer. Just as Christ is not only the historical Jesus who lived two thousand years ago, nor only the mediator, God the Son, sitting at his Father's right hand, but also takes his place in the soul of every Christian so that the Christian himself becomes an "abode of Christ," so likewise Mary is not only the mother of Jesus, not only the eternal *advocata* and *regina coeli* but also lives in the Christian's soul. The Christian soul identifies itself with the Mother of God; in it Christ is forever born anew. One of the medieval mystics, Heinrich von Nördlingen, wrote to his penitent the Dominican Margareta Ebner:

"Open the earth of thine heart and bear to thyself and us the Savior, to grow from thee and blossom and bear new fruit; bear him gently and silently in great pleasure and great joy, in blessed peace and without pain, as Mary bore him."[9] For these mystics, Christ was not born just once in Bethlehem, but is born again and again in every pure soul. To the German mystic this birth of God in the soul is even more important than the birth of God's son in Bethlehem. Meister Eckhart says:

> I say that if Mary had not first given birth to God spiritually, He would never have been born of her physically. A lady once said to our Lord: "Blessed is the womb that bare thee." Then our Lord said: "Not only is the womb that bare me blessed; blessed are they who hear God's word and keep it." It is more worthy of God that He should be born spiritually of every virgin, or of every good soul, than that He should have been born physically of Mary.[10]

Johannes Tauler describes at length this virgin birth of the soul:

> And he who wishes this noble, spiritual birth to take place in his soul as in the soul of Mary, let him perceive what quality Mary had in her; there was a corporeal and spiritual mother. She was a bride, a betrothed virgin, and she was secluded, shut off from everything when the angel came to her. And thus a spiritual mother should be. She should be a pure, chaste maiden. . . . Maiden means that she should be outwardly barren and inwardly bear much fruit. Let this maiden close her outward love and not bear much fruit by it. . . . "All the treasure of the king's daughter is within." Therefore let this virgin be in seclusion; let all her ways, her thoughts, even her omissions, be turned inward, for thus she will bear much fruit and great fruit, God himself, God's Son, God's Word, which is all things and bears all things. . . . And now let us all make room within us for this noble birth; let us become true spiritual mothers, so help us God.[11]

---

9 Philipp Strauch, ed., *Margaretha Ebner und Heinrich von Nördlingen* (Freiburg i.B. and Tübingen, 1882) , p. 195.

10 James M. Clark, ed., *Meister Eckhart: An Introduction . . . with an Anthology of His Sermons* (London, 1957) , p. 212.

11 Johannes Tauler, *Predigten,* ed. Walter Lehmann (Jena, 1923) , I, 5.

Seclusion from the outward, sensory world, inner concentration, the contemplative life in God—these are the virginal womb, from which, according to the German mystics, the son of God is forever born anew. Today more than ever Christianity is often reproached for looking upon the revelation of God as an event that happened just once, for recognizing only one Christ, one Mother of God. And this is true. God erupted into history only once: in Bethlehem and on Golgotha. But this unique event became the type of an event which is enacted over and over, an event which is enacted in each man's soul. Endlessly the unique episode of salvation is repeated and fulfilled in the individual soul of man. When critics assert that Semitic-Christian religion centers around God's unique revelation in history, while Indo-Aryan religion stresses His continuous and multiple revelation in the individual soul, it must be pointed out that here, as in all other matters, Christianity combined the antitheses into a synthesis. And this synthesis was not accomplished by the intervention of Neoplatonic mysticism; we find it in the New Testament, in the writings of the "Semites" Paul and John.

Thus the *Theotokos,* the Mother of God, increased vastly in scope. The queen of heaven, the Mother of God, is manifested in every pure soul and acts upon every pure soul. And this is not all; there is also no end to her manifestations in profane everyday life. In the German Middle Ages, she ceased to be merely the unique woman who bore the son of God, who combined virginity and motherhood; now she was manifested in the face of every woman. Caelius Sedulius, the Latin poet who wrote the oldest extant Latin hymn to the Madonna, prays thus:

> . . . gaudia matris habens cum virginitatis honore,
> nec primam similem visa es nec habere sequentem,
> sola sine exemplo placuisti femina Christo.

> (Along with the honor of virginity thou hast the joys of motherhood. Never has there been a woman like thee and never will there be another. Alone, without a peer, thou, a woman, hast pleased Christ.) [12]

Here there is strong emphasis on the incomparable uniqueness of Mary's womanhood. But in German religious life, poetry, and

[12] Sedulius, *Carmen Paschale,* II, 67–69 (Migne, *PG*, XIX, 599f.) .

369

art a miracle was enacted: the queen of the angels set aside her heavenly crown and descended into the midst of this world's daily life; she became the epitome of what is simplest and most humble, of virginal charm and tender mother's love. In the Saxon *Heliand* and in the *Harmony of the Gospels* of Otfried of Weissenburg, Mary is represented just as a maiden and a mother. She is "the fair maid," "the well-born woman," "the noble lady." In old German Marian hymns the Virgin is consistently addressed as an earthly woman. If she is also called "fairest of women," "best of women," "most precious of women," the meaning is merely that she is the representative of all womanhood. This broadening of the concept of the Blessed Virgin to encompass the whole feminine sex is the most important contribution of the Germanic spirit to the cult of Mary.

This broadening of the Madonna cult was first manifested in old German poetry and old German Christian art. There followed a period of recession, after which the trend re-emerged with full force in art. What moved Otfried and the author of the *Heliand*, what moved the medieval painters of Madonnas, was not primarily the dogmatic, supernatural mother of God, but the human mother with her child. In the *Heliand* the birth of Christ is described as follows: "His mother picked him up and the fairest of women wrapped him in swaddling clothes . . . with both hands she lovingly set down the dear little man in the manger. . . . His mother sat watching beside him, she herself waited, and guarded the holy child."[13] And Otfried's picture of her love for the newborn child is even more plastic:

> And then the mother wrapped the precious child in linen.
> . . . Blissfully she gave the child her virgin breast, and plainly she was glad to be suckling the son of God. O blessedness of the mother's breast kissed by Christ himself. O blessedness of the mother, too, who swaddled him and fondled him. And blessed she who caressed him, who set him on her knees, who rocked him to sleep, who lay down beside him. Yea, blessed she who clothed him, who wrapped him in swaddling clothes, and who slept in one bed with so precious a child. Yea, blessed she who covers him when

13 *Der Heliand*, tr. into modern German by C. W. M. Grein (Cassel, 1869), p. 11.

the frost seeks to harm him, who with her hands and her arms embraces so precious a body.[14]

The reverse of this idyll of *Mater speciosa* is the *Mater dolorosa*, not as shown in the *Stabat Mater*, standing beneath the Cross, participating in the redemption of mankind, but as a symbol for the profound sorrow of a mother grieving for her suffering and dying child. One of the most popular forms of poetry in the Middle Ages was the Lament of Mary, whose echo we find also in Suso. It is the Mother of God who speaks:

> How very lovingly I embraced Him, dead as He was, with my arms, pressing to my maternal heart, my one fair, tender Beloved! Again and again I kissed His fresh flowing wounds, His dead face. . . . I took my tender Son on my lap, and looked at Him. He was dead . . . ; my heart seemed to die once more, and with the mortal wounds it had received it was ready to break into a thousand pieces. Then it uttered many a deep groan. My eyes shed many wretched, bitter tears. My whole appearance became most sad. . . . Alas, I said, . . . my Son, my comfort and my only joy, why hast Thou forsaken me? Where is now the joy I had in Thy birth, the pleasure I had in Thy lovable childhood? . . . All that could ever gladden my heart, whither has it vanished? . . . Alas, my Son, alas, my Son, how I am now deserted by love! How utterly disconsolate my heart has become![15]

A comparison of the laments of Mary with the liturgical *Mater dolorosa* shows the difference between the dogmatic and the universally human picture of the Madonna. But it would be mistaken to view this universally human Madonna worship, which took form in medieval poetry and art, as pure aestheticism; it encompassed a religious faith and an ethical act. The Madonna, as we have said, is compounded of *eros* and *agape*. She is the archetype of the woman; every woman is her image, her representative. But she is not only the beautiful and charming woman painted by the poets and artists, she is everyday woman in her weariness and suffering. "Thou art every mother with child, thou virgin Mary," writes a modern poet (Bockemühl). Just as Christ lies hidden in the poor,

14 *Christi Leben und Lehre, Besungen von Otfred,* tr. into modern German by Johann Kelle (Prague, 1870), p. 33.
15 Suso, *Little Book of Eternal Wisdom,* tr. Clark, pp. 121 ff.

the sick, in strangers, in prisoners, and in them demands the service of humble love, so likewise his mother, Mary. The love of Mary is not aesthetic rapture before a picture of beauty and charm, but the veneration and chivalry that are every woman's due. Of this there is no finer example than Suso, the spiritual troubadour of the Virgin. His biographer reports a touching little incident:

> One day, as he was walking in the country, he happened to meet, on a narrow pathway, a poor, respectable woman; and when the woman drew near him, he gave up to her the dry path, and went himself into the wet at the side, in order to let her go by. The woman, turning around, said to him:—Dear master, how comes it that you, a gentleman and a priest, give way so humbly to me, a poor woman, who ought much more fittingly to have given way to you? He replied:—Oh, dear woman, it is my custom to pay willing deference and honor to all women for the sake of the gentle mother of God in heaven.[16]

A non-canonical saying of Jesus runs: *"Vidisti fratrem, vidisti dominum tuum."* "Hast thou seen thy brother, then thou hast seen thy Lord." Or, as the ancients said: *Homo homini Deus.* Man appears to man as a representative, as an image of God. The conception these sayings embody would seem to negate the dogma of Mary as Mother of God, for Christ and his mother cease to appear as the antithesis to sinful man. And yet this universally human view of the Madonna enters into a profound, an ultimate unity with the dogmatic conception through the mystery of the Incarnation when it is correctly understood: God was manifested in the flesh in Jesus of Nazareth, in the child born of Mary's womb. Through his incarnation, as the Church fathers and Luther made clear, all human flesh and all human souls were purified, hallowed, transfigured, deified. Because the eternal God took flesh from an earthly woman, in order to manifest himself to mankind and redeem mankind, all virginity and all motherhood are hallowed, made into a shining image of divine love.

The Fathers of the first Christian centuries never wearied of contrasting Eve, the seductress, through whom sin came into the world, with Mary the bringer of salvation, the author of redemption. A widely sung hymn has it that Mary reversed the name of

16 *Life of Blessed Heinrich Suso*, tr. Knox, pp. 6of.

Eve—*mutans Hevae nomen;* the angel's *"ave"* is the reverse of "Eva." In her all the sinfulness and weakness of the feminine sex are effaced; the divine aspect of womanhood, diminished and disfigured by original sin, was in her again made manifest in all its radiance. In the Incarnation not only mankind in general, but the femininity of virgin and mother achieved their supreme ennoblement. Just as the whole human race was deified when the son of God became man, so were women ennobled and transfigured by the mother of God, from whom the son of God took his flesh. Just as Christ ascended to heaven with a transfigured human body, and, as it is written in the "Communicantes" of the Ascension Day Mass: "He won a place at the right hand of Thy glory for this frail nature of ours which he had taken upon himself" (*Unitam sibi fragilitatis nostrae substantiam in gloriae tuae dextera collocavit*), so, in the belief of the Church, Mary also rose to heaven with the body which gave flesh to the son of God, and the hosts of the angels rejoiced: *"Assumpta est Maria in coelum, gaudet exercitus angelorum";* the earthly woman with her earthly body has risen up to heaven, where she is exalted even over the incorporeal angels, who bow down to her and serve her.

In all these conceptions the sanctity of the redeemed, purified, transfigured woman is expressed with a wonderful symbolism. Both in her uniqueness as mother of Jesus, and in her universal womanhood, the Madonna is a symbol of divine purity, beauty, love, and gentleness. And around this central symbol cluster any number of secondary symbols taken from nature, from human life, and from the Bible. Nothing has so stimulated the Christian imagination in art, poetry, and the realm of ideas as the Madonna.

But the Madonna is not only a fleeting image which can at any moment be exchanged for another; she is reality, not only in that remote sense in which everything created can operate as a symbol of eternal divine love, but in the sense of a historical revelation of God, the self-revelation of divine love in space and time. Through the mystery of the Incarnation the mother of Jesus, the woman from the house of David, became a created reflection of eternal divine love. Like a magnet this one historical personality drew to itself everything that was great, sacred, and beautiful in Christian —and even non-Christian—faith and ethics. Thus it is meaningless to ask what is historical or nonhistorical in that figure of the Madonna from the standpoint of rational critique. Whatever nonhistorical elements may be involved, the reality of the divine love, which descended upon mankind in Jesus of Nazareth and was diffused through his mother, is incontestable. All the legends of Mary with their imaginative symbolism have their inner share in this reality.

All names and symbols are inadequate. Even in their totality, they cannot entirely encompass the reality of the divine. Even the most wonderful poems and hymns, even the most beautiful pictures, even the clearest theological definitions, all are feeble reflections of the reality of the infinite divine love with which the Virgin-Mother is permeated. And perhaps this inadequacy of symbol and reality in connection with the Madonna cult has nowhere been more beautifully expressed than by Novalis:

> Ich sehe dich in tausend Bildern,
> Maria, lieblich ausgedrückt.
> Doch keins von allen kann dich schildern,
> wie meine Seele dich erblickt.
>
> Ich weiss nur, dass der Welt Getümmel
> seitdem mir wie ein Traum verweht,
> und ein unnennbar süsser Himmel
> mir ewig im Gemüte steht.[17]

(I see thee, Mary, adorably expressed in a thousand images, but none can portray thee as my soul has seen thee. I only know that since then the world's tumult has been wafted away like a dream and a sweet, ineffable heaven has filled my soul forever.) [18]

17 Novalis, *Werke,* ed. H. Friedemann (Berlin, n.d.) , I, 46.
18 For a historical account of the Christian Madonna cult, see "Die Gottesmutter," special issue of *Hochkirche* dedicated to the 1500th anniversary of the Council of Ephesus, ed. Friedrich Heiler (Munich, 1931) . The contents include: F. Heiler, "Die Gottesmutter im Glauben und Beten der Jahrhunderte"; Antiochenus, "Die Gottesmutter in der abendländischen Liturgie"; Anne Marie Heiler, "Die Gottesmutter in der alten deutschen Dichtung"; P. Schorlemmer, "Die Gottesmutter im Bekenntnis des Luthertums"; K. Ramge, "Die Gottesmutter im Gottesdienst des Luthertums" (with bibliography) .

Erich Neumann

Mystical Man

The subject of our present paper is not mysticism but mystical man. We are here concerned not with mysticism in general or with any of the special forms in which it has manifested itself, but with the vehicle of mystical phenomena, man. An understanding of the mystics, the extreme exponents of the mystical process, is, to be sure, one of our principal tasks, but, more than that, we wish here to determine the significance of the mystical for man in general. We may then formulate our problem as follows: To what degree is the mystical a universal human phenomenon, and to what degree is man *homo mysticus?*

These words of clarification are intended to spare you disappointment in case you have expected me to quote familiar or unfamiliar mystical texts or interpret such mystical texts. And perhaps I shall also disappoint you in not attempting to add one more definition of mysticism to all the others, yet it is my hope that at the end of our inquiry you will fully understand what the term "mystical" implies in our present context.

It is in keeping with a twofold limitation that we aim here not at a mystical theology but rather at a mystical anthropology. First, a limitation of a general nature. Modern man's fundamental experience of the relativity of his position and his frames of reference forbids him in principle to make such absolute statements as the naïveté of former times permitted. The second and special limitation consists in this: the psychologist's experience encompasses the human, no less, but also no more, and he may not pass beyond these limits of his experience. But what more than compensates for this twofold limitation is that the psychological area of the human, the area of the *anthropos,* has become so vast and appears so prodigious to our inquiring consciousness that we must almost despair of finding its limits, even though we follow every road, so deep is its law.[1] At the risk of repeating material that is only too familiar, I must in this connection refer to the many things which man formerly experienced as outward world, but which modern man recognizes as inner world within himself.

It is not only the animism of primitive man with his mana-charged places and animals, his spirits and demons, not only the gods of paganism that we have recognized to be projections of inner psychic experience. The Judeo-Christian, as well as the extra-European, religious worlds—with their hierarchies of heaven and hell and all their inhabitants, gods and spirits, angels and devils, redeemers and seducers, with their religious myths of beginning and end, creation, downfall and redemption—have all become intelligible to us as projections of experience that occurs in the psychological inwardness of the *anthropos*. This knowledge follows, of course, the general law that it is very much easier for us to fathom as projections those contents with which we are not unconsciously and affectively involved, but of which only our consciousness has knowledge, than those contents which originate in the depths of our unconsciousness, saturated as they are with affectivity.

This image of the *anthropos* surrounded by circles of heavens and hells which originate within him, resembles the mandala of ancient astrology. But once the phenomenon of projection has been understood, this conception of man's position in the cosmos becomes far more complicated, losing in plasticity what it gains in dynamism.

In our new conception of the *anthropos* system, there is a continuous movement between the central *anthropos,* the man in the middle, and the world as his periphery. The world is the vehicle of the projections of the unconscious, and with the development of the human ego, which takes back and makes conscious these projections into the world, our image both of cosmos and of man changes. The progressive change in the relation between man and world is manifested in a corresponding change in our world picture and brings a new dynamic component into the old mandala of the

---

1 Heraclitus of Ephesus, in H. Diels, *Die Fragmente der Vorsokratiker* (Berlin, 1934), I, Frag. 45.

anthropos; but this is not all, for inwardly as well the *anthropos* is involved in a continuous process of transformation.

This process is based on interrelations between ego, consciousness, and the unconscious, that is, on the fact that the personality is continuously changed from its own center outward, by the spontaneous action of the creative unconscious. Thus the cause of the transformations within the *anthropos* system lies in the human psyche. The initial creative movement which changes man and with him the world implies the inconstancy of world and man, which is experienced as the precariousness of his existence.

Not only is the source of the creative nothingness—which is the point of departure for the autonomous, spontaneous, and unconscious activity of the creative, vital psyche—situated within the psychological domain of the *anthropos,* it is its very center.

The problem of the creative unconscious, the central problem of depth psychology, is at the same time the central problem of mysticism and of mystical man. Since the creative process takes place outside of consciousness and must therefore be looked upon as an experience at the limits of the ego, any attempt to approach this central and primal vortex is a hazardous undertaking. It is in the very nature of such an undertaking that its object cannot be captured by the direct intervention of consciousness, but that one must seek to approach the center in question by a sort of ritual circling, an approach from many sides.

The situation of psychology is so paradoxical because in it the subject of knowledge, the ego as center of consciousness, and the object, the psyche which it strives to understand, are intermeshed, each system forming part of a personality. The interdependence of these systems, their interpenetration, and their relative independence raise fundamental psychological problems.

Any attempt to encompass the phenomenon of mysticism encounters a similar difficulty. Here again man as subject of mystical experience is inseparably and paradoxically bound up with his object, in whatever form it may confront him.

In speaking of a mystical anthropology, that is, a doctrine of mystical man as part of a general theory of man, we are taking a very broad and, one might justifiably say, vague view of mysticism. We recognize mysticism not only in religion and assuredly not only in ecstatic, purely inward mysticism. For us the mystical is rather a fundamental category of human experience which, psychologically speaking, manifests itself wherever consciousness is not yet, or is no longer, effectively centered around the ego.

We find the mystical element in the uroboros stage, the early psychological stage of original unity, in which there is as yet no systematized consciousness, the stage characterized by what Lévy-Bruhl has called *participation mystique*. In this situation, where man and world, man and group, ego and unconscious are intermingled, the mystical element is manifested in the fact that the ego has not yet detached itself from the nonego.

For the original cosmic sense, that which we call outside world and that which we call inner psyche are fused. Stars and trees and animals are psychologically as close to the undelimited ego as fellow clansman, child, and parent; and a mysterious bond unites what is nearest and what is most distant, god, animal, and man. This relation is so fluent because the ego can still everywhere be confounded with the nonego.

The incomplete separation of ego from nonego characterizes the original uroboros state, which lives in the psyche of mankind as the archetype of paradisiacal wholeness. For the ego, lonely and unhappy in consequence of its necessary development, this image of a lost stage of childhood is a symbol of irreparable loss. This image, of course, is always projected back to a time preceding the birth of the ego, which by its very nature is a vehicle of suffering and imperfection. Accordingly, the state of perfection is phylogenetically a paradise placed at the beginning of human history, while it is ontogenetically projected into the beginning of the individual life as the paradise of childhood. But, just as we know that the original condition of mankind was no Rousseauan natural state and that primitive peoples did not inhabit any "happy isles," so we know that childhood is not paradisiacal and happy, but full of problems and perils.

And yet there remains an eternal truth in this image of the perfection of the original situation, even when we understand the projection, even when our insight bids us look on the theological doctrine of the fall of man and the world as a fallacy based upon a false historical projection of this archetype.

378

The question remains open as to what should be done to prevent the ideal of this state of perfection from poisoning mankind. For again and again the arduous heroic path of the ego into consciousness and suffering is endangered by the magic of the temptation to seek, or not to depart from, the state of perfection represented by an egoless unconsciousness.

For modern man existence has split into world and self, the outward and inward which embrace the intervening ego. This split, which is determinant for civilized man, became manifest only with the emergence of the ordering consciousness which posits contradictions, and this can be shown by a study of the development of consciousness.

The growth of humanity is fundamentally the development toward the ego, toward consciousness and individuality. Every step of this road is arduous and fraught with suffering. Only in the course of long historical processes has mankind, following in the wake of the creative precursor, the great individual, succeeded in developing a relatively independent ego as center of a system of consciousness, and, by arduous processes of differentiation, in developing agencies which define the human personality as unity and individuality.

But the development toward the ego, toward individuality and consciousness stands in inexorable conflict with the unconscious. The formation of consciousness and the confirmation of the ego are possible only in battle with the engulfing powers of the unconscious, and this means in detachment from the uroboros stage, from the paradise of undivided unity and perfection. Thus the heroic road of mankind—for heroic it is, in spite of imperfection—is the road to clarity, differentiation, and responsible awareness of the ego.

The road of the human ego is, to be sure, a road to consciousness, but from the very beginning it has not been a road *in* consciousness. What is "given" to man is always the relation of the ego to the unconscious and to a world changed by the projection of unconscious images. Consciousness arises through a process in which the ego comes to grips with the unconscious, is first defeated, and then emerges victorious; the ego must brave the forces of the nonego in order to establish and extend its position. A part of this battle is fought by the heroic action of the ego, which does not depart from its position in consciousness, but takes possession of its contents, draws them into the realm of consciousness, and there elaborates them—i.e. makes the contents accessible to conceptual understanding, subjects them to analysis, and systematically uses them for the construction of a conscious world picture.

But, in spite of everything, this is the easier part of the conflict. What makes the battle perilous, and thus establishes the ego as heroic, is the descent into the depth of the unconscious, the encounter with the nonego.

The development of the ego and of consciousness, in so far as it is a progressive human development, is dependent on the creative— that is, on the spontaneity of the nonego, which manifests itself in the creative process and is by nature numinous. The encounter with the numinous constitutes the "other side" of the development of consciousness and is by nature "mystical."

The origin and development of the human personality, as well as the formation and development of consciousness, are rooted in processes which are mystical in our sense of the word, and which play between the ego, as vehicle of the personal, and the numinous transpersonal. Only modern Western man in the rigidity of his ego, in his imprisonment in consciousness, can fail to recognize man's existential dependence on the force which mystically changes him, the force by which he lives and which lives within him as his creative self.

It is characteristic of the creative process that in it the ego cannot cling to its position in consciousness, but must expose itself to encounter with the nonego. In so doing, the ego renounces conscious reality, in which the world is experienced as contradiction, and an encounter occurs between ego and nonego in which the contradictions of world, ego, and self are suspended. This encounter, wherever it may occur, we designate as mystical.

In order to experience the paradoxical reality which is present before, outside of, or behind the polarization of world and self, the personality must—temporarily at least—transform itself and assume an attitude which leaves open the possibility of a union between ego and nonego.

Every numinous experience, whatever form it may take, is mystical. The numinous content possesses a fascination, a richness beyond the power of consciousness to apprehend and organize, a charge of energy surpassing consciousness. Hence the encounter with it leads always to an upheaval of the total personality and not only of consciousness. In every confrontation of the ego with the numinous, a situation arises in which the ego goes "outside itself"; it falls or is wrenched out of its shell of consciousness and can return "to itself" only in changed form.

The encounter with the numinous paves the way for the emergence of man's creative void, which is nothing other than a state beyond consciousness. This manifestation can take on the character of an epiphany and confront man from outside as a numen; its creative product is then revelation. In this sense the area of revelation extends far beyond the province of religious history, since for primitive man, who takes psychological reality seriously, all the phenomena that we designate as "idea," "inspiration," or "notion" are "revealed." Not only religion, cult, and ritual, but art and morality as well, sprang from revelation, through encounter with the numinous.

Though modern man is familiar with the mystical character of religious revelation, he often fails to recognize that the same phenomenon operates in every creative process and thus determines the whole existence of mankind.

Let us not forget this: The mystical man may be designated as religious, since all his life he consciously or unconsciously confronts the numinous; but he need not necessarily be a believer in God. Our insight into the scope and ubiquity of the mystical phenomenon shows that there are theistic and atheistic, pantheistic and panentheistic, but also materialistic and idealistic, extraverted and introverted, personal and transpersonal forms of mystical experience. The experience of God as a sacred adventure represents only one specific, experimental, form of mysticism; it is by no means the most common and perhaps not even the most significant. But all mystical forms have in common the intensity of experience, the revolutionary, dynamic impetus of a psychological event which takes the ego out of the structure of its consciousness; and in all of them the numinous appears as the antithesis of consciousness.

For every consciousness and ego, the numinous is that which is

"entirely different"; it is indeterminable and free. The psychological
category of autonomy, which the theory of complexes[2] imputes to
the unconscious content, has reference to the prodigious reality that
the numinous is undetermined, thus constantly proving to the ego
its almost total dependence on an overwhelming, incalculable force.

Emerging as it does in a zone diametrically opposed to consciousness, the numen is evasive and indefinable; this accounts for
the uncertainty of man's ego position but also makes possible a
creative revolution of the human personality. For, side by side with
revelation and with the creative achievement which as cultural
phenomenon is characteristic of the human species, stands a third
and decisive form of mystical encounter between ego and nonego:
metamorphosis.

In the process of encounter with a numen, a transformation takes
place; it takes place in the man to whom the numen appears, but
it embraces also the numen itself. The two poles of the encounter
which we designate as mystical, the ego as well as the nonego, are
transformed in a process by which the dividing line between them
is annulled from both sides.

The epiphany of that which had hitherto been hidden requires
not only an ego to which it can manifest itself, but, to an even
greater degree, calls for an act of attention and devotion on the
part of the ego, an aptitude for being "moved," a willingness to see
what wants to appear. Man is the partner of the numinous, for
only in man can the numinous epiphany unfold. Articulated with
the development of mankind is the development of the forms of the
numinous which—like mankind—emerges from anonymous unconsciousness and formlessness to become visible as numen in the
eternal procession of form.

Conversely, human consciousness is dependent on the spontaneity
of the numinous. This interrelation occurs within what we call the
human personality. In this sense, the transpersonal numinous has
its place in man and only in man, for man is the place of the
mystical encounter between ego and nonego. The reality of this
encounter is one of the fundamental facts of man's existence, and
if we designate this encounter and this metamorphosis of ego and

2 See C. G. Jung, "A Review of the Complex Theory," CWJ 8 (1960).

nonego as mystical, the mystical category is a fundamental category of human experience.

The transformation of the personality through the appearance of the numen detaches the ego from its old system of consciousness and also from its old relation to the world, but the price for the connection with the unknown numen, which holds within it the possibility of the creative, is renunciation of the security provided by conscious orientation and entrance into the fundamental paradox of the mystical.

For the ego, this mystical encounter with the nonego is always an extreme experience, for in it the ego always moves toward something which lies outside of consciousness and its rationally communicable world. This area situated outside of consciousness is indeed, from the viewpoint of the total personality which it has transformed, the creative area par excellence, but from the viewpoint of consciousness it is an area of nothingness. This creative area of nothingness in man is the temple and *temenos*, the source and paradise; it is, as in Canaanite mythology,[3] the focal point where El, the great God, sits "at the rising of the streams, in the middle of the source of the two seas." But it is also the center of the mandala[4] with all its symbols, the place of the godhead as of the *anthropos*; it is the area where mystical theology and mystical anthropology coincide.

Man's experience of the creative void is the source experience which led him to project the image of a creation out of nothingness, as he has done not only in Judeo-Christian theology, but, indeed, in all mystical and creative experience. The creative void stands at the center of mystical anthropology as part of a depth psychology concerned with the nature of the creative process, but at the same time it stands at the center of all mystical experience which circles around the hiddenness of the godhead. In view of this central process, which is unknown as such but is for man the profoundest source of creative life, man must be said to be a *homo mysticus*.

Analytical psychology calls this center the self and thus enters

---

3 W. F. Albright, *Archaeology and the Religion of Israel* (Baltimore, 1942).
4 Cf. Richard Wilhelm and C. G. Jung, *The Secret of the Golden Flower* (new edn., New York & London, 1962).

into the very midst of the paradoxical truth that God and man are one image, for the ego is not the self; in its individuation the personality no longer experiences itself as ego, or solely as ego, but at the same time as nonego, as ego-self. The mystic suffers and is tossed about, trying desperately to express this hidden point, the psychological nucleus of the self, which remains unattainable even when the ego plunges into it, which is paradoxically timeless even though it seems to constitute time, which though transpersonal is the center of the personality and which constitutes the numinous essence of man.

Where this paradox, perceived as such by ego-consciousness—though it is not a paradox for the living personality—is manifested, man falls into the dangerous paradox of his own depths. He faces the endless problem of identity, which constitutes the very substance of depth psychology. "Who is who?" becomes the central question, often the question of life or death, sanity or madness. The eternal answer of the East, "Thou art that," has its counterpart in this equally eternal question of the West.

But wherever an encounter with the numinous takes place, the ego is encompassed by the nonego, that is to say, a change takes place in the personality. This change in personality can be a momentary trance or a lasting transformation; it can take the form of an orderly process, or of a seemingly chaotic, directionless eruption, transforming or destroying the personality in a sudden flash; it can manifest itself as a religious experience, as love, artistic creation, a great idea, a delusion—wherever the mystical element is manifested, the hitherto accepted rigidity of a world ordered around the ego is shattered and a dynamically changed and changing world behind the world is revealed.

Whether this revelation is the irruption of a divine, cosmic, or human mystery is here of secondary importance. Thus, for example, one and the same tree may be revered as seat of the godhead, or may as world tree symbolize the mystery of the psychological world; as a world of natural law it may fill a life of scientific effort, or it may reflect in poetry or art the numen that it is. All these are only diverse aspects of the numinous world-content "tree," which we designate as an archetype because to encounter it is to be drawn into a mystical trance and metamorphosis. Experienced in this way, the whole world is numinous: every place, every thing, every situation, and every living creature, for they are all potential bearers of "sparks," as the Hasidim said,[5] capable of kindling and illumining the human personality. The world and its content are numinous, but this is true only because man is by nature a *homo mysticus*.

It may seem at this point that though we have said something of *homo mysticus*, we have said next to nothing of those men who are generally known as "mystics." We intend in the second section of our paper to make good this failing. Moreover, let us recall our opening remarks. Only an insight into the mystical nature of man in general can enable us to understand the specific "mystic," and only through a knowledge of the dialectical relation between the numinous and man can we properly define the area of mystical experience proper.

The extreme tension that is created in the human psyche by the separation between consciousness and the unconscious, the tension upon which human culture is built, can be reduced to the fundamental tension between the ego and the self. The self is associated with the archetypal perfection situation of the uroboros as the source situation of the isolated ego-existence, while the ego is associated with consciousness as the organ of differentiation and isolated experience.

Human development, as we have said, moves toward extension of consciousness and the strengthening of the ego; but, on the other hand, it requires the mystical phenomenon, the creative process inherent in the transforming encounter between the ego and the nonego. The development of consciousness is articulated in a twofold synthesis with the development of the forms of the numinous.

By detaching the ego from the center of consciousness, every experience of the numinous leads to an approximation of the original situation, and hence to a more or less restricted form of the experience of the self. This fact is the basis of primitive religions. The fact that man can experience the numinous and, on a higher plane, the numen, a god or *the* god in anything and everything, is mirrored in the animistic, demonistic, and polytheistic forms of religion. When we refer to this phenomenon as an experience, though a restricted experience, of the self, we mean that although the ego

5 Cf. Martin Buber, *Die chassidischen Bücher* (Hellerau, 1928).

here experiences the nonego in a restricted form, it is nevertheless affected by a numinous experience involving the totality of the psyche.

To the restricted form of the nonego corresponds here an equally restricted form of the ego. The little ego is just as much overpowered by the numinous experience of, let us say, the tree which in the form of a demon has numinously addressed the ego; and the totality of the psyche is just as much set in motion as when a consciousness of greater scope and a more powerful ego are smitten by the epiphany of a godhead.

Here of course we cannot enter into the psychological symptoms of the experience of the numinous self. It always brings with it the intoxication that comes of a changed and heightened feeling of self, a change in the ego-position and consciousness, and this implies also a changed relation to the world and the collectivity.

Since experience of the numinous is always experience of the self and of the "voice" which brings revelation, the ego affected by it comes into conflict with the dogma and agencies of the dominant consciousness. The creative-mystical experience is by nature opposed to the dominant religion and the dominant conscious contents of the cultural canon—that is to say, it is in principle revolutionary and heretical. We may say that wherever a "given," objectified numen is worshiped, the characteristic relation between ego and nonego which defines the mystical phenomenon is destroyed. Consequently, all mystical trends strive to dissolve the traditional forms of religion and worship, although they often disguise this endeavor as a "renewal" of the old religious form. The authentic, fundamental experience of the numinous cannot be other than anticonventional, anticollective, and antidogmatic, for the experience of the numinous is always new.

Thus any mysticism that consists in the experience of dogmatically defined or definable contents is either low-level mysticism or disguised mysticism. It is low-level mysticism when a personality unable to assimilate the cultural canon and the religious dogma is overpowered by one of the archetypal contents of the canon and experiences it mystically—as, for example, when an archetypal content of the Christian cultural canon is mystically experienced by the Negroes in an African mission. Here the mystical experience reveals all the symptoms of primitive mysticism. This, too, is "authentic" mysticism, but it must be called low-level mysticism, because the phenomenology of the mystical experience is regressive in relation to the archetypal cultural canon. But this low-level mysticism, which is not infrequent when a higher cultural canon is imposed on a group whose consciousness is less developed than that of the group to whom the cultural canon belongs, is less significant than the phenomenon of disguised mysticism.

History is replete with examples of mystics who, unwilling to risk the dangerous and often fatal imputation of heresy were driven to compromise and who, consciously or unconsciously, re-dogmatized their authentic mystical experience—i.e., adapted it to the form imposed by the prevailing dogma. Since mystical experience is very largely grounded in archetypes, we should expect the utterances of the mystics to conform with one another. We do indeed find such conformity in the psychological effect of mystical experience, in the transformation it induces in the personality; but as for the content of the experience itself, it is colored more often than not by the prevailing dogma. Seldom do we find authentic Indian symbolism among Catholic mystics, and vice versa. In his discussions of Brother Klaus[6] and of Loyola,[7] C. G. Jung has elucidated this re-dogmatization.[8]

Beyond question, the fear of persecution for heresy drove mystics everywhere into solitude. The anticollective nature of their experience and frequently their typologically extreme introversion also explain why so many mystics preached contempt of the world and flight from the world. We cannot content ourselves with a reductive and personalistic interpretation of these phenomena, although mystical hostility to the world, and the related hostility to women which leads to the practice of celibacy, shows great simi-

---

6 C. G. Jung, "Brother Klaus," CWJ 11 (1958).

7 Jung, "*Exercitia Spiritualia* of St. Ignatius of Loyola," in *The Process of Individuation* (notes on lectures given at the Eidgenössische Technische Hochschule, Zurich, 1939–1940; privately circulated).

8 In this respect the cabala seems to be rather an exception. According to G. Sholem (*Major Trends in Jewish Mysticism*, London, 1955), it clearly reveals archetypal Gnostic symbolism strongly at variance with the Jewish system of consciousness. But why from the first apocalypses to Hasidism the Jewish stream of true, antidogmatic mysticism never ran dry is a matter that cannot concern us here.

larity to familiar symptoms of neurosis. But even in dealing with neurotics we distinguish positive and negative neuroses; if even here the personalistic, reductive approach has proved inadequate, how then can such an approach be adequate to a phenomenon so significant for the history of the human mind as mysticism?

Although we shall attempt only in the second section of our inquiry to give a general picture of the relation between mysticism and neurosis, we must briefly touch on it here. The development toward the ego and consciousness leads in every sense to isolation; it leads to the loneliness and suffering of the ego. But in its extreme, it leads also to the isolation and specialization of consciousness, to its complete absorption by the purely individual, to a split, purely egoist existence, which can no longer apprehend the broad contexts of life or its connection with the creative void and is no longer accessible to mystical experience. The neurotic extreme of imprisonment in a rigid ego and in consciousness is the exact opposite of the primitive or neurotic state of an egoless, unconscious existence.

The mystic's striving to rid himself of the world, his isolation, and his ego—to vanish in the area of creative nothingness and thus recapture the unified experience of self and totality, perfection and paradise—is the understandable countermovement to the movement of the ego into the solitude of consciousness.

But here as everywhere there is a hierarchy of phenomena. Just as we know a lower, somnambulistic, egoless stage of the creative process, of art and prophecy, so also do we find a somnambulistic form of mysticism. And, just as the higher forms of the creative process and of prophecy appear only as syntheses arising from an enhanced tension between the ego and the unconscious, it seems to us, contrary to the current view, that the highest form of mysticism is the synthesis of a heightened tension between the ego and the self. Hence no adequate approach to mysticism is possible unless we can distinguish and evaluate the different forms and degrees of the relationship between the ego, the nonego, and the self.

Any attempt to understand the experience of mystical man as an expression of a varying relation between ego and self must be grounded in a psychology which takes into account the different phases of the ego and consciousness in their development from the unconscious, and thus acquires a system of co-ordinates by which to register the different forms of the ego–self relation.

Such an interpretation of mystical man, taking its orientation from the development of consciousness, makes it possible to distinguish early, high, and ultimate levels of mysticism. This hierarchy has reference both to the stages of human development, in the course of which ego-consciousness arose, and to the stages in the life of the individual, which, in broad outlines at least, recapitulates the phylogenetic development.

We have illustrated the emergence of the mystical element by examples from the uroboros, collective phase of *participation mystique,* and here again reference to this phase may clarify our meaning, though it goes without saying that we can give only a schematic abridgment of a process which we have elsewhere attempted to describe more fully.[9]

The role of archetypal phases in the development of consciousness can be demonstrated; by the study of these phases we can determine how the germ of consciousness frees itself from its original containment in the unconscious, ultimately to achieve the independence that characterizes our personality, divided as it is into a system of consciousness and an unconscious.

The initial, source situation is dominated by the archetypes of the uroboros and the Great Mother, with which are associated a childlike ego and consciousness. The uroboros as symbol of the all-embracing unconscious, which contains the germ of an ego still without independence, characterizes the psychological condition of an early age in human history, known to us today only in rare cases. For reasons we need not go into here, mythology endows this condition with all the symbols of perfection. It is the pleroma, the sphere; it is paradise; it is the prenatal place. Prenatal here means preceding the birth of the ego and consciousness, preceding split, conflict, and suffering.

We call the yearning to return to this stage "uroboros incest," because, in relation to this undeveloped, germinal ego, the uro-

9 For the concept of the uroboros and the following discussion, see Erich Neumann, *The Origins and History of Consciousness* (New York and London, 1954).

boros appears also as archetype of the mother. The ego yearns to enter into this uroboros and thus to lose itself. This phase dominates the existence of the earliest mankind, while ontogenetically it is characteristic of earliest childhood.

But the next phase of the growing consciousness is also dominated by the unconscious, which now takes on the archetypal form of the Great Mother. In childhood and early youth, both mankind and the individual must come to grips with the Mother archetype, who is the terrible, devouring Mother when she represents the conservatism of the unconscious.

This phase ends in the fight with the dragon, which is ontogenetically associated with puberty. In the fight with the dragon, the ego succeeds in overcoming the terrible aspect of the unconscious, the uroboros Mother, and thus becomes a heroic ego. Separation of cosmic parents, fight with the dragon, transfiguration and rebirth, liberation of the ego and of consciousness, acquisition of "higher" manhood—these are the archetypes which constitute the fixed canon pertaining to this phase.

The heroic ego fences itself off against the powers of the unconscious; human and individual development enter on their prime. As the principle of contradiction comes into being through the "separation of the primal parents," the systems of consciousness and the unconscious separate and the ego-consciousness system becomes relatively independent. But at the same time, the fight with the dragon is a mystery of initiation and rebirth; the ego transformed in it is a son of the godhead, a spiritual being, and has achieved "higher" manhood. Only after this metamorphosis is the ego capable of becoming a vehicle of culture and an adult member of society. Here it is a matter of indifference whether the fight with the dragon takes place on the diurnal arc of extraversion, i.e. consists in the defeat of an outward dragon-enemy, into which the archetype is projected, or on the nocturnal arc of introversion, i.e. consists in the defeat of an inner dragon through an initiation or some individual inner event. Both battles are typical battles of rebirth, as Jung has demonstrated.[10]

This phase of the fight with the dragon concludes with the

10 *Symbols of Transformation,* CWJ 5 (1956).

acquisition of a treasure hard to attain, which is the symbol of man's own creative change, and with the *hieros gamos,* the sacred marriage with the prisoner, the anima liberated from the dragon's power. The love motif, with its personal realization on an individual plane, far transcends the personal sphere, for the archetype of the *hieros gamos* determines the adult phase of mankind and the individual man, as type of the creative union of opposites.

The male partner in this sacred marriage is always the hero as higher man. As in myth and ritual, the marriage is "cause" and "prototype" of the world's fertility, that is, of creative life in the world. This fertility of the creative, epitomized in the injunction "Be fruitful and multiply," applies to all phases of life, but presupposes split and differentiation, a polarization of opposites, both without and within. Only a masculine consciousness, an established ego, can be fruitful with the anima; only a male principle which has attained its "higher" form by initiation can be fruitful with the female.

The final and mature phase of human and personal development, which reaches beyond the zenith of the dominant egoconsciousness, is characterized by metamorphosis and integration of the personality, such as we see in the process of individuation. This, too, is prefigured in myth, in the archetypal figure of Osiris. As the sun rises and falls in its path across the sky, so does consciousness develop in every individual as the ages of life unfold, and individuation is the end of its diurnal arc. The metamorphosis of the Horus = sun = ego of this phase, stands under the sign of Osiris, the "first of the Westerly gods." At the end and death of the sun's course, Osiris, the self, receives and Osirifies the ego = Horus = son and transforms him into the self. The mythology and king ritual of the Egyptians contain many accounts of the paradoxical relation between ego and self, Horus and Osiris. The mystery of mysteries: "I and the Father are one," also presides over this final phase of the transformation that is called individuation and which culminates in the death of the ego and the end of life.

Analytical psychology distinguishes three great phases in the development of the personality. Each phase is characterized by the predominance of the same archetypal group which determines the corresponding phase in the development of mankind. It goes without saying that these phases of individual development do not fit into any rigid chronological scheme, but only follow certain approximate age groups. The figures we shall give designate only the culmination of a phase extending over many years.

The stage of infancy and childhood, the period in which the ego and consciousness gradually free themselves from their total containment in the unconscious and achieve independence and systematization, ends with adolescence—that is, approximately at the age of eighteen. The prime of life extends from the end of puberty to approximately the fifty-fourth year. This period we divide into two periods of eighteen years each, between which, at approximately the thirty-sixth year, lies the vital turning point. And finally, we have the end period, concluded by death. Diagrammed, these figures would give us four approximately equal parts. At the initial or eastern end stands the total unconsciousness of the pre-ego stage. At the zenith of adulthood stands a developed consciousness, centered around the ego, which is incorporated into the cultural canon of values prescribed by its group and time. The differentiation of the conscious and unconscious systems has advanced so far that the ego identifies itself almost entirely with consciousness; and the unconscious, precisely because it is unconscious, lies outside its field of vision, from which it is removed or completely split off. This stage, which extends from puberty to the climacteric, is determined by the symbols of the fight with the dragon and the archetypal canon pertaining to it: self-transformation, rebirth, slaying of the dragon, *hieros gamos*, conquest of the treasure, and founding of the kingdom.

The final phase, that of old age, stands under the sign of Osiris and leads from differentiation to integration, from the domination of the ego as center of consciousness to that of the self as center of the personality, and from the split between the conscious and unconscious systems to a new synthesis.

Just as the birth of the ego is preceded by the prenatal world of a pre-ego phase, which is known to the personality only through borderline experience, so is the death of the ego followed by a post-ego phase. This, too, is evident to the personality only in

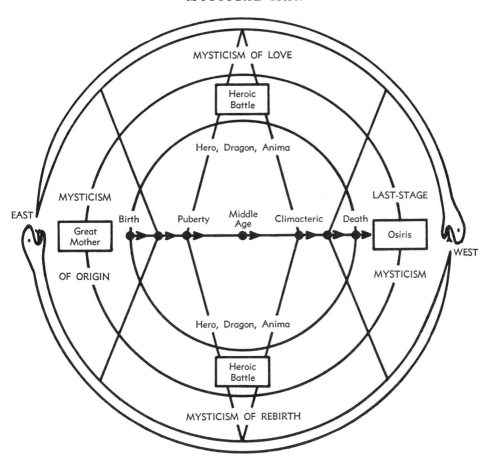

borderline experience. Associated with it are the transformation mystery of Osiris–Horus and the archetypes of the Egyptian ritual of the king and of the dead.

Seen from the limited standpoint of the ego and of consciousness, the pleromatic area of the pre-ego period joins the pleromatic area of the post-ego period. This is symbolized by the uroboros circle, which numinously encompasses life and in which beginning and end meet.

If we contemplate the career of the personality from birth to death, and from total containment in the unconscious to the integration of the final phase, we see that in the course of its transformations it passes through archetypal zones which are

393

manifested in association with the phases of natural life. The solar path of the ego rising from its eastern terminus and descending to its western terminus always passes through a definite sector of the archetypal firmament of the collective unconscious. But the psychocosmic system with which the ego has to do in this process of metamorphosis extends farther, for above and outside the firmament of archetypal images there lies the uroboros area of formless pleroma, preceding form. This is the cosmic mist of godhead, the undefined numinous, the divine void which fills the psychological inwardness of the *anthropos*.

We have endeavored to define the mystical as the encounter of the ego with the archetypal, with the numina, and with the pleromatic, unformed numinous. If we now go farther and attempt to associate the different forms of mysticism with the different life phases of man, it is not in order to satisfy any need of systematization.

The mystical phenomenon is, as we have said, always dependent on the man to whom it manifests itself; the epiphany of the numen is dependent on the personality's stage of development, and the scope of the revelation in which the numen can manifest itself is contingent on the scope of the personality which receives the revelation.

The shaping of the numinous out of the undefined and anonymous into the numen, with its unique utterance, runs parallel to that development of man which leads from the unconscious and anonymous to the conscious and unique.

In the area of the *anthropos,* the diffuse numinous is manifested primarily as an unconscious center which—as in organic life as a whole and perhaps beyond it—operates as a differentiating, centralizing force, directing the vital toward mounting organization. But in man the vitality of the unconscious totality, which we call centroversion, leads to the formation of a new center, a branch center, namely the ego. This ego—for many reasons which we cannot adduce here—is made in the image of the self. Opposed to it is the creative numen as the plenitude of an increasingly formed outward and inward world. To experience this formed numen is the function of the ego as center of the developing consciousness. The end of the process is individuation, in which the ego arrives

394

at a conscious encounter with the self, or, as we might say, with itself.

There is a bold Jewish maxim which says: "God and man are in a sense twins."[11] Our next task will be to suggest at least how in the phases of mysticism this twin nature effects a continuous metamorphosis of mystical man.

II

The mystical encounter between the ego and the nonego is marked by the irruption of the pleromatic uroboros element into the sphere of human life. Or, in the reverse formulation, whenever a mystical phenomenon occurs, the ego penetrates the archetypal heaven and attains the pleromatic uroboros sphere of being. As in every mandala, periphery and center are interchangeable, here, too, the pleromatic uroboros element may be regarded as the surrounding celestial ocean of the godhead, the encompassing sphere, or else as the creative nucleus of nothingness at the center of man. In speaking of the mystical encounter between the ego and the nonego, we may well exclaim: "Descend, or, shall I say, rise!" Ecstasy and penetration to the pleromatic heaven are the same as descent and immersion in the central creative source.

If we disregard those men who are by nature creative, the incursions of the formless or formed numen occur most frequently at times when an archetypal dominant, i.e. a numinous element, is forcing a change in man's momentary ego-form. Such phases and transition points are, as we have seen, potentialities of the human psyche; they lead normally to a change in the personality and a parallel change in the ego and consciousness.

We have said that man is by nature a *homo mysticus*. By this we mean that the development of his natural phases with their archetypal encounters gives a mystical stamp to the inner development of every man, even though he may be unaware of it. This occurs in certain transformation crises of the personality, which, like those of the human organism, are determined by a regular intervention of psychological factors, or archetypes.

We shall now attempt to characterize the various forms of

11 Talmud *Sanhedrin* 46 b.

mysticism in accordance with their relation to the phases of the
life cycle. In this sense we distinguish an early, or source, mysticism; a zenith, or dragon-fight, mysticism characteristic of the
mature age; and a mysticism of the last stage and of death. The
essential criterion is, then, the phase of the ego and the consciousness in which the mystical phenomenon occurs, or, for the
sake of brevity, the ego-phase. Only on this basis will it be possible (though this exceeds the limits of our present project) to
give a psychological interpretation and evaluation of the individual mystical phenomenon.

The early phase of mysticism, source mysticism, is that of
primitive man and of childhood. But here we cannot go into the
primitive mysticism of man's beginnings, which exerts a de-
termining influence on the earliest religion, or the corresponding
mysticism of childhood. It could be elucidated only on the basis
of a depth psychology of childhood, and of such a psychology we
have bare beginnings. Nevertheless, we do know that childhood
is full of mystical experience. The numinous and the archetypal
numina of the collective unconscious are particularly dominant
in this phase, because the child personality, open to both outward
and inward forces, possessing no definite ego and no systematized,
let alone self-contained, consciousness, is still fully receptive to
the transpersonal world. And so the child remains close to the
source and in the macrocosm. Only gradually does the archetypal
experience of his mythological apperception attain secondary
personalization; only gradually is it brought into relation with
the ego and projected into the environment.[12]

The essential interests and contents of this early phase of mankind and of man appear as motifs in the myth of creation, as
answers to the questions of life's whence and whither. Psychoanalysis has contributed much to the understanding of the per-
sonalistically distorted contents of this phase and their relation
to the development of the child. But to a great extent the personalistic prejudice of psychoanalysts has prevented them from
seeing that behind the child's projections into the personal sphere,
characteristic of a later phase of the ego, stands the living world

12 See Neumann, *The Origins and History of Consciousness.*

396

of archetypes. But it is this world which feeds the childlike existence, and in childhood, as in the early phase of mankind, there is a mystical communion with the "great figures" of the collective unconscious. The experience of source mysticism goes far beyond the individual experience of archetypes. Precisely the encounter with the totality, the self, is an essential trait of childhood, as is suggested by children's drawings with their frequent mandala motifs. Consequently the detachment from the self and the development into an ego, which civilization exacts of the child, constitutes one of his greatest difficulties.

We cannot at present concern ourselves with the influence of childhood and its early mystical experience on man's subsequent destinies, but here again we find that the transition points between phases are always points of crisis.

Normally the ego, transformed by the experience of the numinous, returns to the sphere of human life, and its transformation includes a broadening of consciousness. But there is also a possibility that the ego will succumb to the attraction of the numinous and, as a Hasidic maxim puts it, "will burst its shell." This catastrophe can take the form of death in ecstasy, mystical death, but also of sickness, psychosis, or serious neurosis. Disregarding those early childhood experiences which damage the ego-nucleus and its development and whose pathological effects become evident only in later life, we recognize the following phase-initiating points: puberty, life zenith, and climacteric, which are also points of frequent neurotic and psychotic manifestations.

Whenever the ego returns to the sphere of human life, transformed by mystical experience, we may speak of an immanent world-transforming mysticism; but when the ego is torn out of this sphere, or tends to relinquish it or willfully alienate itself from it, we may speak of a nihilistic uroboros mysticism. The decisive factor in this orientation is the condition of the ego *after* its mystical experience. A mystic who passes through all the phases of mystical introversion and attains to nothingness but returns from it in a creative state, that is, with a positive attitude toward the world, may be counted as a representative of this immanent mysticism. He may live in mountain solitude or preach nothingness; provided he thinks he can thus exert a positive influence on the world, he is within the sphere of this mysticism.

In contradistinction to this type, a great number of religious mystics who "live in the world" and perhaps even preach love must, because of their negation of the world, be regarded as nihilistic uroboros mystics. Uroboros mysticism rejects not only the world but also man, the ego, and consciousness; it negates the experience of a differentiated world creatively formed, and with it the differentiation of consciousness, the development of the personality, and consequently the formative power of the creative principle in man.

The anticosmic tendency of the uroboros mystic is nihilistic, because in contrast to those mystics who aim at transforming the world it is a mysticism of disintegration. In its nihilism, creative nothingness is exchanged for the abysmal, deathly womb of the Terrible Mother, which sucks back the newborn babe before it has ever attained life and independence. It is in the nature of the creative principle to let the world take form, to guide the unconscious to consciousness, the anonymous to individuality. The tendency of centroversion[13] as the effective force of the unknown, creative self guides the ego and consciousness out of the unconscious, and only after incurring split and differentiation does the ego-consciousness heroically confront the outward and inward worlds; having proved its strength, it proceeds to synthesize and integrate them. In other words, it is in the very nature of the creative principle to progress from an uroboros world system without ego or consciousness, to a cosmos anthropocentrically ordered round the ego-consciousness. In this creative process not only the world and man are affirmed but also the ego and the historical process in time, for development implies history, both for the individual and the collectivity.

The uroboros mystic rejects all this without realizing that he is thus negating the creative principle itself. Psychologically he remains fixated in the uroboros prenatal stage, in the perfection of total unconsciousness, in the existence of an embryonic ego

13 See Neumann, *Origins*.

preceding world, ego, and consciousness. Living in the image of this prenatal paradise, he denounces the real world. This pleromatic prenatal phase of the uroboros exerts so great a fascination because it offers the joys of the paradise of the unborn. Psychologically it corresponds to a situation in which the tension between consciousness and unconscious is no longer, or rather not yet, present. From this tension between consciousness and the unconscious arises, to be sure, the energy of all psychological life and all conscious experience, but as knowledge of good and evil it is also the source of all doubt and all suffering.

In thus designating the uroboros mystic as infantile, we are merely describing a psychological condition. He yearns to return to, to be gathered into, the maternal womb. His desire is to do away with the creative principle, which begets form, conflict, and suffering, and to achieve beatific nonexistence in the divine womb of nothingness.

In uroboros mysticism the introvert's fear of the world and inability to live in the world becomes ascetic world renunciation; he projects his own inferior, extraverted side into the image of a world that has all the qualities of hell, a world surrendered to the devil. The uroboros saint or gnostic actually lives in a God-forsaken world, a world alienated from God. Since he cannot attain consciousness of his own dark, anima aspect, he is also incapable of experiencing the creative godhead, for the shadow-God and anima-God are inextricably bound up with the creator-God; they are his diabolical and female aspect. Instead, he projects the repressed shadow and anima into the world, which these saints consign to the devil or *māyā*.

Because he is not prepared to accept the creative and abysmal elements in the godhead, he declares the world to be fallen, guilty, seduced, deluded, and corrupted. These saints do not perceive that life and creation must take place in a polarity comprising also the devil, evil, guilt, sin, and death. Accordingly they represent the prenatal, pleromatic condition as the only true being and strive to kill the ego by a process of mystic dissolution, by uroboros incest. They strive not for an integration of the contradictions which make up creative life but for disintegration and regression.

In the last analysis, they look on creation and the creative as a delusion, and, without fully admitting it, they think themselves wiser than the creator.

A great number of uroboros mystics belong to the category of low-level mysticism, that is, they are men with a pathological or fragmentary, primitive, or unstable ego. With them seizure, ecstasy, inflation, depression, or psychosis does not express the overpowering of a mature ego or of an extraordinary total personality by the numinous. Even a high-level mystic can come to grief in his attempt to integrate his experience of the depths. What identifies the low-level mystic is the inferiority of his consciousness and not the overpowering character of the numinous. Hence among uroboros mystics we frequently find men with a psychopathic ego, while world-transforming mysticism presupposes a pronounced development of the ego and a strong tendency toward integration of the personality.

The uroboros mystic, without his knowledge of course, stands under the domination of that very archetype which he most rejects and fears, namely the Terrible Mother. Here we cannot go into the phenomenology of this situation. But precisely the devouring, disintegrating, enfeebling, and diabolically cunning character which he projects into cosmic nature (for this reason considered, it goes without saying, as feminine) is what overpowers him from within. His pseudo-turning to God and his turning-away from the world are expressive of a fixation in the source situation. Behind his hostility to the world, castration by the Great Mother is discernible; the very thing which he outwardly flees in terror has assailed him from within.

We have dealt with this type of mystic at such length, because he is so frequently and unjustifiably regarded as the type of mystical man in general; and also because contrast with the uroboros mystic will help us to elucidate the other phase-types of mysticism, which we shall now briefly discuss.

What uroboros mysticism seeks to avoid is the central element in dragon-fight mysticism, namely, acceptance of life in this world. Since life in split and conflict is creative, it is here affirmed. The fundamental psychological fact that the ego-consciousness system has been detached from the self and the totality of the psyche and has achieved independence is theologically projected into the myth of the fall of man from God and the fall of the world from its original state. This doctrine represents, to be sure, a truth, but it is a purely pedagogic and provisional truth, in other words, not a very profound one. True, the autonomy of the ego always involves dangers, but it is also the basis of human development, for it alone makes possible the realization of the creative "likeness" of man and God.

The achievement of an independent ego and a systematized consciousness would be a fall from the self, if this development were not necessary and willed by the creative self. In reality it is not the evil human ego that falls away from the divine self, but, conversely, it is the self that releases the human ego. Let us recall the concluding words of the Baal-Shem Tov's commentary on the Biblical "Noah walked with God": "And so, when the Father departed from him, Noah knew: It is in order that I may learn to walk."[14]

Reunion with the departed self, that is, individuation, is possible only if, instead of regressively dissolving, the ego consummates its destiny.

Only after accepting the world's split and conflict and the paradoxical nature of life in this world is the ego prepared to fight the dragon. In contrast to the false monism of uroboros, world-hostile mysticism, this mysticism presupposes a dualism of life, an adjustment to the polarity which alone makes possible the life of consciousness and an ethical existence.

An essential trait of the dragon-fight situation, and one which also constitutes the content of the rites of initiation and puberty, is the union of the ego with the "higher man," with the godhead or ancestor. It is this union which establishes the "divine nature" of the hero as premise and consequence of the fight with the dragon. The myth of the hero and of rebirth culminates in the mystical encounter between ego and self, which releases a divinely strengthened ego, an ego which has itself become numinous and in this numinous character faces the battle of life in the world. But this mystical encounter presupposes a strong ego and consciousness, which alone are equal to such an encounter. The actual insig-

14 M. Buber, *Des Rabbi Israel Ben Elieser, genannt Baal-Schem Tow, Unterweisung im Umgang mit Gott* (Hellerau, 1927), p. 45.

nificance and seeming helplessness of the ego confronted by the vast numinosity of the unconscious corresponds to the actual insignificance and seeming helplessness of man confronted by the world. But this situation of minuteness among giants does not prove that the world is disordered and fallen, or ruled by an evil demiurgic principle. It is the mission of the heroic ego to prove itself a David in the presence of Goliath and, despite the objective superiority of the forces of life, to know itself as the godlike center of the world, the seat of the creative principle. By creatively transforming the world, the heroic ego proves that the numinous dwells not only in man, *anthropos,* but also in the godlike ego, vehicle of creative division and decision.

It is only by meeting the challenge with which he is faced, by withstanding the heightened tension between the ego and the self, that the creative man can achieve likeness with God. To bear the cross of this tension is one of the tasks of the heroic ego. Only by clinging to its own position, by thus enlarging consciousness and the personality, can the ego make possible a larger manifestation of the nonego and the world. It is through the ego and its heroic resolve that the creative numinous attains vaster and vaster manifestations.

We must understand hero mysticism in all its scope in order to realize what it means for the development of mankind. All creativeness is mystical, for the individual becomes creative only through its encounter with the numinous, the creative void in the area of the psyche. But since the creative is world-forming and world-generating, it profoundly affirms the world. Hero mysticism is a mysticism of vocation and mission, a mysticism that forms and transforms the world. Hence it matters little whether the encounter is manifested in the religious or the artistic sphere, in outward act or in the inner metamorphosis of the personality. The hero is always the "great individual," great because he realizes in himself the likeness of the creative *anthropos* to God. That is why the king, as prototype of the great individual and hero, is endowed with the attributes of the archetypal canon of Creation, the new year, coronation, and the fight with the dragon. Hence for hero mysticism, world renewal and the founding of a kingdom are symbols of the creative mission, while world and history are the places in which the numinous manifests itself, that numinous which transforms its elect by revelations and mystical encounters and through them renews the world.

We have said that the manifestation of the numinous characteristic of the zenith phase of immanent mysticism requires a stable ego and consciousness. In so saying, we may seem to have excluded from zenith mysticism the vast number of those mystics who are generally regarded as the mystics par excellence and demoted them to the uroboros class. If this were the case, it would reduce our whole analysis to absurdity. In reality the problem is more complicated.

The ecstatic mysticism of the *via negativa*—regardless of whether we have in mind the mysticism of Indian Yoga or Buddhism, the Catholic mysticism of St. Teresa, or the mysticism of prayer and meditation of the cabala—is not uroboros mysticism in the sense characterized by us, but belongs psychologically (although many of its exponents have taken a different view of themselves) to the zenith phase of hero mysticism.

This meditative, acosmic mysticism leading to nothingness—whether it be called godhead, void, or nirvana—by no means represents a regressive process in which the ego is dissolved. The mystics' own accounts often suggest this quite erroneously, because the experience of departing from the old ego-position encourages such an interpretation. But it might easily be shown that the arduous path of zenith, high mysticism, as distinguished from low-level mysticism, is always prepared by a reinforcement of the ego, and not by a drunken disintegration and blurring of consciousness. The essence of acosmic ecstasy is not a pleasurable dissolution of the ego, as in uroboros mysticism, but an extreme exertion of the ego, which, from stage to stage, carries through the hero's fight with the dragon and thus transcends the limits of the old personality. And it is characteristic that ascetic rites and rigorous ethical attitudes are included in the preparations and requirements for these forms of high mysticism. As in the initiation rites of puberty and in the mysteries, these measures serve to reinforce the ego; they are part of its constant striving to follow the inward path with its mounting manifestation of the numinous.

Even when, at the summit of the path, the attractive force of the archetypal self becomes dominant nothingness and the mystic's experience of his own passivity determines the activity of the divine, the mystic is mistaken in supposing that he has destroyed his ego. This final state is attainable only through extreme and gradually mounting activity of the ego. To overcome the gravitational field which attaches the ego to consciousness, to permeate the numinous, archetypal field which surrounds the nothingness at the core of the numinous and resists the ego, demands extraordinary exertions of the ego and of consciousness. Only through extreme concentration of the will and personality can this mystical inward path achieve success. And, paradoxical as it may sound, this means that the ego must increase its charge of energy in order to make possible its own suspension and transposition.

In so far as I, as a layman, am able to judge, it seems to me that Yoga lends itself particularly to an illustration of this point. In telling us of their striving toward a supraconscious state, the mystics seem to confirm our assertion that their mysticism consists not in a dissolution of the ego and of consciousness but in the attainment of a transformed consciousness, the center of which, to be sure, is no longer the ego but the self, around which the ego gravitates. This situation can be understood through analogy with the process of individuation. In this situation, well known to the psychologist, we have to do with an enlarged, not a dissolved consciousness; nevertheless, the ego has to a large extent renounced its autonomy in favor of the self, which now becomes the directing center.

Concerning the psychology of the ego in the last stage of high mysticism, we can say nothing here; it merely seems important to note that from the perspective of hero mysticism, the distinction between the mysticism of the infinite and the mysticism of the personality disappears. Even those states of ecstatic high mysticism, which first take the form of infinity mysticism, culminate in personality mysticism, in a transformation of the personality, and, moreover, in heightened creative activity in the world.

Unquestionably the creative activity of the high mystics is entirely directed inward, so much so that one might doubt whether it is permissible to speak of creative activity in the world. But we should not forget that Christian, Buddhist, and other re-dogmatiza-

tions have given these mystical experiences a world-hostile colora-
tion and have led to world-rejecting formulations which are not at
all in keeping with the true nature of this high mysticism. Not
only the heroic character of these mystics' efforts but also the results at which they aim reveal that these mystics are not uroboros
nihilists. There is a Hasidic maxim which sums up this problem
with popular simplicity. A famous rabbi is said to be a "Zaddik
[a perfectly righteous man] in a fur coat."[15] The explanation is:
"One man buys a fur coat, another buys firewood. And what is
the difference between them? The first wants to warm only himself, the second wants to warm others as well."

Just as it is a basic fallacy to confuse individuation with this
"fur-coat Zaddikism," it is a misunderstanding of the true intention
of the high mystics to regard them as essentially hostile to the
world. In reality, the world-transforming, i.e. the creative, aspect
is always present in the high mystic. The duty of self-sacrifice,
which has the force of law in all high mysticism, demands precisely
that the mystic teach, write, establish schools. In other words, this
mysticism sees itself as a road to the redemption of men. Wherever
this is the case, we have to do with the mysticism of the hero, who
aspires to give the world a new face by his creative rebirth. And,
though Jewish mysticism, for example, strives to "re-create" the
fallen world, to raise it to its original blessed state, the negative
aspect (the conception of the world as fallen) is less important
than the intention of this mysticism to re-create and renew the
world.

Since in this brief sketch we cannot describe all the adventures
of the ego in the mystical encounter with the numinous and the
archetypal situation of heroic battle, it will not be possible to
discuss the particularly important phenomenon of the *hieros gamos*
and the part it plays in the fight with the dragon. This is the
psychological home of love mysticism in all its forms. In the rebirth of the hero, a mystical encounter of the ego with the creative
numinous engenders the new hero by a "higher union." The forms
of mystical *hieros gamos* relationship occurring in this phase are
innumerable, but we can discuss neither the male forms of bride-

15 Buber, *Die chassidischen Bücher*, p. 600.

405

mysticism, in which the ego identifies itself completely with the anima, the soul, in the presence of the numinous, nor the corresponding phenomena among female mystics. Here we find every possible form of archetypal sex symbolism. The male mystic may react as a woman toward a masculine numen, or as a man when confronting a female numinous element. The same is true of the woman mystic. The forms of mystical encounter with the numinous are most numerous of all in love mysticism. By its very nature, the erotic symbolism of the union of opposites which characterizes the love mysticism of the *hieros gamos* must be counted as a part of the encounter between ego and numen, which we have said to be an essential feature of the mystical. This opposition between ego and the numinous is resolved only in the final phase, when the transformation of the total personality, including the ego, becomes predominant over the union of opposites that characterizes the dragon-fight phase.

For the mystics of the highest phase, creative renewal, that is, the life-giving effect of mystical experience, is the essential. In this phase the mystical love-death must therefore be looked upon as a regression and failure if the personality has not contributed its full force to resisting the disintegrating tendencies of the numinous. It does not matter whether this tendency appears as diabolical temptation, as the demonic seduction of power, or in some other form. It is the basic paradox of life that one and the same thing, seen from the perspectives of the ego and of the self, should take on entirely different aspects; and the godlike nature of the ego as opposed to the self is manifested in the determination of the ego to preserve its position as the unique individual for whose sake the world was created, and not to attempt the leap that would make it a hybrid "self." Even where, as in India, the idea of annulling the ego has the force of dogma, this operation of the unique ego cannot be denied, for without it there would be no difference between the saint and the disciples who hold him sacred.

Neither artificial detachment from the world, such as that attempted by the uroboros mysticism that negates creation, nor the fatal love leap into the godhead, which annuls the tension between ego and self, resolves the paradox of life. The hope of solving this paradox seems rather to rest with the immanent, world-transforming type of mysticism, which consists essentially of individuation. For, though high mysticism begins with dragon-fight mysticism, it extends far beyond it, penetrating deep into the province of last-stage mysticism.

We find that in the process of human development, every event which subsequently achieves importance for all men is first enacted in the "Great Individual." The high mystics are "Great Individuals" and as such would seem to be precursors of the process we call individuation, which in the modern world has become typical of men in the second half of their lives. And, as usual when the prototypical process of the Great Individual is generalized, we find here again that the sacral accent which had lifted the mystic above mankind as a saint is not only secularized but also humanized in the last-stage mysticism of the individuation process. (One strong indication that high mysticism represents an anticipation of the individuation process is that the initiation required for it—e.g. in India and among the Jews—is reserved for men past their prime.)

In last-stage mysticism the process of personality integration, known from the work of C. G. Jung, is approached. This kind of mysticism occurs under the sign of the westernmost point; its archetypal master is Osiris, and it is identical with the death and after-death mysticism of the Egyptian and Tibetan Books of the Dead.

In contrast to uroboros mysticism, which says, "Make me free from my selfhood," a fit prayer for world-transforming mysticism might be, "Fill me with my selfhood." And Tersteegen's fine prayer, "Ah, I am still so confused, gather me, thou good shepherd,"[16] could not have been spoken by a hero mystic, and certainly not by an individuation mystic. For in these mysticisms the ego demands to find its own way out of the confusion, to be shepherd over its own sheep, to gather and collect itself. Jung has shown that this very position was the heretical secret of alchemy. But here we shall not discuss this, nor the transformation of the personality in the individuation process, with which I assume you are all familiar. I should prefer to stress another aspect of last-stage mysticism.

The individuation process may be described as a development

16 Friedrich Heiler, *Das Gebet* (4th edn., Munich, 1921) , p. 293.

in which the reality of the self becomes transparent. In it the opaque occlusion of the area of consciousness, in which the ego sees only itself and the contents of its ego-world, is lifted and the constellations of the archetypes, the collective unconscious, rise above the horizon of experience. But then, as the numinous contents are integrated, the self itself becomes transparent in its formless form.

This process is accompanied by another in which one might say that the world becomes transparent. As man becomes transparent to himself as not-only-foreground, not-only-ego, the world also becomes transparent for him as not-merely-foreground and not-merely-nonego. Now neither the extravert's outward vision of the world nor the introvert's inward vision remains in force, but a third type of vision arises. What in the primitive stage was realized as an unconscious bond and mixture between ego and nonego returns now on a higher level as conscious mystical experience, as the possibility of symbolic life. The actualization of Messianism (what the Hasidim formulated as "the redemption of divine sparks in all times and places") belongs to the general experience of this stage.

Originally, Messianism was bound up with a historical process ending in the emergence of a savior who, after the transformation crisis of the apocalypse, ushers in the eschatological age of redemption. This conception can easily be shown to be a projection of an individuation process, the subject of which, however, is the people, the chosen collectivity, and not the individual.

In the collective projection, history appears as the collective representative of destiny; the crisis is manifested in the projection of the wars which characterize the Last Days; and the transformation, as the Last Judgment, death, and resurrection. Similarly, the transfiguration and conquest of the self corresponds to transfiguration in the celestial paradise which in the shape of a mandala gathers in mankind, or else it is projected as life in a re-created and renewed world governed by the king-Adam-*anthropos*-self at its center.

It still remains to clarify the process which we have designated as the actualization of Messianism.

In the cabala, as G. Scholem has made clear, the striving for *tikkun,* the mystical re-creation of the disrupted world, plays a central role. Here the mystic has the mission of advancing the Last Days, the Messianic age, by his activity. It is his task to make the godhead and the world that is bound up with it "whole and complete" again. His work consists in reuniting the parts that have been separated from the godhead—the Shekinah, God's female immanence, which has been wandering about in exile—with God's transcendence. Man's power to accomplish by his mystical actions this great work, which is a creative effort in regard to both world and godhead, constitutes the priestly dignity of man—and in Jewish mysticism, naturally, of the Jew.

This transposition at all times of Messianic activity into the sphere of the individual is what we mean by the actuality of Messianism.

The provisional character of a life spent outside of history in waiting for a millennium is one of the fundamental dangers confronting the intuitive Jew, for it has added an inner to an outer uprootedness. The actualization of Messianism, a process that culminated in the popular mystical movement of Hasidism, overcame this provisional character. Redemption of the sacred sparks in every Now, in every Here, that is the essential task. And this task confronts not only the world, with its general need of redemption, but every individual, for each individual soul has its own particular sparks that demand to be redeemed:

> Before the Day of Atonement the rabbi of Ger spoke to the Hasidim gathered round his table: "Our teacher Hillel said: 'If I am not for myself, who is for me?' If I do not do my duty, who will do it for me? Each must do his duty for himself. And he also said: 'And if not now, when?' When will be the Now? This Now, the moment in which we are speaking, has not been from the creation of the world, and it will never be again. Before it, there was another Now, after it there will be another Now, and every Now has its sacred duty: As it is said in the sacred book, the Zohar: 'The garments of morning are not the garments of evening.' . . . This Now cannot be made good by any other Now, for each moment is encompassed in a special light."[17]

17 Buber, *Die chassidischen Bücher,* p. 637.

This mission of the individual is in its profoundest meaning an actualization of Messianism. As Franz Kafka said: "The Last Judgment is a court-martial." It no longer concerns only the collective but takes in the individual as well. History becomes destiny, the battle and decision remain; but, like redemption and apocatastasis, they are events of individual existence within the psycho-cosmic area of man.

If in every thing and every situation a numinous background can break through, leading to the mystical encounter between the ego and the nonego and thence to illumination, everything in the world becomes a symbol and a part of the numinous, and the world so pilloried by the uroboros mystics becomes prodigiously pregnant with God and godly. It would be a fundamental error to take this for religious pantheism or panentheism, for this form of mature mysticism demands a continuous creative process within the personality. When there is light in man, the light shines without and within; and when it becomes dark and opaque within him, the world too becomes dark and opaque, a world of dead things. The mission of living man is not to plunge himself into the white primal light and lose his identity, but to give transparency to the foregrounds of the world, in order that the primal light of the pleroma may become visible as background and core of the world and thus become intensified in its radiation and efficacy. This he may do by experiencing a symbol, by raising a content to consciousness, by giving form to an archetype, through love for another human being, or in some other way; in any case, we are speaking of an encounter of the self with the self.

This symbolic life is concerned with all the rich destinies of existence in time and not with being outside of time. For in every unique event, in every special situation, the whole of the creative substratum confronts the ego. This is the meaning of the Hasidic saying that if one man wishes to teach another, he should bear in mind "that the soul of his fellow man is also bound to the Creator in devotion, and that he himself stands and teaches before God."[18]

This level synthesizes two attitudes which at first seem mutually exclusive: one which takes seriously the concrete situation in the

---

18 Salomo Birnbaum, *The Life and Sayings of the Baal Shem*, tr. Irene Birnbaum (New York, 1933), p. 18.

actual, given world, and another which looks on its encounter with the numinous substratum as the only authentic reality. Their synthesis constitutes "symbolic life," as is illustrated by a characteristic Hasidic story:

> Once I was present at a conversation between my teacher and a widow. He spoke to her of her widowhood with the kind words of a comforter, and she took his words as comfort for her soul, and gathered strength from them. But I saw him weep and I myself could not help weeping: and then I realized that he was speaking to the widowed glory of God.[19]

It is in this sense that we must understand the last attainable stage of transformation mysticism, and it is everywhere described in similar terms. In Jewish mysticism this stage is known as "adhesion." For the mystic of this phase, life in the world is possible; he needs no heaven, no hereafter, no Messianic kingdom, for all this is present in the world, though veiled and hidden.

In the intermediary phases of mysticism the encounter of the ego with the numinous occurs at points chosen by nature, and even for the creative man the encounter seldom occurs elsewhere. The mature mystic of the final phase, however, lives in a permanent transparence. His self has attained lasting transparence, and so has the world without and within him. With this in mind we shall be in a position to understand the ultimate and central content of last-stage mysticism, its vision of unity.

The radical pursuit of the introverted *via negativa* leads through the experience of a hierarchy of heavens and hells to a merger of the two; it moves farther and farther from consciousness to ecstatic demolition of the ego. The cosmogonic, outward mysticism of extraversion leads to devotion to an external world that embraces all life and culminates in a pantheistic or panentheistic seizure in which the ego is overpowered. But the anthropocentric form of mystical experience, which is the substance of all transformation mysticism, experiences both inner and outer worlds as shells. When these shells become transparent, the multiplicity of the numinous gives way to an experience of unity, in which the self is made

19 Buber, *Die chassidischen Bücher*, p. 505.

manifest as the creative center out of which both man and world are generated.

Wherever there is true mystical experience, the numinous substratum bursts through the given cosmos. But, except in the mature form of mysticism, this transcending of the limit is a seizure that carries the mystic out of humanity and the world into an inhuman sphere outside of the world. When this occurs, the ravished ego falls back into a hostile world fraught with uncertainty and anxiety. But the immanent world-transforming mysticism of the mature phase strives intrinsically to overcome existential uncertainty and anxiety. Only when the world ceases to be filled with hostile, crushing shapes, only when all form has become transparent and a vision of unity has been attained, is its mission completed.

But the vision of unity is bound up with unity of being. Here again the manifestation of the numinous corresponds to the development of the personality. Only in the integrated man, who is attached to a center which is his own creative center and which he experiences as creative center of the world, can the circle close; that circle is peace. For this illumined man the world is transparent and one. But this integration, like everything that happens on this level, is immersed in paradox. The man of this phase is in the world and outside it, at rest and in creative motion, attached to the numinous and also at home in himself. In him lives the creative word and also silence. He lives in multiplicity and unity.

And so it seems that the mystical man, in our broad sense, is the only man who does not content himself with partial aspects of the outward and inward world. He is the only man whose creative unrest cannot be appeased by narcotics which bring him peace within a fragmentary, provisional shell where the ego may take refuge. The mystical man takes seriously the existential fact that man has no shell but is an atom in an infinite universe. But, in spite of all that, he feels that he is not lost and alone. He cannot, to be sure, apprehend the nucleus of human existence, but the numinous in man is also the human in the numinous. Engaged in a dialogue with the self and receiving guidance from the self, a guidance which the ego experiences as meaningful, the ego fashions anew its likeness to the self. This leads to a paradoxical form of intimacy which is often expressed in the symbols of friendship and kinship between the ego and the self and which compensates for the isolation of man in the cosmos.

But also this likeness of the ego to the self is eminently realized in the sphere of the creative.

Just as a creative, numinous force fills the world with living form in an endless hierarchy of manifestations, so does a creative numinous element in man fill the world with living form from within in an equally endless hierarchy of manifestations. The mythological world of early man is itself flooded with forms, and as consciousness develops, these forms enter into a hierarchic order. While in the density of the archetypal figure everything is fused and confused, the prism of consciousness splits the colors and reveals systems of spiritual order and law, a spirit-reality behind all the multiplicity of forms. But beyond the form and in the form the numinous remains at work as center, as nucleus of the creative void. And this occurs not only in the world formed by an extrahuman numen, not only in the tree, the animal, the star, but also in the world of human numinosity—in the poem, the visual representation, the idea. Man's likeness to the creative numen of the world's genesis is the twinlike foundation of mystical man.

The phenomena of mystical anthropology are processes which encompass the self and the ego; and the area of the *anthropos,* in which the central process is enacted, is human, but it is also transcendental. That is why there is here so great a danger of a mythologizing, gnosticizing misunderstanding. What appears as man's likeness to God and also as the formlessness of the godhead is the ego's extreme experience of the self, which can be characterized as extrahuman, superhuman, and divine, but which must also be said to constitute the human as such.

The experience of the self and of its phenomenology, changing in the course of human history and culminating in last-stage mysticism, not only reflects the stages in the development of human consciousness, but also the development of man in his very essence.

The self-revelation of mankind is the revelation of the changing self. To say that with this statement about last-stage mysticism we surpass the limits of psychology is both true and false; the cause of

413

this uncertainty is that though the self is center and central content of the anthropological area, it actually transcends the psychological area.

Here we cannot show to what extent the self is prepsychological and extrapsychological; it suffices to point out that this fact is of crucial importance in death mysticism and in the after-death mysticism which we might call immortality mysticism. The difference between uroboros mysticism and transformation mysticism extends to this mysticism of immortality. Here ecstatic uroboros mysticism attains fulfillment in dissolution of the ego. The drop of water that is the ego sinks back into the sea. "In the drunken, my friends, you can see plainly that there is a link with God, where there is no being of one's own."[20] In contrast to this, the aim of world-transforming mysticism is to carry on life in a continuous mystical frame, so that when in the metamorphoses of the personality and the world the vain and trivial has been banished, "the fixed star, the star of eternal love" may shine.

Just as the individuation process is not a psychological regression but in a certain sense a culmination, accordingly last-stage mysticism is the most comprehensive form of high mysticism. By its achievement of lasting transparency, the stage of discontinuous encounter with the self is transcended. The mystical transparence of the world resembles an all-embracing radiation of the self, and the ego encounters the numinous everywhere and at all times. But it no longer encounters it in the anonymity of the early age, when the numinous was also "radiated." In that age man was unaware of his self and the numinous was anonymously shut up in the object, but now man and godhead meet one another in the open. The world takes form around a united personality, and another expression of this aspect of unity is that the numinous extends beyond the blurred mass of the formless and the indefinable onrush of numinous forms, and takes, or at least is capable of taking, the personal encounter as an encounter with the self. The numinous now speaks as *anthropos*-self to the personality, no longer as a particular numinous phenomenon to an accidental ego.

20 Quoted from F. A. G. Tholuck, *Blühtensammlung aus der morgenländischen Mystik* (Berlin, 1825), p. 219, in Gerardus van der Leeuw, *Phänomenologie der Religion* (Tübingen, 1933), p. 466.

The Egyptian king lives in this world as Horus; his work is the elevation of Osiris, Osirification; when he dies, he dies as Horus and becomes Osiris. Now in immortality mysticism the son as self, as nucleus, as gold, and as product of his life's great work gives himself back to the godhead.

Thus in the mysticism of life's phases, man is transformed in continuously new mystical encounters. At the beginning it seems as though he were effecting the change, at the end as though he were undergoing it. Be that as it may, just as the Horus-king becomes Osiris, the personality is in the end transposed from the ego to the self, and the two are "twins."

Thus from its earliest beginnings the human personality is in constant mystical motion. Reaching inwardly toward the self and outwardly toward the world in ever-new encounters, forever changing, man from childhood onward passes through all the stages of transformation mysticism. And just as the beginning of source mysticism extends back into an unknown sphere prior to the emergence of the ego, so does the end of immortality mysticism extend into an unknown realm beyond the extinction of the ego. The inexplicable fact that man's very center is an unknown creative force which lives within him and molds him in ever-new forms and transformations, this mystery which accompanies him throughout his life, follows him even into death and beyond. So the circle closes, and man ends as he began, a *homo mysticus*.

APPENDICES

Biographical Notes

ERNESTO BUONAIUTI, Ph.D., D.Theol. Born 1880, Rome; died 1946. Professor of the history of early Christianity at the University of Rome from 1915 to 1931, when his appointment ended owing to his refusal to take the Fascist oath of allegiance. After the second World War, in 1945, the Italian Government restored him to his chair, but he had not actually resumed teaching when he died in 1946. A friend of Buonaiuti's has written: "A leading spirit of the Modernist movement, Buonaiuti advocated a return to the primal social values of Christianity implied in the brotherhood of man, values which in his opinion had been obscured by the rigid doctrinalism of an age-old hierarchy. Despite repeated official condemnation of his views, he never in his heart departed from the Catholic Church." He was under the ban of excommunication during the last two decades of his life. Among nearly a hundred publications, the following are chosen for mention here: *Lo gnosticismo* (Rome, 1907); *Il cristianesimo medioevale* (Città di Castello, 1914); *Le Modernisme catholique* (Paris, 1937); *Il cristianesimo nell' Africa romana* (Bari, 1928); *Storia del cristianesimo* (3 vols., Milan, 1942–43); *La fede dei nostri Padri* (Modena, 1944); *I maestri della tradizione mediterranea* (Rome, 1945); *Pellegrino di Roma* (autobiography; Rome, 1945); *Lutero de la Riforma in Germania* (2nd edn., Rome, 1945). Buonaiuti lectured at eight Eranos meetings, the last in 1940.

FRIEDRICH HEILER, Ph.D. (Munich), D.Theol. (hon., Kiel), D.D. (Glasgow). Born 1892, Munich, and died there in 1967. Beginning in 1920, he was professor of the comparative history of religion, Marburg University. In 1934, after resisting the application of the Nuremburg Laws to members of the church, he was transferred to the philosophical faculty at Greifswald University; in 1935, joined the philosophical faculty, Marburg; in 1948, recalled to the theological faculty. Retired 1962. He lectured or served as guest professor at the universities of Uppsala, Lund, Chicago, Salonika, Athens, and Ankara, the Episcopal Seminary in Alexandria, Virginia, and from his retirement to his death at the University of Munich. 1958–59, traveled and lectured in Japan, Java, Siam, Burma, and India, where he became a member of Sanskrit College, Calcutta. 1929, president of the Evangelical-Ecumenical Union; 1953, president of the German branch of the International Union for the History of Religion; 1956, president of the German branch of the World Congress of Faiths. Among many published works on Eastern and Western religion may be mentioned: *Prayer, A Study in the History and Psychology of Religion* (Munich, 1918; tr., London and New York, 1932; paperback, New York, 1958) ; *The Spirit of Worship* (Munich, 1921; tr., London, 1926) ; *The Gospel of Sādhu Sundar Singh* (Munich, 1923; tr., London, 1927) ; *Urkirche und Ostkirche* (Munich, 1937) ; *Die Religionen der Menschheit* (Stuttgart, 1959) ; *Erscheinungsformen und Wesen der Religion (Phänomenologie)* (Stuttgart, 1961). His writings have been translated also into French, Swedish, Dutch, and Japanese. Professor Heiler lectured at the first two Eranos meetings.

WILHELM KOPPERS, Ph.D., professor of ethnology. Born 1886, Menzelen, Lower Rhine; died 1961 in Vienna. Studied Catholic theology and philosophy at St. Gabriel, Mödling, and in Rome; ethnology and Indology at University of Vienna (Ph.D., 1917). Lecturer, Vienna, 1924; assistant professor 1928, full professor 1934, dismissed 1938, reinstated 1945. Founder and director of the Institute for Ethnology. Expeditions to Tierra del Fuego and central India. Publications: *Die ethnologische Wirtschaftsforschung* (1917) ; *Die Anfänge des menschlichen Gemeinschaftslebens in Spiegel der neueren Völkerkunde* (Munich-Gladbach, 1921) ; *Unter Feuerland-Indianer* (with M. Gusinde; Stuttgart, 1924) ; *Völker und Kulturen I: Gesellschaft und Wirtschaft der Völker* (with W. Schmidt; Regensburg, 1924) ; *Gottesglaube und Gebete der Jamana auf Feuerland* (Düsseldorf, 1926) ; *Handbuch der Methode in der kulturhistorischen Ethnologie* (with W. Schmidt; Münster, 1937) ; *Die Bhil in Zentralindien* (Vienna, 1948) ; *Der Urmensch und sein Weltbild* (Vienna, 1949; English, 1952; Italian, 1953). Editor: *Zeitschrift für Ethnologie und Linguistik* (Vienna, 1924–32) ; *Mitteilungen der Anthropologischen Gesellschaft Wien,* since 1929; *Anthropos* (Vienna, 1924–32) ; *Wiener Beiträge zur Kulturgeschichte und Linguistik* (Mödling, 1930–49) ; *Acta ethnologica et linguistica* (Vienna, after 1950). Professor Koppers lectured at the Eranos meeting of 1944.

LOUIS MASSIGNON, Ph.D. Born 1883, Nogent-sur-Marne, France; died 1962, Paris. Professor of Islamic studies, Collège de France; professor, École de Hautes-Études, Sorbonne; president, Institut des études iraniennes, Sorbonne; secretary, Comité France-Islam; vice-president, Comité France-Maghreb. Member, royal academies of Afghanistan, Belgium, Denmark,

Iran, Iraq, Netherlands, and Sweden, academies of Egypt and Damascus, Royal Asiatic Society (London), Russian Academy of Sciences, and American Oriental Society. Legion of Honor; Croix de Guerre (1914–18). Formerly editor, *Revue du monde musulman, Revue des études islamiques,* and *Annuaire du monde musulman.* Resident many years in Arab countries. From an extensive bibliography the following may be cited: *Essai sur les origines du lexique technique de la mystique musulmane* (new edn., Paris, 1954); *La Passion d'al-Hallaj, martyr mystique de l'Islam* (Paris, 1922); *Recueil de textes inédits concernant l'histoire de la mystique en pays d'Islam* (Paris, 1929). Professor Massignon lectured at eleven Eranos meetings, 1937–55.

JEAN DE MENASCE, O.P., D.S.T., B.A., B.Litt. (Oxon.). Born 1902, Alexandria, Egypt. Since 1949, professor of ancient Iranian religion, École des Hautes-Études, Sorbonne. 1938–48, professor of comparative religion, University of Fribourg, Switzerland. 1951 and 1953, Temporary Member, Institute for Advanced Study, Princeton. Chief publications: *Quand Israel aime Dieu* (Paris, 1932); *Shkand-Gumānīk Vicār* (Fribourg, 1945); *Le Livre de Daniel* (Paris, 1953); *Le Denkart: une encyclopédie mazdéenne* (Paris, 1958); *Feux et Fondations Pieuses dans l'Iran Sassanide* (Paris, 1964); articles in *Journal asiatique* (Paris), *Revue de l'histoire des religions* (Paris), *Anthropos* (Fribourg). Father de Menasce lectured at the 1944 and 1945 Eranos meetings.

ERICH NEUMANN, Ph.D. Born 1905, Berlin; died 1960, Tel Aviv, Israel. Studied medicine and completed the examinations in 1933 in Germany. Left Germany in 1933, and after 1934 practiced as an analytical psychologist in Tel Aviv. Patron and lecturer, C. G. Jung Institute, Zurich; lectured elsewhere in Switzerland and the Netherlands. Member International Association for Analytical Psychology and president of The Israel Association of Analytical Psychologists. Publications: *Tiefenpsychologie und neue Ethik* (Zurich, 1949); *The Origins and History of Consciousness* (tr., New York and London, 1954); *The Great Mother* (tr., New York and London, 1954); *Amor and Psyche: The Psychic Development of the Feminine* (tr., New York and London, 1956); *Umkreisung der Mitte* (3 vols., Zurich, 1953–54), partially tr. in *Art and the Creative Unconscious* (New York and London, 1959). Dr. Neumann lectured at all the Eranos meetings from 1948 to 1960.

HENRI-CHARLES PUECH, Ph.D. Born 1902, Montpellier, France. Since 1929, directeur d'études, École des Hautes-Études, Sorbonne: professor of the history of the early Church and patrology and president of the "section des sciences religieuses." Also, since 1952, professor of the history of religion, Collège de France. Member, Institut de France (Académie des Inscriptions et Belles-Lettres), 1962– ; president of the Institut, 1968. Captain of a Zouave regiment in the second World War. Officer of the Legion of Honor (1951). Editor of the *Revue de l'histoire des religions*. Special fields: history of religion and ancient philosophy; patristics; oriental religions (particularly Gnosticism and Manichaeism) in relation to the origin of Christianity. Publications include: with G. Quispel and W. C. van Unnik, *The Jung Codex, A Newly Recovered Gnostic Papyrus: Three Studies* (tr. and ed. Frank Leslie Cross, London, 1955); with A. Vaillant, *Le Traité contre les Bogomiles de Cosmas le Prêtre* (Paris, 1945); *Le Manichéisme: Son fondateur, sa doctrine* (Paris, 1949); editions of Coptic writings found near Nag Hammādi (various, in French and English, 1956–68); and numerous articles in encyclopedias, scholarly journals, and annuals of the Collège de France. Professor Puech lectured at the Eranos meetings of 1936 and 1951.

GILLES QUISPEL, Ph.D. Born 1916, Rotterdam. Since 1952, professor of early Christian literature, University of Utrecht. 1948–49, Bollingen Fellow in Rome; 1951–52, lecturer, C. G. Jung Institute, Zurich. Special interest: Gnosticism. Publications include: *The Jung Codex* (see foregoing note on H.-C. Puech); *Gli Etruschi nel Vecchio Testamento* (Florence, 1939); *De Bronnen van Tertullianus' "Adversus Marcionem"* (Leiden, 1942); *Gnosis als Weltreligion* (Zurich, 1951); *Evangelium Verstatis* (Zurich, 1956); *De Resurrectione* (Zurich, 1963); *La Lettre de Ptolémèe à Flora* (Paris, 1967); *Maharius, das Thomasevangelium und das Lied von der Perle* (Leiden, 1967). He has lectured at seven Eranos meetings between 1947 and 1965.

ERWIN ROUSSELLE, Ph.D., Jur.D. (both Heidelberg). Born 1890, Hanau a. M., Germany; died 1949, Upper Bavaria. Scholar of Semitic and Oriental philology, specializing in Chinese, Tibetan, and Sanskrit and in related studies in Buddhism. 1924–29, professor of German philosophy, Chinese National University, guest professor of comparative linguistics, Tsing Hua University, and director, Sino-Indian Institute, Yenching University. 1931, succeeded Richard Wilhelm as director, China Institute, Frankfurt a. M.; 1935, appointed extraordinary professor, University of Frankfurt. 1938–40, travels in the interior and other parts of China on research for the China Institute. Subsequently removed from both posts at Frankfurt by the Nazi regime, on political grounds; 1943, officially silenced;

1948, restored to both directorate and professorial chair. Publications include *Mysterium der Wandlung: Der Weg zur Verwandlung in den Weltreligionen* (Darmstadt, 1923); a translation of the *Tao Tê Ching* into German (Frankfurt, 1950; an earlier edition was destroyed in the war); and many articles in the China Institute periodical *Sinica*. Professor Rousselle lectured at the first three Eranos meetings, 1933–35.

BORIS PETROVITCH VYSHESLAWZEFF, Jur.D., professor of moral theology. Born 1877, Moscow; died 1954, Geneva. Studied law at the University of Moscow until 1908, continued his studies in Berlin, Rome, Paris, and especially Marburg. Lecturer for philosophy of law and history of philosophy, Moscow 1910, full professor of philosophy of law, Moscow 1917. Expelled 1922, emigrated to Berlin; after 1925, professor of moral theology at the Russian Orthodox Theological Institute, Paris; participated in the ecumenical movement and in founding the Russian religious-philosophical publishing house of the periodical *Put* ("The Way"). Publications (in Russian): *Fichte's Ethics* (Moscow, 1914); *The Russian Nature in Dostoievski's Work* (2nd edn., Berlin, 1923); *The Heart in Christian and Indian Mysticism* (Paris, 1929); *Ethics of the Sublimated Eros* (Paris, 1931); *The Crisis of the Industrial Society* (New York, 1952); *The Philosophical Poverty of Marxism* (pseud. B. Petrov, Frankfurt, 1952); (in French): "Marcel Proust," with R. Honnert, *Cahiers de la Quinzaine*, Ser. 20, No. 5 (Paris, 1930); "Descartes, le Procès du Cartésianisme," with J. Maritain, *Cahiers de la Quinzaine*, Ser. 21, No. 5 (Paris, 1931); editor, *l'Église, l'État et le Monde* (Geneva, 1937). Professor Vysheslawzeff lectured at the Eranos meeting of 1936.

HEINRICH ZIMMER, Ph.D. (Berlin). Born 1890, Greifswald, Germany; died 1943, New York. 1923–38, professor of Indology, Heidelberg University; dismissed because of his anti-Nazi views. 1939–40, guest at Balliol College, Oxford. 1941–43, lecturer, Columbia University. He was son of Heinrich Zimmer, eminent scholar of Celtic philology; was student of Sanskrit, Pali, Pahlavi, Arabic, Chinese, Gaelic, Gothic, Old Norse, Greek, Latin, as well as modern European languages; married Christiane von Hofmannsthal, daughter of the Austrian poet. Influenced the work of C. G. Jung as well as that of Thomas Mann, who dedicated his novel *The Transposed Heads* to him. The first volume of Bollingen Series (1943) was dedicated to his memory; four posthumous works, completed and edited by Joseph Campbell, were subsequently published in the Series: *Myths and Symbols in Indian Art and Civilization* (1946); *The King and the Corpse* (1948); *Philosophies of India* (1951); and *The Art of Indian Asia* (2 vols., 1955).

423

Other posthuma were *Der Weg zum Selbst,* ed. C. G. Jung (Zurich, 1944),
and *Hindu Medicine,* ed. Ludwig Edelstein (Baltimore, 1948). Other
principal works: *Kunstform und Yoga* (Berlin, 1926); *Spiel um den Ele-
fanten* (1929); *Ewiges Indien* (1930); *Indische Sphären* (1955); *Maya:
Der Indische Mythos* (Stuttgart, 1936; 2nd edn., Zurich, 1952); and *Weis-
heit Indiens* (1938). Professor Zimmer lectured at the Eranos meetings of
1933, 1934, 1938, and 1939.

Contents of the *Eranos-Jahrbücher*

The contents of the *Eranos-Jahrbücher*, consisting of thirty-five volumes through 1966, are listed (in translation) for reference. The lectures were delivered in German (chiefly), French, English, and Italian. In the first eight *Jahrbücher*, all the papers were published in German; in later volumes, they were published in their original language. An index of contributors is at the end. In the following list, the titles of papers translated in the present series are indicated by superior numbers for volumes, thus: 1. *Spirit and Nature* (1954); 2. *The Mysteries* (1955); 3. *Man and Time* (1957); 4. *Spiritual Disciplines* (1960); 5. *Man and Transformation* (1964); 6. *The Mystic Vision* (1968).

I: 1933: Yoga and Meditation in the East and the West
> HEINRICH ZIMMER: On the Significance of the Indian Tantric Yoga [4]
> Mrs. RHYS DAVIDS: Religious Exercises in India and the Religious Man
> ERWIN ROUSELLE: Spiritual Guidance in Contemporary Taoism [4]
> C. G. JUNG: A Study in the Process of Individuation
> G. R. HEYER: The Meaning of Eastern Wisdom for Western Spiritual Guidance
> FRIEDRICH HEILER: Contemplation in Christian Mysticism [4]
> ERNESTO BUONAIUTI: Meditation and Contemplation in the Roman Catholic Church

II: 1934: Symbolism and Spiritual Guidance in the East and the West
> ERWIN ROUSSELLE: Dragon and Mare, Figures of Primordial Chinese Mythology [6]
> J. W. HAUER: Symbols and Experience of the Self in Indo-Aryan Mysticism
> HEINRICH ZIMMER: Indian Myths as Symbols
> Mrs. RHYS DAVIDS: On the History of the Symbol of the Wheel
> C. G. JUNG: The Archetypes of the Collective Unconscious
> G. R. HEYER: The Symbolism of Dürer's Melancholia

FRIEDRICH HEILER: The Madonna as a Religious Symbol [6]
ERNESTO BUONAIUTI: Symbols and Rites in the Religious Life of Various Monastic Orders [6]
MARTIN BUBER: Symbolic and Sacramental Existence in Judaism [4]
RUDOLF BERNOULLI: On the Symbolism of Geometrical Figures and of Numbers
SIGRID STRAUSS-KLOEBE: On the Psychological Significance of the Astrological Symbol
M. C. CAMMERLOHER: The Position of Art in the Psychology of Our Time [4]
Swami YATISWARANANDA: A Brief Survey of Hindu Religious Symbolism in Its Relation to Spiritual Exercises and Higher Development

III: 1935: Spiritual Guidance in the East and the West

C. G. Jung: Dream Symbols of the Individuation Process [4]
G. R. HEYER: On Getting Along with Oneself
ERWIN ROUSSELLE: Lao-tse's Journey through Soul, History, and World
Mrs. RHYS DAVIDS: Man, the Search, and Nirvana
RUDOLF BERNOULLI: Spiritual Development as Reflected in Alchemy and Related Disciplines [4]
ERNESTO BUONAIUTI: I. Gnostic Initiation and Early Christianity. II. The Exercises of St. Ignatius Loyola [6]
ROBERT EISLER: The Riddle of the Gospel of St. John
J. B. LANG: Pauline and Analytical Spiritual Guidance

IV: 1936: The Shaping of the Idea of Redemption in the East and the West

C. G. JUNG: The Idea of Redemption in Alchemy
PAUL MASSON-OURSEL: I. The Indian Theories of Redemption in the Frame of the Religions of Salvation. II. The Doctrine of Grace in the Religious Thought of India [2]
Mrs. RHYS DAVIDS: Redemption in India's Past and in Our Present
ERNESTO BUONAIUTI: Redemption in the Orphic Mysteries
HENRI-CHARLES PUECH: The Concept of Redemption in Manichaeism [6]
BORIS VYSHESLAWZEFF: Two Ways of Redemption: Redemption as a Solution of the Tragic Contradiction [6]

V: 1937: The Shaping of the Idea of Redemption in the East and the West

C. G. JUNG: Some Observations on the Visions of Zosimos
LOUIS MASSIGNON: The Origins and Significance of Gnosticism in Islam
PAUL MASSON-OURSEL: I. The Indian Conception of Psychology. II. Indian Techniques of Salvation [1]
JEAN PRZYLUSKI: I. Redemption after Death in the Upanishads and

C. G. JUNG: Transformation Symbolism in the Mass [2]
ERNESTO BUONAIUTI: Christ and St. Paul [6]
MAX PULVER: Gnostic Experience and Gnostic Life in Early Christianity (from the Sources)
ERNESTO BUONAIUTI: Christology and Ecclesiology in St. Paul [6]

IX: 1942: The Hermetic Principle in Mythology, Gnosis, and Alchemy

C. KERÉNYI: Hermes Guide of Souls: The Mythologem of the Masculine Origin of Life
GEORGES NAGEL: The God Thoth according to the Egyptian Texts
MAX PULVER: Jesus' Round Dance and Crucifixion according to the Acts of St. John [2]
C. G. JUNG: The Spirit Mercurius
J. B. LANG: The Demiurge of the Priests' Codex (Gen. 1 to 2 : 4a) and His Significance for Gnosticism

X: 1943: Ancient Sun Cults and Light Symbolism in Gnosticism and Early Christianity

GEORGES NAGEL: The Cult of the Sun in Early Egypt
CHARLES VIROLLEAUD: The God Shamash in Ancient Mesopotamia
C. KERÉNYI: Father Helios
WALTER WILI: The Roman Sun-Gods and Mithras
PAUL SCHMITT: Sol Invictus: Reflections on Late Roman Religion and Politics
MAX PULVER: The Experience of Light in the Gospel of St. John, in the "Corpus hermeticum," in Gnosticism, and in the Eastern Church [4]
LOUIS MASSIGNON: Astrological Infiltration in Islamic Religious Thought
HUGO RAHNER: The Christian Mystery of Sun and Moon

XI: 1944: The Mysteries

C. KERÉNYI: The Mysteries of the Kabeiroi (Appendix: The Castello of Tegna) [2]
WALTER WILI: The Orphic Mysteries and the Greek Spirit [2]
PAUL SCHMITT: The Ancient Mysteries in the Society of Their Time, Their Transformation and Most Recent Echoes [2]
GEORGES NAGEL: The "Mysteries" of Osiris in Ancient Egypt [2]
JEAN DE MENASCE: The Mysteries and the Religion of Iran [2]
FRITZ MEIER: The Mystery of the Ka'ba: Symbol and Reality in Islamic Mysticism [2]
WILHELM KOPPERS: On the Origin of the Mysteries in the Light of Ethnology and Indology [6]
MAX PULVER: On the Scope of the Gnostic Mysteries
JULIUS BAUM: Symbolic Representations of the Eucharist [2]
HUGO RAHNER: The Christian Mystery and the Pagan Mysteries [2]

* Title changed in PEY 1 to "The Phenomenology of the Spirit in Fairy Tales."

XV: 1947: Man

ADOLF PORTMANN: The Problem of Origins
C. KERÉNYI: Primordial Man and Mystery
FRIEDRICH DESSAUER: Man and Cosmos
KARL LUDWIG SCHMIDT: Man as the Image of God in the Old and the New Testament
HUGO RAHNER: Origen's View of Man
GILLES QUISPEL: The Conception of Man in Valentinian Gnosis
LOUIS MASSIGNON: The Perfect Man in Islam and Its Eschatological Originality
VICTOR WHITE: Anthropologia rationalis: The Aristotelian-Thomist Conception of Man
LEO BAECK: Individuum ineffabile

XVI: 1948: Man

HUGO RAHNER: Man as Player
GILLES QUISPEL: Gnostic Man: The Doctrine of Basilides [6]
GERARDUS VAN DER LEEUW: Man and Civilization: The Implications of the Term "Evolution of Man"
C. KERÉNYI: Man and Mask [4]
JOHN LAYARD: The Making of Man in Malekula
C. G. JUNG: On the Self
ERICH NEUMANN: Mystical Man [6]
HERMANN WEYL: Science as Symbolic Construction of Man
MARKUS FIERZ: On Physical Knowledge
ADOLF PORTMANN: Man as Student of Nature

XVII: 1949: Man and the Mythical World

GERARDUS VAN DER LEEUW: Primordial Time and Final Time [3]
C. KERÉNYI: The Orphic Cosmogony and the Origin of Orphism
E. O. JAMES: Myth and Ritual
HENRY CORBIN: The "Narrative of Initiation" and Hermeticism in Iran
ERICH NEUMANN: The Mythical World and the Individual
LOUIS BEIRNAERT: The Mythical Dimension in Christian Sacramentalism
GERSHOM G. SCHOLEM: Cabala and Myth
JULIUS BAUM: Representations of the Germanic Saga of Gods and Heroes in Nordic Art
PAUL RADIN: The Basic Myth of the North American Indians
ADOLF E. JENSEN: The Mythical World View of the Ancient Agricultural Peoples
ADOLF PORTMANN: Mythical Elements in Science

XVIII: 1950: From the World of the Archetypes (Special Volume for C. G. Jung on His Seventy-fifth Birthday, July 26, 1950)

HANS LEISEGANG: The God-Man as Archetype

GERSHOM G. SCHOLEM: On the Development of the Cabalistic Conception of the Shekhinah

GILLES QUISPEL: Man and Energy in Patristic Christianity

ERICH NEUMANN: The Psyche and the Transformation of the Planes of Reality

KARL LÖWITH: The Dynamics of History, and Historicism

HERBERT READ: The Dynamics of Art

MARTIN D'ARCY: The Power of Caritas and the Holy Spirit

ADOLF PORTMANN: The Significance of Images in the Living Transformation of Energy

MAX KNOLL: Quantum Conceptions of Energy in Physics and Psychology

LANCELOT LAW WHYTE: A Scientific View of the "Creative Energy" of Man

XXII: 1953: Man and Earth

ERICH NEUMANN: The Significance of the Earth Archetype for Modern Times

MIRCEA ELIADE: Terra Mater and Cosmic Hierogamies

GILLES QUISPEL: Gnosis and Earth

HENRY CORBIN: Celestial Earth and the Body of the Resurrection according to Various Iranian Traditions: I. Mazdean Imago Terrae. II. Hurqalya's Mystical Earth (Shaikhism)

GERSHOM G. SCHOLEM: The Conception of the Golem and Its Tellurian and Magical Contexts

GIUSEPPE TUCCI: Earth as Conceived of in Indian and Tibetan Religion, with Special Regard to the Tantras

DAISETZ T. SUZUKI: The Role of Nature in Zen

JEAN DANIÉLOU: Earth and Paradise in Greek Mysticism and Theology

ERNST BENZ: I. The Sacred Cave in Eastern Christianity. II. The Charismatic Type of the Russian Saints

ADOLF PORTMANN: The Earth as the Home of Life

XXIII: 1954: Man and Transformation

MIRCEA ELIADE: Mystery and Spiritual Regeneration in Extra-European Religions [5]

FRITZ MEIER: The Transformation of Man in Mystical Islam [5]

HENRY CORBIN: Divine Epiphany and Spiritual Birth in Ismailian Gnosis [5]

ERICH NEUMANN: The Creative Principle in Psychic Transformation

PAUL TILLICH: The Importance of New Being for Christian Theology [5]

DAISETZ T. SUZUKI: The Awakening of a New Consciousness in Zen [5]

LANCELOT LAW WHYTE: The Growth of Ideas [5]

ERNST BENZ: Theogony and the Transformation of Man in Friedrich Wilhelm Joseph Schelling [5]

433

WALTER CORTI: The Platonic Academy Down Through History and as a Task of Our Time

JOSEPH CAMPBELL: The Symbol without Meaning

ADOLF PORTMANN: The Interpretation of Meaning as a Biological Problem

XXVII: 1958: Man and Peace

ERICH NEUMANN: Peace as a Symbol of Life

HENRY CORBIN: Peace and Disquiet of the Soul in the Ṣūfism of Rūzbehān Baqlī of Shīrāz

MIRCEA ELIADE: The "Coincidentia oppositorum" and the Mystery of Totality

GERSHOM G. SCHOLEM: The Doctrine of the Righteous Man in Jewish Mysticism

HERBERT READ: The Flower of Peace

HERBERT W. SCHNEIDER: Peace as Scientific Problem and as Personal Experience

ERNST BENZ: The Idea of Peace in the Present Conflict between Buddhism and Christianity in Asia

CHUNG-YUAN CHANG: Self-Realization and the Inner Process of Peace

HANS KAYSER: The Harmony of the World

ADOLF PORTMANN: Struggle and Peace as a Biological Problem

XXVIII: 1959: The Renewal of Man

ERICH NEUMANN: Genesis, Development, and Renewal in the Psychic Process

HENRY CORBIN: The Hidden Imam and the Renewal of Man

MIRCEA ELIADE: Religious Dimensions of Cosmic Renewal

GERSHOM G. SCHOLEM: A Contribution to the Understanding of the Messianic Idea in Judaism

ERNST BENZ: The Threefold Aspect of the Superman

HERBERT READ: Nihilism and Renewal in the Art of Our Time

WALTER CORTI: Man as an Organ of God

JOSEPH CAMPBELL: Renewal Myths and Rites of the Primitive Hunters and Planters

JOHN LAYARD: The Freeing of the Spirit in Malekula from the Withholding Soul

ADOLF PORTMANN: The Contribution of Biology to a New Image of Man

XXIX: 1960: Man and Creative Form

ERICH NEUMANN: The Psyche as the Place of Creation

HENRY CORBIN: Toward a Morphology of Shī'ite Spirituality

MIRCEA ELIADE: Myths and Symbols of the Rope

GERSHOM G. SCHOLEM: The Mystical Form of the Godhead in the Cabala

HERBERT READ: The Origins of Form in Art

HELLMUT WILHELM: The "Personal City" as the Scene of Creation

HERBERT READ: High Noon and Darkest Night: Some Reflections on Ortega y Gasset's Philosophy of Art
HENRY CORBIN: Comparative Spiritual Hermeneutics. I. Swedenborg. II. Ismailian Gnosis
HELLMUT WILHELM: Journeys of the Spirit
IRA PROGOFF: The Integrity of Life and Death
GILBERT DURAND: Dualisms and Dramatization: The Antithetical Organization and Dramatic Structures of the Imagination
VICTOR ZUCKERKANDL: Circle and Arrow in the Work of Beethoven
GERALD HOLTON: Style and Realization in Physics
ADOLF PORTMANN: The Idea of Evolution as the Destiny of Charles Darwin

XXXIV: 1965: Form as a Challenge of the Mind

GILLES QUISPEL: The Song of the Pearl
GERALD HOLTON: The Metaphor of Space-Time Events in Science
HENRY CORBIN: The Configuration of the Temple of the Ka'aba as Secret of Spiritual Life
STANLEY ROMAINE HOPPER: Symbolic Reality and the Poet's Task
REINHOLD MERKELBACH: The Cosmogony of the Mysteries of Mithra
IRA PROGOFF: Form, Time, and Opus: The Dialectic of the Creative Psyche
GILBERT DURAND: Tasks of the Mind and Imperatives of Being
MAX KNOLL: The World of Inner Luminous Phenomena
SIEGFRIED MORENZ: The Egyptian Cult of the Dead and the Structure of Egyptian Religion
ADOLF PORTMANN: Gestalt as the First and Last Problem of Biology

XXXV: 1966: Creation and Configuration

GERSHOM G. SCHOLEM: Martin Buber's Conception of Judaism
GILBERT DURAND: Artistic Creation as Dynamic Configuration of Structures
IRA PROGOFF: The Man Who Transforms Consciousness: The Inner Myths of Martin Buber, Paul Tillich, and C. G. Jung
REINHOLD MERKELBACH: Content and Form in the Symbolic Tales of Antiquity
HENRY CORBIN: From the Heroic Epic to the Mystic Epic
GILLES QUISPEL: Faust: Symbol of Western Man
JOSEPH GANTNER: L'Immagine del Cour. The Prefigurative Forms of the Imagination and Their Effect in Art
SCHMUEL SAMBURSKY: Phenomenon and Theory: The Physical Thinking of Antiquity in the Light of Modern Physics
JAMES HILLMAN: On Psychological Creativity
ADOLF PORTMANN: Genesis and Development as a Problem of Biology

XXXVI: 1967: The Polarity of Life

GILLES QUISPEL: Man's Divine Double: On the Encounter with the Self in Gnosis

CONTENTS OF THE "ERANOS-JAHRBÜCHER"

437

Index of Contributors

References are to volumes in the foregoing list. Places of residence at the time of publication are noted in parentheses.

Abbreviations

ABA *Abhandlungen der preussischen (deutschen) Akademie der Wissenschaften.* Berlin.

CSEL Corpus Scriptorum Ecclesiasticorum Latinorum. Vienna, 1866– .

CWJ Collected Works of C. G. Jung. New York (from 1967, Princeton; Bollingen Series XX) and London.

GCS *Die griechischen christlichen Schriftsteller der ersten Jahrhunderte.* Deutsche Akademie der Wissenschaften, Kommission für spätantike Religionsgeschichte. Berlin, 1897– .

JA *Journal Asiatique, recueil de mémoires et de notices relatifs aux études orientales.* Paris, 1822– .

JAOS *Journal of the American Oriental Society.* Boston, 1849– .

LCL Loeb Classical Library. London and New York (later, Cambridge, Mass.).

Migne, *PG* J. P. Migne, ed., *Patrologiae cursus completus.*
Migne, *PL* *PG = Patrologia graeca.* 166 vols. Paris, 1857–66.
    PL = Patrologia latina. 221 vols. Paris, 1844–64. (Refs. are to columns.)

NGG *Nachrichten von der Gesellschaft der Wissenschaften zu Göttingen.* Göttingen.

PEY Papers from the Eranos Yearbooks (the present series).

SBA *Sitzungsberichte der preussischen (deutschen) Akademie der Wissenschaften.* Berlin.

INDEX

INDEX

A

Aaron, 354
abbeys, 175, 184; Benedictine, 172
Abel, 137
aboriginals, *see* primitive culture
Abraham, 125, 138, 141, 152–53, 162, 282, 300
Absolute, the, 3–5, 16, 18–19, 28, 339*n; see also* Brahman; God
abstinence, 357; Manichaean, 282, 292, 294, 297; sexual, 282
Abu'l-Barakāt al-Baghdādī, 316
abyss, 105, 116*n*, 244, 258
Academy, Greek, 221
acceptance, of this world, 400
accident, 323; substance and, 11
Achaea, 134, 145
Achamoth, 203
Acta Archelai (Hegemonius), 213–14, 272, 278–79, 293
Acts, apocryphal, 181, 207
Acts of the Apostles, 121, 351
Adam: Christian, 122, 134, 138–40, 142–43, 164, 319, fall of, 140, 365; Manichaean, 256, 258, 276–80, 297, 300–01; redemption of, 277, 279–80, 297
Adamson, Margot R., 330*n*
Ādi Buddha, 86
advaita (nonduality), 21
Advent, 355
Adversus haereses (Irenaeus), 251ff.
advocate/*advocata*, Mary as, 362–63, 367
Aegean region, 50
Aeons, 202, 217–18, 221, 227, 234, 269–70
Aeschylus, 138, 181
aestheticism, 337*n*, 371

Afghan Order of the Čishtīya, 322
Africa, 38–39*n*, 166, 386
afterlife, 176, 323
agape, 155, 200, 365, 371; *see also* love
Agapius, 279*n*
age: groups, 392; old, 6, 17
agrarian society, 35, 48; matriarchy, 63
agriculture, 38; condemned, 293
Aḥmad Shams el-Dīn al-Aflakī, 321
Aḥmad b. Tarkanshāh Aqsarāyī of Cairo, 321
air: animated, 293; son of first man, 270; stratum of universe, 230; zone of, 218, 221
'Ā'isha, 319
akribeia, 211
Akṣobya, 85
Albright, W. F., 383*n*
alchemy, 91, 317, 407
Alcmaeon, 137
alcohol, denial of, 60, 295
Al-Bīrūnī, 247
Alexander the Great, 356
Alexander of Hales, 8, 189, 197
Alexander of Lycopolis, 260*n*, 268*n*–69*n*, 272*n*, 279–80*n*, 283*n*, 294, 306
Alexandria, 173, 210, 216, 218
Alfaric, Prosper, 247*n*, 284*n*, 293–95*n*, 304*n*, 309–10*n*
Alfonsi, Luigi, 221*n*
'Alī, 316
'Alī Ḥusayn Maḥfūẓ, 322*n*
'Alī b. 'Uthmān al-Ḥujwīrī, 317*n*
alien, man as, 261
Allāh, 320–21
allegories, 304; Alexandrian-Platonic, 159

445

446

First Man, *(continued)*
275, 278–80, 297; sons of, five,
270–71
fishes, 104, 112–13, 153, 235
Fitts, Dudley, 168n
flame (s) , 313; tongue of, 123
Flanders, 191
fleece, dewy, 354
flesh, 75, 139, 142, 146, 149, 151,
161, 164; and blood, 337; domination of, 341; Manichaean concept
of, 257, 262, 273, 275, 280, 284,
290, 292, 306
floods, 85, 108, 172
Florand, P. F., 342n
Florenski, Pavel, 354
Flos Sanctorum, 187
flowers, 79, 95, 207, 322, 348, 366;
love of, 262
Flügel, Gustav, 258n–59n, 269n,
272n, 275n, 277n–80n, 294n,
297n, 307n, 312n
flute playing, 322
Folsom cultures, 41
fons amoris, 365
food, 74, 129, 309
force: gift of, 273; primal, 75; universal, 77; virtue of, 285
forgetfulness: demon of, 284; of
soul, 275, 291
forgiveness, 138, 163, 362; Manichaean, 296, 305
formalism, theological, 162
formlessness, 382
forms, 394, 399, 413; eternal procession of, 382; hierarchy of, 8
"forms-of-becoming," 81
fornication, 294
Förster-Streffleur, S., 110n
fortitude, 335; gift of, 341
Fortunatus, 263
fortune, good, 106, 114; goddess of,
70
fragrance, 262, 273
France, 90; pre-Celtic, 91
Francis I, 187
Francis, St., 162
Franciscan Order, 175, 186, 197,
348, 357

fratricide, 137–38
free will, 130, 193, 243, 299
freedom, 86, 142, 151, 160–62, 187,
194, 243, 261, 299; of God, 316;
human, 130; of love, 344; positive, 254; unlimited, 292
Freeman, Kathleen, 24n
Freud, Sigmund, 9
Friedemann, H., 374n
friends, 155, 169, 307
"Friends of Light," 272
friendship, 413
Frigg, 351
fruit, 95, 125–26, 131, 280, 293, 295–
96, 310, 368; forbidden, 30; juice,
295
funeral supper, 154

G

Gabon, 178
Gabriel, angel, 195
Gaffin, R., 254n, 269n
Gahs, A., 32
Galatia, 145, 148–51, 159
Galatians, 135; epistle to, 121, 138
Galilee, 120, 205
Gaṇeśa, 94
Ganges River, 101
Gardeil, A., 346n
garment, 292, 309, 312
Garo, 55
gate, closed, 354, 358
Garuḍa, 87–88
Gaurī, 79, 86
Gaurishankar, 79
Gêhmurd, 277n
Geibel, Emanuel, 350
genesis, 20–21, 413; of world, 233,
266, 271, 413
Genesis, Book of, 137, 168, 204
genetrix, 356
Gentiles, 125
gentleness, of Mary, 351–52, 361,
373
germ, 244–45; of the universe, 230–
32
Germanic peoples, 65

N

472

S

W

X

Y